Feminist Philosophy of Mind

PHILOSOPHY OF MIND SERIES

SERIES EDITOR: David J. Chalmers, *Australian National University*

Feminist Philosophy of Mind

Edited by

KEYA MAITRA AND JENNIFER MCWEENY

OXFORD
UNIVERSITY PRESS

OXFORD
UNIVERSITY PRESS

Oxford University Press is a department of the University of Oxford. It furthers
the University's objective of excellence in research, scholarship, and education
by publishing worldwide. Oxford is a registered trade mark of Oxford University
Press in the UK and certain other countries.

Published in the United States of America by Oxford University Press
198 Madison Avenue, New York, NY 10016, United States of America.

Library of Congress Cataloging-in-Publication Data
Names: Maitra, Keya, editor. | McWeeny, Jennifer, editor.
Title: Feminist philosophy of mind / edited by Keya Maitra and Jennifer McWeeny.
Description: New York, NY, United States of America :
Oxford University Press, [2022] | Series: Philosophy of mind series |
Includes bibliographical references and index.
Identifiers: LCCN 2022000767 (print) | LCCN 2022000768 (ebook) |
ISBN 9780190867621 (pb) | ISBN 9780190867614 (hardback) |
ISBN 9780190867645 (epub)
Subjects: LCSH: Philosophy of mind. | Feminist theory.
Classification: LCC BD418.3 .F46 2022 (print) | LCC BD418.3 (ebook) |
DDC 128/.2—dc23/eng/20220203
LC record available at https://lccn.loc.gov/2022000767
LC ebook record available at https://lccn.loc.gov/2022000768

DOI: 10.1093/oso/9780190867614.001.0001

1 3 5 7 9 8 6 4 2

Paperback printed by Marquis, Canada
Hardback printed by Bridgeport National Bindery, Inc., United States of America

Contents

PART IV. BODY AND MIND

PART V. MEMORY AND EMOTION

Acknowledgments

A collection of essays on feminist philosophy of mind is long overdue in the discipline. We would not have been able to realize this vision without the collaboration, encouragement, and enthusiasm of so many who welcomed the inauguration of this subfield and the expansion of philosophy by centering considerations of gender, race, class, sexuality, age, ability, and other social and experiential categories. Completing this manuscript during a global pandemic at a time when diverse social movements are gaining ground, changing the world, and raising consciousness—waking people up to our widespread participation in systemic injustices and the social structures on which they depend—makes this project even more meaningful. The consideration and discussion of the ways that theories about the nature of mind may support or undermine social movements and the voices and experiences of groups of people at the center of these movements are part and parcel of the sea change that is upon us. Such a project is necessarily a collective one, and we wish to recognize those whose participation was crucial along the way.

We would first like to thank our respective institutions for supporting our research on this project: University of North Carolina Asheville (UNCA) and Worcester Polytechnic Institute (WPI). The University Research Council and Thomas Howerton Distinguished Professorship for the Humanities at UNCA and the Dean of Arts and Sciences and Department of Humanities and Arts at WPI provided financial support. We are especially appreciative of colleagues Melissa Burchard, Ameena Batada, Tracey Rizzo, Wiebke Strehl, and Kate Zubko at UNCA and Jean King, Kate Moncrief, Kris Boudreau, Michelle Ephraim, Roger Gottlieb, Peter Hansen, John Sanbonmatsu, and Ruth Smith at WPI. In addition, many colleagues and friends from the profession have been generous and consistent with their willingness to engage our ideas in conversations over the years. Thank you to Iva Apostolova, Donald Baxter, Nancy Bauer, Asha Bhandary, Ashby Butnor, Arindam Chakrabarti, Vrinda Dalmiya, PJ DiPietro, Paula Droege, Michael Eng, Jay Garfield, Nicole Garner, Mark Johnson, Janine Jones, Noreen Khawaja, Amy Kind, Matt MacKenzie, Emily McRae, Diana Meyers, Dermot Moran, James Morley, Ruth Millikan, Shelley Park, Shireen Roshanravan, Brook Sadler, Naomi Scheman, Susanna Siegel, Margaret A. "Peg" Simons, Elisa Springer, Evan Thompson, Gail Weiss, Naomi Zack, and Kelli Zaytoun.

We developed the idea for this project while attending the 2012 National Endowment for Humanities (NEH) Summer Institute "Investigating Consciousness: Buddhist and Contemporary Philosophical Perspectives." Christian Coseru, Jay Garfield, and Evan Thompson were the directors of the institute, where we benefited from many stimulating conversations with faculty and the other participants across multiple philosophical traditions. When this book was in its early stages, the Pacific Division of the American Philosophical Association invited us to participate in a symposium, "Feminism and Philosophy," on the theme of feminist philosophy of mind, which took place on April 13, 2017, in Seattle, Washington. We are grateful for exchanges with the other panelists in that session, Janine Jones and Amy Kind, and moderator Helen Daly, and for the questions we received from members of the audience, whose enthusiasm for and careful consideration of the subject inspired directions that we pursue in the book.

We presented versions of our own chapters in this book at a number of venues, including the Florida Philosophical Association Annual conference in 2016, where Keya gave a keynote address; the Center for Subjectivity Research in Copenhagen; WoGAP (Workshop on Gender and Philosophy) at MIT; and the Colorado College Philosophy Department Colloquium Series, where Jen delivered lectures. We thank these programs for their hospitality and interest in the subject and the audience members for their insightful comments.

The task of writing the introduction to this book, which defines the scope, content, and history of this new subfield in philosophy, was challenging and required many conversations and revisions. We are lucky to have colleagues who were giving with their time and provided comments on various drafts of the introduction and our individual chapters. Their incisive readings helped us to develop and refine our vision for the book. We are especially grateful to Ashby Butnor, Arindam Chakrabarti, David Chalmers, Vrinda Dalmiya, Paula Droege, Jay Garfield, Janine Jones, Amy Kind, Matt MacKenzie, Naomi Scheman, and Anand Vaidya.

Our editors at Oxford University Press believed in the project from the start and ushered us through each stage of the process with care and sage advice. David Chalmers, editor of the Philosophy of Mind series, could always be leaned upon for guidance and inspiration. Executive Editor Peter Ohlin, Assistant Editors Abigail Johnson and Brent Matheny, and Senior Production Editor Leslie Johnson were a pleasure to work with and provided counsel throughout development and production. We are grateful to the Artists Rights Society (ARS), New York / VEGAP, Madrid for granting us permission to feature Remedios Varo's painting *Alegoría del inverno* (*Allegory of Winter*) on the book's cover, and to Rachel Perkins for her stunning cover design. We would also like to thank our production managers, Nandhini Thanga Alagu and Kavitha Yuvaraj, our copyeditors, Richard Isomaki and Janani Vadivelou, and David Martinez, who meticulously prepared the book's index.

This book is a manifestation of the collective efforts of each of its twenty-one contributors, who brought their unique perspectives and careful thinking to this project. We thank them for their hard work, expertise, and patience throughout the long editing process, and we are honored to be in their company, sharing the pages of this inaugural collection. Susan J. Brison, Judith Butler, Susan James, María Lugones, and Naomi Scheman kindly agreed to our requests to reprint previously published articles. We are appreciative of Princeton University Press, Jeffner Allen, Cambridge University Press, and Rowman & Littlefield for granting the permission rights to reprint their chapters here.

While preparing this manuscript we have experienced invaluable philosophical, professional, and personal growth. We thank our families for their unwavering support in getting us to this point. Keya thanks Mohsin, Abir, baba, bordi, chhordi, Dipakda, Tukun, and Rupun, and members of her Asheville family, Julia Noe, Amy Monroe, Peggy Brooks, Norma Jean Snyder, and Jennifer Fulford for always being there for her. Jen is grateful for her parents, family, and friends, including Emily Stowe, Ashby Butnor, Matt MacKenzie, Quinn MacKenzie, Reid MacKenzie, Sally Wurtzler, Maura McGee, Claudia Tomsa, Matt Allen, and Ture Turnbull.

Finally, and sadly, two of the book's contributing authors passed away before this book appeared in print. Lynne Rudder Baker and María Lugones have each made unparalleled contributions to the discipline of philosophy and will be deeply missed by so many of us. Baker is known for her work in philosophy of mind, metaphysics, and philosophy of religion, where her emphases on personhood and the first-person perspective show philosophy's relevance to the world we live in. To our knowledge, chapter 1 of this book, "Is the First-Person Perspective Gendered?," is the last article that Baker published, and it is one that promises to open a lasting debate on the subject. Lugones is a renowned theorist of coalition, feminism, Women of Color politics, the oppressing ↔ resisting relation, and friendship. Her writings have played a crucial role within the discipline of philosophy and beyond in antiracist, decolonial, and feminist social movements. Her most famous article, "Playfulness, 'World'-Traveling, and Loving Perception," reprinted here as chapter 5, is exemplary both for its theoretical innovation and for its autobiographical honesty. We are extremely grateful to be able to feature the work of these two special and irreplaceable thinkers in *Feminist Philosophy of Mind* and extend their legacies in new directions.

Introduction

What Is Feminist Philosophy of Mind?

Jennifer McWeeny and Keya Maitra

We first conceived of a book that would put feminist philosophy in conversation with philosophy of mind while attending the 2012 National Endowment for Humanities (NEH) Summer Institute "Investigating Consciousness: Buddhist and Contemporary Philosophical Perspectives." The Institute was premised on the idea that the philosophical study of consciousness is furthered by employing resources from diverse disciplines such as cognitive science, phenomenology, analytic philosophy, and Buddhist studies.[1] As philosophers of mind trained by thinkers who were early advocates for interdisciplinarity (Mark Johnson and Ruth Millikan, respectively), we were delighted to see our field approached through these cross-cultural and cross-disciplinary engagements, and we discovered that the juxtaposition of multiple perspectives on consciousness was fecund for our own work, as did many of the Institute's other participants.

At the same time that we were inspired by the Institute's approach to philosophy of mind, as feminist philosophers who work with women of color feminisms and as women situated in postcolonial matrixes (albeit in different ways), we were struck by the conspicuous absence of a prominent feminist or critical social perspective among the Institute's faculty members and readings. Even in a philosophical space that we found to be one of the more inclusive and interdisciplinary we had yet experienced, there were few opportunities for rigorous analysis of feminist perspectives. "Feminist philosophy" is an umbrella concept that holds together multiple manners of doing philosophy that share the following feature: they regard the voices and experiences of women and members of underrepresented groups such as people of color, LGBTQ individuals, working-class people, and people with disabilities as philosophically significant.[2] Because this regard is not proportionally distributed across these groups in individual instances of feminist philosophy, and because such approaches span diverse motivations and literatures, the plural form, feminist philosoph*ies*, is more apt to describe this type of work.[3]

Noticing the absence of feminist philosophies at the NEH Summer Institute, and the corollary tendency on the part of discussants to talk about minds in the

Jennifer McWeeny and Keya Maitra, *Introduction* In: *Feminist Philosophy of Mind*. Edited by: Keya Maitra and Jennifer McWeeny, Oxford University Press. © Oxford University Press 2022.
DOI: 10.1093/oso/9780190867614.003.0001

abstract as "*the* [universal] mind" rather than "*this* [particular person's] mind" or "*my, your, his, her,* or *their* mind," generated a series of provocative questions that ultimately led to the present study: Would contemporary debates in philosophy of mind be furthered by taking note of feminist insights? Would feminist philosophical projects benefit from employing theories and vocabularies from philosophy of mind? Would new philosophical questions, topics, and phenomena be revealed by an integration of the two fields? This book demonstrates affirmative answers to these questions by featuring twenty essays that combine insights from feminist philosophies and philosophies of mind.

Philosophy of mind is that subfield of philosophy that seeks to answer the question "What is the mind?" (Chalmers 2002, xi).[4] Philosophers of mind look for identifying features of the mind—features that are shared among minds and are therefore universal. They ask what conditions a thing must fulfill in order for it to be a mind (or a particular component of minds such as consciousness or memory), and they frequently employ thought experiments, conceivability problems, and appeals to empirical data to reveal these conditions in fine-grained ways.[5] This focus has resulted in careful accounts of events and episodes of minds such as thoughts, desires, and dreams; contents of minds such as beliefs and feelings; functions of minds such as perception, attention, imagination, and emotion; and properties of minds such as intentionality, consciousness, and intelligence.[6] Explanations of mind-body interaction, mind-world interaction, self-knowledge, and knowledge of other minds have been central preoccupations of the field and have led to the development of a number of its prominent views, including dualism, physicalism, functionalism, individualism, externalism, enactivism, and many others.

Although they rarely use the same vocabularies as philosophers of mind, feminist philosophers have written extensively on the natures of consciousness, the self, personal identity, and agency, and have attended to differential experiences of these phenomena across social groups.[7] Analyses of the roles of first-person and third-person perspectives in the constitution of self-consciousness in oppressive contexts have played an important part in feminist, critical race, and trans studies, as has the question of whether the self is unitary or plural.[8] Scholars have also considered whether cognitive science, and in particular neuroscience, can explain phenomena such as sex, gender, and sexual orientation, as well as illnesses that predominantly affect women.[9] Critical social theorists have developed original theories of emotion, reason, memory, perception, imagination, belief, and desire that attend to the social and relational nature of these mental phenomena.[10] In addition, they have crafted alternative ontologies and accounts of mind-body relations that grow from unique criticisms of naturalism, physicalism, and dualism that are not readily voiced in philosophy of mind.[11] Many of these feminist views foreground the context and particularity of minds. They follow from asking questions such as "Whose mind is the model for the theory?" and "Are some groups of people attributed minds (or certain mental capacities) more readily than others?"

Studies of mental phenomena undertaken by feminists bring new perspectives to standard accounts in philosophy of mind, just as advancements in philosophy of mind offer important resources to feminist philosophers. For example, the vocabularies of philosophy of mind can be useful when describing the ways that oppression takes root in thoughts, beliefs, desires, and emotions. Naomi Scheman's classic paper "Individualism and the Objects of Psychology" offers a paradigmatic example of this approach (Scheman 1983). Here Scheman argues against "individualism," or the idea that factors internal to an individual alone produce the meaning and content of mental phenomena. She expands upon criticisms of individualism expressed by Hilary Putnam and Tyler Burge in order to reveal an original theory of mental content that sees beliefs and desires as social and relational phenomena, and that implicates a method for cultivating liberatory rather than oppressive beliefs and desires in a population (Putnam 1975a; Burge 1979).

Ned Block's article "Sexism, Racism, Ageism, and the Nature of Consciousness" indicates the benefits of dialogue between feminist philosophy and philosophy of mind in a different way and thus serves as another precursor to the field (Block 1999). Block presents a critique of representationism, the view that the phenomenal character of an experience is captured fully in its representational content, by emphasizing variations in color vision across populations demarcated by gender, race, and age. This paper demonstrates how thinking about the particularity of minds in relation to social categories can contribute to ongoing debates in philosophy of mind. Similarly, a number of topics that have recently gained attention in philosophy of mind, such as embodiment, social cognition, the extended mind, enactivism, externalism, mindreading, empathy, and cross-cultural approaches highlight the context and particularity of minds, and thus dovetail with feminist projects.[12]

Defining Feminist Philosophy of Mind

Feminist philosophy of mind is an area of study that investigates the nature of mind with reference to social locations marked by categories such as gender, race, class, sexuality, nationality, and ability, and/or investigates the nature of social locations with reference to theories about the mind.[13] Although this emerging field grows from seeds of its parent disciplines and speaks to their central debates, it is ultimately distinct from them because it takes the three focal questions already mentioned—*What* is the mind? *Whose* mind is the model for the theory? *To whom* is mind attributed?—and treats them collectively rather than separately.

Asking "*Whose mind?*" and "*To whom is mind attributed?*" alongside "*What is the mind?*" brings much complexity to theorizing about the mind, as recent attention to topics such as artificial intelligence, animal cognition, and panpsychism has shown. Conceiving of "*Whose?*" and "*To whom?*" not only in terms of *species* categories such as humans, bats, and machines, but also *intraspecies* categories delineated by gender, race, class, and so on, likewise promises to bring further innovation. The interrogative triad of *What? Whose?* and *To whom?* forms a method for investigating the mind that invites theorists to think beyond their own perspectives and discourages them from confusing their own socially and culturally situated views and disciplinary intuitions with universal human experiences. This is a method attentive to the philosophical consequences of assuming third-person perspectives when studying the minds and bodies of others, and of subsuming the first-personal perspectives of others under our own.

Alternating between these frames of *What? Whose?* and *To whom?*, feminist philosophy of mind does not prematurely foreclose the questions of whether minds are uniform across beings and groups of beings, and of when and whether sameness or difference among distinct minds should be prioritized in our theorizing about the mind. It welcomes the expertise that comes with disciplinary and subdisciplinary specializations in a particular area while also questioning the habitual assumptions and conventional practices that accompany such specializations. This field is born of the conviction that considering multiple perspectives and methods together will generate more nuanced understandings of the mind and its various components than would otherwise be possible.

The differences between the three guiding questions at the center of feminist philosophy of mind are aptly illustrated by the following foundational claims in the history of philosophy: René Descartes's "I am. I exist . . . as long as I am thinking" (1984, 19); Simone de Beauvoir's "I am a woman" (2010, 5); and Sojourner Truth's "Ain't I a woman?" (Gage 2005, 104).[14] It does not seem to us a coincidence that these claims are respectively associated with distinct social locations and philosophical literatures.

For Descartes, his certainty in his own experience of thinking demonstrates that mind is immaterial and therefore distinct from the body (and, by implication, his sex); it is defined by its action, thought, which in turn is a hallmark of the human. Notably, Descartes's experience also implicates an individuated mind, one that is essentially private and bounded rather than social and relational.

On the contrary, Beauvoir's social location is inescapably primary in her experience.[15] Noting the difference between a man's relation to his sex and her own, she explains, "If I want to define myself, I first have to say 'I am a woman'; all other assertions will arise from this basic truth" (2009, 5). The concept "woman" must therefore be analyzed philosophically in order for Beauvoir to have the same certainty in her first-personal experience as Descartes does, *before* she can theorize about consciousness and the mind in the style of her countrymen, Descartes, Jean-Paul Sartre, and Maurice Merleau-Ponty. Her skepticism is about the internal world rather than the external one, and about the integrity of her own experience when it has been shaped in contexts of sexist and economic oppression. The divergence between third-person and first-person accounts of womanhood that Beauvoir respectively chronicles in the two volumes of *The Second Sex*, "Facts and Myths" and "Lived Experience," shows the importance of asking "*Whose mind is the model for the theory?*" and, another variation of the "whose" question: "*Whose theory is modeling the mind?*"

Sojourner Truth's call, "Ain't I a woman?" begins at a different place still. Bell hooks's interpretation of Truth's sentiment emphasizes that the dictates of racism and sexism establish Black men as representative of Black people and White women as representative of women, thus discounting the lived experiences of Black women.[16] In this context, Truth's status as both a human *and* a woman is always in question, rendering invisible or irrelevant her first-personal experiences, her subjectivity, and her mind: "In the eyes of the 19th century white public, the black female was mere chattel, a thing, an animal" (hooks 1981, 159). Rather than begin with a statement or proposition that is self-evident and self-certain like those of Descartes and Beauvoir, Truth's experiential starting point is interrogative. She asks why what is self-evident to her is not self-evident to others; her skepticism is fueled by this irrational discrepancy in attitudes toward her own existence. Hooks's analysis stresses that even feminist theorizing that foregrounds the particularity of social locations can repeat the mistake of confusing the experiences of certain individuals—White, bourgeois women, for example—with those of all individuals in the group "women," a criticism that has often been levied against Beauvoir (hooks 1981, 7).[17] Such moves evade the fact that a long-standing justificatory strategy of oppressions has been to attribute mind differentially—to code racial and cultural Others as either mentally deficient ("primitive") or altogether lacking a mind in the Cartesian or Kantian sense ("animal" or "bestial").[18] Concepts of mind inevitably tally with this social history: the "primitive" helps define the "rational"; what is "animal" helps to define what is "human"; beings who are seen as "uncivilized" help to define what a "woman" is (hooks 1981; Spillers 1987; Oyěwùmí 1997; Lugones 2007).

At the same time that we characterize feminist philosophy of mind as a field that considers the *What? Whose?* and *To whom?* questions about mind collectively, we also recognize that these questions are interpreted in different ways and engaged in varying degrees across individual instances of the category, as the diversity among the chapters in this collection attests. Nonetheless, the twenty chapters in *Feminist Philosophy of Mind* reveal five predominant themes for this new philosophical area that are respectively detailed in each of the book's parts: "Mind and Gender&Race&," "Self and Selves," "Naturalism and Normativity," "Body and Mind," and "Memory and Emotion."[19]

We chose these themes for this inaugural collection because, with the exception of the first one, they already populate the literatures of *both* feminist philosophy and philosophy of mind. The first chapter of parts II–V therefore consists in a reprint of a classic article that has in some way set the stage for current research on these topics. Further, representing each theme with a paired set of terms rather than one term evokes the different histories and emphases of feminist philosophy and philosophy of mind and raises crucial questions of interaction and integration between the terms. What is the relationship, if any, between mind and gender&race&? The self and other selves? Naturalistic explanations and normative standards? Bodies and minds? One faculty of mind such as memory and another such as emotion? In what follows, we trace how and why each of these subjects has come to be a central thematic for feminist philosophy of mind with reference to the existing literature in its parent fields and discuss the original interventions that this book makes to contemporary debates.

Part I: Mind and Gender&Race&

Folk understandings of mind often suggest that minds are gendered and raced like people are; they can be classified into different types that mirror gender-categories or race-categories.[20] For example, Louann Brizendine's bestseller *The Female Brain* attributes personality differences between men and women to hormonal fluctuations that effect differences between the groups' respective brain structures (Brizendine 2006). Brizendine claims that women may be better at expressing emotions and remembering events because the hippocampus in the female brain is larger than it is in the male brain (Brizendine 2006, 5). The male brain, for its part, has a larger amygdala and "two and a half times the brain space devoted to sexual drive" (Brizendine 2006, 5). Studies undertaken from a feminist perspective frequently argue that minds are gendered from the other direction: it is not that biological differences in brain structure produce gendered minds, but that society and culture act differently on minds in ways that eventually yield different ways of perceiving, reasoning, feeling, and thinking between men and women, including different ways of conceiving of what mind is (Gilligan 1982; Belenky et al. 1986).

Stephen Jay Gould's *The Mismeasure of Man* famously details how widespread social and cultural biases have shaped purportedly scientific claims about differential capacities for intelligence and cognitive function among different races (Gould 1981).[21] Whether appealing to biological factors or cultural influences, a number of recent book titles continue to reflect concepts of raced and racialized minds. These include *The Chinese Mind* (De Mente 2009), *The Indian Mind* (Moore 1967), *The Black Mind* (Dathorne 1974), *The African Mind* (Chinweizu 1987), *The Crisis of the European Mind* (Hazard 2013), and *For Indigenous Minds Only* (Waziyatawin and Yellowbird 2012). Everyday language also implies that in folk psychology minds are tied to other identity categories such as class, sexuality, and ability. Claims such as "That's how poor people think" or "Gay men are more emotional than straight men" repeat this tendency to see minds as personalized in ways that mirror features of social identities.

In contrast to these popular ideas about minds, philosophers of mind more often than not presume that minds are *not* the kinds of things that are influenced by gender, race, culture, and society in constitutive or structural ways, though they may admit that minds may be gendered or raced contingently in terms of their content.[22] Even recent work that considers the embodied, embedded, enactive, extended, and social components of cognition rarely conceives of embodiment or socialization in terms of gender or race. This trend may be linked to a presumption that whatever it is that makes a mind a mind is likely to be gender- and race-neutral. It may also reflect a political fear of making space for discriminatory claims that would suggest that women and people of color have different mental capacities than men and White people.

Though not usually referenced in the philosophy of mind literature, W. E. B. Du Bois's notion of double consciousness presents what is likely the most formidable challenge to the idea that mental structure is universal among different social groups. In *The Souls of Black Folk*, Du Bois writes that Black people living in a racist world lack a true self-consciousness (Du Bois 1903, 3). Instead, they possess a "double consciousness," which he defines as "a sense of always looking at oneself through the eyes of others" (Du Bois 1903, 3).[23] This description suggests that oppression can alter the very structure of an individual's consciousness to the point where a third-person perspective eclipses the first-person perspective.[24] Frantz Fanon's well-known criticism of Sartre's theory of consciousness makes the point emphatically: "ontology does not allow us to understand the being of the black man" (Fanon 2008, 90). Moreover, double consciousness afflicts *all* Black people in a racist world (and arguably all marginalized people), and so it is a broader and different phenomenon than mental "disorders" such as dissociative identity.

Each chapter in part I brings questions about the connections between social location and mental architecture out from the margins of the field and sows seeds for a vibrant contemporary debate. Are minds gendered in terms of their content, their structure, or not at all? At what point specifically (or in which faculty/ capacity) do factors like gender, race, class, sexuality, culture, social context, and ability become relevant to investigations into the nature of mind? Is gender only a matter of third-person ascription, or does it live in first-personal structures of a consciousness? Do our ways of conceiving of mental properties such as intelligence reflect our ways of conceiving of social or physical properties such as sex and race? How does recognizing the differential attribution of mind across racial groups affect our understanding of the problem of other minds?

Chapter 1, by Lynne Rudder Baker, enters this conversation with a careful consideration of the first-person perspective, or the capacity to "conceive of oneself as oneself in the first-person." In "Is the First-Person Perspective Gendered?" she argues that although the first-person perspective may be de facto gendered within certain cultural contexts, it is not gendered de jure. Even though language is embedded with ideas about gender and the first-person perspective requires language, Baker suggests that gender identity is formed only after the first-person perspective has already been established. Contrary to thinkers who would claim that this aspect of mental structure is *necessarily* gendered, Baker claims that it is only contingently so.

In chapter 2, "Computing Machinery and Sexual Difference: The Sexed Presuppositions Underlying the Turing Test," Amy Kind argues that our standard ways of conceiving of the attributes of thought and intelligence are implicitly modeled on how we understand the attribute of sex. Kind's discussion reminds us of an oft-forgotten element of the Turing test; namely, that the original Imitation Game involves convincing a neutral questioner that a man is a woman. Kind concludes that our tendencies to think about intelligence as an all-or-nothing affair and to value superficial markers of intelligence are related to the way sex attributes were conceived in the mid-twentieth century.

Keya Maitra's contribution, chapter 3, "Toward a Feminist Theory of Mental Content," shows that the feminist emphasis on the experiences of women and other underrepresented groups pushes in the direction of content externalism. While most externalist theories fail to account for the roles of social organization and social power in the production of mental content, Maitra argues that Millikan's teleosemantic theory offers a promising foundation. A feminist theory of content allows us to appreciate the nuanced role that historical and sociocultural forces play in shaping the content of our languages and minds.

In chapter 4, "Disappearing Black People through Failures of White Empathy," Janine Jones reveals a difficulty with the classic problem of other minds: namely, if racism entails that Black people are not recognized as having minds in the first place, or are recognized as having "attenuated" minds in comparison with White people, then empathy between members of the two groups cannot proceed as it would in a context where they are equally attributed minds. Jones argues that the construction of Black people's minds in Manichaean opposition to that of White people's renders White empathy for Black people improbable, and that therefore self-empathy on the part of White people is a more productive project for countering racism. Jones's theory of empathy thus departs from models that rely solely on the self's positive perceptions, memories, and imagination, and includes what the self could *not* have perceived, remembered, or imagined in experience.

From these summaries, we see how jointly engaging the questions of *What? Whose?* and *To whom?* leads to new insights. The chapters in part I answer "*What is the mind?*" by respectively proposing theories of the first-person perspective, intelligence, mental content, and other minds. They do so largely by asking "*Whose mind?*"—by considering these aspects of minds in relation to different groups of people, including women and men, immigrants and citizens, and Black people and White people. The question "*To whom is mind attributed?*" (and the variation "*How* is mind attributed?") is crucial to Kind's explanation of how we think of the property of intelligence as a property akin to sex discussed in chapter 2, and to Jones's development of the multidimensional description of empathy offered in chapter 4. Moreover, in chapter 3, Maitra suggests that the analysis of mental content is furthered by looking at whose content it is, that is, the social and historical context that shapes content over time and that grounds the meaning of concepts such as "whiteness."

Part II: Self and Selves

Whereas the chapters in part I consider a range of mental phenomena in light of social location, those in part II discuss the self in particular, addressing questions about the ontology of the self, self-consciousness, agency, and personal identity. This theme in philosophy of mind has been attended to by feminist philosophers more so than any other and so it is fitting that it be addressed after the introductory chapters illuminating certain relationships between mind and the social categories of gender, race, sexuality, and nationality.

In the existing literature on the self, feminist philosophers have explored a wide variety of topics, including how experiences of self and agency are influenced by sexism, racism, and other traumas (Anzaldúa 1999; Brison 2003; Alcoff 2011); how boundaries between one's self and others may become confused in relationships of care and dependence (Kittay 1999; Meyers 2014; Dalmiya 2017); how a woman's consciousness of her self affects her possibilities for liberation (Butnor 2011; Fatima 2012; Maitra 2014; Leboeuf 2018); how agency and autonomy are structured in oppressive situations (Veltman and Piper 2014; Herr 2018); and how studies of oppressed consciousnesses like those described by Du Bois and Beauvoir often prioritize a self's inherent multiplicity or plurality over its unity (Barvosa 2008; Ortega 2016; McWeeny 2017).

By contrast, philosophy of mind's engagement with the question of self has largely come through one particular lens, namely, the lens of personal identity, which may be a marginal topic in the field due to its association with metaphysics. The question of personal identity considers which mental structures make a person the same person from one moment to the next and what unites diverse experiences together into one consciousness. Philosophers of mind have recognized a variety of phenomena as central to identity and consciousness, from memory (Locke 1996), to causal dependence (Shoemaker 1984), to the first-person perspective (Zahavi 2005; Baker 2013; Ganeri 2012), a lack of first-personal perspective (Albahari 2007, 2009), a feeling of ownership or intimacy (de Vignemont 2007), and the self-reflective character of consciousness (MacKenzie 2015). They have also questioned whether an enduring self or ego exists at all beyond the flow of consciousness, and sought to explicate the relationship between agency and personal identity.[25]

Ian Hacking, who is known for emphasizing the importance of social context in his work in philosophy of science, ironically suggests that examples involving dissociative identity disorder, for instance, do not undermine the unity of consciousness because the central question of personal identity is not "*who* I am, but *what* I am" (Hacking 1995, 221; emphasis added). As long as the "what" of self is universal, philosophers need not bother with experiences of discontinuity or multiplicity implicated by "who" one is.[26] When discontinuity and fragmentation of the self is acknowledged in philosophy of mind, this is often taken to signal the existence of a different self rather than plurality and contradiction *within* one self (Nagel 1971; Lewis 1976). For example, even though Galen Strawson's book on the self is titled *Selves*, he nonetheless stresses that "the idea of any such experience of separate interests [multiple points of view in one self] is unimaginable and bewildering. . . . I find it hard to believe that anyone really has such experience" (Strawson 2009, 16).

Contrary to Hacking's claim, feminist theory often begins with the idea that the "who" of self is inextricable from the "what" of self, and that therefore the possibility of a plural self is an empirical and phenomenological question, not merely a logical one (Radden 2011). For this reason, feminists have generally preferred to analyze real-life, concrete examples of fractured or multiple selves in contexts of oppression, trauma, and human rights abuses rather than hypothetical thought experiments.[27] Further, feminists frequently understand the self to be both "embodied" and "relational"—constitutively linked to the body and constitutively dependent on its relations to others.

The four chapters in part II engage questions about the self's relationality and embodiment and, in so doing, significantly extend theorizing about the self in philosophy of mind. How is the self affected by its social context and the particularity of the body to which it is tied? Is a person's sense of self or self-consciousness gendered, raced, classed, or otherwise marked by social location? Is the self singular or plural? To what extent is agency facilitated or hindered by one's gender and race? Does taking account of social location affect the ways that we think about the continuity of self over time?

In chapter 5, "Playfulness, 'World'-Traveling, and Loving Perception," first published in 1987, María Lugones articulates her landmark notion of " 'world'-traveling." "World"-traveling involves traversing oppressive social structures, such as when one moves between communities where one is respectively seen with and without racist perceptions. In such cases, it seems that the same person is capable of possessing two contradictory properties *at the same time*: playfulness and seriousness. Lugones explains how this is possible by arguing that properties of self are *world-dependent*, and that, contrary to how the self has generally been conceived in the history of philosophy, the self is actually "a plurality of selves" insofar as it is keyed into a plurality of "worlds" or social structures.

Chapter 6, "Symptoms in Particular: Feminism and the Disordered Mind," offers a critique of unitary, ahistorical, and reductive accounts of self. Here Jennifer Radden presents a theory of mental disorder that reconsiders the role symptoms play in medical and cognitivist models of mind. Instead of treating symptoms as mere downstream effects of brain dysfunction, she takes them as moments of voiced distress of a self embedded in a particular network of social relationships. The first-person experience of the sufferer thus becomes decisive for articulating the nature of the disorder and its diagnostic process, as well as for understanding at which point multiplicity becomes a sign of disorder.

Presumptions of agency and activity often follow from the idea of a freestanding, unitary self. Challenging this presumption, recent feminist accounts have valorized the roles of passivity and relational receptivity in autonomy, maintaining that these features are just as important as activity and agency. Diana Tietjens Meyers's essay, chapter 7, "Passivity in Theories of the Agentic Self: Reflections on the Views of Soran Reader and Sarah Buss," reveals why such approaches are problematic and emphasizes the roles of interactivity and capacity over and above passivity in establishing relational forms of agency. When dependency is understood in terms of capacities rather than passivity, respect for the agency of victims of human rights abuses is not compromised.

In "The Question of Personal Identity," chapter 8, Susan James criticizes analytic accounts of personal identity that too hastily embrace the hierarchical and gendered opposition between mind and body. According to these views, personhood and its survival are treated as a matter of *psychological* continuity, that is, continuity of psychological states such as desires, intentions, beliefs, and memory, and *bodily* continuity (or discontinuity) remains irrelevant. Drawing from feminist research on memories of bodily trauma including Susan J. Brison's pathbreaking work featured in chapter 17, James points out that although in such cases psychological unity can be shattered, it can also be restored through practices of bodily respect and recognition by others.

Part II shows us how the recognition of feminist philosophy of mind's core triad of questions advances existing debates and theories about personal identity and selfhood. Lugones's response to the *What?* question is an original account of identity—the self is a "plurality of selves"—that she develops by attending to the *To whom?* question: she examines the differential attribution of properties such as playfulness across diverse national and social contexts. In a similar fashion, Radden's and James's analyses center the consideration of women's minds (the *Whose?* question) in order to get at the "*What?*" of mental disorder and bodily continuity in ways that recognize women's experiences of their own selves. Meyers's theory of agency is likewise dependent on thinking about agency in the context of human rights abuses, thus taking up the questions of "*Whose* agency?" and "*To whom* is agency attributed?"

Part III: Naturalism and Normativity

The preceding two parts raise questions about the relationship between social location and certain types of mental phenomena. Part III shifts our focus to the mind's embodiment and, in particular, how best to conceive of the brain and the rest of the physical body in our theories about the mind. The chapters in this part each consider the place of naturalism in philosophy of mind, but they do so from diverse angles, respectively appealing to the methods and literatures of phenomenology, enactivism, cognitive science, and philosophy of language. Philosophers of mind often link the concepts of naturalism and normativity by asking whether or not normative aspects of experience, such as morality, judgments, or values can be "naturalized."[28] Feminist philosophers frequently approach this question from an inverse direction; they reveal mechanisms whereby normative values regarding gender and race creep into naturalistic explanation.[29]

For our purposes, we can define naturalism broadly as the view that the mind can be fully explained by the sciences. In a recent article titled "Naturalisms in Philosophy of Mind," Stephen Horst writes that "naturalism has become a kind of ideology in philosophical circles—that is, it is a widely shared commitment to a way of believing, speaking and acting whose basic assumptions are seldom examined or argued for" (Horst 2009, 221).[30] Current disagreements within philosophy of mind over naturalism generally arise over *how* best to fulfill these kinds of commitments and not over *whether* or not naturalistic approaches to mind should be pursued in the first place.[31] Notably, new naturalisms that interpret the requirement about scientific explanation more loosely than others have been developed. These include nonreductive naturalism (Millikan

1984), naive naturalism (Hornsby 2001), and liberal naturalism (De Caro and Macarthur 2004).

The automatic acceptance of naturalism in philosophy of mind contrasts sharply with the place of naturalism in feminist circles. As Sally Haslanger and Ásta observe, "Feminists tend to be wary of any suggestion that a category is 'natural,' or that what's 'natural' should dictate how we organize ourselves socially" (2017). We can define naturalism about sex as the view that sexual categories can be fully explained by the sciences and/or that sex is constitutively related to physiological and/or anatomical aspects of the body. Feminist philosophers largely reject the folk tendency to see sex as a "natural" phenomenon in these senses of the term.[32] Likewise, biological conceptions of race are widely criticized (Appiah 1985; Haslanger 2000; Zack 2002), as are physiological explanations of sexual orientation (Stein 1999; Johnston 2008).

Feminist criticisms of naturalism emphasize the pragmatic concern that science is not a socially and politically neutral enterprise. As many mainstream philosophers of science have pointed out, observation and interpretation are situated in social and historical contexts (Kuhn 1970; Latour and Wooglar 1986). Insofar as science does not incorporate methods to keep its social assumptions in check, it will be ripe for reading current social arrangements into scientific data.[33] We must note, however, that feminist criticisms of naturalism do not necessarily lead to social construction, the view that social factors play a causal role in the existence of the phenomenon. Nor do they inevitably lead to the sex-gender distinction, often used to shield naturalistic ideas about sex from amendment or criticism by relegating considerations of social and cultural factors to the concept of "gender."[34]

The essays in part III inhabit the tense intersection between philosophy of mind's embrace of naturalism and feminist philosophy's skeptical attitude toward natural categories. In so doing, they take a wider view on mental phenomena than is common in either field, attending to both the "natural" and "sociocultural" aspects of mind, and, more important, questioning presumptions of hard and fast divisions between nature and culture, fact and value, and science and phenomenology. How do we best eliminate social bias and falsely normative standards when relying on third-person scientific descriptions? How can 4E cognition theory better take account of the social and political contexts of minds? What can neuroscience and evolutionary biology contribute to theories of gender? To what extent can feminist methods make science more rigorous? What kinds of metaphysical views are implicated by the language that we use to talk about the body and its sex(es) and gender(s)?

In chapter 9, "Sexual Ideology and Phenomenological Description: A Feminist Critique of Merleau-Ponty's *Phenomenology of Perception*," first published in 1989, Judith Butler notes that naturalistic accounts of sexual desire partake in an

obvious category mistake: they attempt to explain first-person experiential phenomena purely with reference to third-person scientific studies of the objective
body. However, a phenomenological approach, which begins in first-personal
experience, also invites the false universalization of particular social biases. For
example, Maurice Merleau-Ponty conceives of "normal" or "non-pathological"
sexual desire only in terms of a male subject who is aroused by a female object.[35]
Butler emphasizes that not only does this normative and normalizing view of
sexual desire apply only to a subset of humans (namely, heterosexual men), but
that it is also wielded politically to pathologize those who do not conform to the
presumed standard.[36]

Chapter 10, "Enactivism and Gender Performativity," answers Butler's call to
develop a theoretical framework that is capable of attending to the social particularity and individuality of the subject in question by providing an enactivist account of gender. Ashby Butnor and Matthew MacKenzie argue that enactivism,
or the view that cognition is a product of the dynamic interaction between organism and environment, has not yet gone far enough in its recognition of the
social, cultural, and intersubjective nature of cognition. To address this gap, feminist theories can provide enactivism with ways to account for the role power
plays in shaping cognition and an individual's life-world. Inversely, enactivism
can offer feminists an account of how gender is produced by the confluence of
relational, pragmatic, and biological processes.

Anne Jacobson's chapter, "Norms and Neuroscience: The Case of Borderline
Personality Disorder," addresses the question of whether dominant practices
of cognitive neuroscience are shaped by patriarchal values. She focuses on the
case of borderline personality disorder, a syndrome that is predominantly diagnosed in women and whose distinguishing features include gender-associated
characteristics such as a fragile sense of self and a deficit in empathy. Jacobson
argues that neuroscience can be useful for feminist analysis due to its focus on
explaining a being's well-functioning within a given niche, which provides a
way to take account of an organism's values and interests while still employing a
third-person investigatory framework.

Chapter 12, "Embodiments of Sex and Gender: The Metaphors of Speaking
Surfaces," by Gabrielle Benette Jackson highlights a problem with much feminist
literature on embodiment: most theorists appeal to metaphors—"the metaphors
of speaking surfaces"—to capture the ways that social forces mold bodily behavior into sexes and genders. Using verbs such as "manifest" or "generate,"
feminists represent women's bodies as "texts," "scripts," "surfaces," and "sites."
This move misleads in regard to the underlying ontology of sex and gender because it implies that human experience should be categorized reductively, according to exclusive dichotomies between the internal and external, subjective
and objective, active and passive, and natural and cultural.

By asking "*Whose mind?*" and "*To whom is mind attributed?*" the chapters in part III not only provide unique accounts of *what* the mind is, but also foreground important methodological considerations when working with third-person and first-person perspectives on mental phenomena. Butler's chapter exposes the tendency in both science and phenomenology to take examples of male, heterosexual desire as models for all sexual desire. In chapter 10, Butnor and MacKenzie reveal that the methods of 4E cognition theory often evade the question of "*Whose mind?*" by employing too narrow meanings of concepts such as "embodiment," "embeddedness," and the "social." Jacobson's observation in chapter 11 that borderline personality disorder is not proportionally distributed among men and women leads to a theory about how best to account for values using neuroscientific explanation. Finally, Jackson's chapter shows us how using certain metaphors to describe the body can ironically instill a neglect of bodily and social context in theories about the mind, a separation that feminist scholars have long sought to overcome.

Part IV: Body and Mind

Most anthologies in philosophy in mind begin with a part on mind-body dualism. In contrast, we have placed this part near the end of our book because the problems and vocabularies respectively employed by philosophers of mind and feminist philosophers have traditionally implicated different conceptions of "mind" and "body." Having first familiarized ourselves with differences between individualist and relational notions of mind, as well as naturalist and phenomenological notions of body in parts I–III, we are better able to see how the arguments in part IV employ these broadened perspectives on "mind" and "body" in order to make original contributions to a centuries-old debate.

The prevalence of naturalism in philosophy of mind goes hand in hand with the prevalence of physicalism, the view that the mind is entirely physical in nature.[37] Gilbert Ryle's idea that the mental realm is connected to the observable realm via dispositions to behave in certain ways is a precursor to present-day approaches such as eliminativism, functionalism, and computationalism that likewise insist, contrary to Descartes's dualism, that there is nothing occult about the mind (Ryle 1949).[38] Various versions of physicalism attempt to explain the mental in terms of its identity with, reducibility to, or supervenience on, the physical.[39] The physical is in turn conceived of as a brain state, which shifts the focus from the external observations of behaviorism to internal functionings of the brain and thus to empirical data derived from brain-imaging technologies.

The question of the nature and basis of consciousness parallels the question of the body-mind relationship because providing a theoretical account of experience, including its phenomenal or "what it's like" aspects, presents the hardest problem for physicalism. The "hard" problem of consciousness is the problem of explaining consciousness in physical terms (Chalmers 1995, 1996). It highlights what many have called the "explanatory gap" between matter and consciousness, the idea that no amount of explanation at the level of matter can yield an understanding of our phenomenal experience (Levine 1983; Drayson 2015). Many recent accounts in philosophy of mind offer suggestions for how to close or bypass this gap.[40]

Ironically, contemporary physicalisms often embrace the terms of Descartes's dualism even as they are rejecting the position overall; they deny that an immaterial mind exists while also preserving the Cartesian/Newtonian conception of matter as that which is passive, unthinking, divisible, and knowable by science. By contrast, some philosophers of mind challenge both Cartesian dualism and materialism by theorizing in terms of mental and nonmental properties instead of mental and physical categories (Russell 2004; Montero 2001).[41]

Feminist philosophers share with contemporary philosophers of mind the tendency to seek ontological possibilities beyond mind-body dualism.[42] Unlike many philosophers of mind, however, they are critical of a reductive physicalism that would identify mind with a physical, biological, anatomical, or neurological state. Feminists and other theorists who are likewise invested in fostering liberatory social change have long argued that mind-body dualism enables not only sexist oppression, but also racism, colonialism, heterosexism, ableism, and speciesism.[43] Such views maintain that dualism entails a hierarchical ordering of mind and body that has inevitably been mapped on to social groups such as men and women, colonizers and the colonized, White people and people of color, and upper-class and working-class peoples, thereby facilitating social mechanisms of differentiation, discrimination, and oppression. Moreover, dualism seems inconsistent with the experiences of the oppressed.[44] Reductive physicalism has also been deployed historically to justify the use and abuse of nature and the subordination of women (Merchant 1980).

Like the scholarly terrain in philosophy of mind, a careful examination of consciousness has gone hand in hand with feminist considerations of the mind-body relationship. Feminist interest in the content and structure of consciousness is as much practical as it is theoretical due to the fact that "consciousness-raising" has been the primary method for inciting political mobilization in women's movements in the United States since the 1970s (Garry and Pearsall 1989, 251). Consciousness-raising is a collective practice whereby women generate awareness of the structural conditions that restrict their freedom by sharing with each other descriptions of their first-personal experiences, especially those experiences that society refutes or silences. This practice works to expose "false consciousness" (a consciousness that harbors false perceptions of reality as if they were true) and cultivate "feminist consciousness" (a consciousness that is skilled in sorting true perceptions of reality from illusions that are part and parcel of the dictates of a sexist social system) (Bartky 1975; MacKinnon 1989, 108, 115–116; King 1988, 69–72). Such analyses of consciousness are related to the Marxist project of examining how material conditions shape the form and contents, and thus the epistemic and cognitive capacities, of particular minds. Articulating this relationship between the internal/experiential and external/material is one of the hardest problems for feminism, just as describing subjective experience in objective terms is the hardest problem for philosophy of mind.

Part IV features questions and arguments that emerge at the intersections of these two different literatures that investigate the relationship between body and mind. Is physicalism compatible with the idea that beliefs, desires, and emotions are social and relational, constituted in part by external factors? Does a "materialist feminism," or a "feminist materialism," suggest a contradiction in terms? How are views about who (or what) has a mind related to theories about the nature of minds and their connections to bodies? Would studies of animal cognition benefit from employing feminist methods for theorizing across disciplines and power relations? Is sexual orientation a mental disposition, a biological urge, or a mix of both?

In chapter 13, "Against Physicalism," first published in 2000, Naomi Scheman builds on her early critique of individualism to present a unique argument against physicalism (Scheman 1983). She begins by challenging philosophers' unexamined conviction that mental events, states, and processes enter into psychological explanation as particulars. Given this faith, the reasonableness of the physicalist project seems irresistible. By contrast, Scheman brings to the fore the irreducibly relational nature of our mental lives by acknowledging the role of social practices and their patterns of salience in shaping the meaning of beliefs, desires, and emotions. She concludes that physicalism is not necessarily false, but that it is empty or vacuous because mental objects are not particulars.

Chapter 14, "Why Feminists Should Be Materialists and Vice Versa," by Paula Droege places feminism in conversation with cognitive ethology in order to mount an argument against Scheman's critique of physicalism. Droege believes that taking a materialist approach to reality can help feminists gain an understanding of the physical forces that contribute to our beliefs and values. Likewise, materialists gain from feminism an array of epistemic and ethical tools for examining faulty assumptions that misdirect research, as well as strategies for surmounting common obstacles to interdisciplinary collaboration.

In chapter 15, "Which Bodies Have Minds? Feminism, Panpsychism, and the Attribution Question," Jennifer McWeeny reframes the classic metaphysical problem of how the mind interacts with the body in terms of the question of mental attribution: Which bodies have minds? She develops a taxonomy of possible answers to the question by jointly examining critical social theorists' descriptions of experiences of mental attribution associated with the bodies of women, Black people, laborers, and others and theories of physicalist panpsychism from the philosophy of mind. McWeeny's analysis reveals that our theories about what a mind is are inextricably connected with our beliefs about who (or what) has a mind.

E. Díaz-León's contribution, chapter 16, "Sexual Orientation: The Desire View," argues that, contrary to accounts that would locate sexual orientation in physiology, orientation is a complex mental state grounded in a person's relational beliefs, desires, and dispositions. She maintains that the ordinary concept of sexual orientation is determined by a combination of two factors: (1) one's own sex and gender, and (2) the sex and gender of the persons for whom one is disposed to have sexual desires. In a move not unlike Scheman's, Díaz-León's view of sexual orientation builds on the idea that the link between a certain mental state and a certain behavior cannot be specified independently of other mental states.

Part IV highlights how thinking about *to whom* mind should be attributed spurs innovative "*what*" positions that shed a different light on the mind-body relationship. Scheman develops a formidable argument against physicalism by questioning the entrenched habit of construing mental events and states as particulars that belong to one person rather than to a society or culture. Droege's discussion of nonhuman minds leads her to advance a form of feminist materialism. Through the juxtaposition of feminism and panpsychism, McWeeny shows how mental attribution patterns reflect views about whether bodies are the types of things can exist without minds and vice versa. Moreover, the *whose* question is presupposed in the concept of sexual orientation that is the focus of Díaz- León's study. Inversely to those who seek a physical explanation for mental phenomena, Díaz- León traces what is standardly thought to be a physiological phenomenon, namely, sexual urges, to the content of desire.

Part V: Memory and Emotion

The four chapters in the final part of *Feminist Philosophy of Mind* generate accounts of specific mental phenomena by appealing to notions from the book's other parts, including the ideas of a gendered mind, a raced and encultured mind, the relational self, relational agency, and the embodied mind. How does thinking of mind as a gendered and raced phenomenon yield new ways of thinking about the structure and function of emotions? How does trauma affect the continuity of memory and thus personal identity? How does thinking of the self in relational terms complicate traditional accounts of memory and emotion in philosophy of mind? How does thinking of grief and love specifically as they occur in the experiences of non-Western women and women of color alter our accounts of the natures of these emotions?

Philosophers of mind are increasingly interested in memory. They generally theorize about memory in three main ways. First, it is discussed in the context of theories about the continuity of self and personal identity. Second, taxonomies of different kinds of memory have been developed with particular emphasis placed on "episodic" memory, or the memory of past events that one has experienced (Tulving 1983; Droege 2012; Cheng and Werning 2016). Third, considerable effort has been devoted to constructing causal theories of memory. One of its most comprehensive articulations connects mental representations through memory traces (Bernecker 2009). Finally, the need to study memory and emotions together given their functional similarities has also been proposed (Goldie 2012; de Sousa 2017).

Somewhat similar to memory, emotions had received a cursory treatment in analytic philosophy of mind until the 1970s. This early lack of interest in emotions as mental phenomena likely resulted from the folk belief that emotions are unintelligent bodily impulses structurally opposed to thought and reason (Rorty 1980). However, the recent embrace of interdisciplinarity in philosophy of mind, and related engagements with developmental psychology, social psychology, and neuroscience, have opened the study of emotions in exciting ways. For example, contemporary emotion theory delineates a variety of parts to emotional experience including evaluative, physiological, phenomenological, expressive, behavioral, and mental components (Ben-Ze'ev 2000; Scherer 2009). Philosophers have also focused on assessing emotions' appropriateness and rationality, in addition to determining their role in motivating action (de Sousa 1987; Zhu and Thagard 2002). Others have argued that emotions are best theorized in terms of their similarity with perceptions (Prinz 2004; Döring 2007; Tappolet 2016).

Like contemporary philosophy of mind, feminist literature has paid special attention to developing theoretical descriptions of the faculties of memory and emotion. Such work has feminist import since women's accounts of states of affairs are often put into question on the purported grounds that women are emotional, irrational, and prone to cognitive inaccuracies. For instance, several feminists have formed theories of memory by looking to concrete examples of the way that memory functions in traumas that disproportionately affect women and other demographic groups, such as rape, sexual abuse, racism, colonization, and genocide (Brison 2003; Alexander 2005; Alcoff 2011).

A primary aim of feminist theories of emotion is to consider how particular emotions are differentially cultivated and experienced by members of different social categories (Lorde 1984; Narayan 1988; Jaggar 1989). For example, anger has been a frequent object of feminist analysis given its gender-specificity and race-specificity in oppressive societies: the anger of women and people of color is readily dismissed as irrational and unfounded, while the anger of men and White people is often celebrated as rational and righteous (Scheman 1980; Frye 1983; Lorde 1984). Other emotions including love, shame, disgust, rage, and hope have been theorized with a feminist lens.[45]

In the opening chapter of this part, chapter 17, "Outliving Oneself: Trauma, Memory, and Personal Identity," first published in 1997, Susan J. Brison lays the groundwork for current work on memory in a number of ways. First, she references real-life cases rather than thought experiments. Second, the trauma she discusses in relation to theories of memory is her own. It is thus a breakthrough piece where a woman has the courage to analyze her first-personal experience of trauma philosophically, and where the communicative and narrative practice of philosophy helps her and others heal. Finally, she shows how her sense of self and her memory are constitutively affected by her relationships, so it cannot be that self and memory are nonsocial, nonrelational phenomena.

Chapter 18 by Iva Apostolova, "Does Neutral Monism Provide the Best Framework for Relational Memory?" builds on Sue Campbell's argument in favor of a relational model of memory as opposed to an archival one. Apostolova suggests that Bertrand Russell's theory of neutral monism offers the best epistemological and metaphysical framework for relational memory because it charts a solution to the problem of "semantic contagion," a term first used by Ian Hacking to signify the phenomenon that occurs when a condition seems to spread immediately after it is publicly identified and described (Hacking 1995, 238). This concept is often used to discredit the memories of survivors of sexual assault and so developing an alternative explanation is crucial for a feminist response to this dismissal.

In chapter 19, "The Odd Case of a Bird-Mother: Relational Selfhood and a 'Method of Grief,'" Vrinda Dalmiya offers an account of selfhood that centers on the perspective of a bereaved mother. Experiencing extreme forms of being out of control due to grief, the bereaved mother's self emerges from a pervasive self-*mistrust* that then goes on to ground the acceptance of herself as dispositionally open to being undone by grief. In its ability to capture the opacity of the self, Dalmiya's "method of grief" turns out to be a far more effective means for self-awareness than Descartes's method of doubt, which operates according to epistemic certainty.

Chapter 20, "Equanimity and the Loving Eye: A Buddhist-Feminist Account of Loving Attention," focuses on loving attention, which Emily McRae defines as a way of paying attention to others that is motivated by care, respect, and kindness. This way of attending, integral to Mahayana Buddhist philosophy of mind and ethics, is also central to many influential feminist conceptions of moral perception. McRae shows how Buddhist skills of equanimity and mindfulness are necessary for cultivating loving attention in feminist realms. She also highlights their roles in effecting a person's self-transformation from an arrogant perceiver to someone who can lovingly attend to others.

Employing an approach that thinks the *What? Whose?* and *To whom?* aspects of mind together brings different perspectives to familiar philosophical topics, as we have already witnessed in parts I–IV. The authors of part V theorize memory, grief, love, and attention not merely in abstract terms, but as phenomena associated with particular bodies situated in specific social locations. In chapter 18, Apostolova observes that different capacities for memory are often attributed to women than to men. Brison and Dalmiya analyze concrete examples of women's trauma and grief to emphasize the relational nature of the self and self-knowledge. McRae's chapter concentrates on different modes of attending carried out by different social actors in contexts of oppression, and this perspective illuminates the interconnectedness of faculties of attention, perception, and love.

The Future of Feminist Philosophy of Mind

When we consider the twenty essays in this book collectively rather than individually, we begin to see feminist philosophy of mind not merely as a trending topic of interest but as a recognizable field or tradition with its own distinctive set of core questions, methods, and internal conversations. Together, the chapters in *Feminist Philosophy of Mind* establish a basis for further inquiry and future growth of the field, and for new ways of combining the questions *What is the mind? Whose mind is the model for the theory?* and *To whom is mind attributed?*, as well as adding others to the method. We expect that subsequent research will not only extend the themes and debates pursued in this book, but will also utilize the fecundity of these methodological approaches to grow in new, not-yet-imagined directions. Here are a few that seem most obvious.

First, it is likely that a more direct and expansive debate will soon take shape over the question of whether minds are necessarily or contingently gendered, raced, oriented, classed, cultured, and so on. While theorists may agree that the mind is relational and situated, they will likely disagree about the mechanisms and consequences of social situation. The parallels between the theoretical landscapes surrounding theories of mind and theories of gender are liable to come into greater relief (for example, that there are physicalists, eliminativists, dispositionalists, extensionists, externalists, and so on, in both areas). Moreover, we expect that more "mental" theories of sex, gender, and other social categories will be developed that identify specific genders with a particular structure of consciousness, disposition, functional attitude, or mental content rather than with physiology, behavior, or performance (Ayala and Vasilyeva 2015; Dembroff 2016; McWeeny 2017). We likewise predict that considerations of the differential attributions of mind across social groups, such as men and women and White people and people of color, will incite fresh theories about the mind and its components that go beyond the insights of this book.

Second, and as a consequence of the first point, the future of feminist philosophy of mind demands looking at the relationship between mind and a diverse array of social locations, and centering the experiences of a diverse array of people. We believe that developing feminist philosophy of mind in a robustly intersectional way requires more work that takes up the interplay between philosophy of mind and philosophy of race.[46] For example, it would be important to articulate an account of mind that could underwrite phenomena such as epistemologies of ignorance (Tuana and Sullivan 2007; Medina 2013; McRae 2019) and other cognitive consequences of the racial contract (Mills 1999). In addition, an obvious trajectory for feminist philosophy of mind is to theorize about disabilities and neurally diverse cognitive abilities in ways that do not reduce such experiences to "pathology" or "exception."[47] Thinking about the mind with reference to examples of transgender experience and gender transitioning also holds much promise for the field (Bettcher 2009; Shrage 2009). Additionally, we think that studies of the relationship between mind and socioeconomic class are warranted (Charlesworth 2000).

Third, there are a number of topics in feminist philosophy of mind that have so far been underexplored and undertheorized. For instance, while many have noted the relationship between perception and the mechanisms of sexism and racism, more in-depth analysis is needed (Rohrbach 1994; Ngo 2017; Ortega 2019). We also expect that many emotions such as joy, regret, frustration, and equanimity that have not yet been examined in detail, as well as mental processes, such as sensation, attention, and imagination, will be further explored with a feminist perspective (Jones 2012; Kind 2013). Extending existing theories of action, agency, and autonomy also constitutes a rich horizon for feminist philosophy of mind (Veltman and Piper 2014; Brancazio 2018). Additionally, developing the intersections between feminist philosophy of mind and epistemology, metaphysics, ethics, aesthetics, as well as interdisciplinary areas such as neuroscience and global health is an obvious next step (Dalmiya 2017; Rippon 2019).

Fourth, the topics of artificial intelligence and posthumanism are evident points of overlap for feminist philosophy and philosophy of mind since they entail the consideration of the *To whom?* question and the need to examine social and political concepts like "human," "natural," "man-made," "object," "thing," and their relations with social categories like "women," "people of color," and "trans" (Haraway 1991; Braidotti 2013; Weheliye 2014; Schneider 2019). Inversely, smart technologies and artificial intelligences along with technological and genetic enhancements are now part of our contemporary milieu and have already had an enormous impact upon social relations, as well as the contours of political and economic life.

As we look to the future of feminist philosophy of mind, our sincere wish is that more and more philosophers begin to approach philosophical questions not merely from the purview of one specialization, but with the compound eye that follows from a willingness to build on insights from multiple domains of inquiry and multiple framing questions. Though the professional practice of surrounding oneself with others who are fluent in a specialized vocabulary and who predominantly share a social and cultural demographic has generated many important innovations throughout the history of philosophy, it has also limited us—herded our creativity into certain myopic channels.

The authors of *Feminist Philosophy of Mind* push against these barriers and beckon us to explore fertile landscapes where mind and social location, self and selves, naturalism and normativity, body and mind, rationality and emotion, and other historically opposed pairings are not cordoned off from one another by fiat, but mingle unchecked in the reality of everyday experience and everyday theorizing. This new space of inquiry is both an opening in the ossified edifice of our ancient and modern discipline and a precipice from where we can begin to see the promise of a professional milieu that values the search for truth and illumination above adherence to disciplinary conventions and the comfort of known professional practices and discourses. Feminist philosophy of mind makes explicit that multidimensional theorizing requires considerable self-reflection on the part of the theorist so that he/she/they are aware of the ways his/her/their membership in a certain species, race, gender, sexuality, nationality, class, and ability is imbricated in both the oppression of others and the very fabric of theorizing. We all must be wary of the ways social location can inadvertently direct theorists to take up and guard certain positions for reasons other than philosophical ones.

Because the concept of mind is a keystone aspect of most philosophical theories from ethics to epistemology, from language to action, from logic to aesthetics, we believe that the insights generated by feminist philosophers of mind in the coming decades will have reverberations across our discipline and beyond. This potential for impact coupled with the openness of the field at this early moment in its development makes it a most exciting time to pursue the themes taken up in *Feminist Philosophy of Mind*. We invite you, the reader, whatever your professional training, cultural background, gender&race& to find your own ingresses into this evolving terrain, to explore the rich philosophical questions posed by the authors in this book, and to participate in shaping this nascent field into a widespread and indispensable philosophical project.

Notes

1. The list of faculty members for the Institute reflects this orientation and included Miri Albahari, Dan Arnold, Katalin Balog, David J. Chalmers, Christian Coseru, Shaun Gallagher, Jonardon Ganeri, Jay Garfield, Uriah Kriegel, Alva Noë, Mark Siderits, Susanna Siegel, Charles Siewert, Evan Thompson, and Dan Zahavi.

2. Here we adapt a definition from Butnor and McWeeny (2014, 4). See also Alcoff and Kittay (2007), Tuana (2007, 21–22), Lugones and Spelman (1983), Collins (1990), and Kishwar (1990), all of whom question the inclusivity of the term "feminism."

3. Examples of feminist philosophy span a diverse array of philosophical traditions, approaches, and topics, from analytic philosophy to Continental philosophy, pragmatism, and comparative philosophy, and from ethics and political philosophy to epistemology, metaphysics, logic, philosophy of science, and aesthetics. These engagements are also informed by different kinds of feminisms, including, for example, Black, Latina, Asian American, intersectional, transnational, Third World, queer, trans, and crip feminisms.

4. For descriptions of philosophy of mind, see McLaughlin, Beckerman, and Walter (2009) and Kim (2011).

5. Paradigmatic approaches of this kind include Hilary Putnam's Twin Earth thought experiment, designed to show that mental content is dependent on factors external to the mind (Putnam 1975); Derek Parfit's teletransporter problem, which emphasizes psychological connectedness over personal identity (Parfit 1984); and David J. Chalmers's zombie conceivability problems that challenge physicalist accounts of consciousness (Chalmers 1996).

6. On thought and mental content see Harman (1973), Fodor (1975), Millikan (1984), Kriegel (2002); on belief see Churchland (1981), Stitch (1983), Schwitzgebel (2002); on perception see Armstrong (1961), Siegel (2010), Coseru (2012); on imagination see Kind (2001, 2013), Schellenberg (2013); on attention see Mole (2011), Ganeri (2017); on emotion see Rorty (1980), Goldie (2000), Prinz (2004); on intentionality see Brentano (1973), Dretske (1981), Crane (1998), Arnold (2012); on consciousness see Dennett (1991), Chalmers (1996), Siewert (1998), Zahavi (2005), Baker (2013); on intelligence see Turing (1950); on dreams see Flanagan (2000), Gerrans (2012).

7. On consciousness see Bartky (1975), King (1988), Wynter (2001), Maitra (2014); on self and personal identity see Anzaldúa (1999), Meyers (1997, 2014), Shotwell and Sangrey (2009), Shrage (2009); on agency see Veltman and Piper (2014), Herr (2018), Brancazio (2018).

8. See Fanon (2008), Young (1980), Bordo (1994), Gordon (1995), Alcoff (2006), Bettcher (2009), Ortega (2016), McWeeny (2017).

9. See Hegarty (1997), Fine (2010), Bluhm, Jacobson, and Maibom (2012), Joel (2012), Rippon (2019).

10. See Scheman (1980, 1983), Frye (1983), Lorde (1984), Antony and Witt (1993), Rohrbach (1994), Campbell (1998), Alexander (2005), Medina (2013).

11. See Daly (1990), Plumwood (1993), Quijano (2000), Barad (2007), Alaimo and Hekman (2008), Coole and Frost (2010), Weheliye (2014), Wilson (2015), Grosz (2017).

12. See Lakoff and Johnson (1980), Johnson (1987), Jackson and Petit (1988), Varela, Thompson, and Rosch (1991), Baier (1997), Garfield, Peterson, and Perry (2001), Tomasello (1999), Clark (2008), Thompson (2007), Hutto and Myin (2013), Ganeri (2012), Gallagher (2017), Newen, de Bruin, and Gallagher (2018), Kiverstein (2019), Schneider (2019).

13. See also McWeeny (2021).

14. The phrase "Ain't I a woman?" is attributed to Sojourner Truth. However, there are competing accounts of her 1851 speech at the Akron Women's Suffrage Convention. See Painter, who questions the accuracy of Frances D. Gage's account, which includes the famous phrase (Painter 1997, 164–178).

15. On the relationship between Beauvoir's and Descartes's views, see Bauer (2001, 46–77).

16. hooks's idea can be considered a precursor to contemporary discussions of intersectionality in feminist theory. See also Combahee River Collective (1978), Davis (1983), and King (1988). The term "intersectionality" was developed in the context of Black feminist theorizing in part to emphasize the invisibility of Black women's experiences in feminist and antiracist organizing, but also to express a unique ontological situation associated with Black women's social locations. For more on the concept's meaning and history, see Crenshaw (1991) and Carasthasis (2016).

17. See also Collins (1990, 6) and King (1988, 43–46).

18. See Spivak (1988), Oyěwùmí (1997), Quijano (2000), Lugones (2007), Taylor (2015), Harfouch (2018), Pickens (2019), Tullman (2019).

19. We use the neologism "gender&race&" as a placeholder for a list of social locations. "Gender&race&" is thus shorthand for "gender&race&class&sexuality&nationality &ability&etc." The word is intended to remind readers that "feminist philosophy" as we define it embraces a robustly intersectional understanding of social location, and rejects the unthinking prioritization of gender in its analyses, especially insofar as gender is naively equated with White, upper-class, western, cisgendered, heterosexual, and able-bodied women's experiences. At the same time, the ambiguous "&" that both connects and separates "gender" and "race" emphasizes that not all instances of feminist philosophy of mind employ intersectional methods, and leaves open the possibility of multiple conceptions of the relationship between gender and race (and other social locations), from that of a juxtaposition of analytically discrete categories to an interweaving of mutually constitutive ones. See also note 16.

20. Here and throughout *Feminist Philosophy of Mind*, we employ the term "gender" in the broadest sense to signify a person's *genre* or type in regard to social categories such as woman, man, intersex, transgender, agender, gender nonbinary, and gender-queer. In this usage, "gender" is not necessarily distinct from "sex"; it does not specify the cultural as opposed to the natural, nor does it indicate the psychological as opposed to the physical or anatomical. For criticisms of the sex-gender distinction, see Gatens (1991) and Heinämaa (1997).

21. See also Appiah (1985) and Zack (2002).

22. For thinkers who discuss gender and race see Block (1999) and Siegel (2017, 170–196). See Yergeau (2013) for an argument that philosophers of mind often construe the mind in ableist terms.

23. On multiple consciousness, see also King (1988).

24. See also Fanon (2008, 90) and Beauvoir's discussion of women's "divided" consciousness (2010, 67, 302, 572, 749), summarized in McWeeny (2017). Margaret A. Simons argues that Beauvoir's theory of woman in *The Second Sex* was influenced by Du Bois's idea, as well as Richard Wright's view of racial oppression (Simons 2001, 176–178).

25. See Parfit (1984), Korsgaard (1989), Albahari (2007), Strawson (2009), Siderits, Thompson, and Zahavi (2011), Ganeri (2015).

26. See also Parfit (1984, 245–280).

27. See Wilkes (1988) for an exception.

28. See Putnam (1982), Papineau (1993), De Caro and Macarthur (2010), Churchland (2011), Díaz-León (2016), Hufendiek (2016), and Tomasello (2016).

29. See Harding (1986), Hubbard (1990), Longino (1990), Haraway (1991), Nelson (1992), Fausto-Sterling (2000), Zack (2002), Code (2006), Fine (2012), Vidal (2012), Rippon (2019). This approach is not incompatible with certain strains in philosophy of mind that emphasize the interplay of fact and value, such as Hacking (1999) and Marchetti and Marchetti (2017).

30. Horst provides a classification of naturalistic views, which includes philosophical naturalisms that see mind as a natural phenomenon that can be explained by the sciences, and empirical naturalisms that see philosophical inquiry as a special type of empirical inquiry (Horst 2009, 222).

31. For example, theorists are divided between those that believe a naturalistic explanation of mind requires causal closure (Papineau 1993) and those that do not (Davidson 1970; Baker 2009). Another disagreement lies between those who believe a physicalist explanation of mind is best served by mind-brain identity theory (Smart 1959) and those who advocate multiple realizability (Fodor 1974; Kim 1992).

32. See Beauvoir (2010), Butler (1990), Wittig (1992), Heinämaa (1997), Fausto-Sterling (2000), Warnke (2007), and Garry (2011). A common criticism of naturalistic views of sex is that a set of physical features circumscribes too narrow a group to capture a phenomenon like womanhood; there will always be individuals who are regarded as women but nonetheless lack the relevant determinant, or who possess the determinant but are not regarded as women.

33. For salient examples of this phenomeon, see Gould (1981), Martin (1991), Fausto-Sterling (2000), and Fine (2010).

34. Phenomenological accounts of sexual difference are often critical of both naturalistic explanation and social constructionism due to their shared reliance on problematic notions of causality. See Beauvoir (2010), Gatens (1991), Heinämaa (1997, 2003), McWeeny (2017).

35. See also Beauvoir's criticisms of Sigmund Freud's and Alfred Adler's views about women's psychology (2010, 49–61).

36. See also Weiss (2015).

37. Naturalism and physicalism should not be conflated even if they are complimentary to one another. Those who believe in the existence of nonphysical forces or nonphysical laws in nature may be naturalists without being physicalists.
38. For functionalism, see Putnam (1975) and Jackson and Petit (1988); for computationalism, see Fodor (1975).
39. See Smart (1959) for a classic version of identity theory; Paul Churchland (1981), Patricia Churchland (1986), Dennett (1987) for reductionism and eliminativism; Davidson (1970), van Cleve (1990), Garfield (2001) for supervenience accounts. See also note 32.
40. See, for example, Dennett (1991, 2013), Block (2002), and Strawson (2006).
41. See also the critical alternatives to dualism cited in note 11.
42. See note 12.
43. See, for example, Anzaldúa (1999), Bordo (1987), Daly (1990), Plumwood (1993), Quijano (2000). Cf. Gertler (2002).
44. Anzaldúa's description of "mestiza consciousness" provides a classic example of this incompatibility (Anzaldúa 1999). See also Du Bois (1903), Beauvoir (2010), Fanon (2008), and King (1988).
45. See Ahmed (2004), Dalmiya (2009), Kim (2014), Whitney (2015), Green (2018), Malantino (2019).
46. See note 16.
47. For some recent examples, see Nicki (2001), Kafer (2013), Yergeau (2013), Taylor (2015), Larson (2018), and Pickens (2019).

References

Ahmed, Sara. 2004. *The Cultural Politics of Emotion*. New York: Routledge.

Alaimo, Stacy, and Susan Hekman, eds. 2008. *Material Feminisms*. Bloomington: Indiana University Press.

Albahari, Miri. 2007. *Analytical Buddhism: The Two-Tiered Illusion of Self*. London: Palgrave Macmillan.

Albahari, Miri. 2009. "Witness Consciousness: Its Definition, Appearance and Reality." *Journal of Consciousness Studies* 16 (1): 62–84.

Alcoff, Linda Martín. 2006. *Visible Identities: Race, Gender, and the Self*. New York: Oxford University Press.

Alcoff, Linda Martín. 2011. "Experience and Knowledge: The Case of Sexual Abuse Memories." In *Feminist Metaphysics: Explorations in the Ontology of Sex, Gender and the Self*, edited by Charlotte Witt, 209–224. Dordrecht: Springer.

Alcoff, Linda Martín, and Eva Feder Kittay. 2007. "Introduction: Defining Feminist Philosophy." In *The Blackwell Guide to Feminist Philosophy*, edited by Linda Martín Alcoff and Eva Kittay, 1–13. Malden, MA: Blackwell.

Alexander, M. Jacqui. 2005. *Pedagogies of Crossing: Meditations on Feminism, Sexual Politics, Memory, and the Sacred*. Durham, NC: Duke University Press.

Antony, Louise, and Charlotte Witt, eds. 1993. *A Mind of One's Own: Feminist Essays on Reason and Objectivity*. Denver, CO: Westview Press.

Anzaldúa, Gloria. 1999. *Borderlands / La Frontera: The New Mestiza*. 2nd ed. San Francisco, CA: Aunt Lute Books.

Appiah, Anthony. 1985. "The Uncompleted Argument: Du Bois and the Illusion of Race." *Critical Inquiry* 12 (1): 21–37.

Armstrong, D. M. 1961. *Perception and the Physical World*. London: Kegan Paul.

Arnold, Dan A. 2012. *Brains, Buddhas, and Believing: The Problem of Intentionality in Classical Buddhist and Cognitive-Scientific Philosophy of Mind*. New York: Columbia University Press.

Ayala, Saray, and Nadya Vasilyeva. 2015. "Extended Sex: An Account of Sex for a More Just Society." *Hypatia* 30 (4): 725–742.

Baier, Annette C. 1997. *The Commons of the Mind*. Chicago: Open Court.

Baker, Lynne Rudder. 2009. "Non-reductive Materialism." In *Oxford Handbook in Philosophy of Mind*, edited by Ansgar Beckermann, Brian P. McLaughlin, and Sven Walter, 109–127. New York: Oxford University Press.

Baker, Lynne Rudder. 2013. *Naturalism and the First-Person Perspective*. New York: Oxford University Press.

Barad, Karen. 2007. *Meeting the Universe Halfway: Quantum Physics and the Entanglement of Matter and Meaning*. Durham, NC: Duke University Press.

Bartky, Sandra. 1975. "Toward a Phenomenology of Feminist Consciousness." *Social Theory and Practice* 3 (4): 425–439.

Barvosa, Edwina. 2008. *Wealth of Selves: Multiple Identities, Mestiza Consciousness, and the Subject of Politics*. College Station: Texas A&M University Press.

Bauer, Nancy. 2001. *Simone de Beauvoir, Philosophy & Feminism*. New York: Columbia University Press.

Beauvoir, Simone de. 2010. *The Second Sex*. Translated by Constance Borde and Shiela Malovany-Chevallier. New York: Knopf.

Belenky, Mary Field, Blythe McVicker Clinchy, Nancy Rule Goldberger, and Jill Mattuck Tarule. 1986. *Women's Ways of Knowing: The Development of Self, Voice, and Mind*. New York: Basic Books.

Ben-Ze'ev, Aaron. 2000. *The Subtlety of Emotions*. Cambridge, MA: MIT Press.

Bernecker, Sven. 2009. *Memory: A Philosophical Study*. New York: Oxford University Press.

Bettcher, Talia Mae. 2009. "Trans Identities and First-Person Authority." In *You've Changed! Sex Reassignment and Personal Identity*, edited by Laurie Shrage, 98–120. New York: Oxford University Press.

Block, Ned. 1999. "Sexism, Racism, Ageism, and the Nature of Consciousness." *Philosophical Topics* 26 (1–2): 39–70.

Bluhm, Robyn, Anne Jaap Jacobson, and Heide Lne Maibom. 2012. *Neurofeminism: Issues at the Intersection of Feminist Theory and Cognitive Science*. New York: Palgrave Macmillan.

Bordo, Susan. 1987. *The Flight to Objectivity: Essays on Cartesianism and Culture*. Albany: State University of New York Press.

Bordo, Susan. 1994. *Unbearable Weight: Feminism, Western Culture, and the Body*. Berkeley: University of California Press.

Braidotti, Rosi. 2013. *The Posthuman*. Malden, MA: Polity.

Brancazio, Nick. 2018. "Gender and the Senses of Agency." *Phenomenology and the Cognitive Sciences* 18 (2): 425–440.

Brentano, Franz. 1973. *Psychology from an Empirical Standpoint*. Translated by Antos C. Rancurello, D. B. Terrell, and Linda L. McAlister. New York: Routledge and Kegan Paul.

Brison, Susan J. 2003. *Aftermath: Violence and the Remaking of a Self*. Princeton: Princeton University Press.

Brizendine, Louann. 2006. *The Female Brain*. New York: Harmony Books.

Burge, Tyler. 1979. "Individualism and the Mental." *Midwest Studies in Philosophy* 4 (1): 73–122.

Butler, Judith. 1990. *Gender Trouble: Feminism and the Subversion of Identity.* New York: Routledge.

Butnor, Ashby. 2011. "Cultivating Self, Transforming Society: Embodied Ethical Practice in Feminism and Zen Buddhism." In *Buddhism as a Stronghold of Free Thinking? Social, Ethical and Philosophical Dimensions of Buddhism*, edited by Siegfried C. A. Fay and Ilse Maria Bruckner, 56–74. Nuestall, Germany: Ubuntu.

Butnor, Ashby, and Jennifer McWeeny. 2014. "Feminist Comparative Philosophy: Performing Philosophy Differently." In *Asian and Feminist Philosophies in Dialogue: Liberating Traditions*, edited by Jennifer McWeeny and Ashby Butnor, 1–35. New York: Columbia University Press.

Campbell, Sue. 1998. *Interpreting the Personal: Expression and the Formation of Feelings.* Ithaca: Cornell University Press.

Carastathis, Anna. 2016. *Intersectionality: Origins, Contestations. Horizons.* Lincoln: University of Nebraska Press.

Chalmers, David J. 1995. "Facing Up to the Problem of Consciousness." *Journal of Consciousness Studies* 2 (3): 200–219.

Chalmers, David J. 1996. *The Conscious Mind: In Search of a Fundamental Theory.* New York: Oxford University Press.

Chalmers, David J., ed. 2002. *Philosophy of Mind: Classical and Contemporary Readings.* New York: Oxford University Press.

Charlesworth, Simon. 2000. *A Phenomenology of Working-Class Experience.* Cambridge: Cambridge University Press.

Cheng, Sen, and Markus Werning. 2016. "What Is Episodic Memory If It Is a Natural Kind?" *Synthese* 193 (5): 1345–1385.

Chinweizu. 1987. *Decolonising the African Mind.* London: Sundoor.

Churchland, Patricia Smith. 1986. *Neurophilosophy: Toward a Unified Science of the Mind-Brain.* Cambridge, MA: MIT Press.

Churchland, Patricia Smith. 2011. *Braintrust: What Neuroscience Tells Us about Morality.* Princeton: Princeton University Press.

Churchland, Paul M. 1981. "Eliminative Materialism and the Propositional Attitudes." *Journal of Philosophy* 78: 67–90.

Clark, Andy. 2008. *Supersizing the Mind: Embodiment, Action, and Cognitive Extension.* New York: Oxford University Press.

Code, Lorraine. 2006. *Ecological Thinking: The Politics of Epistemic Location.* New York: Oxford University Press.

Collins, Patricia Hill. 1990. *Black Feminist Thought: Knowledge, Consciousness, and the Politics of Empowerment.* Boston: Unwin Hyman.

Combahee River Collective. 1978. "A Black Feminist Statement." In *Capitalist Patriarchy and the Case for Socialist Feminism*, edited by Zillah Eisenstein, 362–372. New York: Monthly Review Press.

Coole, Diana, and Samantha Frost, eds. 2010. *New Materialisms: Ontology, Agency, and Politics.* Durham, NC: Duke University Press.

Coseru, Christian. 2012. *Perceiving Reality: Consciousness, Intentionality, and Cognition in Buddhist Philosophy.* New York: Oxford University Press.

Crane, Tim. 1998. "Intentionality as the Mark of the Mental." In *Contemporary Issues in the Philosophy of Mind*, edited by Anthony O'Hear, 229–252. Cambridge: Cambridge University Press.

Crenshaw, Kimberlé Williams. 1991. "Mapping the Margins: Intersectionality, Identity Politics, and Violence against Women of Color." *Stanford Law Review* 43 (6): 1241–1299.

Dalmiya, Vrinda. 2009. "The Metaphysics of Ethical Love: Comparing Practical Vedanta and Feminist Ethics." *Sophia* 48 (3): 221–235.

Dalmiya, Vrinda. 2017. *Caring to Know: Comparative Care Ethics, Feminist Epistemology, and the Mahābhārata.* New York: Oxford University Press.

Daly, Mary. 1990. *Gyn/Ecology: The Metaethics of Radical Feminism.* Boston: Beacon Press.

Dathorne, O. R. 1974. *The Black Mind: A History of African Literature.* Minneapolis: University of Minnesota Press.

Davidson, Donald. 1970. "Mental Events." In *Experience and Theory*, edited by Lawrence Foster and J. W. Swanson, 79–102. New York: Humanities Press.

Davis, Angela Y. 1983. *Women, Race & Class.* New York: Vintage Books.

De Caro, Mario, and David Macarthur. 2004. *Naturalism in Question.* Cambridge, MA: Harvard University Press.

De Caro, Mario, and David Macarthur, eds. 2010. *Naturalism and Normativity.* New York: Columbia University Press.

Dembroff, Robin. A. 2016. "What Is Sexual Orientation?" *Philosophers' Imprint* 16 (3): 1–27.

De Mente, Boyé Lafayette. 2009. *The Chinese Mind: Understanding Traditional Chinese Beliefs and Their Influence on Contemporary Culture.* Rutland, VT: Tuttle Publishing.

Dennett, Daniel. C. 1987. *The Intentional Stance.* Cambridge, MA: MIT Press.

Dennett, Daniel. C. 1991. *Consciousness Explained.* New York: Little, Brown.

Descartes, René. 1984. *Meditations on First Philosophy.* In *The Philosophical Writings of Descartes, Volume 2*, translated and edited by John Cottingham, Robert Stoothoff, and Dugald Murdoch, 1–62. Cambridge: Cambridge University Press.

de Sousa, Ronald. 1987. *The Rationality of Emotion.* Cambridge, MA: MIT Press.

de Sousa, Ronald. 2017. "Memory and Emotion." In *The Routledge Handbook of Philosophy of Memory*, edited by Sven Bernecker and Kourken Michaelian, 154–165. New York: Routledge.

de Vignemont, Frédérique. 2007. "Habeas Corpus: The Sense of Ownership of One's Own Body." *Mind and Language* 22 (4): 427–449.

Díaz-León, E. 2016. "Norms of Judgement, Naturalism, and Normativism about Content." *Philosophical Explorations* 19 (1): 48–58.

Döring, Sabine A. 2007. "Seeing What to Do: Affective Perception and Rational Motivation." *Dialectica* 61 (3): 363–394.

Drayson, Zoe. 2015. "The Philosophy of Phenomenal Consciousness: An Introduction." In *The Constitution of Phenomenal Consciousness: Toward a Science and Theory*, edited by Steven M. Miller, 273–292. Amsterdam: John Benjamins.

Dretske, Fred. 1981. *Knowledge and the Flow of Information.* Cambridge, MA: MIT Press.

Droege, Paula. 2012. "Assessing Evidence for Animal Consciousness: The Question of Episodic Memory." In *Experiencing Animal Minds: An Anthology of Human-Animal Encounters*, edited by Julie A. Smith and Robert W. Mitchell, 231–245. New York: Columbia University Press.

Du Bois, W. E. B. 1903. "Of Our Spiritual Strivings." In *The Souls of Black Folk: Essays and Sketches* by W. E. B. Du Bois, 1–12. Chicago: A. C. McClurg.

Fanon, Frantz. 2008. *Black Skin, White Masks.* Translated by Richard Philcox. New York: Grove Press.

Fatima, Saba. 2012. "Presence of Mind: A Political Posture." *Social Philosophy Today* 28: 131–146.

Fausto-Sterling, Anne. 2000. *Sexing the Body: Gender Politics and the Construction of Sexuality*. New York: Basic Books.

Fine, Cordelia. 2010. *Delusions of Gender: How Our Minds, Society, and Neurosexism Create Difference*. New York: Norton.

Fine, Cordelia. 2012. "Explaining, or Sustaining, the Status Quo? The Potentially Self-Fulfilling Effects of 'Hardwired' Accounts of Sex Differences." *Neuroethics* 5: 285–294.

Flanagan, Owen. 2000. *Dreaming Souls: Sleep, Dreams, and the Evolution of the Conscious Mind*. New York: Oxford University Press.

Fodor, Jerry A. 1974. "Special Sciences: Or the Disunity of Science as a Working Hypothesis." *Synthese* 28: 97–115.

Fodor, Jerry A. 1975. *The Language of Thought*. New York: Thomas Y. Crowell.

Frye, Marilyn. 1983. *The Politics of Reality: Essays in Feminist Theory*. Berkeley, CA: Crossing Press.

Gage, Frances D. 2005. "Reminiscences by Frances D. Gage of Sojourner Truth." In *The Concise History of Woman Suffrage*, edited by Mari Jo Buhle and Paul Buhle, 103–105. Urbana: University of Illinois Press.

Gallagher, Shaun. 2017. *Enactivist Interventions: Rethinking the Mind*. New York: Oxford University Press.

Ganeri, Jonardon. 2012. *The Self: Naturalism, Consciousness, and the First-Person Stance*. New York: Oxford University Press.

Ganeri, Jonardon. 2017. *Attention, Not Self*. New York: Oxford University Press.

Garfield, Jay L. 2001. "Nārgārjuna's Theory of Causality: Implications Sacred and Profane." *Philosophy East & West* 51 (4): 507–524.

Garfield, Jay L., Candida Peterson, and Tricia Perry. 2001. "Social Cognition, Language Acquisition and the Theory of Mind." *Mind and Language* 16 (9): 494–541.

Garry, Ann. 2011. "Intersectionality, Metaphors, and the Multiplicity of Gender." *Hypatia* 26 (4): 826–850.

Garry, Ann, and Marilyn Pearsall, eds. 1989. *Women, Knowledge, and Reality: Explorations in Feminist Philosophy*. Boston: Unwin Hyman.

Gatens, Moira. 1991. "A Critique of the Sex/Gender Distinction." In *A Reader in Feminist Knowledge*, edited by Sneja Gunew, 139–157. New York: Routledge.

Gerrans, Philip. 2012. "Dream Experience and a Revisionist Account of Delusions of Misidentification." *Consciousness and Cognition* 21 (1): 217–227.

Gertler, Brie. 2002. "Can Feminists Be Cartesians?" *Dialogue* 41: 91–112.

Gilligan, Carol. 1982. *In a Different Voice: Psychological Theory and Women's Development*. Cambridge, MA: Harvard University Press.

Goldie, Peter. 2000. *The Emotions: A Philosophical Exploration*. New York: Oxford University Press.

Goldie, Peter. 2012. *The Mess Inside: Narrative, Emotion, and the Mind*. New York: Oxford University Press.

Gordon, Lewis R. 1995. *Bad Faith and Antiblack Racism*. New York: Humanity Books.

Gould, Stephen Jay. 1981. *The Mismeasure of Man*. New York: Norton.

Green, Rochelle. 2018. "Cultivating Hope in Feminist Praxis." In *Theories of Hope: Exploring Alternative Affective Dimensions of Human Experience*, edited by Rochelle Green, 111–128. Lanham, MD: Lexington Books.

Grosz, Elizabeth. 2017. *The Incorporeal: Ontology, Ethics, and the Limits of Materialism*. New York: Columbia University Press.

Hacking, Ian. 1995. *Rewriting the Soul: Multiple Personality and the Sciences of Memory*. Princeton: Princeton University Press.

Hacking, Ian. 1999. *The Social Construction of What?* Cambridge, MA: Harvard University Press.

Haraway, Donna J. 1991. *Simians, Cyborgs, and Women: The Reinvention of Nature*. New York: Routledge.

Harding, Sandra. 1986. *The Science Question in Feminism*. Ithaca: Cornell University Press.

Harfouch, John. 2018. *Another Mind-Body Problem: A History of Racial Non-being*. Albany: State University of New York Press.

Harman, Gilbert. 1973. *Thought*. Princeton: Princeton University Press.

Haslanger, Sally. 2000. "Gender and Race: (What) Are They? (What) Do We Want Them to Be?" *Noûs* 34 (1): 31–55.

Haslanger, Sally, and Ásta. 2017. "Feminist Metaphysics." *The Stanford Encyclopedia of Philosophy*, edited by Edward N. Zalta. https://plato.stanford.edu/entries/feminism-metaphysics/.

Hazard, Paul. 2013. *The Crisis of the European Mind: 1680–1715*. Translated by J. Lewis May. New York: NYRB Classics.

Hegarty, Peter. 1997. "Materializing the Hypothalamus: A Performative Account of the 'Gay Brain.'" *Feminism Psychology* 7: 355–372.

Heinämaa, Sara. 1997. "Woman, Nature, Product, Style." In *Feminism, Science, and the Philosophy of Science*, edited by Lynn Hankinson Nelson and Jack Nelson, 289–308. Dordrecht: Kluwer Academic.

Heinämaa, Sara. 2003. *Toward a Phenomenology of Sexual Difference: Husserl, Merleau-Ponty, Beauvoir*. Lanham, MD: Rowman & Littlefield.

Herr, Ranjoo Seodu. 2018. "Islamist Women's Agency and Relational Autonomy." *Hypatia* 33 (2): 195–215.

hooks, bell. 1981. *Ain't I a Woman: Black Women and Feminism*. Boston: South End Press.

Hornsby, Jennifer. 2001. *Simple Mindedness: In Defense of Naïve Naturalism*. Cambridge, MA: Harvard University Press.

Hubbard, Ruth. 1990. *The Politics of Women's Biology*. New Brunswick, NJ: Rutgers University Press.

Hufendiek, Rebekkah. 2016. *Embodied Emotions: A Naturalist Approach to a Normative Phenomenon*. New York: Routledge.

Hutto, Daniel D., and Erik Myin. 2013. *Radicalizing Enactivism: Basic Minds without Content*. Cambridge, MA: MIT Press.

Jackson, Frank, and Philip Petit. 1988. "Functionalism and Broad Content." *Mind* 97 (387): 381–400.

Jaggar, Alison M. 1989. "Love and Knowledge: Emotion in Feminist Epistemology." *Inquiry* 32 (2): 151–176.

Joel, Daphna. 2012. "Genetic-Gonadal-Genitals Sex (3G-Sex) and the Misconception of Brain and Gender, or, Why 3G-Males and 3G-Females Have Intersex Brain and Intersex Gender." *Biology of Sex Differences* 3: 27.

Johnson, Mark. 1987. *The Body in the Mind: The Bodily Basis of Meaning, Imagination, and Reason*. Chicago: University of Chicago Press.

Johnston, Rebekah. 2008. "The Trouble with Inversion: An Examination of Science and Sexual Orientation." *Les Ateliers d'Éthique* 3 (2): 72–84.

Jones, Janine. 2012. "Can We Imagine *This* Happening to a White Boy?" In *Pursuing Trayvon Martin: Historical Contexts and Contemporary Racial Dynamics*, edited by George Yancy and Janine Jones, 141–154. Lanham, MD: Lexington Books.

Kafer, Alison. 2013. *Feminist, Queer, Crip*. Bloomington: Indiana University Press.

Kim, David Haekwon. 2014. "Shame and Self-Revision in Asian American Assimilation." In *Living Alterities: Phenomenology, Embodiment, and Race*, edited by Emily S. Lee, 103–132. Albany: State University of New York Press.

Kim, Jaegwon. 1992. "Multiple Realization and the Metaphysics of Reduction." *Philosophy and Phenomenological Research* 52: 1–26.

Kim, Jaegwon. 2011. "Introduction." In *Philosophy of Mind* by Jaegwon Kim, 1–30. 3rd ed. New York: Routledge.

Kind, Amy. 2001. "Putting the Image Back in Imagination." *Philosophy and Phenomenological Research* 62 (1): 85–109.

Kind, Amy. 2013. "The Heterogenity of the Imagination." *Erkenntnis* 78 (1): 141–159.

King, Deborah K. 1988. "Multiple Jeopardy, Multiple Consciousness: The Context of a Black Feminist Ideology." *Signs* 14 (1): 42–72.

Kittay, Eva. 1999. *Love's Labor: Essays on Women, Equality, and Dependency*. New York: Routledge.

Kishwar, Madhu. 1990. "Why I Do Not Call Myself a Feminist." *Manushi* 61: 2–8.

Kiverstein, Julian, ed. 2019. *The Routledge Handbook of Philosophy of the Social Mind*. New York: Routledge.

Korsgaard, Christine M. 1989. "Personal Identity and the Unity of Agency: A Kantian Response to Parfit." *Philosophy & Public Affairs* 18 (2): 101–132.

Kriegel, Uriah. 2002. "Phenomenal Content." *Erkenntnis* 57: 175–198.

Kuhn, Thomas. 1970. *The Structure of Scientific Revolutions*. 2nd ed. Chicago: University of Chicago Press.

Lakoff, George, and Mark Johnson. 1980. *Metaphors We Live By*. Chicago: University of Chicago Press.

Larson, Stephanie R. 2018. "Survivors, Liars, and Unfit Minds: Rhetorical Impossibility and Rape Trauma Disclosure." *Hypatia* 33 (4): 681–699.

Latour, Bruno, and Steve Woolgar. 1986. *Laboratory Life: The Construction of Scientific Facts*. 2nd ed. Princeton: Princeton University Press.

Leboeuf, Céline. 2018. "Reforming Racializing Body Habits: Affective Environment and Mindfulness Meditation." *Critical Philosophy of Race* 6 (2): 164–179.

Levine, Joseph. 1983. "Materialism and Qualia: The Explanatory Gap." *Pacific Philosophical Quarterly* 64: 354–361.

Lewis, David. 1976. "Survival and Identity." In *The Identities of Persons*, edited by Amélie Okensberg Rorty, 17–40. Berkeley: University of California Press.

Locke, John. 1996. *An Essay Concerning Human Understanding*. Indianapolis: Hackett.

Longino, Helen. 1990. *Science and Social Knowledge: Values and Objectivity in Scientific Inquiry*. Princeton: Princeton University Press.

Lorde, Audre. 1984. *Sister Outsider: Essays and Speeches*. Berkeley, CA: Crossing Press.

Lugones, María. 2007. "Heterosexualism and the Colonial/Modern Gender System." *Hypatia* 22 (1): 186–209.

Lugones, María, and Elizabeth V. Spelman. 1983. "Have We Got a Theory for You! Feminist Theory, Cultural Imperialism, and the Demand for 'the Woman's Voice.'" *Women's Studies International Forum* 6 (6): 573–581.

MacKenzie, Matt. 2015. "Reflexivity, Subjectivity, and the Constructed Self: A Buddhist Model." *Asian Philosophy* 25 (3): 1–18.

MacKinnon, Catherine. 1989. *Toward a Feminist Theory of the State*. Cambridge, MA: Harvard University Press.

Maitra, Keya. 2014. "Mindfulness, *Anātman*, and the Possibility of a Feminist Self-Consciousness." In *Asian and Feminist Philosophies in Dialogue: Liberating Traditions*, edited by Jennifer McWeeny and Ashby Butnor, 101–122. New York: Columbia University Press.

Malatino, Hilary. 2019. "Tough Breaks: Trans Rage and the Cultivation of Resilience." *Hypatia* 34 (1): 121–140.

Marchetti, Giancarlo, and Sarin Marchetti, eds. 2017. *Facts and Values: The Ethics and Metaphysics of Normativity*. New York: Routledge.

Martin, Emily. 1991. "The Egg and the Sperm: How Science Has Constructed a Romance Based on Typical Male-Female Roles." *Signs* 16 (3): 485–501.

McLaughlin, Brian P., with Ansgar Beckerman and Sven Walter, eds. 2009. *The Oxford Handbook of Philosophy of Mind*. New York: Oxford University Press.

McRae, Emily. 2019. "White Delusion and *Avidyā*: A Buddhist Approach to Understanding and Deconstructing White Ignorance." In *Buddhism and Whiteness*, edited by Emily McRae and George Yancy, 43–59. Lanham, MD: Lexington.

McWeeny, Jennifer. 2017. "The Second Sex of Consciousness: A New Temporality and Ontology for Beauvoir's 'Becoming a Woman.'" In *"On ne naît pas femme: on le devient . . .": The Life of a Sentence*, edited by Bonnie Mann and Martina Ferrari, 231–273. New York: Oxford University Press.

McWeeny, Jennifer. 2021. "Feminist Philosophy of Mind." In *The Oxford Handbook of Feminist Philosophy*, edited by Kim Q. Hall and Ásta, 169–183. New York: Oxford University Press.

Medina, José. 2013. *The Epistemology of Resistance: Gender and Racial Oppressions, Epistemic Injustice, and Resistant Imaginations*. New York: Oxford University Press.

Merchant, Carolyn. 1980. *The Death of Nature: Women, Ecology, and the Scientific Revolution*. New York: Harper & Row.

Meyers, Diana Tietjens, ed. 1997. *Feminists Rethink the Self*. Boulder, CO: Westview Press.

Meyers, Diana Tietjens. 2014. "Corporeal Selfhood, Self-Interpretation, and Narrative Selfhood." *Philosophical Explorations* 17 (2): 141–153.

Millikan, Ruth G. 1984. *Language, Thought and Other Biological Categories: New Foundations for Realism*. Cambridge, MA: MIT Press.

Mills, Charles W. 1999. *The Racial Contract*. Ithaca: Cornell University Press.

Mole, Christopher. 2011. *Attention Is Cognitive Unison: An Essay in Philosophical Psychology*. New York: Oxford University Press.

Montero, Barbara. 2001. "Post-physicalism." *Journal of Consciousness Studies* 8 (2): 61–80.

Moore, Charles A, ed. 1967. *The Indian Mind: Essentials of Indian Philosophy and Culture*. Honolulu: University of Hawaii Press.

Nagel, Thomas. 1971. "Brain Bisection and the Unity of Consciousness." *Synthese* 22 (3–4): 396–413.

Narayan, Uma. 1988. "Working Together across Difference: Some Considerations on Emotions and Political Practice." *Hypatia* 3 (2): 31–47.

Nelson, Lynn Hankinson. 1992. *Who Knows? From Quine to a Feminist Empiricism*. Philadelphia: Temple University Press.

Newen, Albert, Leon de Bruin, and Shaun Gallagher, eds. 2018. *The Oxford Handbook of 4E Cognition*. New York: Oxford University Press.

Ngo, Helen. 2017. *The Habits of Racism: A Phenomenology of Racism and Racialized Embodiment*. New York: Routledge.

Nicki, Andrea. 2001. "The Abused Mind: Feminist Theory, Psychiatric Disability, and Trauma." *Hypatia* 16 (4): 80–104.

Ortega, Mariana. 2016. *In-Between: Latina Feminist Phenomenology, Multiplicity, and the Self*. Albany: State University of New York Press.

Ortega, Mariana. 2019. "Spectral Perception and Ghostly Subjectivity at the Colonial Gender/Race/Sex Nexus." *Journal of Aesthetics and Art Criticism* 77 (4): 401–409.

Oyĕwùmí, Oyèrónkę. 1997. *The Invention of Women: Making an African Sense of Western Gender Discourses*. Minneapolis: University of Minnesota Press.

Painter, Nell Irvin. 1997. *Sojourner Truth: A Life, a Symbol*. New York: W. W. Norton.

Papineau, David. 1993. *Philosophical Naturalism*. Oxford: Blackwell.

Parfit, Derek. 1984. *Reasons and Persons*. New York: Oxford University Press.

Plumwood, Val. 1993. *Feminism and the Mastery of Nature*. New York: Routledge.

Pickens, Therí Alyce. 2019. *Black Madness :: Mad Blackness*. Durham, NC: Duke University Press.

Prinz, Jesse. 2004. *Gut Reactions: A Perceptual Theory of Emotion*. New York: Oxford University Press.

Putnam, Hilary. 1975a. "The Meaning of 'Meaning.'" In *Mind, Language, and Reality: Philosophical Papers, Volume 2*, by Hilary Putnam, 215–271. Cambridge: Cambridge University Press.

Putnam, Hilary. 1975b. "The Nature of Mental States." In *Mind, Language, and Reality: Philosophical Papers, Volume 2*, by Hilary Putnam, 429–440. Cambridge: Cambridge University Press.

Putnam, Hilary. 1982. "Why Reason Can't Be Naturalized." *Synthese* 52: 3–24.

Quijano, Aníbal. 2000. "Coloniality of Power, Eurocentrism, and Latina America." *Nepantla: Views from the South* 1 (3): 533–580.

Radden, Jennifer. 2011. "Multiple Selves." In *The Oxford Handbook of the Self*, edited by Shaun Gallagher, 547–570. New York: Oxford University Press.

Rippon, Gina. 2019. *The Gendered Brain: The New Neuroscience That Shatters the Myth of the Female Brain*. London: Vintage Books.

Rohrbach, Augusta. 1994. "Violence and the Visual: The Phenomenology of Vision and Racial Stereotyping." *International Studies in Philosophy* 26 (1): 71–82.

Rorty, Amélie Oksenberg. 1980. "Explaining Emotions." In *Explaining Emotions*, edited by Amélie Oksenberg Rorty, 103–126. Berkeley: University of California Press.

Russell, Bertrand. 2004. "What Is the Soul?" In *In Praise of Idleness and Other Essays* by Bertrand Russell, 159–164. London: Routledge Classics.

Ryle, Gilbert. 1949. *The Concept of Mind*. Chicago: University of Chicago Press.

Schellenberg, Susanna. 2013. "Belief and Desire in Imagination and Immersion." *Journal of Philosophy* 110 (9): 497–517.

Scheman, Naomi. 1980. "Anger and the Politics of Naming." In *Women, Language, and Society*, edited by Sally McConnell-Ginet, Ruth Borker, and Nelly Furman, 174–187. New York: Praeger.

Scheman, Naomi. 1983. "Individualism and the Objects of Psychology." In *Discovering Reality: Feminist Perspectives on Epistemology, Metaphysics, Methodology, and*

Philosophy of Science, edited by Sandra Harding and Merrill B. Hintikka, 225–244. Dordrecht: Kluwer.

Scherer, Klaus R. 2009. "The Dynamic Architecture of Emotion: Evidence for the Component Process Model." *Cognition and Emotion* 23(7): 1307–1351.

Schneider, Susan. 2019. *Artificial You: AI and the Future of Your Mind*. Princeton: Princeton University Press.

Schwitzgebel, Eric. 2002. "A Phenomenal, Dispositional Account of Belief." *Noûs* 36: 249–275.

Shoemaker, Sydney. 1984. "Personal Identity: A Materialist's Account." In *Personal Identity* by Sydney Shoemaker and Richard Swinburne, 67–132. Oxford: Basil Blackwell.

Shotwell, Alexis, and Trevor Sangrey. 2009. "Resisting Definition: Gendering through Interaction and Relational Selfhood." *Hypatia* 24 (3): 56–76.

Shrage, Laurie, ed. 2009. *You've Changed! Sex Reassignment and Personal Identity*. New York: Oxford University Press.

Siderits, Mark, Evan Thompson, and Dan Zahavi, eds. 2011. *Self, No Self? Perspectives from Analytical, Phenomenological, and Indian Traditions*. Oxford: Oxford University Press.

Siegel, Susanna. 2010. *The Contents of Visual Experience*. New York: Oxford University Press.

Siegel, Susanna. 2017. *The Rationality of Perception*. New York: Oxford University Press.

Siewert, Charles. 1998. *The Significance of Consciousness*. Princeton: Princeton University Press.

Simons, Margaret A. 2001. "Richard Wright, Simone de Beauvoir, and *The Second Sex*." In *Beauvoir and "The Second Sex": Feminist, Race, and the Origins of Existentialism* by Margaret A. Simons, 167–184. Lanham, MD: Rowman & Littlefield.

Smart, J. J. C. 1959. "Sensation and Brain Processes." *Philosophical Review* 68 (2): 141–156.

Spillers, Hortense J. 1987. "Mama's Baby, Papa's Maybe: An American Grammar Book." *Diacritics* 17 (2): 64–81.

Spivak, Gayatri. 1988. "Can the Subaltern Speak?" In *Marxism and the Interpretation of Culture*, edited by Cary Nelson and Lawrence Grossberg, 271–313. Urbana: University of Illinois Press.

Stein, Edward. 1999. *The Mismeasure of Desire: The Science, Theory, and Ethics of Sexual Orientation*. New York: Oxford University Press.

Stitch, Stephen. 1983. *From Folk Psychology to Cognitive Science: The Case against Belief*. Cambridge, MA: MIT Press.

Strawson, Galen. 2006. "Realistic Monism: Why Physicalism Entails Panpsychism." *Journal of Consciousness Studies* 13 (10–11): 3–31.

Strawson, Galen. 2009. *Selves: An Essay in Revisionary Metaphysics*. New York: Oxford University Press.

Tappolet, Christine. 2016. *Emotions, Values, and Agency*. New York: Oxford University Press.

Taylor, Ashley. 2015. "The Discourse of Pathology: Reproducing the Able Mind through Bodies of Color." *Hypatia* 30 (1): 181–198.

Thompson, Evan. 2007. *Mind in Life: Biology, Phenomenology, and the Sciences of Mind*. Cambridge, MA: Belknap Press.

Tomasello, Michael. 1999. *The Cultural Origins of Human Cognition*. Cambridge, MA: Harvard University Press.

Tomasello, Michael. 2016. *A Natural History of Human Morality*. Cambridge, MA: Harvard University Press.

Tuana, Nancy. 2007. "What Is Feminist Philosophy?" In *Philosophy in Multiple Voices*, edited by George Yancy, 21–48. Lanham, MD: Rowman & Littlefield.

Tuana, Nancy, and Shannon Sullivan, eds. 2007. *Race and Epistemologies of Ignorance*. Albany: State University of New York Press.

Tullmann, Katherine. 2019. "The Problem of Other Minds: What Problem? Whose Mind?" *Metaphilosophy* 50 (5): 708–728.

Tulving, Endel. 1983. *Elements of Episodic Memory*. New York: Oxford University Press.

Turing, Alan. 1950. "Computing Machinery and Intelligence." *Mind* 59: 433–460.

Van Cleve, James. 1990. "Mind-Dust or Magic? Panpsychism versus Emergence." *Philosophical Perspectives* 4: 215–226.

Varela, Francisco J., Evan Thompson, and Eleanor Rosch. 1991. *The Embodied Mind: Cognitive Science and Human Experience*. Cambridge, MA: MIT Press.

Veltman, Andrea, and Mark Piper, eds. 2014. *Gender, Oppression, and Autonomy*. New York: Oxford University Press.

Vidal, Catherine. 2012. "The Sexed Brain: Between Science and Ideology." *Neuroethics* 5 (3): 295–303.

Warnke, Georgia. 2007. *After Identity: Rethinking Race, Sex, and Gender*. Cambridge: Cambridge University Press.

Waziyatawin and Michael Yellow Bird. 2012. *For Indigenous Minds Only: A Decolonisation Handbook*. Santa Fe, NM: School for Advanced Research.

Weheliye, Alexander G. 2014. *Habeus Viscus: Racializing Assemblages, Biopolitics, and Black Feminist Theories of the Human*. Durham, NC: Duke University Press.

Weiss, Gail. 2015. "The Normal, the Natural, and the Normative: A Merleau-Pontian Legacy to Feminist Theory, Critical Race Theory, and Disability Studies." *Continental Philosophy Review* 48: 77–93.

Whitney, Shiloh. 2015. "The Affective Forces of Racialization." *Knowledge Cultures* 3 (1): 45–64.

Wilkes, Kathleen V. 1988. *Real People: Personal Identity without Thought Experiments*. New York: Oxford University Press.

Wilson, Elizabeth A. 2015. *Gut Feminism*. Durham, NC: Duke University Press.

Wittig, Monique. 1992. *The Straight Mind and Other Essays*. Boston: Beacon Press.

Wynter, Sylvia. 2001. "Towards the Sociogenic Principle: Fanon, Identity, the Puzzle of Conscious Experience, and What It Is Like to Be 'Black.'" In *National Identities and Sociopolitical Changes in Latin America*, ed. Mercedes F. Durán-Cogan and Antonio Gómez-Moriana, 30–66. New York: Routledge.

Yergeau, Melanie. 2013. "Clinically Significant Disturbance: Theorists Who Theorize Theory of Mind." *Disability Studies Quarterly* 33 (4): 1–26.

Young, Iris Marion. 1980. "Throwing Like a Girl: A Phenomenology of Feminine Body Comportment, Motility, and Spatiality." *Human Studies* 3 (2): 137–156.

Zack, Naomi. 2002. *Philosophy of Science and Race*. New York: Routledge.

Zahavi, Dan. 2005. *Subjectivity and Selfhood: Investigating the First-Person Perspective*. Cambridge, MA: MIT Press.

Zhu, Jing, and Paul Thagard. 2002. "Emotion and Action." *Philosophical Psychology* 15 (1): 19–36.

PART I
MIND AND GENDER&RACE&

1

Is the First-Person Perspective Gendered?

Lynne Rudder Baker

The first-person perspective, as I have argued at length elsewhere, is an essential property of persons (Baker 2013, 2000, 2015).[1] What I am concerned with here is the bearing of the first-person perspective—in particular, the robust first-person perspective—on one's gender identity. The structure of my chapter is simple: first to discuss the ideas of sex, gender, and gender identity; then to discuss the first-person perspective; and finally to discuss various questions about the relation between the robust first-person perspective and gender identity.

Sex, Gender, Then Gender Identity

The concepts of sex and gender are murky. Traditionally, a sharp and seemingly simple distinction has been made between gender and sex: sex is determined by the biological equipment that you were born with, usually categorized as male or female, indicated by external genitalia and by internal indicators such as reproductive organs, sex chromosomes, and gonads. Gender refers to "the attitudes, feelings, and behaviors that a given culture associates with a person's biological sex" (American Psychological Association 2011). Since there are other construals of sex and gender and their relations, I will use this fairly straightforward construal as a starting point for launching my own view of the first-person perspective. However, my view can accommodate other accounts of sex and gender or a critique of the distinction altogether.[2]

Moreover, the construal I started with is trebly imprecise: First, it presumes that a culture determines a definite set of attitudes, feelings, and behaviors associated with a person's sex, and that these attitudes, feelings, and behaviors are not in conflict with each other. (Is being a tomboy part of a girl's gender? Aren't some girls, but not others, tomboys in our society's eyes?) Second, this definition of "gender" obscures the normative dimension of the attitudes, feelings, and behaviors that a society associates with a person's biological sex. There is not so much an empirical correlation between certain attitudes, for example, and a person's sex; rather the attitudes, feelings, and behaviors reflect society's expectations about a person of one biological sex or the other. (Some societies expect

Lynne Rudder Baker, *Is the First-Person Perspective Gendered?* In: *Feminist Philosophy of Mind.*
Edited by: Keya Maitra and Jennifer McWeeny, Oxford University Press. © Oxford University Press 2022.
DOI: 10.1093/oso/9780190867614.003.0002

girls to gravitate toward "helping" professions and to shy away from combative sports.) To frustrate these expectations can be costly: a girl who wants to be a placekicker on a football team must be ready to endure rejection. Third, and perhaps most interestingly, this construal of gender makes gender dependent on there being clear answers about a person's biological sex and about society's expectations for a person of that sex.

That the two-sex system of sex is not exhaustive is suggested by the existence of intersexuals (Fausto-Sterling 2000, 31). Intersexuals are people whose bodies "mix together anatomical components conventionally attributed to both males and females," people who are neither clearly male nor female or are both at once (for example, an XX child with masculine external genitalia) (Fausto-Sterling 2000, 47).

We cannot, and morally should not, pass off this indeterminacy of sex by saying that it is the result of a malfunction in fetal development. Some intersexuals may appreciate having, say, both male and female anatomical features, and I don't think that we should call an identity that people endorse a "malfunction"—any more than I think that the Roman Catholic Church should call homosexuality an "objective disorder." Perhaps we should consider intersexuals more like albinos (just different) than like hemophiliacs (abnormal). In nature, there is a biological series at the ends of which are clear males and females (Fausto-Sterling 2000, 31). Although the two-sex system is not in nature, it can be maintained by modern surgery. Since gender concerns social attitudes toward sex, the murkiness introduced by the existence of intersexuals carries over into gender.

The unclarity of the notions of gender and of sex is magnified when it comes to the notion of gender identity, defined by the American Psychological Association as "one's sense of oneself as male, female or transgender" (American Psychological Association 2011). There are gender roles, which may be accepted or rejected, and stereotypical gender behaviors, which people of each gender may or may not display. One may even reject one's assigned sex. Transgendered people—"trans"—do not identify with the sex assigned to them at birth. "Trans" may be used both as designating either a gender identity or a sex or both. A transgendered woman was born a biological male, but thinks of herself as a woman, and a transgendered man was born a biological female, but thinks of himself as a man. The gender identity of trans does not accord with their assigned biological sex. Some trans go on to have surgery and to have many of the distinguishing biological features of someone of the other biological sex. Some trans men freeze their eggs before completing the transition. Some conceive and give birth.

The notions of sex, gender, and gender identity are tied in different ways to embodiment. For convenience, I'll suppose that sex is a matter of particular biological organs (parts of bodies); gender is a matter of attitudes and behaviors that a culture associates with a biological sex; and gender identity is a matter of one's psychological and social attitudes and behaviors toward one's own gender or sex. These attitudes and behaviors, along with sexual feelings, concern the whole embodied person. If (per impossibile!) there were disembodied persons, they would have neither sex nor gender nor gender identity.

So sex is biological; gender is social; gender identity is psychological. Despite the unclarity and complications of both the notions of gender and sex, my concern here is primarily with gender identity, the way that one regards (or does not regard) oneself as a sexual being. Attitudes and feelings about one's own sex may be confused or conflicted, in which case one's gender identity may be confused or conflicted. I shall consider gender identity to be attitudes and feelings—even if confused or conflicted—toward one's own biological sex, along with behaviors that manifest them, regardless of their causal antecedents (implicit social conditioning, explicit teaching, experience, deliberation, and so forth). With this understanding, I'll construe the topic of this chapter to be whether or not having a first-person perspective brings with it any particular kind of gender identity, where gender identity is taken to pertain to the whole person, rather than to any subpersonal features of the person (for example, sexual organs or DNA). One's attitudes, behaviors, and feelings toward one's sex clearly concern the whole person, embodied and embedded in an environment.

What Is a Robust First-Person Perspective?

Since the robust first-person perspective is a central idea of my view of persons, I'll explain it at some length. The purpose of this (seemingly irrelevant?) exposition is to consider its relation to gender identity. So please bear with me.

I take a first-person perspective to be a two-stage dispositional property. It begins with a rudimentary stage, which babies are born with. The rudimentary stage provides its bearer a first-person perspective on the environment and allows its bearer to act intentionally on nearby objects. The rudimentary stage, which comprises consciousness and intentionality, is shared by many nonhuman mammals (chimpanzees) and prelinguistic human persons (for example, infants). The robust stage, which is unique to language users, is a capacity to conceive of oneself in the first person, to think of oneself as oneself.

The robust stage of the first-person perspective—for brevity, I'll call it "a robust first-person perspective"—confers innumerable causal powers, such as the capacity to enter into contracts, to write memoirs, to make commitments, to cultivate new habits, and on and on. None of these characteristic human activities would be possible without robust first-person perspectives. The causal powers conferred by the robust first-person perspective are so vast that they make the difference between persons and animals a difference in kind (Baker 2013).

This capacity has two substantive presuppositions: First, a robust (or rudimentary) first-person perspective requires embodiment. One must have a body located in space, with a functioning brain, that interacts with the environment and allows one to negotiate and act on the environment. The normally functioning brain supplies the mechanisms that support one's mental life, and the robust first-person perspective is a sophisticated feature of a person's mental life. Second, and of greater importance here, to have a robust first-person perspective, one must have a language of some grammatical complexity, and only persons can acquire such a language. Only persons have robust first-person perspectives. Your cat, no matter how lovable, is incapable of having the attitudes that make up gender identity. This is so because such attitudes require one to be able to conceive of herself qua first-personal, to conceive of herself in the first person, and this ability in turn requires that she have a language that allows her to express many empirical concepts as well as a concept of herself in the first person (Baker 2013, 130–140). In greater detail:

The language required for someone to have a robust first-person perspective must have room for a self-concept—often marked by a "*" as in "I*" (pronounced "I-star"). To have a robust first-person perspective, one must be able to entertain thoughts like "I wonder how I* am going to die." In "I wonder how I* am going to die," with the first occurrence of "I," I refer to myself, and with the second occurrence of "I"—the "I*," I attribute to myself a first-person reference. The first occurrence of "I" is transparent; any co-referring term can be substituted for it salva veritate; but the second occurrence of "I" is opaque. It is not transparent, but entails that the thinker or speaker conceives of herself or himself from the first person. The second occurrence of "I" expresses a self-concept.

Following Héctor-Neri Castañeda, I call such thoughts "I* thoughts" (Castañeda 1966, 1967). I* thoughts are complex first-personal thoughts with linguistic or psychological main verbs in which the second occurrence of "I" is not transparent. (Although all I* thoughts manifest a first-person perspective, not all thoughts that manifest a robust first-person perspective are I* thoughts. If you are looking at an old school picture and exclaim, "That's me. I'm the one in the red dress," you manifest a robust first-person perspective just as surely as if you had said, "I believe that I* am the one in the red dress.") Nevertheless, in order to have a robust first-person perspective, one must be able to think I* thoughts, and hence one must have a self-concept, signaled by "I*."

Each of us who has a robust first-person perspective has a self-concept. The self-concept refers to the thinker or speaker conceived of from the first person. No sentence in the third person has the same truth conditions as an "I*" sentence. My wondering how I am going to die is not equivalent to LB's wondering how LB is going to die. No "I wonder how I am going to die" entails that I have a first-personal conception of myself as myself.

A self-concept—the vehicle of the robust first-person perspective—cannot stand alone. One cannot just think of oneself without thinking something about oneself. (This is where Hume was right when he said, "When I enter most intimately into what I call *myself*, I always stumble on some particular perception or other" [Hume 1896, 252]. Although I agree with Hume that there is no entity that is a self, his famous passage seems to me only to imply that one does not experience oneself in isolation; a self-concept cannot stand alone.)

One attributes thoughts to oneself, and in order to do that, one must have a battery of empirical concepts ("I wish that I had a truck" contains a self-concept [expressed by the second occurrence of "I"] and the concepts *wish* and *truck*.) So one must have empirical concepts in order to have I* thoughts. In order to acquire empirical concepts, one must have a public language.

This is so, because (1) empirical concepts can be both correctly applied and misapplied to various things, and (2) the difference between correct and incorrect application of an ordinary empirical concept is grounded in public language. As Wittgenstein said, without a public language, there would be no application conditions to ground a difference between using a concept correctly and using it incorrectly.

To see this, suppose that a nonlinguistic Ms. Brown had never had any interactions with other people, and was stranded alone in a jungle clearing. Could it occur to her to begin to name the things around her—birds, trees, and so on? If Wittgenstein is right, the answer is no: without a good deal of linguistic and prelinguistic preparation, Ms. Brown, could not decide to name anything at all. One could not decide to refer to anything until one had had countless interactions with language users.

Let's put that problem aside and suppose (per impossible) that it occurs to her to call some birds she sees circling around, "crows." How could Ms. Brown's use of the sound "crow" express any concept at all? She could not have formed the intention to refer to crows by "crow" unless she already has significant parts of a natural language. She could not have formed the intention to refer to the kind of creature that she is seeing by vocalizing "crows"; in her languageless state, she could not have acquired the concept of *a kind of creature*.

In the absence of a public language—with a community of language users—there would be nothing that would make it the case that any of Ms. Brown's mental events or vocalizations expressed any concept—*crow* or *bird* or anything else. Suppose that one day a raven started flying around, and Ms. Brown vocalized "crow!" Did she mistake a raven for a crow? How could she? There would be no difference whatever between her emitting what sounds like "crow" in the presence of crows and her emitting what sounds like "crow" in the presence of ravens. Even if she could mean something by her vocalization of "crow," there would be no difference between her meaning *crow* and her meaning *crow-or-raven* or her meaning *bird*—unless she already had mastered a language.

Ms. Brown's putative concept does not have an extension that would make her use of what sounds like "crow" on a given occasion right or wrong. Any record that Ms. Brown tried to make of her observations (by, say, marking a tree when she saw what she wanted to call "crow") would be right. Whatever seems right to her is right: "And that only means that here we can't talk about 'right'" (Wittgenstein 1953, 92e). So what sounds like "crow" in the mouth of an isolated Ms. Brown does not express any qualitative concept.

What's true of the concept expressed by the English word "crow" is also true of the mundane empirical concepts that are needed for thoughts that contain a self-concept. For example, if I wonder whether I* have enough income to retire, I must have a self-concept and the qualitative concepts *income* and *retirement*. Acquisition of those concepts requires a public language. If I thought that *income* was only what was in my bank account, I would be corrected by my financial adviser.

In short: in order to have a robust first-person perspective, one must have a self-concept (expressed by "I*"); and in order to have a self-concept, one must have a store of empirical concepts whose acquisition depends on a public language—at least for beings like us.

Before turning to issues concerning gender, let me emphasize the importance of the robust first-person perspective. Not only is it unique to persons, but it is presupposed by many (perhaps most) recognizably human activities. For example, we vote, we pursue graduate degrees, we make wills, we perform speech acts like pledging allegiance to the flag, swearing to tell the truth, making commitments. All of these activities—the list is endless—presuppose that the speaker or thinker has a robust first-person perspective. For example, the voter must be thinking of herself (qua herself) as voting; the person pursuing a graduate degree must think of herself as one pursuing a graduate degree, the person making a will not only must think of herself as making a will, but she must certify that she made that will. And if one pledges allegiance to the flag, one pledges her *own* allegiance.

The Relation of the Robust First-Person Perspective to Gender Identity

In this section, I shall show the relevance of the robust first-person perspective to gender identity. I shall argue that any having attitudes whatever toward one's gender depends on having a robust first-person perspective. (Although in the past, I have presented the first-person perspective as an essential property of persons, my essentialism is not relevant to the issues at hand. So, in deference to the overwhelming number of feminists who are antiessentialists, I'll regard the first-person perspective here as simply an important property of persons.)

The robust first-person perspective is presupposed even by the meanings of such neutral phrases as "attitudes toward one's biological sex." This phrase means attitudes toward one's own biological sex conceived of from the first person as one's own. Such attitudes entail that there are robust first-person perspectives. Moreover, if everyone has some attitudes or other toward his or her biological sex—even if the attitude is one of indifference or rejection or bewilderment— then we have the general proposition: "For all x, if x is a person, then x has some attitude toward her (own) biological sex." This may look like an impersonal claim, but it's not. The claim embeds attribution of a first-person reference; since "attitude toward her (own) biological sex" requires that the subject have a self-concept, one cannot have an attitude about her own biological sex unless she has a robust first-person perspective. The relation between one's gender identity and one's self-concept is that having a gender identity—having *any attitudes at all* toward one's biological sex—itself presupposes having a self-concept.

Although one cannot have any gender identity without having a robust first-person perspective, can one have a robust first-person perspective without having gender identity? On my view, one essentially has a body, but in certain pathological cases, one may believe oneself to be disembodied. In that case, if one might (wrongly) believe that one was disembodied, one could have a robust first-person perspective without a gender identity. However, in normal cases, where one knows that one has a body, having a robust first-person perspective brings with it attitudes toward one's body, and hence attitudes toward one's biological sex. Of course, this puts no constraints on the content of the attitudes (pride, revulsion); it is only that in psychologically normal cases, anyone with a robust first-person perspective has gender identity. Indeed, gender identity may well develop along with the robust first-person perspective. Some research is needed here.

My point here is that the robust first-person perspective and the language that manifests it are immediately relevant to issues of gender identity, inasmuch as one's attitudes about one's sex all require a robust first-person perspective, and other people's attitudes toward one as an exemplar of a gender are conveyed by means of language. So we have good reason to ask further:

Is the Robust First-Person Perspective Itself Gendered?

To ask whether the robust first-person perspective is gendered is to ask whether the robust first-person perspective itself introduces the attitudes, feelings, and behaviors that one's society associates with one's biological sex. To see how a robust first-person perspective could be marked for gender, recall that to acquire a robust first-person perspective, one must have mastered language of a certain complexity. To learn a language is not just to match words and things. To learn a language is, in effect, to learn a world; a young child learns what it is proper to do and to say and under what conditions it is to be done or said.[3] And without realizing it, people pick up almost-hidden differences in gender. For example, women giggle (silly creatures), while men chuckle (they acknowledge attempts at wit). No one is explicitly taught to say more often of women that they giggle, not chuckle, or of men that they chuckle, not giggle. And chuckling is ostensibly not normative. Nevertheless, to say "men chuckle" where "women giggle" is to convey a stereotype: men are taken more seriously than women. Another example, from which I would draw the same conclusion: men yell (righteous indignation) and women shriek (out-of-control emotion).

In learning a language, one learns norms and expectations, as well as the way things are (Wittgenstein 1953). Language is a repository of "gender schemas," construed as "sets of largely unconscious beliefs about men and women that condition our perceptions and shape our normative expectations" (Antony 2012, 227). And the world that young children get to know via language learning comes laden with implicit gender bias. For example, women "are subject to a gendered norm that assigns to them primary responsibility for childcare, elder care, socializing, and housework" (Antony 2012, 237). Young girls and young boys learn such norms as they learn a language; and as they acquire robust first-person perspectives, they learn to apply the norms to themselves.

So one acquires attitudes as one learns a language. Nevertheless, the language (English, say) may be home to a plethora of inconsistent attitudes, and which particular attitudes a child acquires depends on the local norms. But even knowledge of the local norms is insufficient to predict which particular attitudes a child will acquire: Two sisters, brought up among the same local norms, may acquire very different attitudes toward gender by the time that they reach the robust stage of the first-person perspective. Although both sisters may know that playing with dolls is approved behavior for girls and climbing trees is not, one sister may see herself as a future mother who plays with dolls, while the other sister sees herself as a tomboy who climbs trees. Both these attitudes manifest the robust first-person perspective, and both these behaviors—playing with dolls and acting as a tomboy—are associated with girls. So even though gender-specific ideas seep into the language that is the vehicle for the robust first-person perspective, the robust first-person perspective itself is not responsible for which gender-specific language attitudes a child acquires.

One reason for this is that the robust first-person perspective is a (stage of) a formal property. Although a dispositional property, it is not like being disposed to tell the truth or being disposed to eat apples. The robust first-person perspective itself has no qualitative character whatever. It is simply the (nonqualitative) capacity to conceive of oneself as oneself in the first person. This capacity is manifested in any array of attitudes that a person has about herself as herself*.

The robust first-person attitudes that one has toward oneself are manifestations of one's self-concept. The self-concept itself is merely the concept-of-oneself-as-oneself*. How one manifests a self-concept depends on numerous environmental circumstances. We inherit all sorts of attitudes, feelings, and behavior from the language(s) we learn. Before a child reaches maturity, some of these attitudes, feelings, and behavior make up their gender schemas. Gender identity is a mixture of attitudes one has about oneself* (the robust first-person perspective again) and attitudes about female and male genders.

The same capacity (the robust first-person perspective) may be manifested in inconsistent ways by (perhaps) different people. For example, one sister is disposed to become a pathologist, and the other is disposed to become a stay-at-home mother who keeps a lovely and welcoming house. There's no difference here in the capacity at issue; the difference resides only in its manifestations. And of course, one's attitudes may change dramatically as one has wider experience and learns more about the world. However, attitudes that define gender may be especially intransigent, and harder to change than, say, attitudes about Georgian architecture.

Having seen that gender identity of any sort entails having a robust first-person perspective, let's ask the converse question: Does one's first-personal concept of oneself entail one's gender identity? Clearly, no. For one thing, some people do, and others do not, regard their gender as part of who they are. For some people, one's identity is closely tied to gender (think of macho cowboys swaggering down the street, or coy girls flirting), but for others, one's gender is just a contingent fact, like the color of one's hair. A robust first-person perspective is a necessary, but not a sufficient, condition for one's gender identity.

In sum, although gender identity, as a matter of attitudes along with associated feelings and behaviors about oneself, clearly presupposes a robust first-person perspective, the particular attitudes that one has are not a result of the robust first-person perspective per se. (This point holds no matter how we end up individuating sexes, whether in a binary or along a "continuum.")

That is, it is not the robust first-person perspective that determines one's gender or one's attitudes toward gender. The robust first-person perspective just makes it possible to have such attitudes. The role of the robust first-person perspective with respect to gender identity is to give us the resources to have and to exhibit whatever gender identity-related attitudes that we have.

How the Robust First-Perspective Underwrites
Gender Freedom

I'll use the neologism "gender freedom" to be the view that one has some control over the gender schemas that one manifests. To some extent, perhaps after reflection, therapy, or just life experience, one can choose between gender schemas that carry implicit bias against girls and women on the one hand, and those that accord to girls and women equal respect and dignity on the other hand. Since the robust first-person perspective is not a qualitative property, it can stand behind any attitude that manifests one's capacity to think of oneself as oneself*. Even if the language that one first learns as a toddler—the language that initially shapes manifestations of one's self-concept—carries with it gender norms that undervalue being a girl, one need not be saddled with debilitating norms—at least this is so if one is fortunate enough to be brought up in a (relatively) free local environment.

Maturity, I believe, is to a certain extent a matter of coming to understand the worldview that one has unconsciously absorbed, especially the parts pertaining to gender (along with the parts concerning race and class), then evaluating the inherited worldview, and perhaps trying to change one's outlook with more or less success. As we grow up, our attitudes relating to gender may change, and hence our gender identity changes. Reflective people may consciously try to change their attitudes and behaviors. The gender identity of transgender people does not match some or all of their biological and anatomical features. Intersexual persons are almost always taught to identify themselves* as either male or female. Whether they deal with the mismatch by undergoing surgery or by trying to change their attitudes and hence their gender identity, maturity means that they come to terms with the mismatch and take responsibility for what they do about it. (Even when there is no mismatch, but certain privileges are built in to being cisgender, people should come to terms with what their privileged position means.)

Can There Be Robust First-Person Perspectives
without Gender?

The multiplicity of biological sexes leads to a final question: Could we change society in such a way that there are people with robust first-person perspectives but without any gender schemas at all? Could "I*" play a role in thought and action, as it does now, if there were no gender at all? Can we even imagine such a possibility?

I think that a world without gender schemas, and hence without gender differences, is conceptually possible (though not, I suspect, desirable). Here is a thought experiment that at least suggests that society could be reconfigured in such a way that we would have no need for gender schemas, in which case perhaps the gender distinction between men and women—or rather, between masculine and feminine—would wither away.

I am thinking of two changes—one social-normative, the other technological-normative. First the social-normative change: complete equality of men and women, with respect to sex and gender, and with respect to sexual partners. Any two mutually consenting adults would be welcome to choose each other as a long-term or short-term sexual partners. There would be no gender roles; there would be no difference in pay for men and women; a person would be eligible for any job that he or she could do. The roles of mother and father would (perhaps slowly) change into a single role of parent. The race really would be to the swift.

Besides this social-normative change, imagine a technological-normative change introducing machines that can produce new people with almost no involvement of existing people. In effect, artificial insemination would be augmented by artificial gestation. The technological part of the technological-normative change would be to harvest eggs and sperm from people at puberty. (Think of a mature person as a castrato or a female who has undergone infertility-inducing surgery.) Human eggs that had been harvested from pubescent girls would be fertilized in machines by sperm harvested from pubescent boys and men, and then implanted in an artificial uterus, where they would develop as fetuses do now.

The normative part of the technological-normative change, of course, would be inducing puberty-aged boys and girls and their parents as well as grown people to undergo what we might call "sex-harvesting." With these two (imaginary!) changes, there would be no need for gender identity or gender attitudes at all. Maybe there would be a period during which gender attitudes would just be vestigial, followed by their disappearance altogether. I do not suppose that such changes would be either likely or desirable, but they seem to be conceptually and metaphysically possible. Still, even if the technological and normative changes envisaged by the thought experiment are possible, given the kind of entities that we are, they may be impossible for us. (Analogously, it may be logically and conceptually possible for everyone to ignore all their offspring, or "to sit quietly (but comfortably?) on a chair of nails," without its being possible for entities like us [Cavell 1979, 111].) Since we do not know whether the changes envisaged by the thought experiment are really possible for us, perhaps the best response is to leave open the question of whether it is possible to enact the robust first-person perspective without gender.

This thought experiment seems conceptually and metaphysically possible (and perhaps even physically possible). If so, then we would continue to have I*-thoughts without any distinctions of gender whatever. In that case, we could conclude that the first-person perspective really is gender-free.

If the (fantastical) changes are not possible for us, then perhaps the robust first-person perspective is gendered in the sense that everyone who has it has some gender or another. In that case, we should conclude that the robust first-person perspective is gendered, but not in a way that automatically leads to gender inequality. Rather, it could lead to a myriad of ways of organizing human activity, many of which would be explicitly liberatory.

The Upshot

To sum up, it is not the robust first-person perspective per se that confers gender schemas, but rather environmental factors that affect one as one learns a language and acquires a robust first-person perspective. The robust first-person perspective, from which we can conceive of ourselves *as* ourselves in the first person, confers on us myriad unique abilities: we can imagine different ways of life; we can enter into others' experience; we can think about (and misrepresent) our own inner states. We can lie; we can play-act; we can try to become more empathetic. Importantly, we can envisage ourselves and our world in ways that are not in fact actual. This capacity, which any of us may use to shape ourselves, makes gender contingent, and (up to a point) discretionary for us.

People with robust first-person perspectives may divide into two (or more) groups that are distinguished by being stereotypically feminine (for example, seeing oneself as a housekeeper rather than as a football player) or by being stereotypically masculine (for example, seeing oneself as a navy SEAL rather than an elder-caregiver). However—and this is at the heart of my view—such division is not inherent in the first-person perspective itself: de facto at any given time, we all may be one of two genders, but de jure we are not. The robust stage of the first-person perspective makes room for a gender-fluid, gender-nonbinary, gender-free, or freely gendered world.

So I conclude that we can join Dostoyevsky in saying that life may be a messy affair, but at least it is life and not a series of extractions of square roots (Dostoevsky 1988, 35).

Notes

1. I am enormously grateful to Keya Maitra and Jennifer McWeeny for incisive comments and guidance.
2. There is a vast feminist literature that treats issues relevant to my chapter. See, for example, Gatens (1991) and Heinämaa (1997).
3. See Lugones (this volume).

References

American Psychological Association. 2011. "Definition of Terms: Sex, Gender, Gender Identity, Sexual Orientation." http://onlineresourcesalex.weebly.com/uploads/1/7/2/9/17295132/gender_vs._sex.pdf.

Antony, Louise. 2012. "Different Voices or Perfect Storm: Why Are There So Few Women in Philosophy?" *Journal of Social Philosophy* 43 (3): 227–55.

Baker, Lynne Rudder. 2000. *Persons and Bodies: A Constitution View*. Cambridge: Cambridge University Press.

Baker, Lynne Rudder. 2013. *Naturalism and the First-Person Perspective*. Oxford: Oxford University Press.

Baker, Lynne Rudder. 2015. "Human Beings as Social Entities." *Journal of Social Ontology* 1 (1): 77–87.

Castañeda, Héctor-Neri. 1966. "He: A Study in the Logic of Self-Consciousness." *Ratio* 8 (4): 130–57.

Castañeda, Héctor-Neri. 1967. "Indicators and Quasi-Indicators." *American Philosophical Quarterly* 4 (2): 85–100.

Cavell, Stanley. 1979. *The Claim of Reason*. Oxford: Clarendon Press.

Dostoevsky, Fyodor. 1988. *Notes from Underground*. Translated by Jesse Coulson. London: Penguin.

Fausto-Sterling, Anne. 2000. *Sexing the Body: Gender Politics and the Construction of Sexuality*. New York: Basic Books.

Gatens, Moira. 1991. "A Critique of the Sex Gender Distinction." In *A Reader in Feminist Knowledge*, edited by Sneja Gunew, 139–57. New York: Routledge.

Heinämaa, Sara. 1997. "What Is a Woman? Butler and Beauvoir on the Foundations of Sexual Difference." *Hypatia* 12 (1): 20–39.

Hume, David. 1896. *A Treatise on Human Nature*. Edited by Selby-Bigge. Oxford: Clarendon Press.

Wittgenstein, Ludwig. 1953. *Philosophical Investigations*. Translated by G. E. M. Anscombe. New York: Macmillan.

2

Computing Machinery and
Sexual Difference

The Sexed Presuppositions Underlying the Turing Test

Amy Kind

In his 1950 paper "Computing Machinery and Intelligence," Alan Turing proposed that we can determine whether a machine thinks by considering whether it can succeed at a simple imitation game.[1] A neutral questioner communicates with two different systems, one a machine and one a human being, without knowing which is which. If after some reasonable amount of time the machine is able to fool the questioner into identifying it as the human, the machine wins the game, and we should conclude that it thinks. This imitation game, now known as the Turing test, has been much discussed by philosophers of mind, and for more than half a century there has been considerable debate about whether it is an adequate test for thinking. But what has not been much discussed are the sexed presuppositions underlying the test. Too often forgotten in the philosophical discussion is the fact that Turing's imitation game is modeled on an imitation game in which a neutral questioner communicates with two different humans, one a man and one a woman, without knowing which is which. In this original imitation game—what I'll call the "man/woman imitation game"—the man wins if he is able to fool the questioner into identifying him as the woman.

Thus arises the question motivating this chapter: How has philosophical engagement with the issue of computer intelligence been influenced by the comparison to sexual differentiation—what I will call "the sex analogy"—on which it is based? In what follows, I begin with two competing interpretations of the Turing test that we find in the literature, one that ignores the man/woman imitation game altogether and another that does not. As I will suggest, however, even on the interpretation that acknowledges Turing's reliance on the man/woman imitation game, the significance of the sex analogy has not been adequately explored. In the second half of this chapter, I thus turn to such an exploration. As we will see, the fact that the Turing test was modeled on a man/woman imitation game seems to have led us astray in various ways in our attempt to conduct an effective investigation and assessment of computer intelligence.

Amy Kind, *Computing Machinery and Sexual Difference* In: *Feminist Philosophy of Mind*.
Edited by: Keya Maitra and Jennifer McWeeny, Oxford University Press. © Oxford University Press 2022.
DOI: 10.1093/oso/9780190867614.003.0003

The Standard Interpretation

The original imitation game involves a man and a woman serving as the two contestants plus a neutral questioner who may be either a man or a woman. Turing uses the labels "A" for the man, "B" for the woman, and "C" for the neutral questioner. Each participant is in a separate room and they communicate with one another electronically. C, who does not know which participant is in which room, aims to make this determination. While A's object is to try to fool C into identifying him as the woman, B's object is to try to help C. In describing the kind of exchange that might take place as the questioner attempts to determine which participant is which, Turing supposes that C might ask about the length of the participants' hair. Were C to ask this of A—the participant who, though actually a man, is trying to convince the questioner that he is a woman—Turing reports that A might respond with something like the following: "My hair is shingled and the longest strands are about nine inches long" (Turing 1950, 434). (We will return to this specific example later on in the section titled "The Exegetical Question.")

Only once the man/woman imitation game is fully described does Turing move on to introduce his now famous test. The test emerges directly from the original man/woman imitation game with just one simple change: the machine replaces participant A. Interestingly, however, though Turing himself relies heavily on the man/woman imitation game in developing his test, this reliance has been largely ignored in the secondary literature. Looking at various prominent overviews of the Turing test, for example, one finds that they explain the test without any reference whatsoever to the fact that it arises within a context involving a focus on sex (or sex and gender).[2]

Consider, for example, the entry on the Turing test in the *Stanford Encyclopedia of Philosophy*, perhaps the most highly regarded philosophical reference work available today.[3] The fact that the human/machine imitation game is modeled on a man/woman imitation game receives no mention at all when the game is described:

> Turing (1950) describes the following kind of game. Suppose that we have a person, a machine, and an interrogator. The interrogator is in a room separated from the other person and the machine. The object of the game is for the interrogator to determine which of the other two is the person and which is the machine. (Oppy and Dowe 2016, 5)

We see a similar omission in discussion of the Turing test in the relevant entries of the *Routledge Encyclopedia of Philosophy* (Moor 1998), Blackwell's *A Companion to Philosophy of Mind* (Guttenplan 1994), the *Oxford Companion to*

Consciousness (French 2009), and many comparable reference works. Even when it is acknowledged that Turing's own description of the game proceeds slightly differently from the description being provided, or in the rare cases when it is acknowledged that Turing's man/machine imitation game is based on a man/woman imitation game, these facts are dismissed as unimportant or irrelevant to the key matter at hand. As French puts it, though Turing provides a description that is "slightly more complicated" than the one that he himself provides, "there is essentially universal agreement that the additional complexity of the original version adds nothing of substance to its slightly simplified reformulation that we refer to today as the Turing test" (French 2009, 642).[4]

French's claim of nearly universal agreement is perhaps something of an overstatement, as we will see in just a moment. But it is certainly true that such agreement is widespread. Indeed, even Turing's biographer dismisses the original formulation of the game in terms of a man/woman imitation game as a "red herring" (Hodges 1983, 415). We thus arrive at what is often called *the standard interpretation* of the Turing test, an interpretation that treats it as an imitation game in which a computer aims to imitate a human being. According to the standard interpretation, the question at issue for the neutral interrogator is one of *species-differentiation*: Which of the two beings with whom I am communicating is a member of the human species and which is not?[5]

A Minority Interpretation

Against the standard interpretation, a small cadre of philosophers have offered a different interpretation of the Turing test, one that takes the original man/woman imitation game to have considerably more significance.[6] On this minority interpretation, Turing aims not to offer a species-differentiation test but a sex-differentiation test. Just as the man in the original imitation game aims to convince the neutral questioner that he is a woman, so too the computer in the revised imitation game aims to convince the neutral questioner that it is a woman. This interpretation gains at least partial support from Turing's initial description of the test. Consider the key passage from Turing:

> We now ask the question, "What will happen when a machine takes the part of A [the man] in this game?" Will the interrogator decide wrongly as often when the game is played like this as he does when the game is played between a man and a woman? These questions replace our original, "Can machines think?" (Turing 1950, 434)

In shifting from the man/woman imitation game to the imitation game involving the machine, Turing notes explicitly that the man is to be replaced with the machine. Since the man's aim in the original game is to fool the interrogator into identifying him as the woman, and since Turing does not say anything about the aim of the game having changed, philosophers who offer this minority interpretation claim that the Turing test is not intended to be a species test at all.

As Saul Traiger argues, referring specifically to the passage from Turing just quoted:

> The interpretation of this paragraph is crucial. We are to substitute a machine, specifically a digital computer, for A in the game. But substituting one player for another in a game presupposes the identity of the game. So nothing about the game has changed. We merely have a different individual, one who happens to be a digital computer, taking on the role of A. The machine, as A, is to cause C to believe that A is a woman. (Traiger 2000, 565)

Likewise, as Judith Genova puts it:

> Obviously, those who eliminate gender from the game assume that when Turing says, "Will the interrogator decide wrongly as often as when the game is played like this," he means by 'this' something like, between a computer and a person, with the object now being to discover which is machine and which is human. However, there is no prima facie reason to change the basic question of the game. 'Like this,' can just as well mean, with the machine imitating a man with the object remaining to distinguish between genders. (Genova 1994, 314)

Thus, on this minority interpretation, Turing did not intend for the interrogator to try to figure out which being is the human but rather to try to figure out which being is the woman.[7] Here the test for intelligence is an indirect one. The machine can be said to pass the test—and thus to count as intelligent—if it manages to fool the interrogator into identifying it as the woman as often as the man had managed to fool the interrogator into identifying him as the woman. The thought seems to be something like this: If a computer is as good at this kind of sophisticated imitation task as a man is, then we can infer intelligence on the part of the computer.

What's the upshot of interpreting Turing in this fashion? Several of the philosophers who offer this minority interpretation take the primary significance to lie in the difficulty of the task facing the machine. That's not to say that they take imitating a woman to be easier than imitating a human of unspecified sex. Rather, the difficulty lies in the fact that in the species-differentiation test the interrogator knows that one of the participants is the machine whereas in the sex-differentiation test, this thought does not even enter the interrogator's mind.[8]

Unlike proponents of the standard interpretation, then, proponents of the minority interpretation argue that the man/woman imitation game cannot be ignored when understanding the Turing test. In doing so, however, such proponents deny that we should assign any particular importance to sex. While this may initially seem surprising, it actually coheres nicely with their explanation of the significance of their interpretation. If the important difference between the minority interpretation's view of the Turing test and the standard interpretation's view of the Turing test is that only the former keeps the interrogator ignorant of the fact that one of the contestants in the game is a machine, then there needn't be any special reason that we model the Turing test on a game involving participants of two different sexes as opposed to different nationalities or political alignments. Granted, we may not be able to sub in just any pair of contrasting identities here. Traiger suggests that it be important that there be some sort of cultural alignment among participants (Traiger 2000, 570), while Sterrett suggests that the contrasting identities must be such that the imitator is required to reflect critically on what kinds of responses to give (Sterrett 2000, 550). But the fact remains that, even on the minority interpretation, the focus on sex itself is not seen as an especially important one.

Here Genova's work constitutes a notable exception. As is by now well known, Turing struggled with his sexual identity throughout his lifetime, and this struggle is often thought to have played a direct role in his suicide.[9] Drawing on these biographical details, Genova argues that Turing's work "confirms the belief in a close interaction between the personal and the intellectual affirmed by many feminist and cultural critics today" (Genova 1994, 324). In particular, Turing's use of the man/woman imitation game enabled him to confuse men, women, and machines, and thereby demonstrate "that no boundaries were sacred or unbreachable. All rules, all categories, all boundaries were made to be transgressed" (Genova 1994, 317). Indeed, Genova sees Turing's inclusion of the machine in the man/woman imitation game as enabling him to deconstruct this binary and, moreover, that "the evolution of thinking machines might provide a solution to the strangling binarism" that comes along with the differentiation between the sexes (Genova 1994, 315–316).

In this way, Genova sees Turing's initial use of a man/woman imitation game as both deliberate and essential, and she thereby takes a position that sets her apart not only from both the proponents of the standard interpretation but also from other proponents of the minority interpretation. Yet this also reveals something interesting. In bringing sex to the forefront of the discussion, Genova's reflections suggest a way in which our thinking about sex might be influenced by the analogy with computer intelligence. Importantly, however, this still tells us nothing about the ways in which our thinking about computer intelligence might be influenced by the analogy with sex. Thus, even here, in a paper rare among the philosophical literature on the Turing test for its assignment of importance to Turing's invocation of the sexes qua the sexes, the question that motivates the discussion of this chapter—how the sex analogy has influenced our thinking about computer intelligence—remains unaddressed.

The Exegetical Question

Now that we have distinguished the minority interpretation from the standard interpretation, the question naturally arises as to which interpretation is the correct one. Though I will not here attempt to settle this exegetical question, it's worth noting some important textual evidence in support of the standard interpretation over the minority interpretation. In particular, it's difficult to make sense of some of the discussion of "Computing Machinery and Intelligence" if Turing did not have a species-differentiation test in mind. Consider, for example, this passage concerning the appropriate strategy for the machine to adopt in attempting to win the game:

> It might be urged that when playing the "imitation game" the best strategy for the machine may possibly be something other than imitation of the behaviour of a man. This may be, but I think it is unlikely that there is any great effect of this kind. In any case there is no intention to investigate here the theory of the game, and it will be assumed that the best strategy is to try to provide answers that would naturally be given by a man. (Turing 1950, 435)

If Turing intended a sex-differentiation test, then the machine (who is taking the place of A, the man, in the original man/woman imitation game) would be aiming to convince the neutral questioner that it is a *woman*. Thus, one would expect to see Turing here talking about the *behavior of a woman* and *answers that would naturally be given by a woman*.

While passages like this are by no means decisive, they are at least strongly suggestive that Turing had a species-differentiation test in mind. But, as noted above, I won't here attempt to settle the exegetical question. Ultimately the question of which interpretation is the correct one is something of a red herring for the issue I here pursue, that is, the issue of how the sex analogy has influenced the subsequent discussion of computer intelligence. Whatever Turing himself intended, the vast majority of philosophical engagement with the Turing test has proceeded against the backdrop of the standard interpretation. Our exploration of the sex analogy must thus operate within that framework, that is, within the

framework of the Turing test understood as a species test. This gives us the following formulation of the question in which I am interested: How has our understanding of that species-differentiation test been influenced by the fact that it was
modeled on a sex-differentiation test?

As I will argue in what follows, thinking of a questioner's determination of intelligence on the model of a questioner's determination of sex has had several unfortunate consequences for philosophical thinking about computer intelligence.
I'll focus on three such consequences in particular:

(1) The sex analogy has encouraged us to think of intelligence as a certain
    kind of all-or-nothing, fixed property;
(2) The sex analogy has encouraged us to think about superficial markers of
    intelligence; and
(3) The sex analogy has encouraged us to think of the machine as pretending
    to be something that it is not.

In the next three sections, I take up each of these consequences in turn.

Intelligence as All or Nothing

In thinking about all three of the consequences that I will be exploring, it's important to remember that Turing was operating with a mid-twentieth-century
conception of one's sex. This point is especially critical in thinking about the first
of our three consequences. According to the conception operative in the middle
of the twentieth century, people fall into exactly one of two categories when it
comes to sex: man or woman. Moreover, which category someone falls into was
not considered to be open to change. Though neither of these assumptions currently holds much sway, at the time Turing was writing, sex was thought to be
both binary and fixed.[10]

In taking the man/woman imitation game to be an appropriate model for a
test for intelligence, Turing thereby seems to be thinking of intelligence in an
analogous way as both binary and fixed. The very setup of the test seems to presuppose that there are exactly two categories a machine could fall into. Either
the machine is intelligent or it is not intelligent. It also seems to presuppose that
which category a machine falls into is not open to change.

In fact, it takes only a moment's reflection to see how problematic these two
presuppositions are. In other contexts where we talk about intelligence, we are
much more likely to recognize an *intelligence continuum*. Consider discussions
of animal intelligence, for example—or more specifically, consider Koko, an
eastern lowland gorilla who has been taught American Sign Language as part

of her participation in the Gorilla Language Project. According to her handlers, Koko has a working vocabulary of over 1,000 signs and is said to understand approximately 2,000 spoken English words. On IQ tests, where a score of 100 is considered normal for humans, Koko has scored between 70 and 95. In discussions of Koko, her mental capacities are often compared to those of a young child (Patterson and Gordon 1993). The discussion is not framed in terms of *whether* she is intelligent, all or nothing, but rather *how much* intelligence we should say that she has. We see a similar dialectic in discussions of intelligence in other animal species. To give just one other example: Alex, an African Grey parrot studied extensively by Irene Pepperberg, is often described as having the intelligence of a five-year old (Pepperberg 2009).

When we step away from a computer-related context to other contexts in which intelligence is discussed, we also see an important sensitivity to the idea that where one falls on the intelligence continuum can change. Animals like Koko and Alex may, with guidance from trainers and teachers, develop new skills and capacities that incline us to count them as more intelligent than they were before. This point is also an obvious one in discussions of human intelligence. Intelligence develops as one grows from infant to child to adult—though also, in some unfortunate cases, accident or illness can lead to intelligence loss. In none of these non-computer-related contexts do we see an assumption that intelligence is fixed. Why, then, do we make such an assumption in the case of computer intelligence? Why do we see such an assumption built into the notion of the Turing test?[11] As I am here suggesting, this problematic assumption traces directly to the sex analogy.

Having fleshed out the problematic nature of these two presuppositions, however, we are now led to what may seem to be a counterintuitive result. It turns out that it's precisely because the Turing test has been taken to be a species-differentiation test (as assumed by proponents of the standard interpretation), rather than a sex-differentiation test (as assumed by proponents of the minority interpretation), that considerations of sex end up exerting an important influence in the discussion of computer intelligence. To see this, it will be helpful first to recall that proponents of the minority interpretation claim that Turing intended the game to stay the same when the machine substituted in for player A, that is, that we should see the Turing test as a sex-differentiation test. In this way, the neutral questioner is ignorant of the fact that one of the contestants in the game is a machine. As we saw, however, proponents of this interpretation also point out that Turing need not have started with a man/woman imitation game in order to achieve the requisite ignorance on the part of the neutral questioner. A nationality imitation game, or a political alignment imitation game, would have worked just as well. In the context of the standard interpretation, however, the differences between modeling the species-differentiation test on a sex-differentiation test and modeling it on a test aimed at differentiating nationality or political alignment test turn out to be critical ones.

Let's focus on nationality for a moment, and let's suppose that the questioner in the nationality imitation game has to figure out which participant is the American. Here we could have many different kinds of contestants in the role of A: a Canadian, a Mexican, an Australian, a Korean, and so on. When the questioner identifies one of the contestants as being the American, this identification thus carries no further implication about what nationality the other contestant is. Nationality is not binary. The same point would apply to a political alignment game, since political alignment also fails to be binary.

Because these characteristics are nonbinary, we also see more clearly a network of overlapping similarities and differences among the various choices. The Canadian and Australian might share a native language with the American, the Canadian and the Mexican share geographical proximity with the American, and so on. On some questions, then, it will likely be easier for the Australian to imitate the American than for the Mexican, whereas on other questions it will likely be easier for the Mexican to imitate the American than for the Australian. Matters are similar with respect to political alignment. With respect to some beliefs a Republican will resemble the Libertarian more than the Democrat, but with respect to other beliefs they will resemble the Tea Partier more than the Libertarian. So again, on some questions it will likely be easier for the Tea Partier to imitate the Republican, whereas on other questions it will likely be easier for the Libertarian to do so.

In fact, then, the two-contestant imitation game format seems somewhat unnatural when thinking about nationality or political alignment. If we were starting from scratch in an effort to design a game whose aim was to unmask the American, say, it seems we'd be much more likely to adopt a different format. Perhaps we might use something more like the *Dating Game* setup, where there are three contestants behind the curtain—one American and two not. Or we might even begin with a much larger group. By careful interaction and well-designed queries, the neutral questioner might eliminate possible contestants one by one until the field is narrowed to just a single contestant left standing—not quite the original *Dating Game*, perhaps, but instead more like an anonymized version of its millennial counterpart, *The Bachelorette*.

Even in these kinds of setups, there is still only one winner. Only one panelist gets the date, and only one contestant gets the rose. But suppose we were to develop a Turing test based on one of these other kinds of models. I don't know exactly what such a test would look like, but we might naturally think that there would be an important sense in which a computer who placed in the middle of the pack—who came in second among three panelists, or who lasted into a late round in the one-by-one elimination of a larger group—could still be said to be victorious.

The point here should in some sense be obvious: One doesn't have to come in first in an intelligence contest to count as intelligent. But when we're thinking of intelligence on the model of sex, this point gets lost. When the model at work is one of sex, and when sex is taken to be all or nothing, intelligence too looks like an all-or-nothing property. Indeed, intelligence looks like the kind of property that species-membership is. Either you are a human or you're not, and likewise, either you're intelligent or you are not. In neither case is there any middle ground. In this way, the test seems to encourage a way of thinking about intelligence that unnecessarily prejudices us against the computer participant.

Unsurprisingly, perhaps, many of the influential criticisms of the Turing test in the philosophical literature can be seen as pointing to something like this prejudice. To take just one example, consider Robert French's argument that "the Test provides a guarantee not of intelligence but of culturally-oriented human intelligence" (French 1990, 54). In an effort to establish this point, French offers the analogy of what he calls "the seagull test" for flight: a machine is said to be capable of flight if a neutral observer is unable to differentiate the machine from a real seagull by way of a three-dimensional radar screen. While it seems true that any system that passes the seagull test is flight-capable—that is, while it seems true that passing the seagull test is sufficient for flight-capability—it also seems true that many flight-capable systems will be unable to pass the test, as the test sets the bar too high. The point here seems clear: Just as flight-capability should not be linked to being indistinguishable from a seagull, so too should intelligence not be linked to being indistinguishable from a human. To assume otherwise is to be humancentric. But while this kind of humancentric prejudice has been previously noticed, what hasn't yet been noticed is how such prejudice can be seen as a natural consequence of the sex analogy with which Turing began.[12]

There's a certain irony here, since one of Turing's main aims in proposing the test was precisely to sidestep a certain kind of prejudice that would arise from tackling the question of computer intelligence head on. Given a mid-century definition of "thinking," Turing worried a computer might be conceptually excluded from counting as thinking. The concept "thinking" might simply not have been a concept that could be applicable to a computer. The Turing test was a way to circumvent this problem, or at least, a way to postpone direct consideration of the question, "Can a computer think?" until such time as the definition of thinking had become sufficiently expansive to allow for a genuine assessment.[13] In modeling his test on a man/woman imitation game, however, Turing showed himself to be victim of some of the same prejudices that he was trying to avoid.

Superficial Markers of Intelligence

The previous section helped us to see how the sex analogy misleadingly encourages us to think of intelligence as all or nothing. In this section, we will look at a second way in which the sex analogy is misleading. But while the first problem arises primarily from a way in which the sex analogy encourages a problematic characterization of intelligence itself, this problem arises from a way in which the sex analogy encourages a problematic way of detecting intelligence. In particular, the sex analogy seems to encourage a superficial line of questioning by the neutral questioner, and it thus correspondingly encourages us to focus on superficial rather than deep markers of intelligence.

Recall the kinds of question that Turing thinks the neutral questioner might ask in the original man/woman imitation game, namely, questions about hair length. Even from a 1950s perspective one would expect that hair length and other matters of appearance would be viewed as a superficial marker of sex and not a central aspect of it. In fact, the contestants are separated from the neutral questioner precisely so matters of appearance don't influence the questioner's judgment.

Of course, the questioner might choose to probe in a different way. By forcing the contestants to answer questions about moral dilemmas or about matters of social justice, a questioner might be able to uncover subtle patterns of sexed thinking lurking beneath the surface. Insofar as an awareness of such patterns requires a nuanced understanding that would be difficult for an unsophisticated participant to fake, we might think that these lines of questioning would ultimately prove more fruitful than lines of questioning about more superficial matters. But these lines of questioning are not among the most obvious ones that come to mind. Rather, in an imitation game involving sex, we're likely to be inclined toward questions about appearance, occupation choice, favorite pastimes and so on—an inclination that is promoted by Turing's own choice of sample question.

Ultimately, though Turing could perhaps have chosen to highlight more illuminating examples of sex-related questions, to some extent the problem here may be largely unavoidable, that is, the focus on superficial markers may well be endemic to the very concept of a sexed imitation game. Much contemporary work on sex and gender suggests that many of the apparent differences between the sexes are not biologically based but rather are the products of various kinds of socialization. As such, these differences are at least in principle changeable and thus might not be thought to run very deep. But insofar as there are no deep facts about sex that could manifest in a conversation with a neutral questioner, there are no deep facts for which to test. In this respect, sex seems quite unlike intelligence. Whether a being has intelligence does seem like a deep fact about the being. Were we not thinking about testing for intelligence on the model of testing for sex, we might naturally focus our attention more effectively on rooting out that deep fact. With sex as the model, however, our attention is naturally diverted to more superficial markers. Worries, for example, are explicitly raised in Turing's discussion about how fast or how flawlessly the computer might answer questions about calculation. Too quick or too flawlessly, and the computer might be inadvertently unmasked. Here we bump up against a certain irony: it's the computer's *superiority* with respect to these superficial markers of intelligence that might keep it from passing the test.

This irony brings us back to an issue that we encountered in the previous section: Turing's species test seems to constrain intelligence to a human mold.[14] And here again, we can see how the sex analogy helps to impose this constraint. To convince a questioner that they are a woman, participants in the man/woman imitation game will likely fall back on traditional conceptions of femininity and womanhood. This will be true not only for contestant A, who is not the woman, but also for contestant B, who is. Suppose contestant B is 5 foot 10 inches tall or has very short hair or that she has some other physical characteristics that are not traditionally viewed as feminine. Or suppose that she is a race car driver or an actuary or a member of some other profession dominated by men. Speaking truthfully about any of these characteristics will likely make it harder for B to win the game. In this way, the man/woman imitation game constrains sex to a very traditional or stereotypical—indeed, superficial—mold. It's thus no surprise that a species test modeled on it would likewise constrain intelligence to a very traditional or stereotypical—indeed, superficial—mold. The ability to answer questions quickly and flawlessly matters no more to intelligence than profession and hair length matter to sex. But, in both cases, it's these kinds of superficial characteristics that end up looming large.

At this point, however, an objection to my line of reasoning might naturally arise. In describing the Turing test, Turing himself gives three different examples of questions that might be put to the participants. The first asks the participant to produce a sonnet; the second asks the participant to solve an addition problem, and the last asks the participant to solve a chess problem. Since facility with poetry, math, and/or chess doesn't seem in any way a superficial marker of intelligence, the point pushed in this section might well seem unfounded.

In response to this potential objection, I think it's useful to return to a point that I made in the previous section, namely, that the notion of intelligence being employed in discussions of computer intelligence seems quite different from the notion being employed in other contexts, for example, in discussions of animal intelligence. The fact that Koko the gorilla and Alex the parrot cannot compose poetry or play chess does not count against their having intelligence. Passing the Turing test seems to require not only being able to respond like a human, but being able to respond like a human over an extremely wide range of subjects. Though having such a wide-ranging capacity for response might well be a good indicator of intelligence, it is by no means essential to intelligence, and a focus on it moves us away from the deep facts about intelligence, whatever those may be.

The Pretense of Intelligence

In addition to the two problematic influences already discussed, in this final section I'll briefly consider an additional problem that arises from the kind of contrast that the sex analogy sets up. In the man/woman imitation game, the man is pretending to be something that he is not. The whole point of the game is for him to try to fool the questioner into identifying him as something that he's not. If he wins the game, we certainly aren't entitled to conclude that he is a woman but rather that he's a good pretender—or at least that he's a good pretender when it comes to his sex.

This encourages us to think about the computer's performance the same way: just as the man is pretending to be something that he is not, the model of the man/woman imitation game thus encourages us to think of the computer participating in the Turing test as pretending to be something that it is not. If the computer wins the game, why would we conclude that it is intelligent? Wouldn't the appropriate conclusion simply be that it is a very good pretender, analogous to the appropriate conclusion in the man/woman imitation game?[15]

In fact, the issue of pretense has played a significant role in criticisms of the Turing test. Consider, for example, the so-called Chinese Room thought experiment proposed by John Searle. Searle offers a case in which a system might pass the Turing test for speaking a language like Mandarin without having any understanding of Mandarin, a fact that each of us is supposed to be able to determine for ourselves by imagining ourselves instantiating a computer program for the production of Mandarin outputs (Searle 1980).

At this point, one might plausibly protest that the problem of pretense arises not from the fact that Turing modeled his test on an imitation game involving sex but that he modeled it on an imitation game at all. In any imitation game, the issue of pretense will be a salient one. Worries about pretense—that the computer was not actually intelligent but was merely pretending to be so—would have just as naturally arisen had Turing chosen to focus on political alignment of nationality. While this point seems undoubtedly correct, I don't think it undermines the point that I mean here to be making. For I think there's good reason to believe that it's the focus on sex that leads us to think about imitation games in the first place.

The philosophical exploration of computer intelligence prompted by Turing's introduction of his test is by now almost seventy years in. And while the discussion has in many ways moved away from the test itself, with numerous commentators vehemently arguing that it has led the conversation astray, until now little attention has been paid to the respect in which the sex analogy underlying the test has played a part in that conversation. As I have aimed to show in this chapter, its part has been not only significant but also in various ways problematic. Of course, it's impossible at this point to unwind the clock and wipe the slate clean. But even if we cannot entirely erase the problematic influences of the sex analogy, we can only begin to address them and work toward a corrective once they have been identified. Though there is thus considerably more work to be done, this chapter should serve as an important first step toward this ongoing project.

Notes

1. An earlier version of this chapter was presented at a session on "Feminist Philosophy of Mind" at the Pacific Division meeting of the American Philosophical Association in 2017. I am grateful to the audience there for helpful feedback. Thanks also to Keya Maitra and Jennifer McWeeny for their incisive and helpful feedback.

2. Though I here say "sex and gender," it is important to note that Turing was writing at a time before the sex/gender distinction was in place. (The distinction is often traced to Stoller (1968); see Mikkola (2017) for a useful overview.) In order to avoid anachronism, and also to better capture what Turing had in mind, I tend to talk in terms of "sex" rather than "gender" in what follows.

3. For a discussion of the prominence of the *Stanford Encyclopedia of Philosophy*, see Sonnad (2015).

4. See also Saygin et al. (2000, 467).

5. In addition to the writers mentioned in the text above, the standard interpretation is also offered by Jack Copeland and Diane Proudfoot, two philosophers who have (both jointly and individually) written extensively on Turing's work. See, for example, Proudfoot and Copeland (2012).

6. See Genova (1994), Hayes and Ford (1995), Sterrett (2000), Traiger (2000), and Lenat (2008).

7. Interestingly, Lenat suggests that we can attribute the dominance of the standard interpretation to "political correctness." See Lenat (2008, 273–274). I do not have the space to engage this suggestion here.

8. See, for example, Hayes and Ford (1995, 972), Traiger (2000, 565), and Lenat (2008, 274).

9. See Hodges (1983) for extensive discussion of Turing's struggles with his sexuality.

10. Indeed, the view that gender is both fixed and binary was still the prevailing view in the 1990s. In pushing back against this binarism in her famous article "The Five

Sexes," Anne Fausto-Sterling notes that "Western culture is deeply committed to the idea that there are only two sexes" (Fausto-Sterling 1993, 20).

11. Of course, subsequent to the publication of Turing's paper, there has been considerable work in computer science and artificial intelligence toward enabling machines to learn. The existence of such work, however, does not undermine my point in the text above about the presuppositions built into the Turing test. Whatever the progress on learning computers that has been made, such presuppositions have nonetheless exerted an influence in the philosophical exploration of computer intelligence.

12. French, for example, argues persuasively that part of the problem with the Turing test is that it "admits of no degrees" in its determination of intelligence and that there is a problem with any kind of test that fails to recognize an intelligence continuum (French 1990, 57). But in making this argument, French does not seem to notice the way in which this failure on the part of the Turing test seems to trace to the sex analogy on which it is based.

13. See, for example, the following passage: "The original question, 'Can machines think?' I believe to be too meaningless to deserve discussion. Nevertheless I believe that at the end of the century the use of words and general educated opinion will have altered so much that one will be able to speak of machines thinking without expecting to be contradicted" (Turing 1950, 442).

14. In fact, the constraint is even narrower than this, since there seems a presumption that the human contestant is a Western, neurotypical adult.

15. In fact, this issue of pretense might well be one reason why the model of the man/woman imitation game often drops out of the discussion. Insofar as it seems plausible that simulating intelligence may be good enough for intelligence, while still remaining implausible that simulating being a woman is good enough for being a woman, we have reason to think that the analogy should be dismissed as irrelevant—as just a way to get the conversation started.

References

Fausto-Sterling, Anne. 1993. "The Five Sexes: Why Male and Female Are Not Enough." *The Sciences* 33 (2): 20–25.

French, Robert. 1990. "Subcognition and the Limits of the Turing Test." *Mind* 99 (393): 53–65.

French, Robert. 2009. "The Turing Test." In *Oxford Companion to Consciousness*, edited by Timothy Bayne, Axel Cleeremans, and Patrick Wilken, 641–643. Oxford: Oxford University Press.

Genova, Judith. 1994. "Turing's Sexual Guessing Game." *Social Epistemology* 8 (4): 313–326.

Guttenplan, Samuel. 1994. "Alan Turing." In *A Companion to the Philosophy of Mind*, edited by Samuel Guttenplan, 594–596. Oxford: Blackwell.

Hayes, Patrick, and Kenneth Ford. 1995. "Turing Test Considered Harmful." *Proceedings of the Fourteenth International Joint Conference on Artificial Intelligence IJCAI 95* (1): 972–977.

Hodges, Andrew. 1983. *Alan Turing: The Enigma*. New York: Simon and Schuster.

Lenat, Douglas B. 2008. "Building a Machine Smart Enough to Pass the Turing Test: Could We, Should We, Will We?" In *Parsing the Turing Test: Philosophical and Methodological Issues in the Quest for the Thinking Computer*, edited by Robert Epstein, Gary Roberts, and Grace Beber, 261–282. Dordrecht: Springer.

Mikkola, Mari. 2017. "Feminist Perspectives on Sex and Gender." In *Stanford Encyclopedia of Philosophy*, edited by Edward N. Zalta. https://plato.stanford.edu/archives/sum2 017/entries/feminism-gender/.

Moor, James H. 1988. "Turing, Alan Mathison (1912–54)." In *The Routledge Encyclopedia of Philosophy*, edited by Tim Crane. https://www-rep-routledge-com.ccl.idm.oclc.org/articles/biographical/turing-alan-mathison-1912-54/v-1.

Oppy, Graham, and David Dowe. 2016. "The Turing Test." In *Stanford Encyclopedia of Philosophy*, edited by Edward N. Zalta. https://plato.stanford.edu/archives/spr2016/entries/turing-test/.

Patterson, Francine, and Wendy Gordon. 1993. "The Case for the Personhood of Gorillas." In *The Great Ape Project*, edited by Paola Cavalieri and Peter Singer, 58–75. New York: St. Martin's Griffin.

Pepperberg, Irene M. 2009. *Alex and Me*. New York: Harper.

Proudfoot, Diane, and Jack Copeland. 2012. "Artificial Intelligence." In *The Oxford Handbook of Philosophy of Cognitive Science*, edited by Eric Margolis, Richard Samuels, and Stephen P. Stich, 147–182. Oxford: Oxford University Press.

Saygin, Ayse Pinar, Ilyas Cicekli, and Varol Akman. 2000. "Turing Test: 50 Years Later." *Minds and Machines* 10 (4): 463–518.

Searle, John. 1980. "Minds, Brains, and Programs." *Behavioral and Brain Sciences* 3 (3): 417–424.

Sonnad, Nikhil. 2015. "This Free Online Encyclopedia Has Achieved What Wikipedia Can Only Dream Of." *Quartz*. September 21. https://qz.com/480741/this-free-online-encyclopedia-has-achieved-what-wikipedia-can-only-dream-of/.

Sterrett, Susan G. 2000. "Turing's Two Tests for Intelligence." *Minds and Machines: Journal for Artificial Intelligence, Philosophy, and Cognitive Science* 10 (4): 541–559.

Stoller, Robert. 1968. *Sex and Gender*. London: Hogarth Press.

Traiger, Saul. 2000. "Making the Right Identification in the Turing Test." *Minds and Machines: Journal for Artificial Intelligence, Philosophy, and Cognitive Science* 10 (4): 561–572.

Turing, Alan. 1950. "Computing Machinery and Intelligence." *Mind* 59 (236): 433–460.

3

Toward a Feminist Theory
of Mental Content

Keya Maitra

This chapter grows out of my dual conviction that a theory of mental content needs to be shaped by feminist concerns, *and* feminist theorizing and activism need to be informed by a feminist theory of mental content.[1] A feminist theory of content allows us to appreciate the nuanced role that historical and sociocultural forces play in shaping the content of many of our terms—a hitherto underexplored dimension of a major topic in philosophy of mind.[2] Using as an example José Jorge Mendoza's analysis of how the history of US immigration and citizenship law has shaped the term "whiteness," my chapter argues that feminist theorizing and activism stand to benefit from the possibility of a feminist theory of mental content that makes explicit how the contents of many terms with social and political import are determined and held stable.

Interestingly though, the question of mental content—arguably one of the central topics in philosophy of mind—seems to get very little attention from feminist philosophers. Feminist reluctance to engage with the discussion of mental content in philosophy of mind is fair. Insofar as the social and political makings of our reality have been treated as mostly irrelevant to the objective understanding of mental phenomena that philosophers of mind pursue, feminists would find little incentive in joining that journey. Further, attempted feminist engagements have garnered very little attention. Take for example, the article "Individualism and the Objects of Psychology" that Naomi Scheman published in 1983.[3] In this piece, Scheman offers a sustained and incisive critique of what she calls "the individualist assumption" in much of mainstream philosophy of mind and develops a thoroughgoing anti-individualist account of the mental. In spite of being published in a widely used feminist anthology, this chapter exerted little influence either in feminist theory or in traditional analytic philosophy (Golumbia 1999, 202).

David Golumbia argues that the traditionalism and sexism of much of analytic philosophy of mind and its technical and scientistic character have alienated and discouraged feminists (Golumbia 1999, 202–203). While there is truth in this reasoning, it cannot be the entire truth. After all, areas like philosophy

Keya Maitra, *Toward a Feminist Theory of Mental Content* In: *Feminist Philosophy of Mind*.
Edited by: Keya Maitra and Jennifer McWeeny, Oxford University Press. © Oxford University Press 2022.
DOI: 10.1093/oso/9780190867614.003.0004

of science and epistemology are every bit as technical and scientistic and just as "heavily guarded fortresses of philosophy," yet they have cultivated significant feminist contributions (Golumbia 1999, 203).[4] I propose that the lack of feminist engagement here might be due to the fact that a theory of content's benefits have not been clearly articulated. To rectify the situation, we need to address the question, "What kind of externalism would work for the feminist project?".

I open my argument by considering the externalist theory of meaning and mental content. Externalism is the view that factors outside of one's mind at least partially determine the content of mental phenomena. Given feminist interest in understanding the sociopolitical factors underlying systems of oppression, and the fact that most of these factors exist outside of one's mind, it would seem that the externalist approach would be the best option for feminist purposes. However, not every externalism is compatible with feminism. Indeed, an important aspect of my central argument consists in exposing how and why classical externalist accounts in the philosophy of mind literature remain ineffectual for feminist purposes. In treating the social world as a transparent given, and not a malleable product of various interacting power dynamics, the typical externalist account remains inadequate for capturing *how* factors outside of us are responsible for the contents of our thoughts and aspirations. This observation opens the need to outline a few features that a feminist theory of content should have. The final part of my argument develops the first approximation of a feminist theory of content. In this regard, I will use Ruth Garrett Millikan's "consumer" account of meaning and mental representation as a template. While Millikan's theory does not feature directly within the philosophy of mind literature on mental content per se, given its focus on evolutionary functioning of cognitive systems, its externalist elements are unmistakable. In the process, I will highlight this theory's potential for feminism and outline how it needs to be amended and adjusted in order to achieve a feminist theory of content.

Externalism about Mental Content: A Classic Version

Philosophers of mind have used the notion of content as a clear way of distinguishing between mental and nonmental phenomena. The blooming Olivia rose bush in my neighbor's garden is nonmental, while my thought that it is breathtaking is mental. This much seems obvious. But the notion of content allows us to clarify this distinction. The blooming Olivia bush is not about anything else beyond itself. True, it gives a lot of enjoyment to passersby but in itself it is simply itself. My thought that the blooming Olivia rose bush is breathtaking, however, *is* about something else, namely, the bush. Franz Brentano is credited with underscoring this distinction between nonmental and mental phenomena and introducing the notion of intentionality to characterize what he took to be the "mark of the mental." He observes that things in a mind are about something else. The question that becomes primary then is *how* a thought or desire comes to be about whatever it is. How is such aboutness determined? The debate over mental content is about what factors determine the contents of mental items.

A good place to start a quick review of the debate over mental content is with the causal theories of meaning and reference in analytic philosophy of language that were proposed by Hilary Putnam and Saul Kripke in 1960s and 1970s. Countering the description theory of meaning that associates the meaning of a term with various descriptions, proponents of the causal theory of reference argue that the object referred to by a term ultimately determines the meaning of the term. For example, description theory maintains that the meaning of "water" is determined and learned by its associated description as a thirst-quenching, colorless, odorless liquid that fills our lakes, rivers, and oceans, and is good for bathing. Proponents of causal theories, on the other hand, argue that the meaning of "water" is determined by the chemical makeup of whatever stuff one interacts with in using the term "water." This idea motivates Putnam's proclamation, " 'meanings' just ain't in the *head*" (Putnam 1975, 227). The structure of the world determines meaning, not the description in one's mind. He contrives his classic Twin Earth example to drive this point home. In this example, we are asked to imagine a remote planet in our universe, the Twin Earth, exactly like Earth except for a few critical differences. One difference is that instead of water (H_2O), Twin Earth has a different stuff, whose complex chemical compound is abbreviated as XYZ. We are to imagine further that the macro properties of XYZ, properties one would encounter under normal Earth temperatures and pressures, are indistinguishable from the properties of water. One implication of this example is that the descriptions we use to describe our phenomenological interactions with either Earth water or Twin Earth water would be indistinguishable.

Still, according to Putnam, anyone using the term "water" on Earth would be referring to H_2O and not XYZ. This is simply because it is H_2O that English language users interact with when using "water." Further, let us assume that folks on Twin Earth, who in the example speak English, also use the term "water" to refer to the clear liquid that they find in their lakes and reservoirs. But since they only interact with XYZ in their Twin Earth environment, their term "water" refers to XYZ and not H_2O (Putnam 1975, 223). Thus, in a causal theory of reference, what determines the meaning of a term is the object in the world to which the term first refers and this content is then subsequently passed down using a causal chain. Further, Putnam clarifies, "Every linguistic community exemplifies the . . . division of linguistic labor . . . : that is, possesses at least some terms whose associated 'criteria' are known only to a subset of the speakers who acquire the terms, and whose use by the other speakers depends upon a structured cooperation between them and the speakers in the relevant subsets" (Putnam 1975, 228). He distinguishes between the criteria of acquiring the use of a term, for example "gold," and acquiring the method of recognizing whether something is gold or not (Putnam 1975, 227). There might be certain situations where only the experts can recognize that a piece of metal is gold. A common speaker might not be able to tell whether her term "gold" applies in those situations. But such a speaker will still know the meaning of the term "gold" given the cooperative feature of language use.

The discussion about mental content in philosophy of mind in many ways parallels the discussion on the nature of meaning just outlined. Focusing on mental "representation"—understood simply as mental items with semantic properties—philosophers of mind discuss which factors determine the contents of representations: what they are about. The main discussion is framed in terms of the contrast between externalism and internalism or individualism and anti-individualism.[5] Internalism or individualism maintains that the content of a mental state is determined by factors and properties internal to the subject's mind. Tyler Burge characterizes individualism as "philosophical treatments that seek to see a person's intentional mental phenomena ultimately and purely in terms of what happens to the person, what occurs within him, . . . without any essential reference to the social context in which he or the interpreter of his mental phenomena are situated" (Burge 2007, 132–133).[6] An externalist or anti-individualist view, on the other hand, argues that the content of a mental state is determined at least in part by factors outside the subject's mind. Using the Twin Earth example, an internalist would argue that the respective mental state of Sam on Earth, that is, "Earth Sam," and his Twin Earth doppelganger, "Twin Earth Sam," containing the term "water" are identical given their phenomenological indistinguishability. An externalist, on the contrary, would argue that they are not the same since their relevant external environments—Earth with H_2O and Twin Earth with XYZ—are different. Putnam's version of externalism focuses on natural kind terms, that is, terms referring to kinds we encounter in our physical environment, like "water" and "gold." Tyler Burge extends this idea through his social anti-individualism that maintains that if our words get deployed in different social and linguistic environments, then they have different meanings correspondingly. As his arthritis example shows, Burge also deploys Putnam's insights explicitly to the question of ascription of mental content or what he calls "content attribution" (Burge 2007, 127).

In his famous example involving the term "arthritis," Burge asks us to imagine an English-speaker, let us call her "Jane," who experiences pain in her thigh and thinks that she has arthritis in her thigh. Since Jane is not a doctor according to the example, she is unaware that arthritis is a condition that afflicts joints only, and therefore she cannot have it in her thigh. So in thinking that she has arthritis in her thigh, she entertains a false thought. Burge then asks us to imagine another situation where our same Jane is part of a linguistic community where the term "arthritis" is used to refer to a different ailment, say "tharthritis," which is not just a condition of the joints but also includes the thighs. Under this imaginary social situation, when Jane thinks that she has arthritis in her thigh, she is entertaining a true thought. Since by hypothesis Jane is the same person in both these situations—her mental states and experience of her physical ailment are identical, the difference in her respective thought is due to the difference in her respective linguistic community (Burge 2007, 123–124). Burge uses this example to demonstrate that mental content is determined at least in part by communal linguistic and social contexts. Burge specifies that the role the social environment plays in content determination is "constitutive" (Burge 2007, 151). He unpacks the idea of "constitutive" in terms of the mental content of a term depending on its "underlying network of relations to the environment" (Burge 2007, 154). As he writes, "the natures and correct individuation of many of an individual person's intentional, or representational, mental states and events commonly depend in a constitutive way on relations that the individual bears to a wider social environment" (Burge 2007, 151).

Ingredients for a Feminist Theory of Content

The constitutive emphasis on communal and social determinants of mental content should make the externalist theory of mental content tailor-made for feminist theorizing. Indeed, feminists seem to share the wide-ranging externalist criticism of internalism within mainstream philosophy of language and mind for neglecting the world.[7] Interestingly, however, feminists who *are* critical of individualism and internalism do not take the extra step of constructing a positive externalist theory. Why not? Most likely they find little feminist potential in the typical ways anti-individualist or externalist theories get worked out in philosophy of language and mind. As Jennifer Saul and E. Díaz-León write:

> One might well suggest that philosophers of language have generally attended only to aspects of the social world that are not of particular interest to feminists. While causal theories of reference undeniably involve social elements, these social elements don't seem to be of the sort that concern feminists; while Putnam's division of linguistic labour arguably involves some power relations (experts have a special sort of linguistic power that non-experts lack), the political aspects of these power relations—if any—have been ignored. (Saul and Díaz-León 2018, 18)

In other words, classic theories of externalism fail to point out *how* the individualist accounts of mental content neglect the *social* (and political) world and the extent of the damage such a neglect exacts on one's theory. Further, even though Burge says relations that an individual bears to a wider social environment are responsible for determining the contents of that individual's thoughts and beliefs, his theoretical framework doesn't allow any room or need for understanding those relations in terms of social categories such as gender and race. For these reasons, feminist perspectives have little to gain from engaging with this version of externalism given where it stops.

Moreover, externalist theorizing that draws its intuitive force from thought experiments fails to take certain dimensions of the real world seriously, and understanding these dimensions is crucial to understanding how social contexts can impact our thoughts and beliefs. The Twin Earth example is set up in a way such that everything is hypothetically kept exactly the same except the fact that "water" on Earth is causally connected to samples of H_2O, while on Twin Earth it is connected to samples of XYZ. Setting up the experiment such that the twins are in indistinguishable psychological states would have the implication that their respective behavior and/or action generating from those states would need to remain indistinguishable as well. This way of setting up the thought experiment, however, underestimates the relation between content, behavior, context, and environment. Earth Sam and Twin Earth Sam would both drink the liquid they find in their kitchen faucet when thirsty. But if we imagine the chemical compound XYZ to be toxic for inhabitants of Earth, and also that Earth Sam finds herself in Twin Earth, a possibility that Putnam's example clearly imagines, then her beliefs involving "water" and other related mental states would come to differ significantly from that of Twin Earth Sam. So the hypothetical setup of this example and its capacity to serve as the main argument in defense of externalism become far less obvious on closer examination.

Further, the use of the example "water" and its framing in terms of its causal relation to H_2O or XYZ seem to overestimate the viability of its application to terms of social and political import like "gender," "whiteness," or "immigrant."[8] These terms are entangled in an ongoing constitutive fashion with the phenomena they refer to and not passively "dangling at the other end of a long causal chain" (Clark and Chalmers 1998, 9). Thus it is no wonder that externalism's potentials for social and political philosophy remain underexplored (Haslanger 2012, 395). Such implications seem hard to articulate when externalism's central argument is modeled after the Twin Earth example. As Millikan writes, "Historical entities— actual world entities, not possibilities—are what are at the center of cognitive life. They are the main structures that make thought and language possible. 'Meanings' do not carve up possible worlds. They are structured and maintained almost entirely by the actual world, their degree of determinateness is contingent on *actual historical processes*" (Millikan 2017, 21; emphasis added). As a result, an adequate theory of content would need to be informed by the social and political concerns that require us to take currently existing, structurally and historically embedded patterns of oppression and marginalization into account. A theory of content so informed—a *feminist* theory of content, given feminist theorists' nuanced analyses of these patterns—would be a welcome engagement from the perspective of philosophy of mind.

In the conclusion of "The Meaning of 'Meaning,'" Putnam writes, "Traditional philosophy of language, like much traditional philosophy, leaves out other people and the world; a better philosophy and a better science of language must encompass both" (Putnam 1975, 271). What I noted earlier, however, is that typical externalist theories leave both "other people and the world" unproblematized. They thus fail to recognize the complex patterns of embeddedness that many of our terms have in social and political structures of power and dominance (Haslanger 2005, 12). This oversight is costly since such a typical externalist account could still "be taken to legitimate a white male paradigm of meanings: X means Y because the (white, male) power structure has taken it to mean Y" (Pappas 1999, 218). Referring to the "neoconservative defenders" of culture who appeal to the need to "preserve past unity" in arguing against any pluralistic explorations into the nature of meaning and mind, Nickolas Pappas alerts us that "'the social' can be as opaque, hence as susceptible to strategic manipulations, as 'the mental'" (Pappas 1999, 218). This is why Golumbia suggests that feminist theory "offers a far more unsettling picture, in which not just meanings but minds, in an important sense, aren't in the head—instead, they are part of the general social and cultural, which is to say political, fabric" (Golumbia 1999, 209).

Scheman offers a clear defense of a *minds-aren't-in-the-head* thesis through her attack on the individualist assumptions that "psychological objects are particular states of individuals" and that they "attach to us singly (no matter how socially we might acquire them)" (Scheman 1983, 227). Even though in these formulations Scheman's critique seems directed at the location of a mental state, they also highlight that psychological objects cannot exist independently of the ways the world turns out. For her, the ways of the world necessarily include our experience of inextricable interdependence, that is to say, of being "constitutively dependent on other things," events, people, and their voices in one's social realities (Scheman 1983, 229). She takes this interdependence to be a salient feature of women's everyday experience. An anti-individualist or externalist theory that takes women's experiences as real, she argues, has to accept "human beings as socially constituted, as having emotions, beliefs, abilities, and so on only insofar as they are embedded in a social web of interpretation that serves to give meaning to the bare data of inner experience and behavior" (Scheman 1983, 232). Further, she criticizes the "individualism of *method*, a counting of each as one and only one," that for her is continuous with content individualism and foundational to liberal political theory (Scheman 1983, 231). Scheman proposes that objects of psychology do not belong to the "political confines of our own heads and hearts and guts" (Scheman 1983, 241). Finally, Scheman writes, "we are responsible for the meaning of each other's inner lives, that our emotions, beliefs, motives, and so on are what they are because of how they—and we—are related to the objects in our world—not only those we share a language with, but those we most intimately share our lives with" (Scheman 1983, 241). Earlier I noted Burge's characterization of anti-individualism as the idea that content is constitutively determined by social environment. However, the "anti-individualism" that Scheman is proposing here is distinctly different. For her individualism denotes "a respect for separateness" that her anti-individualism rejects (Scheman 1983, 231). Burge's anti-individualism, in using an unproblematized notion of social environment that conceives of society as a collection of separate individuals, fails to take into account the interdependence and interrelatedness that Scheman considers to constitute our social reality.

So the anti-individualist or externalist theory of content that feminist theorizing requires has to have the feature of inextricable interdependence of our languages and minds on our social and political world. Only when we acknowledge this nature, and further how this interdependence is undervalued in the dominant structures of power, do we begin to appreciate another aspect of this theory of content: in the recognition that our minds are constitutively dependent on our sociopolitical realities lies the first "important step in the process of changing them" (Golumbia 1999, 209). This brings us to the most important aspect of a feminist theory of content, namely, that our theorizing has to enable us to imagine a different and more equitable reality. It is important to note that "naming and defining reality are among the ways in which the dominant group takes and keeps possession of its world" (Garry and Pearsall 1989, 48). Or, as Scheman elaborates, "what purports to be a statement about how things naturally are is instead an expression of a historically specific way of structuring some set of social interactions" that furthers the dominant status quo (Scheman 1983, 230–231). Any possibility of subverting this domination has to start with an understanding of its underlying mechanism.

Putnam-Burge externalism falls short of this target because it remains confined to a status quo understanding of various linguistic and mental concepts. But in so doing, it "fails to understand how our current concepts have structured our practices, distribute power and authority, and bring with them false assumptions of legitimacy" (Haslanger 2005, 15). A theory of content for feminist purposes would not only tell us *how*—through the process located in a particular sociopolitical history—these concepts come to have their content, but also *what* would be required to transform their content. In the next section,

I argue that a feminist theory of content inspired by Millikan's teleosemantic theory will be able to do both.

Millikan's Teleosemantic View

All teleosemantic theories of mental content argue that the content of a representation—its aboutness—depends on the teleological notion of function. "Function" here is typically understood in terms of its etiology since it is determined by the history of the item or system possessing it (Millikan 1994, 245).[9] For example, the function of a human heart to pump blood is determined by its being selected for, that is, reproduced or copied for, pumping blood in the evolutionary history of the human biological system. While in this case the heart was "selected for" given its role in the history of biological evolution, other histories such as "modern history" where functions are determined by recent selection and sociocultural histories, among others, can also serve as the location for reproduction and selection (Godfrey-Smith 1994).

Given this understanding of "function," the content of a representation becomes what it is supposed to or designed to represent. A simple teleological theory thus maintains that a mental representation "R" represents R when the cognitive system that "R" is a part of "was designed to react to Rs by producing 'Rs'" (Millikan 1994, 243). Evolutionary selectionist history is taken to tell us the story of why the cognitive system evolved to produce "R" in response to R in its environment. But what exactly determines that R is the content of "R"? What mechanism makes my thought this morning, for example, that hemlock woolly adelgid are back, about the hemlock tree I see outside my window and the characteristic white markings that I see on its leaves?[10] Millikan argues that two adjustments have to be made to the teleosemantic framework if our account is to answer this question with sufficient precision.

First, we need to foreground how a cognitive system *uses* a representation. This is because simply focusing on the evolutionary (and other, for example, cultural) history which grounds the functioning of a cognitive system as it produces a representation fails to hit the mark of what that representation is about. As Millikan proposes, we need to consider the cognitive system

> as divided into two parts or two aspects, one of which produces representations for the other to consume. What we need to look at is the consumer part, at what it is to use a thing *as* a representation. Indeed, a good look at the consumer part of the system ought to be all that is needed to determine not only representational status but representational content. (Millikan 1994, 246)

This emphasis on the "consumer part," on how a representation is *used* as determining its content, not only sets Millikan's "consumer" account apart from other teleosemantic accounts and the classic externalisms of Burge and Putnam, but, as I will argue in the final section, also makes it the correct mold for a feminist theory of content.

In addition to the shift in focus from simple evolutionary history to the consumer function, Millikan's account also redirects our attention from functions to "normal conditions for those functions" (Millikan 1994, 249). Normal conditions are those that allowed the function to be historically performed when it was performed properly. Again using the example of the human heart, normal conditions would include being part of a viable biological system where pumping blood led to the system's survival, reproductive potential, and selective advantage. In the case of mental representation, normal conditions are those that support the correspondence between the representation and the world outside. My thought that the hemlock woolly adelgid are back on the hemlock outside my window requires that the hemlock woolly adelgid are indeed back on the hemlock outside my window if the representations involved are to participate in the functioning of my cognitive system. On this theory of content, then, what the consumers of "R" require is that "R" corresponds to appropriate situations "in order to perform *their* [consumers'] tasks" (Millikan 1994, 250). There are many more nuances to Millikan's teleosemantic view, but this brief outline should suffice for our purpose of building toward a feminist theory of content.

Toward a Feminist Theory of Content

Before offering ways to modify Millikan's consumer account to fit the needs of a feminist theory of content, let me address a few concerns regarding this account's compatibility with feminist orientations. First, Millikan is no different from other externalist philosophers of mind who omit social and political concerns. Since her primary focus is to develop a realist account of intentionality that understands language and thought as biological categories with functions, these concerns are not central to her project. However, I believe nothing precludes a theoretical framework from being adapted for feminist theorizing. I am inspired in this regard, for example, by Judith Butler's adaptation of Merleau-Ponty's phenomenological model even though "Merleau-Ponty does not write his theory of sexuality within an explicitly political framework" (Butler, this volume, 175). Thus even though Millikan doesn't write within an explicitly political framework, her model can be extended in a way that offers arguments useful for feminist purposes. Indeed, I will argue that Butler's theoretical tools allow us to appreciate another interesting feature of Millikan's theory that makes its adaptation for feminism especially worthwhile.

A more serious unease about the effectiveness of Millikan's framework for our purposes might result from its general and evolutionary naturalistic framing. This concern stems from feminist worries about naturalism and requires a layered response. Feminist denunciation of certain versions of naturalism, such as those that obliterate historical situatedness, is absolutely crucial. Such obliteration is evident, for example, in the "naturalist ideology" of mainstream theorizing about sexuality that offers a "normative model [of sexuality] against which individual instances can be gauged" (Butler, this volume, 175). This naturalism thus turns prescriptive and ideological, and reflects the social situation of the theorist more than an objective reality. Instead, as Butler points out, what we need is an account of sexuality "which restores both the historical and volitional components of sexual experience and, consequently, opens the way for a fuller description of sexuality and sexual diversity" (Butler, this volume, 175).

Clarifying the nature of Millikan's naturalism would allow us to show why it is not a prescriptive or ideological naturalism. Millikan's goal is to offer an account of mental content without already assuming some semantic notion like meaning or intention. So her point is to offer an account of intentionality in nonintentional terms, as Chalmers notes while introducing Millikan's chapter titled "Biosemantics" in his philosophy of mind anthology (Chalmers 2002, 474). This approach does not necessitate a specific "naturalist ideology" since the aim is not to offer a standard that every instance is evaluated against. More importantly, Millikan's account, though naturalistic, is not blind to historically situated information. Indeed, history of use—how a term has been used by the language system that has contributed to that system's survival and flourishing under selectionist pressures—is a central determining feature of Millikan's theory of content.[11]

How do I propose to modify Millikan's teleosemantic account? First, by highlighting that Millikan is clear from her very first articulation that functions can also result from the cultural and social context of meme selection (Millikan 1984). As she clarifies more recently, the term "biological" in her *Language, Thought and Other Biological Categories* (1984) "was a metaphorical reference to selectionist principles of every kind. Well known analogs of natural selection are found, for example . . . in some kinds of cultural selection" (Millikan 2017, 5). Meme is the unit of selection in the context of cultural evolution. Human preferences, what Elizabeth Anderson calls "contextual interests and values" over the span of the history of a culture, influence which meme gets reproduced while serving a specific function (Anderson 1995, 46). Words, for example, are memes reproduced and selected for their function in the relevant linguistic cultures.[12] Human preferences in the form of dominant preferences within a cultural context play a role in determining the contents of our mental items by shaping the mechanism through which a term gets used to correspond to certain features of our cultural and social reality. These mechanisms thus can help us explain how our terms, for example, terms with political import, such as "immigrant" and "whiteness," come to have the contents they do in the context of contemporary US culture.

Millikan has also argued that what a cognitive system can do "in accordance with evolutionary design" can be "very novel and surprising" given these systems' ability to learn and adapt (Millikan 1994, 251). Thus the "specific principles of generalization and discrimination, etc., which have been built into the system by natural selection" can be used for purposes these principles were not designed for originally (Millikan 1994, 251). They have helped us learn new ideas such as those of economic recession and the Global Positioning System. In the history of many societies and cultures, these generalizing and discriminative apparatuses have also been used to dominate, marginalize, and oppress others. Such dominating functions can become the norm for a certain culture under certain favorable and historical conditions. This apparatus can explain, for example, how racism has become the norm for US and global culture by getting "in the structure of our society and the invisible crannies of our mind" (Brooks 2019).

My proposal is that Millikan's basic model gives us a way of understanding the conditions underlying oppressive social structures that enabled the propagation of their historical function of maintaining the status quo of domination. This way of approaching the discussion reveals the forces that have been operational in keeping stable certain oppressive structural conditions that determined the contents of many of our terms. This understanding can then allow us to imagine a transformative reality; a sociocultural reality where, under changing conditions and levels of awareness that undermine the stabilizing forces of the oppressive status quo, our terms can come to have, over time, transformed egalitarian content. In the following I offer a modified teleosemantic view for content for the terms "immigrant," "whiteness," and "illegal alien," whose current meanings in the US context were forged and reproduced in the sociocultural and political history that stabilized their function for white supremacy. Using the teleosemantic model to understand these terms allows us to expose the mechanism undergirding that dominant agenda.

In his illuminating article "Illegal: White Supremacy and Immigration Status," José Jorge Mendoza looks at the history of US citizenship and immigration law to expose how the concept of "whiteness" is implicated in the current dominant discussion of illegal immigration. His analysis shows how "whiteness" in the US context corresponds to a "braid of three interwoven strands" of race, ethnicity, and nationality (Mendoza 2016, 201). He also outlines the process through which the content or meaning of "whiteness" is determined and held stable. He shows how one or more of these strands account for the ways "white" status has been granted to different social groups at different moments of the US political history and how this differential status in turn determined that group's eligibility for US citizenship. For example, the very first Naturalization Act that the US passed in 1790 stipulated that "only 'white persons' would be eligible for naturalization" (Mendoza 2016, 208). This requirement for "white" status does not end with the amendments adopted at the end of the Civil War. Mendoza traces how "white" status continued to be required for US citizenship historically. It is emphasized through the ethnicity strand, for example, in the Chinese Exclusion Act of 1882 that excluded Chinese nationals from US citizenship. Similarly, the nationalism strand is at play in the Johnson-Reed Act of 1924 that "introduced a system of 'national origin' quotas" (Mendoza 2016, 211). Interestingly, 1890 census numbers were used to determine the quotas for the 1924 Act, even though later census numbers were available, since it was argued that the 1890 census "captured the true composition of the United States before it was deformed by a large wave of Southern and Eastern European immigrants" (Mendoza 2016, 211). With this brief outline of Mendoza's main points, let me now turn to how his account helps us clarify the process that stabilizes the content of "whiteness" in the US political and social contexts.

Mendoza's analysis helps us identify the "consumer" and "normal conditions"—two important elements in Millikan's teleosemantic model— that determine the content of "whiteness." The consumer of this representation, whose survival and propagation was its function, has been the political power structure dominant in the United States since the ratification of the US Constitution. The normal conditions, to remind ourselves, are the conditions under which the function of a term is performed historically that help specify the correspondence relation between the term and its referent. In the case of "whiteness," the normal conditions are the various US government acts and related Supreme Court decisions, listed in Mendoza's article, that allowed its function of undergirding white privilege to be performed and replicated, and that ensured that the meaning of "whiteness" corresponds to actual political conditions. Through this process, "whiteness" comes to correspond to the interwoven reality of race, ethnicity, and nationality that Mendoza takes to make "American *whiteness*" (Mendoza 2016, 208).

Another intriguing feature of Mendoza's analysis is how the history of words such as "Caucasian" and "illegal" in common speech gets implicated in how the Supreme Court makes its decisions (Mendoza 2016, 213). Knowing the history of these terms and the forces that solidified their meanings—for example, the 1817 and 1824 Immigration Acts, the 1848 Treaty of Guadalupe Hidalgo, the 1965 Naturalization and Immigration Act, and various related US Supreme Court decisions—helps us understand how the contents of these terms are selected,

reproduced, and stabilized. These examples thus offer an illustration of how political, social, and cultural forces work in the historical timeline to determine the
content of terms we use. The feminist theory of content I am developing here
helps us appreciate the concrete way that power shapes the very structures that
our cognitive systems use to navigate our social and political realities. Exposing
the forces of power that keep conceptual structures stable and resistant to change
also helps us imagine what is required to change them. It therefore demonstrates
the effectiveness of discussion in philosophy of mind for answering questions
more readily located in the areas of social and political philosophy. Ashby
Butnor and Matthew MacKenzie write, "we have the capacity to revise social
meanings and enact different kinds of worlds—worlds that are more conducive
to individual and social flourishing, rather than harm and oppression" (Butnor
and MacKenzie, this volume, 191). I agree wholeheartedly and believe that by
exploring how terms and concepts have come to have their meanings, including
oppressive ones, we can also start the process of imagining how they can have
content conducive to social flourishing.

Thinking about the question of content, especially in relation to feminist topics
using Millikan's framework, has one obvious advantage: it allows us to focus on
these concepts/meanings in terms of their historical selection and reproduction.
Further, understanding them through this framework also helps us uncover the
forces that keep them stable. Putnam-Burge externalism, in the case of "whiteness," focuses on how the term is used in the linguistic community of English
speakers in the United States (more specifically, one might argue, the community
of white, male, bourgeois academics), and thus is unequipped to capture the relational or historical dynamics of factors that play a role in the determination of
content. It is here that Millikan's teleosemantic theory becomes useful.

Let me conclude by acknowledging that combining feminism and philosophy
of mind, fields that might appear to have incompatible goals, methodologies, and
audiences, requires confrontation on the way to possible resolution. I hope to
have shown that the conflict is productive, that feminists and philosophers of
mind have good reason to take steps toward one another.

Notes

1. I am grateful to Jennifer McWeeny, Paula Droege, Brook Sadler, Arindam Cakrabarti,
   and Ruth Millikan for many helpful comments and conversations.
2. My search attempts to find sources involving mental content and feminism returned
   no result at the online databases of the Philosopher's Index and PhilPapers.
3. Golumbia writes, "Indeed, along with Hilary Putnam's 'The Meaning of "Meaning"'
   and Tyler Burge's 'Individualism and the Mental,' I think of Scheman's essay as one of

the most important essays in philosophy of mind to have appeared in recent times" (Columbia 1999, 202).

4. See, for example, Alcoff and Potter (1993), Kourany (2010), and Grasswick (2011).
5. While the contrasting positions are most commonly referred to as "externalism" and "internalism" in the philosophy of mind literature, Burge has been one of the prominent exceptions in preferring the names "individualism" and "anti-individualism" instead. Burge outlines his reasons for his preference (Burge 2007, 154). However, given how widely the name "externalism" is used in the literature, I have decided to stick with this name while also noting its intimate overlaps with "anti-individualism."
6. Burge proposes his anti-individualist theory in "Individualism and the Mental," originally published in 1979. This paper is later reprinted in Burge (2007) along with a postscript. All page references here are from Burge (2007).
7. See, for example, Saul and Díaz-León (2018) and Scheman (1983). However, not every feminist theorist agrees. Antony (1995), for example, offers a defense of individualism for the feminist project.
8. However, as Jennifer McWeeny pointed out, "water" can also be a socially and politically loaded term. Imagine being a resident in one of the slums in Chennai, India, during its acute water crisis in June 2019 when private water tankers were the only source of reliable water. One's ability to buy that water would definitely influence one's understanding and use of the term "water."
9. Millikan's "Biosemantics" was originally published in 1989.
10. These are tiny aphid-like insects that attack North Carolina hemlock trees.
11. However, while Butler takes "historical" to mean "individual acts of appropriation" (Butler, this volume, 180) located in individual histories, for Millikan "historical" stands for "historically optimal conditions" located in the selectionist history (Millikan 1994, 246).
12. See, for example, Dennett (2017) for a recent account of the role of memes in the development of human minds.

References

Alcoff, Linda, and Elizabeth Potter, Elizabeth, eds. 1993. *Feminist Epistemologies*. New York: Routledge.
Anderson, Elizabeth. 1995. "Knowledge, Human Interests, and Objectivity in Feminist Epistemology." *Philosophical Topics* 23 (2): 27–58.
Antony, Louise. 1995. "Sisters, Please, I'd Rather Do It Myself." *Philosophical Topics* 23 (2): 59–94.
Brooks, David. 2019. "The Racial Reckoning Comes." *New York Times*. June 6. https://nyti.ms/31hssCa.
Burge, Tyler. 2007. "Individualism and the Mental (1979) and Postcript to 'Individualism and the Mental' (2006)." In *Foundations of Mind: Philosophical Essays, Volume 2*, by Tyler Burge, 100–181. New York: Oxford University Press.
Chalmers, David J., ed. 2002. *Philosophy of Mind: Classical and Contemporary Readings*. Oxford: Oxford University Press.
Clark, Andy, and David Chalmers. 1998. "The Extended Mind." *Analysis* 58 (1): 7–19.

Dennett, Daniel. C. 2017. *From Bacteria to Bach and Back: The Evolution of Minds*. New York: Norton.

Garry, Ann. and Marilyn Pearsall, eds. 1989 *Women, Knowledge, and Reality: Explorations in Feminist Philosophy*. New York: Routledge.

Godfrey-Smith, Peter. 1984. "A Modern History Theory of Functions." *Noûs* 28 (3): 344–362.

Golumbia, David. 1999. "Feminism and Mental Representation: Analytic Philosophy, Cultural Studies, and Narrow Content." In *Is Feminist Philosophy Philosophy?*, edited by Emanuala Bianchi, 202–211. Evanston: Northwestern University Press.

Grasswick, Heidi E., ed. 2011. *Feminist Epistemology and Philosophy of Science: Power in Knowledge*. Dordrecht: Springer.

Haslanger, Sally. 2005. "What Are We Talking About? The Semantics and Politics of Social Kinds." *Hypatia* 20 (4): 10–26.

Haslanger, Sally. 2012. *Resisting Reality: Social Construction and Social Critique*. New York: Oxford University Press.

Kourany, Janet A. 2010. *Philosophy of Science after Feminism*. New York: Oxford University Press.

Mendoza, José Jorge. 2016. "Illegal: White Supremacy and Immigration Status." In *The Ethics and Politics of Immigration*, edited by Alex Sager, 201–220. London: Rowman & Littlefield.

Millikan, Ruth Garrett. 1984. *Language, Thought, and Other Biological Categories: New Foundations for Realism*. Cambridge, MA: MIT Press.

Millikan, Ruth Garrett. 1994. "Biosemantics." In *Mental Representation: A Reader*, edited by Ted. A. Warfield and Stephen Stich, 243–258. Cambridge: Basil Blackwell.

Millikan, Ruth Garrett. 2017. *Beyond Concepts: Unicepts, Language, and Natural Information*. New York: Oxford University Press.

Pappas, Nickolas. 1999. "Replies to Hass and Golumbia." In *Is Feminist Philosophy Philosophy?*, edited by Emanuala Bianchi, 212–218. Evanston: Northwestern University Press.

Putnam, Hilary. 1975. "The Meaning of 'Meaning.'" In *Mind, Language and Reality: Philosophical Papers, Volume 2*, by Hilary Putnam, 215–271. Cambridge: Cambridge University Press.

Saul, Jennifer, and Esa Díaz-León. 2018. "Feminist Philosophy of Language." *Stanford Encyclopedia of Philosophy*, edited by Edward N. Zalta. https://plato.stanford.edu/archives/fall2018/entries/feminism-language/.

Scheman, Naomi. 1983. "Individualism and the Objects of Psychology." In *Discovering Reality: Feminist Perspectives on Epistemology, Metaphysics, Methodology, and Philosophy of Science*, edited by Sandra Harding and Merrill B. Hintikka, 225–244. Dordrecht: D. Reidel.

4

Disappearing Black People
through Failures of White Empathy

Janine Jones

Empathy is sometimes thought to be, if not a moral panacea for crimes against humanity, then a moral motivator to work against them. Notwithstanding the fact that anti-black racism is a structural problem, it is conceptually and practically problematic to propose that black people, in the United States, depend on the morality and affection of white people for social justice, when justice *for black people*, in the US context, is rooted in and endures through the legacy of a legal tradition whereby black enslaved people were subjected to the absolute power of white masters, and where their relief from cruelty inflicted upon them by white people depended on the benevolent feeling and affection between master and slave (Hartman 1997, 132–133). Moreover, white empathy for black people tends to fail.[1] In this chapter, I argue that the construction of black people's minds in Manichaean opposition to that of white people's is at the root of white failures of empathy for black people. I propose that rather than seek to empathize with black people, white people self-empathize.

My departure from traditional philosophy of mind can be discerned along two dimensions. First, I introduce an essential consideration into the debates about other minds; namely, that it is nearly impossible to perceive or to know some other minds as minds within contexts of oppression. Since the advent of the modern era, one of the central ways that white patriarchal groups have wielded colonial-enslavement-subjection power is through constructions of mind inextricably interwoven with constructions of humanity and personhood. The minds of members of oppressed groups are constructed as a priori *knowable*. The result is that such minds become a posteriori unknowable, or nearly so, to the dominant group who claims to know them. Black people, the subject of this chapter, fit the description of this general problem. White supremacist constructions of black people's minds emerge from historical conditions of black enslavement and subjection that determined the scope and extent of constructed black mentality. If a black enslaved person *moved*—in thought, in body—beyond the movements allowed or directed by white people, she was known, a priori to possess a *criminal* mind, with criminal intent (Hartman 1997, 80–87). If a black

Janine Jones, *Disappearing Black People through Failures of White Empathy* In: *Feminist Philosophy of Mind*.
Edited by: Keya Maitra and Jennifer McWeeny, Oxford University Press. © Oxford University Press 2022.
DOI: 10.1093/oso/9780190867614.003.0005

girl or woman was subjected to what we would call rape, she was known, a priori, *in such instance*, as possessing mind—a *willfully* submissive mind (Hartman 1997, 80–87). Hence, she could not have been raped.

Second, the model of self-empathy I propose introduces the reconstruction of historical selves as essential to empathetic practice. Such construction effects a departure from models of empathy that rely solely on the self's perception, memory, and imagination, and includes what the self could *not* have perceived or remembered *in experience*. Introducing historical reconstruction of selves into empathetic practice opens up possibilities for what a person can imagine about herself—among other things, that she is not in a socio-ontological position apt for imagining black people empathetically.

When exploring conceptions of Western mind-body dualism, we tend to focus on the disconnect between mind and body at the expense of considering intricate connections conceptualized between the two. In medieval and early modern literary and nonliterary texts, black skin was fixed as permanent and compared with the "indurate heart of heretics." Such comparison anchored the heart as also being fixed as permanent (Loomba 2009, 505). Arguably, aspects of what was called the heart became theorized as mind. Such a consideration compels us to reconsider the tradition in Western thought of theorizing the body as reflecting the nature of mind and/or character. Thus, even if we speak of embodied minds, the problem of black minds cannot be divorced from the problem of black bodies.

Black bodies signal the problematic-defective nature of black mind. Excess has been an essential device for conceptualizing black bodies. Excess and/or hypercorporeality indicates that a mind has failed to set limits and order on its body: it is, par excellence, a nonrational mind. Further, the excess black is conceptually correlated with violence. Excess black *materiality* requires violence in the form of forced labor for the emergence of discontinuous (countable) black bodies (Jones 2016, 325). The black body is thought to *emerge* through work because work is invested with reason: "Though black bodies cannot access reason, through work . . . they would be involved in endeavors possessing utility, and operations of cause and effect" (Jones 2016, 328). The excess body demands that the mind that enables such excess be scrutinized. Inspection reveals the nature of black mind as something practically nonexistent, but criminal or submissive when in existence.

Significantly, the black mind has been theorized as incapable of making gender distinctions (Curry 2016, 565). Two ideas might emerge from this claim. First, it might be thought that black minds were incapable of distinguishing gender, *tout court*, one of the most basic categories in Western thought. Is this consistent with the historical evidence provided by the persisting fear of black *males* raping white girls and women—a criminal intent and action, *arguably* requiring the capacity to distinguish gender? A second idea should be considered—namely, that black minds cannot distinguish gender with respect to their own inchoate bodies. Mental incapacity for distinguishing gender, coupled with inchoate uncategorizable materiality, which cannot be the object of Western gender distinctions, invites the idea that black bodies can be placed anywhere, and require outside, rational direction to find places.

Arguably, excess black bodies are thought of as reflecting minds with what Dan Zahavi has conceptualized as a "minimal" form of self-consciousness, which "precedes the mastery of language and the ability to form full-blown rational judgements and propositional attitudes . . . [and which] is not something unique to, or distinctive of, adult human beings, but something all phenomenally conscious creatures possess" (Zahavi 2014, 14). Possessing thin consciousness through work would be thought insufficient for endowing black bodies with full-fledged minds (Jones 2016, 328). Combining this picture of mind and body yields black beings who lack rational minds, who can only be invested with reason through their laboring bodies. As stated above, the mental states of such beings—and what needs to be done with them—is indicated by the excess their bodies manifest. Such bodies require, indeed, call forth, violence to counter their excess. Michael Brown's murder, Eric Garner's murder, and Taji Rice's apprehension (Tamir Rice's sister was handcuffed at the scene of her brother's murder, and thrown in the back of a squad car) have been so explained in terms of excess (Ritskes 2015).

The nonmind/body connection described above renders black people fungible. It reduces them to the socio-ontological condition of interchangeable multipurpose tools in the service of humanity, without the kind of loss or gain in value thought to occur within economies of whiteness when the uniqueness of a genuine individual is acquired, exchanged, mutated, or otherwise destroyed. My discussion requires an introduction of the concept of white fungibility (which I attribute to Philip Harper) in contradistinction to black fungibility. It is primarily due to this Manichaean-structured opposition that white people's ability to successfully perceive or empathize with black people is impeded. My view understands white and black fungibility as grounded in and derived from the nature of the kinds of minds constructed through anti-black, white supremacist logics. Black fungibility is derivatively attributed to black bodies, and implemented directly through them.

In the remainder of this chapter I proceed first by providing a discussion of black fungibility and its knowable-unknowable black mind, followed by an elucidation of white fungibility. Subsequently, I offer three (concise) accounts of empathy, each of which presents a particular mode of disappearing black people. The first—the Experience/Analogue-Construction Model—underscores white fungibles' inability to access or construct experiences that are structurally similar to that of black fungibles, which is the reason for empathetic failure. The experience of the black fungible disappears from the field of white people's experience. There, on the empathetic horizon, she becomes empathetically imperceptible.

The second—the *Direct Perception Model*—points to how failure of white empathy for black people may begin in perceptual encounters. Recall what Officer Darren Wilson said regarding his encounter with Michael Brown. When Wilson grabbed Brown, the only way he could describe the feeling was "I felt like a five-year-old holding on to Hulk Hogan." (Wilson is 6′4″ and 210 lbs.). Wilson stated that Brown tried to go for his gun.

> Then after he did that he looked up at me and had the most intense aggressive face. The only way I can describe it, it looks like a demon. That's how angry he looked . . . it almost looked like he was bulking up to run through the shots, like it was making him mad that I am shooting at him. And the face he had was looking straight through me, like I wasn't even there, I wasn't even anything in his way. (Sanburn 2014)

Alleged black bodily excess triggers perception of *mindless* violence, a threatening representation, which is exchanged (without loss of value) for the black person. Being able to perceive black people in the world is a reasonable condition to demand for the possibility of imagining *them* empathetically. With so many black people killed because they are exchanged in perception for scary-monster threats, the Direct Perception Model seems far from promising, underscoring as it does how easily black people's fungible exchange value—during white perceptual experience—can lead to their deaths. This model illustrates perspicaciously the problem of the knowable, unknowable black mind. Wilson's a priori knowledge of Brown overdetermines who or what Brown (allegedly) is, thereby determining that Wilson cannot know who Brown is a posteriori.

The *Transference Model of Empathy* is closest to that which Saidiya V. Hartman has in mind. She makes her case for the disappearance of black people through white acts of empathy using the case of John Rankin (1793–1886), an American Presbyterian minister, educator, and abolitionist—who worked actively on the Underground Railroad. Rankin unquestionably possesses the bona fides of a goodwill white person.[2] Rankin wrote a letter to his slave-owning brother in order to persuade him of the evils of slavery. His epistle engages an empathetic exercise, during which he substitutes himself and his family, as victims on the coffle, for black people experiencing the coffle. He writes about how he feels about his own pain.

> I began in reality to feel for myself, my wife, and my children—the thoughts of being whipped at the pleasure of a morose and capricious master, aroused

the strongest feelings of resentment; but when I fancied the cruel lash was approaching my wife and children, and my imagination depicted in lively colors, their tears, their shrieks, and bloody stripes, every indignant principle of my bloody nature was excited to the highest degree. (Hartman 1997, 18)

This example illustrates how easily black people can be exchanged for something else, without seeming loss of value in the eyes of the white empathizer. Rankin did not deem his empathetic exercise a failure simply because he replaced his empathetic objects with himself. This model may illustrate the problem of the knowable, unknowable black mind. Supposing Rankin thinks he knows black people's pain, and he knows his own, he might as well substitute himself for them, without loss of value. At the same time, there is the sense that it is because Rankin does not know black people that he must substitute himself for them, so as to discover pain that he can deeply understand—his own and that of other white people.

The three models I present do not exhaust models of empathy. However, they cover three important conditions which, in fact, work together in any act of successful empathetic engagement. Being able to *understand* the object of empathy assumes that the empathizer has succeeded in perceiving the *right object* and placing it within the empathetic act. Being able to *perceive* the object of empathy is a condition underscoring the importance of the problem of misrecognition and misnaming (and hence, misunderstanding) in empathy. Finally, empathetic acts, if they are to be about a particular object, must, as for other imaginative acts, retain *the object of the imagining*. Otherwise, the imaginative or empathetic act fails.

In the last section, I propose that white people self-empathize. I sketch a two-stage model, which relies upon the reconstruction of historical selves. A word of caution: I do not move *beyond* the black-white binary paradigm, countenanced in much of the literature. The thinking behind such a move is misguided, in many ways.[3] That said, let's be clear: this chapter does not address all forms of oppression. It does not address *foundational* forms of oppression, such as indigenous land dispossession and loss of sovereignty, let alone their spatialized convergence with abject black racialization. This chapter concerns a certain Western understanding of the construction, existence, and value of mind through *abject racialization*. Arguably, blackness is at rock bottom in terms of abject racialization, in the US context. Thus, my work, here, falls within the contours of a black/white *Manichaeanism* that "shapes [Western] aesthetic and moral valuations" while also infiltrating non-Western aesthetic and axiomatic systems through processes of Western colonization (Deliovsky and Kitossa 2013, 165). Reflecting "a process of negative and positive racialization," this Manichaeastic structure "is a symbolic matrix (of inclusion and exclusion) that incorporates other racial/ethnic (and class) categories, albeit in a manner both contingent and hierarchical" (Deliovsky and Kitossa 2013, 165).

I focus entirely on modes of disappearing black people through white empathy. In keeping with this, I attend only to the Manichaean black fungibility/white fungibility structure it engenders.

Black Fungibility and White Fungibility in Manichaean Opposition

Hortense Spillers's and Hartman's works provide the foundations for theorizing black fungibility. The central idea they advance is that no restriction is placed on what a fungible black body can be exchanged for. It can be exchanged for a commodity, for an idea, or even for space, as Tiffany Lethabo King argues in "The Labor of (Re)reading Plantation Landscapes Fungible(ly)" (2016). According to Hartman, it is black fungibility's "abstractedness and immateriality" that makes it possible for black people to serve as vehicles for "white self-exploration, renunciation, and enjoyment" (Hartman 1997, 26). She states further that "The fungibility of the commodity makes the captive body an abstract and empty vessel vulnerable to the projection of others' feelings, ideas, desires, and values" (Hartman 1997, 21). Spillers's scholarship addresses "Black bodies as open spaces of shifting 'signification and representation' which humans use to make meaning of their lives" (Spillers, 1987, 75, cited in King 2016, 1025).

Thus, the core features of black fungibility are (1) its abstractedness and immateriality, (2) the commodity-like/empty vessel status of black bodies, and (3) the exchangeability of the black body for anything white people can imagine. Now suppose it is thought that rational minds direct their well-*formed* bodies to engage in rational, human endeavors (see above). Suppose that an inchoate, black body is thought not to possess a mind—and when it does, it is thought to possess not a rational but a criminal or submissive one. Such a body could not be rationally directed by its own mind. For all rational and virtuous intents and purposes, it wouldn't have one. I propose therefore that the *empty vessel* status of the excess black body is best understood as deriving from its empty-mind status. Similarly, the abstractedness and *immateriality* of the black body's fungibility is best understood as derivative, where, in the first instance these qualities attach to the absent mind. Observe: when the criminal mind of the black person is recognized when the black person moves outside of a white person's will and direction, such criminal movement undermines the white person's ability to make the black person's body captive for fungible endeavors. One significant repercussion then is that when black people possess mind during alleged criminal moments, they undermine white people's ability to use them fungibly. The concept of excess plays a role here as well. Black bodies perceived as black excess indicate that there is *no end* not only to the various uses that can be made of a black body, but there is no end to the amount, degree, and quantity of black-body-use that can be enjoyed by white people. The black criminal mind that directs itself *limits* (or seeks to limit) what can be done to her body in her moment of criminality. Effecting a limit undermines the perception that there is no end to what can be done with her alleged excess. I conjecture that when black bodies are punished, they are punished not merely for their "crime" but for undermining the perception that they are infinitely fungible and bringing to light that they have ideas of their own about their selves.

My general claim is that the ground for the perception of black bodies as fungible empty vessels, exchangeable for anything, is the construction of black people as lacking the kind of minds that invest bodies with their own rational will and intention. Such perception leaves black bodies open and empty for occupation and direction from rational white male minds, and their close associates.

A goodwill white person today would not assert that black people are not rational or claim that black people possess mind only when criminal or when willfully submissive. But possessing rationality can be thought of in terms of degrees. Thus, a contemporary goodwill white person does not have to be committed to the idea that black people possess no rationality whatsoever. Further, they never have to make such statements. Consider what Paul Bloom says about Martin Luther King in his book *Against Empathy: The Case for Rational Compassion* (2016). He distinguishes between "moral heroes" and "rational maximizers"— "people of the heart" as opposed to "people of the head." "From Huckleberry Finn to Pip to Jack Auer, from Jesus to Gandhi to Martin Luther King Jr., they are individuals of great feeling (of the heart). Rationality gets you Hannibal Lecter and Lex Luther" (Bloom 2016, 6).

We need not deny that Martin Luther King was a man of great feeling in order to understand that he was a great strategist, which I would suppose requires rationality. Knowing a bit of history should make it difficult to place MLK squarely on the heart side of Bloom's binary. Bloom appears to have done so with relative ease. I have no reason to assume that his intentions were not among the best when he did so. Similar modes of thinking are in play when goodwill white people use black people to gather *experiential* data for their theoretical projects, for which they believe themselves uniquely qualified to be the framers and interpreters. These are everyday behaviors of goodwill white people in the academy and elsewhere. Such behaviors place black people on the side of body, and away from the side of mind and rationality. When goodwill white people place the responsibility for constructions of defective black cognition on egregious anti-black individuals and organizations (for example, David Duke or the KKK), they resort to tactics of obfuscation or, bad faith at worst, or they need to engage self-empathetic acts in order to discover that their other is not an other from another mother (or father).

Let's now contrast black fungibility with white fungibility. I believe that Phillip Harper, in *Abstractionist Aesthetic*, conceptualizes white fungibility and contrasts it with black fungibility. I will not, however, saddle him with this claim, as he does not use the term *fungibility* and the claim may be controversial. Importantly, white fungibility does not include that constitutive concept of commodity necessary to the concept of black fungibility, because the black body has functioned as a marketable product produced to satisfy white people's needs and desires. Central to all forms of fungibility is the concept of exchangeability, and the concept of abstraction, which allows for it. Mind (or lack of mind) is the key component effecting the abstraction required for both white and black fungibility. Harper correctly observes that

> abstraction is neither good nor bad *per se, its value instead depending on the functions it is made to serve and the perspective from which it is assessed.* Indeed, at the very moment that plantation slavery was being consolidated as the foundation of the U.S.-national economy (and leaving aside that from this angle black people's abstraction constituted an absolute boon), abstraction provided the conceptual means whereby certain members of the population saw their own personhood optimized rather than negated, with all the benefits that implies. (Harper 2015, 31; emphasis added)

Harper argues that white men have been constructed as generic exemplars of rationality. Because white men are thought of as individuals who represent rationality, and thereby represent humanity, *each can replace the other* in representing rational, human projects. To support his claim, Harper offers the example of Benjamin Franklin, who in 1773 devised a repeatable thirteen-week course for "'acquir[ing] the *Habitude*' of the thirteen specific 'virtues' of which he understood" moral perfection to consist (Harper 2015, 32). Franklin allotted a page for each virtue. He drew a grid on each page where days of the week were represented by columns, with each column marked with a letter for the day. Thirteen red lines crossed these columns, forming rows, which represented virtues. The beginning of each row was marked with the first letter of a name of a virtue. For example, the row representing Order was marked with an "O" (Harper 2015, 32).

Harper writes that Franklin gave us "a distinct form for the ideal 'clean book' he theoretically might have achieved" (Harper 2015, 33).

> Recruited to the project of figuring the moral perfection of the proto-republican citizen, its consummate blend of faultless uniformity and ordered regularity aptly emblematizes not only the noble genericism but also

the supreme rationality that citizen was understood to epitomize. *By the same token, of course, it also figures the absolute exclusion of black (and other non-white-male persons) from the polity,* inasmuch as they were considered incapable of either sublimating their particular interests or eradicating their vicious tendencies (both of which were held to be intractable elements of their blackness itself), and deemed wholly devoid of the capacity for reason. (Harper 2015, 34)

Here, Harper is describing a primary *and* the *restricted* manner in which white men are fungible (that is, interchangeable). White men's fungibility is inextricably linked to their individuality, which they possess through the kind of minds they possess—rational ones. Conversely, the kind of minds white men possess entail that they are individuals. Thus, the individuality of white men is not undermined by the genericity that enables their fungibility. As individuals they are still, to use Tom Regan's phrase, "subjects of a life" (Regan 2004). Moreover, their noble fungibility, with respect to humanity, is what accounts for the universal aspect of their existences. Such representative capacity entails that white men, in general, are fungible with respect to being interchangeable representatives of rationality and humanity.[4]

We are now at a point where we can understand why John Rankin (see above) might have failed had he used two of the models of empathy under consideration, and why he did fail when he tried to use the third.[5]

The Experience/Analogue-Construction Model for Empathetic Understanding

Allison Barnes and Paul Thagard understand empathy as a system of mapping the structure of an empathizer's experience onto the structure of the experience of the individual with whom the empathizer seeks to empathize—"the target." Such a mapping allows an empathizer to infer, predict, or explain the target's emotions based on the goals the empathizer has attributed to the target, given the situation the empathizer has described the target as being in. This model of empathy has nothing to do with having or seeking compassion or sympathy for a target. It leaves open the possibility that we might engage in empathetic exercises in order to understand how best to harm a target. Barnes and Thagard's model makes explicit how failures can occur. Empathetic understanding fails to the extent that the empathizer cannot retrieve or construct a source analogue corresponding to the structure of the target's situation. Thus, an empathetic response will be weak to the extent that the source analogue of the empathizer

(a) has disparate situations, goals, and emotions from those in the target analog;
(b) has a causal relation with structure different from that of the target analog;
(c) does not contribute to the cognitive purposes of the empathizer, which may include problem solving, explanation, or communication. (Barnes and Thagard 1997)

Rankin would have failed had he used this model. He shares neither experiences nor structures of experience with black people. Further, had Rankin constructed an analogue, it would have failed with respect to (a) and (b), and perhaps with respect to (c). Here I have space only to raise a crucial question regarding (c). Does empathizing with black people's pain contribute to *Rankin's* cognitive purposes? What are his cognitive purposes as a fungible white man? We might also ask: Had Rankin tried to construct an analogue, could he have known, without understanding his white fungibility, that his analogue was a failure? Not being able to recognize such empathetic failure is a serious problem for white empathizers.

The Direct Perception Model

Zahavi understands empathy as fundamental to any kind of access to other people. He restricts it to basic understanding of another person—the target—who, as in perception, must be present in order for the success of the empathetic act. Zahavi aims to conceive of empathy in analogy to perception. However, his model must then recognize empathy as a special form of perception because of a critical difference between mental states and external objects: mental states, unlike external objects, have aspects accessible only to the person that has them. Monika Dullstein observes in "Direct Perception and Simulation: Stein's Account of Empathy" that in order to deal with this problem, Zahavi makes the weaker claim that we *experience* rather than perceive others' mental states (Dullstein 2013).[6] It would seem then that just as we would fail to perceive a person P if the person were unavailable for our perception, on Zahavi's view of empathy, empathy would be unsuccessful if the target is unavailable for the empathetic experience. In other words, no experience of the target, no experience of the target's mental states.

In order to think about whether Rankin would have failed had he used this model of empathy, we must consider whether he really experienced black people and their pain in perceptual experience. Although Rankin's statements suggest that he *knows* that black people are in a mental state of suffering, I would like to cast doubt (not conclusive, by any means) on the idea that he knows or even believes any such thing *about them*. We cannot understand the situation of the coffle, black pain, and black enslavement without considering the fundamental historical conditions in which black pain was perceived by white people, and black enslavement implemented by white people.

Hartman provides an in-depth, detailed analysis of the problematics around black pain *for white people*, in light of, among other things, their enjoyment of black pain. Here I mention one problem only, which Hartman calls "the disavowing of claims of pain." Black people were forced to dance and sing as they marched along in chains. The threat of the whip made sure they "stepped it up lively." Given such *theatrics* (and the spectacle and the enjoyment of the spectacle thereby produced, along with the perceived mindless/excess *nature* of black people), it was difficult for white people to perceive black people's pain. The legacy of misperception has continued. White perception of black pain has been evidenced throughout American medical history. Black enslaved women suffered gynecological surgeries without the benefit of anesthesia.[7] Recent studies link disparities in pain management to racial bias (Samarrai 2016). Hartman quotes Abraham Lincoln, who having encountered a coffle delivered some pithy statements about black pain:

> And yet amid all these distressing circumstances, as we would think of them, they were the most cheerful and apparently happy creatures on board. One whose offence for which he had been sold was an over-fondness for his wife, played the fiddle almost continually; and others danced, sung, cracked jokes, and played various games with cards from day to day. How true it is that "God tempers the wind to the shorn lamb," or in other words, that He renders the worst of the human condition tolerable, while He permits the best, to be nothing but tolerable. (Hartman 1997, 34)

What Lincoln seems to be telling us is that the pain a black person feels on the coffle is about as tolerable (or intolerable) as the pain of those living the best of the human condition—that is, white people, in particular, white men. Above, we stated: no experience of target, no experience of target's mental states. Considering the case of Rankin, I propose another condition (to that of Zahavi) for success on this model. If the mental state the empathizer is trying to imagine is identical with the mental state M through which she seeks to empathize with the target, but the empathizer cannot experience apperceptively (in experience) the target's mental state M, then the empathizer cannot empathetically imagine the target's mental state M. The historical conditions surrounding the coffle and its intended effects on white people, as evidenced by Lincoln's words, in addition to the substitution Rankin found it necessary to make, should give us pause regarding his ability to experience apperceptively their pain. Therefore, we should be skeptical of Rankin's success—had he tried—in empathetically imagining black people's pain on this model.

The Transference Model of Empathy

De Vignemont and Jacob's simulation-based model of empathy, which is restricted to affective states only, offers five conditions for empathy. First, we suppose that an empathizer E* is in some affective state A*. Second, we assume that E*'s affective state A* stands in some similarity relation to the affective state A that a target T would be in. E*'s being in state A* is caused by T's being in state A. E*'s being in A* makes E* aware that her being in A* is caused by T's being in A. Thus, E* must care about T's affective life. Representing another's pain is carried out by running offline one's own pain systems, where an affective pain system will be activated, but not the sensory-motor system that typically accompanies standard pain. This model understands empathy as a way of gaining a deeper understanding of the target's experiences in the situation in which she finds herself, rather than a means by which the empathizer becomes aware of the target's mental state in the first place. Empathy fails if the empathizer is not imagining the other's pain, but her own (Dullstein 2013, 335–337).

Of the three models, this one best describes the one Rankin attempted to deploy. Again, we might ask why Rankin substituted himself for black people, as if by doing so he could get a deeper understanding of their suffering? Rankin wrote, "We are naturally too callous to the sufferings of others, and consequently prone to look upon them with cold indifference, until, in imagination we identify ourselves with the sufferers, and make their sufferings our own" (quoted in Hartman 1997, 18). These thoughts suggest that Rankin is already aware of the mental states of black enslaved people with whom he seeks to empathize, in which case he was seeking deeper understanding. But by Rankin's own account, he felt his own pain. Hence, according to the model, as understood by its authors, he failed in imagining black people's pain. He succeeded only in imagining his own.

Self-Empathy

Disappearing black people in perception or in the imagination constitutes a harm, whether intended or not. Such imaginative acts reproduce, in imagination, the logic of black fungibility—that is, the exchange of black people for whatever a white person manages to exchange a black person for, without loss of value. Such acts exercise habits of mind that are anti-black. I think it's fair to suppose that goodwill whites do not want to practice, even imaginatively, disappearing black people or honing their anti-black mental capacities. I propose that they try self-empathy, which may allow them, first, to understand the forms of racism they participate in, and second, to see why, for the most part, they cannot empathize with black people.

Philosophers have found much to reject in Theodor Lipps's understanding of empathy, in particular, his imitation view of empathy (Moran 2004, 282). However, Lipps's view that self-understanding involves empathy is, I believe, to be retained and developed. The self of past and future and imagined states might be recognized as one's self, by the self. Following Lipps, self-objectivation, which occurs when imagining one's self, renders the imagined self an other. But the otherness in question may be understood, with respect to our problem, as also deriving from the lack of acknowledging one's self as one's self, and not simply from the logic of self-objectivation. I propose a two-stage process of self-empathy. In the *first stage* the self becomes aware of an other self. In the *second stage*, the self comes to understand herself—who she is—through historical reconstruction, and is thereby able to see the alleged other as her own self.

I have in mind, here, subjects who encounter a self they reject as being their own. Empathetic understanding would be engaged in order to understand, through first-person perception of shared mental states, that the other self is identical with one's own. To begin, the target self is *perceived* as an other via mental states one does not perceive as being one's own, but of which one has become aware because one has given voice to ideas that express those mental states (or perhaps through an implicit bias test). (We might think of this as an epistemic other.) We can imagine a person in such a situation saying, "Who said that?" Or even, "What (or who) *possessed* me to say that?" The American civil rights activist, journalist, and educator Ann Braden recounts, in *Southern Patriot* how, when having breakfast downtown before making her way to the newspapers to work on the first edition of the afternoon paper, a friend who had joined her asked, "Anything doing?" Ann Braden replied, "*no, just a colored murder*" (Branden 2006, 3). The meaning—that black lives don't matter—the callousness of expressing the words in front of the black waitress serving them, may have struck Braden as not coming from her self, although the words had come from her.

In the first stage, the empathizer seeks to build an analogue of the other encountered. In the example at hand, our Braden character encountered the other in first-person perceptual experience, and might begin to construct an analogue with the words used, the meaning(s) they expressed, the easy callousness with which they were spoken, and whatever else she might divine from memories about this other.

The goal of second stage is for the empathizer to recognize that the alleged other is her self. Hence, the empathizer engages in a reconstruction of her good self, whereby she comes to understand, through historical reconstruction of her good white self, the way(s) and the degree to which she is a white fungible. She will be able to do this, in part, by becoming aware of the historical conditions, structures, and systems required for the full enjoyment of her white fungibility. Not to be left to rely on her own *selective* memory and choices, the empathizer, in most cases, may require the intervention of historical documents and analyses, which can provide plausible elucidations of both explicit and implicit components present in the construction of her self. Broadening our ideas about what legacies are, how they are transmitted, and what role they may play in the construction of selves, we may then ask, for example: How might the construction of white women's selves be related to structures, systems, and practices, including white slave-owning women's participation in the marketplace of black enslavement and in the mistress-making of their own daughters, especially within a context in which "historians have neglected these women because their behaviors toward, and relationships with, their slaves do not conform to prevailing ideas about white women and slave mastery"? (Jones-Rogers 2019, xi–xii.) The process of discovering and understanding the self I'm theorizing is antipodal to that of first-person introspection for discovering the self, and what the self is. One important condition the white empathizer must examine is black fungibility, and her relation to it.

Understanding her enjoyment of black fungibility as a white fungible creates an opening for the empathizer to see how it is possible for the alleged other's words to express *her* meanings and her emotions, and vice versa (Ann Braden's alleged other is unmistakably a white fungible.) In this way, the empathizer comes to deeply understand her good white self. From this point, it is up to the good white self to overcome its fragility, use its reason and concede that the best explanation for the situation at hand is that the words in question and their meanings came from someone who is none other than and *deeply* her self.

Understanding the nature of white fungibility in relation to black fungibility, recognizing her other as a white fungible, and then through historical reconstruction of her self, coming to understand that she (too) is a white fungible, the empathizer may come to see that the callous white fungible and she possess the same mental states—they think the same way, say the same things, and mean the same things!—and they do so within the same first-person mental space. Hence, the empathizer no longer denies herself. But the good white self could fail at this juncture. Being more committed to understanding her self as good (or perhaps unwilling to give up the pleasures of black fungibility), she could fail to see the evidence, or to use it. In such case, she continues to deny, in the empathetic act, that her self is herself.

Our Ann Braden character did not fail. Because she *desired to truly be good and not just think herself good*, she, like the real Ann Braden, changed her good, white fungible self, not by empathizing with black people, but through self-empathy, which was key to her future, active commitment to challenging structural anti-black racism.

Notes

1. Plausibly, my general claim about white empathy holds across geopolitical space. Cashing it out in other contexts requires engaging the historical specifics pertaining to the construction of black and white people in those contexts.
2. The name "goodwill whites" for good-willed white people is theorized in Jones (2004).
3. See Deliovsky and Kitossa (2013, 159–160).
4. Arguably, in the US context, white women also generically stand in as representatives of humanity. When black men were lynched for allegedly raping white women, the criminal acts they purportedly committed were crimes against symbols of humanity. If one imagines that this claim pertains to white, bourgeois women only, reconsider the case of the Scottsboro Nine. See Jones (2014).
5. Assuming that black people possess minds and rationality, my view leaves us with the unsettling plausible conclusion that black people, who do see themselves as human beings—but also understand white people through white fungibility—will be able to empathize with white people, to the extent to which they do not understand themselves as black fungibles.
6. See Zahavi (2010, 295) and Dullstein (2013, 341).
7. See Washington (2008).

References

Barnes, Allison, and Paul Thagard. 1997. "Empathy and Analogy." http://cogsci.uwater loo.ca/Articles/Pages/Empathy.html.

Bloom, Paul. 2016. *Against Empathy: The Case for Rational Compassion.* New York: HarpersCollins.

Braden, Anne. 2006. "Southern Patriot." http://www.newsreel.org/transcripts/Anne-Bra den-Southern-Patriot-transcript.pdf.

Curry, Tommy J. 2016. "Ethnological Theories of Race/Sex in Nineteenth-Century Black Thought: Implications for the Race/Gender Debate of the Twenty-First Century." In *The Oxford Handbook of Philosophy and Race,* edited by Naomi Zack, 565–575. Oxford: Oxford University Press.

Deliovsky, Katerina, and Tamari Kitossa. 2013. "Beyond Black and White: When Going Beyond Make Take Us Out of Bounds." *Journal of Black Studies* 44 (2): 158–181.

Dullstein, Monika. 2013. "Direct Perception and Simulation: Stein's Account of Empathy." *Review of Philosophy and Psychology* 4 (2): 333–350.

Harper, Phillip Brian. 2015. *Abstractionist Aesthetics: Artistic Form and Social Critique in African American Culture.* New York: New York University Press.

Hartman, Saidiya V. 1997. *Scenes of Subjection: Terror, Slavery, and Self-Making in Nineteenth Century America*. New York: Oxford University Press.

Jones, Janine. 2004. "The Impairment of Empathy in Goodwill Whites for African Americans." In *What White Looks Like: African-American Philosophers on the Whiteness Question*, edited by George Yancy, 65–86. New York: Routledge.

Jones, Janine. 2014. "Caster Semenya: Reasoning Up Front with Race." In *Why Race and Gender Still Matter: An Intersectional Approach*, edited by Namita Goswami, Maeve M. O'Donovan, and Lisa Yount, 133–155. London: Pickering and Chatto.

Jones, Janine. 2016. "To Be Black, Excess, and Non-recyclable." In *The Oxford Handbook of Philosophy and Race*, edited by Naomi Zack, 319–330. Oxford: Oxford University Press.

Jones-Rogers, Stephanie E. 2019. *They Were Her Property: White Women as Slave Owners in the American South*. New Haven: Yale University Press.

King, Tiffany Lethabo. 2016. "The Labor of (Re)reading Plantation Landscapes Fungible(ly)." *Antipode* 48 (4): 1022–1039.

Loomba, Ania. 2009. "Race and Possibilities of Comparative Critique." *New Literary History* 40 (3): 501–522.

Moran, Dermot. 2004. "The Problem of Empathy: Lipps, Scheler, Husserl and Stein." In *Recherches de théologie et philosophie médiévales: Bibliotheca 6: Amor amicitiae: On the Love That Is Friendship: Essays in Medieval Thought and Beyond in Honor of the Rev. Professor James McEvoy*, edited by Thomas A. F. Kelly and Phillip W. Rosemann, 269–312. Leuven, Belgium: Peeters.

Regan, Tom. 2004. *The Case for Animal Rights*. Berkeley: University of California Press.

Ritskes, Eric. 2015. "The Fleshy Excess of Black Life: Mike Brown, Eric Garner, and Tamir Rice." *Decolonization: Indigeneity, Education, and Society*. January 2. https://decolon ization. wordpress.com/2015/01/02/the-fleshy-excess-of-black-life-mike-brown-eric-garner-and-tamir-rice/.

Samarrai, Fariss. 2016. "Study Links Management in Pain Management to Racial Bias." *UVA Today*. April 4. https://news.virginia.edu/content/study-links-disparities-pain-management-racial-bias.

Sanburn, Josh. 2014. "All the Ways Darren Wilson Described Being Afraid of Michael Brown." *Time*. November 25. http://time.com/3605346/darren-wilson-michael-brown-demon/.

Spillers, Hortense. 1987. "Mama's Baby, Papa's Maybe: An American Grammar Book." *Diacritics* 17 (2): 65–81.

Washington, Harriet A. 2008. *Medical Apartheid: The Dark History of Medical Experimentation on Black Americans from Colonial Times to Present*. New York: Doubleday.

Zahavi, Dan. 2010. "Empathy and Direct Social Perception: A Phenomenological Proposal." *Review of Philosophy and Psychology* (2) 3: 541–558.

Zahavi, Dan. 2014. *Self & Other: Exploring Subjectivity, Empathy, and Shame*. Oxford: Oxford University Press.

PART II
SELF AND SELVES

5

Playfulness, "World"-Traveling, and Loving Perception

María Lugones

This chapter weaves two aspects of life together. My coming to consciousness as a daughter and my coming to consciousness as a woman of color have made this weaving possible.[1] This weaving reveals the possibility and complexity of a pluralistic feminism, a feminism that affirms the plurality in each of us and among us as richness and as central to feminist ontology and epistemology.

The chapter describes the experience of "outsiders" to the mainstream of, for example, white/Anglo organization of life in the United States and stresses a particular feature of the outsider's existence: the outsider has necessarily acquired flexibility in shifting from the mainstream construction of life where she is constructed as an outsider to other constructions of life where she is more or less "at home." This flexibility is necessary for the outsider. It is required by the logic of oppression. But it can also be exercised resistantly by the outsider or by those who are at ease in the mainstream. I recommend this resistant exercise that I call " 'world'-traveling" and I also recommend that the exercise be animated by an attitude that I describe as playful.

As outsiders to the mainstream, women of color in the United States practice "world"-traveling, mostly out of necessity. I affirm this practice as a skillful, creative, rich, enriching, and, given certain circumstances, loving way of being and living. I recognize that much of our travel is done unwillingly to hostile white/Anglo "worlds." The hostility of these "worlds" and the compulsory nature of the "traveling" have obscured for us the enormous value of this aspect of our living and its connection to loving. Racism has a vested interest in obscuring and devaluing the complex skills involved in it. I recommend that we affirm this traveling across "worlds" as partly constitutive of cross-cultural and cross-racial loving. Thus, I recommend to women of color in the United States that we learn to love each other by learning to travel to each other's "worlds." In making this recommendation, I have in mind giving a new meaning to coalition and propose "Women of Color" as a term for a coalition of deep understanding fashioned through "world"-traveling.

María Lugones, *Playfulness, "World"-Traveling, and Loving Perception* In: *Feminist Philosophy of Mind*. Edited by: Keya Maitra and Jennifer McWeeny, Oxford University Press. © Oxford University Press 2022. DOI: 10.1093/oso/9780190867614.003.0006

According to Marilyn Frye, to perceive arrogantly is to perceive that others are for oneself and to proceed to arrogate their substance to oneself (Frye 1983, 66). Here, I make a connection between "arrogant perception" and the failure to identify with persons that one views arrogantly or has come to see as the products of arrogant perception. A further connection is made between this failure of identification and a failure of love, and thus between loving and identifying with another person. The sense of love is not the one Frye has identified as both consistent with arrogant perception and as promoting unconditional servitude. "We can be taken in by this equation of servitude with love," Frye says, "because we make two mistakes at once: we think of both servitude and love that they are selfless or unselfish" (Frye 1983, 73). The identification of which I speak is constituted by what I come to characterize as playful " 'world'-traveling." To the extent that we learn to perceive others arrogantly or come to see them only as products of arrogant perception and continue to perceive them that way, we fail to identify with them—fail to love them—in this particular way.

Identification and Love

As a child, I was taught to perceive arrogantly. I have also been the object of arrogant perception. Though I am not a white/Anglo woman, it is clear to me that I can understand both my childhood training as an arrogant perceiver and my having been the object of arrogant perception without any reference to white/Anglo men. This gives some indication that the concept of arrogant perception can be used cross-culturally and that white/Anglo men are not the only arrogant perceivers.

I was brought up in Argentina watching men and women of moderate and of considerable means graft the substance of their servants to themselves. I also learned to graft my mother's substance to my own. It was clear to me that both men and women were the victims of arrogant perception and that arrogant perception was systematically organized to break the spirit of all women and of most men. I valued my rural gaucho ancestry because its ethos has always been one of independence, courage, and self-reliance in the midst of poverty and enormous loneliness. I found inspiration in this ethos and committed myself never to be broken by arrogant perception. I can say all of this in this way only because of what I have learned from Frye's "In and Out of Harm's Way: Arrogance and Love" (1983). She has given me a way of understanding and articulating something important in my own life.

Frye is not particularly concerned with women as arrogant perceivers but as the objects of arrogant perception. Her concern is, in part, to enhance our understanding of women "untouched by phallocratic machinations," by understanding the harm done to women through such machinations (Frye 1983, 53). In this case, she proposes that we could understand women untouched by arrogant perception through an understanding of what arrogant perception does to women. Frye also proposes an understanding of what it is to love women that is inspired by a vision of women unharmed by arrogant perception. To love women is, at least in part, to perceive them with loving eyes. "The loving eye is a contrary of the arrogant eye" (Frye 1983, 75).

I am concerned with women as arrogant perceivers because I want to explore further what it is to love women. I want to begin by exploring two failures of love: my failure to love my mother and white/Anglo women's failure to love women across racial and cultural boundaries in the United States. As a consequence of exploring these failures I will offer a loving solution to them. My solution modifies Frye's account of loving perception by adding what I call "playful 'world'-travel." Then I want to take up the practice as a horizontal practice of resistance to two related injunctions: the injunction for the oppressed to have our gazes fixed on the oppressor and the concomitant injunction not to look to and connect with each other in resistance to those injunctions through traveling to each other's "worlds" of sense. Thus, the first move is one that explores top-down failures of love and their logic; the second move explores horizontal failures.

It is clear to me, that at least in the United States and Argentina, women are taught to perceive many other women arrogantly. Being taught to perceive arrogantly is part of being taught to be a woman of a certain class in both the United States and Argentina; it is part of being taught to be a white/Anglo woman in the United States; and it is part of being taught to be a woman in both places: to be both the agent and the object of arrogant perception. My love for my mother seemed to me thoroughly imperfect as I was growing up because I was unwilling to become what I had been taught to see my mother as being. I thought that to love her was consistent with my abusing her: using, taking her for granted, and demanding her services in a far-reaching way that, since four other people engaged in the same grafting of her substance onto themselves, left her little of herself to herself. I also thought that loving her was to be in part constituted by my identifying with her, my seeing myself in her. Thus, to love her was supposed to be of a piece with both my abusing her and with my being open to being abused. It is clear to me that I was not supposed to love servants: I could abuse them without identifying with them, without seeing myself in them.

When I came to the United States I learned that part of racism is the internalization of the propriety of abuse without identification. I learned that I could be seen as a being to be used by white/Anglo men and women without the possibility of identification (that is, without their act of attempting to graft my substance onto theirs rubbing off on them at all). They could remain untouched, without any sense of loss.

So, women who are perceived arrogantly can, in turn, perceive other women arrogantly. To what extent those women are responsible for their arrogant perceptions of other women is certainly open to question, but I do not have any doubt that many of them have been taught to abuse women in this particular way. I am not interested in assigning responsibility. I am interested in understanding the phenomenon so as to understand a loving way out of it. I am offering a way of taking responsibility, of exercising oneself as not doomed to oppress others.

There is something obviously wrong with the love that I was taught and something right with my failure to love my mother in this way. But I do not think that what is wrong is my profound desire to identify with her, to see myself in her; what is wrong is that I was taught to identify with a victim of servitude. What is wrong is that I was taught to practice servitude of my mother and to learn to become a servant through this practice. There is something obviously wrong with my having been taught that love is consistent with abuse, consistent with arrogant perception.

Notice that the love I was taught is the love that Frye speaks of when she says, "We can be taken in by this equation of servitude with love" (Frye 1983, 73). Even though I could both abuse and love my mother, I was not supposed to love servants. This is because in the case of servants one is supposed to be clear about their servitude and the "equation of servitude with love" is never to be thought clearly in those terms. So, I was not supposed to love and could not love servants. But I could love my mother because deception (in particular, self-deception) is part of this "loving."

In the equation of love with servitude, servitude is called abnegation and abnegation is not analyzed any further. Abnegation is not instilled in us through an analysis of its nature but rather through a heralding of it as beautiful and noble. We are coaxed, seduced into abnegation not through analysis but through emotive persuasion. Frye makes the connection between deception and this sense of loving clear. When I say that there is something obviously wrong with the loving that I was taught, I do not mean to say that the connection between this loving and abuse is obvious. Rather, I mean that once the connection between this loving and abuse has been unveiled, there is something obviously wrong with the loving given that it is obvious that it is wrong to abuse others.

I am glad that I did not learn my lessons well, but it is clear that part of the mechanism that permitted my not learning well involved a separation from my mother: I saw us as beings of quite a different sort. It involved abandoning my mother even while I longed not to abandon her. I wanted to love my mother, though, given what I was taught, "love" could not be the right word for what I longed for.

I was disturbed by my not wanting to be what she was. I had a sense of not being quite integrated, my self was missing because I could not identify with her,

I could not see myself in her, I could not welcome her "world." I saw myself as separate from her, a different sort of being, not quite of the same species. This separation, this lack of love, I saw, and I think that I saw correctly, as a lack in myself (not a fault, but a lack). I also see that if this was a lack of love, love cannot be what I was taught. It has to be rethought, made anew.

There is something in common between the relation between me and my mother as someone I did not used to be able to love and the relation between women of color in the United States like me and white/Angla women: there is a failure of love. As I eluded identification with my mother, white/Angla women elude identification with women of color, identifications with beings whose substance they arrogate without a sense of loss. Frye helped me understand one of the aspects of this failure—the directly abusive aspect. But I also think that there is a complex failure of love in the failure to identify with another woman, the failure to see oneself in other women who are quite different from oneself. I want to begin to analyze this complex failure.

Notice that Frye's emphasis on independence in her analysis of loving perception is not particularly helpful in explaining these failures. She says that in loving perception, "the object of the seeing is another being whose existence and character are logically independent of the seer and who may be practically or empirically independent in any particular respect at any particular time" (Frye 1983, 77). But this does not help me understand how my failure of love toward my mother (when I ceased to be her parasite) left me not quite whole. It is not helpful since I saw her as logically independent from me. And it also does not help me understand why the racist or ethnocentric failure of love of white/Angla women—in particular of those white/Angla women who are not pained by their failure—should leave me not quite substantive among them.

I am not particularly interested here in cases of white women's parasitism onto women of color but more pointedly in cases where the relation is characterized by failure of identification. I am interested here in those many cases in which white/Angla women do one or more of the following to women of color: they ignore us, ostracize us, render us invisible, stereotype us, leave us completely alone, interpret us as crazy. All of this *while we are in their midst*. The more independent I am, the more independent I am left to be. Their "world" and their integrity do not require me at all. There is no sense of self-loss in them for my own lack of solidity. But they rob me of my solidity through indifference, an indifference they can afford and that seems sometimes studied. But many of us have to work among white/Anglo folk and our best shot at recognition has seemed to be among white/Angla women because many of them have expressed a *general* sense of being pained at their failure of love.

Many times white/Angla women want us out of their field of vision. Their lack of concern is a harmful failure of love that leaves me independent from them in a way similar to the way in which, once I ceased to be my mother's parasite, she became, though not independent from all others, certainly independent from me. But, of course, because my mother and I wanted to love each other well, we were not whole in this independence. White/Angla women are independent from me, I am independent from them; I am independent from my mother, she is independent from me; and none of us loves each other in this independence. I am incomplete and unreal without other women. I am profoundly dependent on others without having to be their subordinate, their slave, their servant.

Identification and Women of Color

The relations among "Women of Color" can neither be homogenized nor merely wished into being as relations of solidarity. To the extent that Women of Color names a coalition, it is a coalition in formation against significant and complex odds that, though familiar, keep standing in our way. The coalition or interconnecting coalitions need to be conceptualized against the grain of these odds. Audre Lorde is attentive to the problem of homogenization in coalition formation when she tells us to explore our relations in terms of "non-dominant differences" (Lorde 1984b, 111). The epistemological shift to nondominant differences is crucial to our possibilities. To the extent that we are "created different" by the logic of domination, the techniques of producing difference include divide and conquer, segregation, fragmentation, instilling mistrust toward each other for having been pitted against each other by economies of domination, instilling in us the distinction between the real and the fake. Here I will not address each one of these techniques of keeping us focused on dominant differences among each other, that is differences concocted by the dominant imagination. Rather, I will emphasize the epistemological shift to nondominant differences.

To the extent that in resistance to oppressions, both men and women have historically fashioned resistant "communities," resistant socialities that have made meanings that have enabled us to endure as resistant subjects in the oppressing ↔ resisting relation, we have created alternate historical lines that are in connection with each other—they do not exist in isolation—lines that we do not understand, as nothing requires that we understand the spatio-temporal differences among us. Systems of domination construct women of color as subordinate, inferior, servile. We can see each other enacting these dominant constructions, even when we do it against our own desire, will, and energy. We can see and understand these animations of the dominant imaginary, but we are not sufficiently familiar with each other's "worlds" of resistance to either cross, or travel to them, nor to avoid what keeps us from seeing the need to travel, the enriching of our possibilities through "world"-travel.

There is an important sense in which we do not understand each other as interdependent and we do not identify with each other since we lack insight into each other's resistant understandings. To put the point sharply, the resistant understandings do not travel through social fragmentation. Separatism in communities where our substance is seen and celebrated, where we become substantive through this celebration, combines with social fragmentation to keep our lines of resistance away from each other. Thus, it is difficult for women of color to see, know each other, as resistant rather than as constructed by domination. To the extent that we face each other as oppressed, we do not want to identify with each other, we repel each other as we are seeing each other in the same mirror.[2] As resistant, we are kept apart by social fragmentation. To identify with each other, we need to engage in resistant practices that appear dangerous. We have not realized the potential lying in our becoming interdependently resistant. As resistant, we appear independent from each other to each other. The coalition sense of "Women of Color" necessitates this identification that comes from seeing ourselves and each other interrelating "worlds" of resistant meaning. To the extent that identification requires sameness, this coalition is impossible. So, the coalition requires that we conceive identification anew. The independence of women of color from each other performed by social fragmentation leaves us unwittingly colluding with the logic of oppression.

"Worlds" and "World"-Traveling

Frye says that the loving eye is "the eye of one who knows that to know the seen, one must consult something other than one's own will and interests and fears and imagination" (Frye 1983, 75). This is much more helpful to me so long as I do not understand her to mean that I should not consult my own interests nor that I should exclude the possibility that my self and the self of the one I love may be importantly tied to each other in many complicated ways. Since I am emphasizing here that the failure of love lies in part in the failure to identify, and since I agree with Frye that one "must consult something other than one's own will and interests and fears and imagination," I will explain what I think needs to be consulted. It was not possible for me to love my mother while I retained a sense that it was fine for me and others to see her arrogantly. Loving my mother also required that I see with her eyes, that I go into my mother's "world," that I see both of us as we are constructed in her "world," that I witness her own sense of herself from within her "world." Only through this traveling to her "world" could I identify with her because only then could I cease to ignore her and to be excluded and separate from her. Only then could I see her as a subject, even if one subjected, and only then could I see how meaning could arise fully between us. We are fully dependent on each other for the possibility of being understood and without this understanding we are not intelligible, we do not make sense, we are not solid, visible, integrated; we are lacking. So traveling to each other's "worlds" would enable us to *be* through loving each other.

I hope the sense of identification I have in mind is becoming clear. But to become clearer, I need to explain what I mean by a "world" and by "traveling" to another "world." In explaining what I mean by a "world," I will not appeal to traveling to other women's "worlds." Instead, I will lead you to see what I mean by a "world" the way I came to propose the concept to myself: through the kind of ontological confusion about myself that we, women of color, refer to half-jokingly as "schizophrenia" (we feel schizophrenic in our goings back and forth between different "communities") and through my effort to make some sense of this ontological confusion.

Some time ago I came to be in a state of profound confusion as I experienced myself as both having and not having a particular attribute. I was sure I had the attribute in question and, on the other hand, I was sure that I did not have it. I remain convinced that I both have and do not have this attribute. The attribute is playfulness. I am sure that I am a playful person. On the other hand, I can say, painfully, that I am not a playful person. I am not a playful person in certain "worlds." One of the things I did as I became confused was to call my friends, far away people who knew me well, to see whether or not I was playful. Maybe they could help me out of my confusion. They said to me, "Of course you are playful," and they said it with the same conviction that I had about it. Of course I am playful. Those people who were around me said to me, "No, you are not playful. You are a serious woman. You just take everything seriously."[3] They were just as sure about what they said to me and could offer me every bit of evidence that one could need to conclude that they were right. So I said to myself, "Okay, maybe what's happening here is that there is an attribute that I do have but there are certain 'worlds' in which I am not at ease and it is because I'm not at ease in those 'worlds' that I don't have that attribute in those 'worlds.' But what does that mean?" I was worried both about what I meant by "worlds" when I said, "In some 'worlds' I do not have the attribute" and what I meant by saying that lack of ease was what led me not to be playful in those "worlds." Because, you see, if it was just a matter of lack of ease, I could work on it.

I can explain some of what I mean by a "world." I do not want the fixity of a definition at this point, because I think the term is suggestive and I do not want to close the suggestiveness of it too soon. I can offer some characteristics that serve to distinguish between a "world," a utopia, a possible "world" in the philosophical sense, and a "world" view. By a "world" I do not mean a utopia at all. A utopia does not count as a "world," in my sense. The "worlds" that I am talking about are possible. But a possible "world" is not what I mean by a "world" and I do not mean a "world"-view, though something like a "world"-view is involved here.

For something to be a "world" in my sense, it has to be inhabited at present by some flesh and blood people. That is why it cannot be a utopia. It may also be inhabited by some imaginary people. It may be inhabited by people who are dead or people that the inhabitants of this "world" met in some other "world" and now have in this "world" in imagination.

A "world" in my sense may be an actual society, given its dominant culture's description and construction of life, including a construction of the relationships of production, of gender, race, and so on. But a "world" can also be such a society given a nondominant, a resistant construction, or it can be such a society or a society given an idiosyncratic construction. As we will see, it is problematic to say that these are all constructions of the same society. But they are different "worlds."

A "world" need not be a construction of a whole society. It may be a construction of a tiny portion of a particular society. It may be inhabited by just a few people. Some "worlds" are bigger than others.

A "world" may be incomplete. Things in it may not be altogether constructed or some things may be constructed negatively (they are not what "they" are in some other "world"). Or the "world" may be incomplete because it may have references to things that do not quite exist in it, references to things like Brazil, where Brazil is not quite part of that "world." Given lesbian feminism, the construction of "lesbian" is purposefully and healthily still up in the air, in the process of becoming. What it is to be a Hispanic in this country is, in a dominant Anglo construction, purposefully incomplete. Thus, one cannot really answer questions like "What is a Hispanic?" "Who counts as a Hispanic?" "Are Latinos, Chicanos, Hispanos, black Dominicans, white Cubans, Korean Colombians, Italian Argentinians, Hispanic?" What it is to be a "Hispanic" in the varied so-called Hispanic communities in the United States is also yet up in the air. "We" have not yet decided whether there is something like a "Hispanic" in our varied "worlds."[4] So, a "world" may be an incomplete visionary nonutopian construction of life, or it may be a traditional construction of life. A traditional Hispano construction of northern New Mexican life is a "world." Such a traditional construction, in the face of a racist, ethnocentric, money-centered Anglo construction of northern New Mexican life, is highly unstable because Anglos have the means for imperialist destruction of traditional Hispano "worlds."

In a "world," some of the inhabitants may not understand or hold the particular construction of them that constructs them in that "world." So, there may be "worlds" that construct me in ways that I do not even understand. Or, it may be that I understand the construction, but do not hold it of myself. I may not accept it as an account of myself, a construction of myself. And yet, I may be *animating* such a construction.[5]

One can "travel" between these "worlds" and one can inhabit more than one of these "worlds" at the same time. I think that most of us who are outside the mainstream of, for example, the United States' dominant construction or organization of life are "world"-travelers as a matter of necessity and of survival. It seems to me that inhabiting more than one "world" at the same time and "traveling" between "worlds" is part and parcel of our experience and our situation. One can be at the same time in a "world" that constructs one as stereotypically Latina, for example, and in a "world" that constructs one as simply Latina. Being stereotypically Latina and being simply Latina are different simultaneous constructions of persons who are part of different "worlds." One animates one or the other or both at the same time without necessarily confusing them, though simultaneous enactment can be confusing if one is not on one's guard.

In describing my sense of a "world," I am offering a description of experience, something that is true to experience even if it is ontologically problematic. Though I would think that any account of identity that could not be true to this experience of outsiders to the mainstream would be faulty, even if ontologically unproblematic. Its ease would constrain, erase, or deem aberrant experience that has within it significant insights into nonimperialistic understanding between people.

Those of us who are "world"-travelers have the distinct experience of being different in different "worlds" and of having the capacity to remember other "worlds" and ourselves in them. We can say, "That is me there, and I am happy in that 'world.'" So, the experience is of being a different person in different "worlds" and yet of having memory of oneself as different without quite having the sense of there being any underlying "I." When I can say, "That is me there and I am so playful in that 'world,'" I am saying, "That is *me* in that 'world'" not because I recognize myself in that person; rather, the first-person statement is noninferential. I may well recognize that that person has abilities that I do not have and yet the having or not having of the abilities is always an "I have . . ." and "I do not have . . ." (that is, it is always experienced in the first person).

The shift from being one person to being a different person is what I call "traveling." This shift may not be willful or even conscious, and one may be completely unaware of being different in a different "world," and may not recognize that one is in a different "world." Even though the shift can be done willfully, it is not a matter of acting. One does not pose as someone else; one does not pretend to be, for example, someone of a different personality or character or someone who uses space or language differently from the other person. Rather, one is someone who has that personality or character or uses space and language in that particular way. The "one" here does not refer to some underlying "I." One does not *experience* any underlying "I."

Being at Ease in a "World"

In investigating what I mean by "being at ease in a 'world,' " I will describe different ways of being at ease. One may be at ease in one or in all of these ways. There is a maximal way of being at ease, namely, being at ease in all of these ways. I take this maximal way of being at ease to be somewhat dangerous because it tends to produce people who have no inclination to travel across "worlds" or no experience of "world"-traveling.

The first way of being at ease in a particular "world" is by being a fluent speaker in that "world." I know all the norms that there are to be followed. I know all the words that there are to be spoken. I know all the moves. I am confident.

Another way of being at ease is by being normatively happy. I agree with all the norms, I could not love any norms better. I am asked to do just what I want to do or what I think I should do. I am at ease.

Another way of being at ease in a "world" is by being humanly bonded. I am with those I love and they love me, too. It should be noticed that I may be with those I love and be at ease because of them in a "world" that is otherwise as hostile to me as "worlds" get.

Finally, one may be at ease because one has a history with others that is shared, especially daily history, the kind of shared history that one sees exemplified by the response to the "Do you remember poodle skirts?" question. There you are, with people you do not know at all and who do not know each other. The question is posed and then everyone begins talking about their poodle skirt stories. I have been in such situations without knowing what poodle skirts, for example, were, and I felt ill at ease because it was not *my* history. The other people did not know each other. It is not that they were humanly bonded. Probably they did not have much politically in common either. But poodle skirts were in their shared history.

One may be at ease in one of these ways or in all of them. Notice that when one says meaningfully, "This is *my* 'world,' " one may not be at ease in it. Or one may be at ease in it only in some of these respects and not in others. To say of some "world" that it is "*my* world" is to make an evaluation. One may privilege one or more "worlds" in this way for a variety of reasons: for example, because one experiences oneself as an agent in a fuller sense than one experiences oneself in other "worlds." One may disown a "world" because one has first-person memories of a person who is so thoroughly dominated that she has no sense of exercising her own will or has a sense of having serious difficulties in performing actions that are willed by herself and no difficulty in performing actions willed by others. One may say of a "world" that it is "my world" because one is at ease in it (that is, being at ease in a "world" may be the basis for the evaluation).

Given the clarification of what I mean by a "world," " 'world'-travel," and being at ease in a "world," we are in a position to return to my problematic attribute, playfulness. It may be that in this "world" in which I am so unplayful, I am a different person than in the "world" in which I am playful. Or it may be that the "world" in which I am unplayful is constructed in such a way that I could be playful in it. I could practice, even though that "world" is constructed in such a way that my being playful in it is kind of hard. In describing what I take a "world" to be, I emphasized the first possibility as both the one that is truest to the experience of "outsiders" to the mainstream and as ontologically problematic because the "I" is identified in some sense as one and in some sense as a plurality. I identify myself as myself through memory and I retain myself as different in memory.

When I travel from one "world" to another, I have this image, this memory of myself as playful in this other "world." I can then be in a particular "world" and have a double image of myself as, for example, playful and as not playful. This is a very familiar and recognizable phenomenon to the outsider to the mainstream in some central cases: when in one "world" I animate, for example, that world's caricature of the person I am in the other "world." I can have both images of myself, and, to the extent that I can materialize or animate both images at the same time, I become an ambiguous being. This is very much a part of trickery and foolery. It is worth remembering that the trickster and the fool are significant characters in many nondominant or outsider cultures. One then sees any particular "world" with these double edges and sees absurdity in them and so inhabits oneself differently.

Given that Latins are constructed in Anglo "worlds" as stereotypically intense—intensity being a central characteristic of at least one of the Anglo stereotypes of Latinas—and given that many Latinas, myself included, are genuinely intense, I can say to myself "I am intense" and take a hold of the double meaning. Furthermore, I can be stereotypically intense or be the real thing, and, if you are Anglo, you do not know when I am which *because* I am Latin American. As a Latin American I am an ambiguous being, a two-imaged self: I can see that gringos see me as stereotypically intense because I am, as a Latin American, constructed that way but I may or may not *intentionally* animate the stereotype or the real thing knowing that you may not see it in anything other than in the stereotypical construction. This ambiguity is funny and is not just funny; it is survival-rich. We can also make the picture of those who dominate us funny precisely because we can see the double edge, we can see them doubly constructed, we can see the plurality in them. So we know truths that only the fool can speak and only the trickster can play out without harm. We inhabit "worlds" and travel across them and keep all the memories.

Sometimes, the "world"-traveler has a double image of herself and each self includes as important ingredients of itself one or more attributes that are *incompatible* with one or more of the attributes of the other self: for example, being playful and being unplayful. To the extent that the attribute is an important ingredient of the self she is in that "world" (that is, to the extent that there is a particularly good fit between that "world" and her having that attribute in it, and to the extent that the attribute is personality or character central, *that "world" would have to be changed if she is to be playful in it*). It is not the case that if she could come to be at ease in it, she would be her own playful self. Because the attribute is personality or character central and there is such a good fit between that "world" and her being constructed with that attribute as central, *she* cannot become playful, she is unplayful. To become playful would be, for her, to become a contradictory being.

I suggest, then, that my problematic case, the being and not being playful, cannot be solved through lack of ease. I suggest that I can understand my confusion about whether I am or am not playful by saying that I am both and that I am different persons in different "worlds" and can remember myself in both as I am in the other. I am a plurality of selves. This explains my confusion because *it is to come to see it as of a piece* with much of the rest of my experience as an outsider in some of the "worlds" that I inhabit and of a piece with significant aspects of the experience of nondominant people in the "worlds" of their dominators.

So, though I may not be at ease in the "worlds" in which I am not constructed playful, it is not that I am not playful *because* I am not at ease. The two are compatible. But lack of playfulness is not caused by lack of ease. Lack of playfulness is not symptomatic of lack of ease but of lack of health. I am not a healthy being in the "worlds" that construct me unplayful.

Playfulness

I had a very personal stake in investigating this topic. Playfulness is not only the attribute that was the source of my confusion and the attitude that I recommend as the loving attitude in traveling across "worlds." I am also scared of ending up a serious human being, someone with no multidimensionality, with no fun in life, someone who is just someone who has had the fun constructed out of her. I am seriously scared of getting stuck in a "world" that constructs me that way, a "world" that I have no escape from and in which I cannot be playful.

I thought about what it is to be playful and what it is to play and I did this thinking in a "world" in which I only remember myself as playful and in which all of those who know me as playful are imaginary beings. It is a "world" in which I am scared of losing my memories of myself as playful or have them erased from me. Because I live in such a "world," after I formulated my own sense of what it is to be playful and to play, I decided that I needed to go to the literature. I read two classics on the subject: Johan Huizinga's *Homo Ludens* (1968) and Hans-Georg Gadamer's chapter on the concept of play in his *Truth and Method* (1975). I discovered, to my amazement, that what I thought about play and playfulness, if they were right, was absolutely wrong. Though I will not provide the arguments for this interpretation of Gadamer and Huizinga here, I understood that both of them have an agonistic sense of play. "Play" and "playfulness" have—in their use—ultimately, to do with contest, with winning, losing, battling. The sense of playfulness that I have in mind has nothing to do with agon. So, I tried to elucidate both senses of play and playfulness by contrasting them to each other. The contrast helped me see the attitude that I have in mind as the loving attitude in traveling across "worlds" more clearly.

An agonistic sense of playfulness is one in which *competence* is central. You'd better know the rules of the game. In agonistic play there is risk, there is *uncertainty*, but the uncertainty is about who is going to win and who is going to lose. There are rules that inspire hostility. The attitude of *playfulness is conceived as secondary to or derivative from play*. Since play is agon, then the only conceivable playful attitude is an agonistic one: the attitude does not turn an activity into play, but rather presupposes an activity that is play. One of the paradigmatic ways of playing for both Gadamer and Huizinga is role-playing. In role-playing, the person who is a participant in the game has a *fixed conception of him- or herself*. I also think that the players are imbued with *self-importance* in agonistic play since they are so keen on winning given their own merits, their very own competence.

When considering the value of "world"-traveling and whether playfulness is the loving attitude to have while traveling, I recognized the agonistic attitude as inimical to traveling across "worlds." The agonistic traveler is a conqueror, an imperialist. Huizinga, in his classic book on play, interprets Western civilization as play. That is an interesting thing for Third World people to think about. Western civilization has been interpreted by a white Western man as play in the agonistic sense of play. Huizinga reviews Western law, art, and any other aspects of Western culture and sees agon in all of them. Agonistic playfulness leads those who attempt to travel to another "world" with this attitude to failure. Agonistic travelers cannot attempt travel in this sense. Their traveling is always a trying that is tied to conquest, domination, reduction of what they meet to their own sense of order, and erasure of the other "world." That is what assimilation is all about. Assimilation is an agonistic project of destruction of other people's "worlds." So, the agonistic attitude, the playful attitude given Western man's construction of playfulness, is not a healthy, loving attitude to have in traveling across "worlds." Given the agonistic attitude, one *cannot* travel across "worlds," though one can kill other "worlds" with it.[6] So, for people who are interested in crossing racial and ethnic boundaries, an arrogant Western man's construction of playfulness is deadly. One cannot cross the boundaries with it. One needs to give up such an attitude if one wants to travel.

What, then, is the loving playfulness that I have in mind? Let me begin with one example: We are by the riverbank. The river is very low. Almost dry. Bits of water here and there. Little pools with a few trout hiding under the rocks. But it is mostly wet stones, gray on the outside. We walk on the stones for a while. You pick up a stone and crash it onto the others. As it breaks, it is quite wet inside and it is very colorful, very pretty. I pick up a stone and break it and run toward the pieces to see the colors. They are beautiful. I laugh and bring the pieces back to you and you are doing the same with your pieces. We keep on crashing stones for hours, anxious to see the beautiful new colors. We are playing. The playfulness of our activity does not presuppose that there is something like "crashing stones" that is a particular form of play with its own rules. Instead, *the attitude that carries us through the activity, a playful attitude, turns the activity into play.* Our activity has no rules, though it is certainly intentional activity and we both understand what we are doing. The playfulness that gives meaning to our activity includes uncertainty, but in this case the uncertainty is an *openness to surprise.* This is a particular metaphysical attitude that does not expect the "world" to be neatly packaged, ruly. Rules may fail to explain what we are doing. We are not self-important, we are not fixed in particular constructions of ourselves, which is part of saying that we are *open to self-construction.* We may not have rules, and when we do have them, *there are no rules that are to us sacred.* We are not worried about competence. We are not wedded to a particular way of doing things. While playful, we have not abandoned ourselves to, nor are we stuck in, any particular "world." We *are there creatively.* We are not passive.[7]

Playfulness is, in part, an openness to being a fool, which is a combination of not worrying about competence, not being self-important, not taking norms as sacred, and finding ambiguity and double edges a source of wisdom and delight.

So, positively, the playful attitude involves openness to surprise, openness to being a fool, openness to self-construction or reconstruction and to construction or reconstruction of the "worlds" we inhabit playfully, and thus openness to risk the ground that constructs us as oppressors or as oppressed or as collaborating or colluding with oppression. Negatively, playfulness is characterized by uncertainty, lack of self-importance, absence of rules or not taking rules as sacred, not worrying about competence, and lack of abandonment to a particular construction of oneself, others, and one's relation to them. In attempting to take a hold of oneself and of one's relation to others in a particular "world," one may study, examine, and come to understand oneself. One may then see what the possibilities for play are for the being one is in that "world." One may even decide to inhabit that self fully to understand it better and find its creative possibilities.

There are "worlds" we enter at our own risk, "worlds" that have agon, conquest, and arrogance as the main ingredients in their ethos. These are "worlds" that we enter out of necessity and that would be foolish to enter playfully in either the agonistic sense or in my sense. In such "worlds," *we* are not playful. To be in those "worlds" in resistance to their construction of ourselves as passive, servile, and inferior is to inhabit those selves ambiguously, through our first-person memories of lively subjectivity.

But there are "worlds" that we can travel to lovingly, and traveling to them is part of loving at least some of their inhabitants. The reason I think that traveling to someone's "world" is a way of identifying with them is that by traveling to their "world" we can understand *what it is to be them and what it is to be ourselves in their eyes*. Only when we have traveled to each other's "worlds" are we fully subjects to each other. (I agree with Hegel that self-recognition requires other subjects, but I disagree with his claim that it requires tension or hostility.)

Knowing other women's "worlds" is part of knowing them and knowing them is part of loving them. Notice that the knowing can be done in greater or lesser depth, as can the loving. Traveling to another's "world" is not the same as becoming intimate with them. Intimacy is constituted in part by a very deep knowledge of the other self. "World"-traveling is only part of the process of coming to have this knowledge. Also, notice that some people, in particular those who are outsiders to the mainstream, can be known only to the extent that they are known in several "worlds" and as "world"-travelers.

Without knowing the other's "world," one does not know the other, and without knowing the other, one is really alone in the other's presence because the other is only dimly present to one.

By traveling to other people's "worlds," we discover that there are "worlds" in which those who are the victims of arrogant perception are really subjects, lively beings, resisters, constructors of visions even though in the mainstream construction they are animated only by the arrogant perceiver and are pliable, foldable, file-awayable, classifiable. I always imagine the Aristotelian slave as pliable and foldable at night or after he or she cannot work anymore (when he or she dies as a tool).[8] Aristotle tells us nothing about the slave *apart from the master*. We know the slave only through the master. The slave is a tool of the master. After working hours, he or she is folded and placed in a drawer until the next morning.

My mother was apparent to me mostly as a victim of arrogant perception. I was loyal to the arrogant perceiver's construction of her and thus disloyal to her in assuming that she was exhausted by that construction. I was unwilling to be like her and thought that identifying with her, seeing myself in her, necessitated that I become like her. I was wrong both in assuming that she was exhausted by the arrogant perceiver's construction of her and in my understanding of identification. I do not think I was wrong in thinking that identification was part of loving and that it involved in part my seeing myself in her. I came to realize through traveling to her "world" that she is not foldable and pliable, that she is not exhausted by the mainstream Argentinian patriarchal construction of her. I came to realize that there are "worlds" in which she shines as a creative being. Seeing myself in her through traveling to her "world" has meant seeing how different from her I am in her "world."[9]

So, in recommending "world"-traveling and identification through "world"-traveling as part of loving other women, I am suggesting disloyalty to arrogant perceivers, including the arrogant perceiver in ourselves, and to their constructions of women and to their constructions of powerful barriers between women. As Women of Color, we cannot stand on any ground that is not also a crossing. To enter playfully into each other's "worlds" of subjective affirmation also risks those aspects of resistance that have kept us riveted on constructions of ourselves that have kept us from seeing multiply, from understanding the interconnections in our historico-spatialities. Playful "world"-travel is thus not assimilable to the middle-class leisurely journey nor the colonial or imperialist journeys. None of these involve risking one's ground. These forms of displacement may well be compatible with agonistic playfulness, but they are incompatible with the attitude of play that is an openness to surprise and that inclines us to "world"-travel in the direction of deep coalition.

Notes

1. This chapter was first published in 1987 and reprinted in María Lugones's *Pilgrimages/Peregrinajes: Theorizing Coalition Against Multiple Oppressions*, 77–100 (Lanham, MD: Rowman & Littlefield, 2003). It is reprinted here with slight modifications with the permission of the author and press.

2. See Audre Lorde's treatment of horizontal anger in "Eye to Eye: Black Women, Hatred, and Anger" (Lorde 1984a). Lorde understands black women seeing the servile construction of themselves in each other with anger, hatred.

3. It is important that I have been thought a person without humor by whites/Anglos inside the US academy, a space where struggles against race/gender and sexual oppression require an articulation of these issues. I have been found playful by my companions in struggles against white/Anglo control of land and water in the US Southwest. Those struggles have occurred in the space-time of Chicano communities. Being playful or not playful becomes in those two contexts deep traits, symptomatic of larger incongruities.

4. This "we" embraces the very many strands of Latinos in the United States. But this "we" is unusually spoken with ease. The tension in the "we" includes those who do not reject "Hispanic" as a term of identification.

5. Indeed people inhabit constructions of themselves in "worlds" they refuse to enter. This is true particularly of those who oppress those whose resistant "worlds" they refuse to enter. But they are indeed inhabitants of those "worlds." And indeed those who are oppressed animate oppressive constructions of themselves in the "worlds" of their oppressors.

6. Consider the congruities between the middle-class leisurely journey that Janet Wolff describes and the agonistic sense of play (Wolff 1992).

7. One can understand why this sense of playfulness is one that one may exercise in resistance to oppression when resistance is not reducible to reaction. Nonreactive resistance is creative; it exceeds that which is being resisted. The creation of new meaning lies outside of rules, particularly the rules of the "world" being resisted.

8. But I can also imagine the Aristotelian slave after hours as an animal without the capacity to reason. In that case, roaming in the fields, eating, and copulating would be distinctly passionate activities where passion and reason are dichotomized. Imagining people who are taken into servility in this manner is what leads oppressors to think of those they attempt to dominate both as dangerous and as nonpersons.

9. The traveling also permitted me to see her resistances in plain view in my daily life. She did not hide resistance.

References

Frye, Marilyn. 1983. "In and Out of Harm's Way: Arrogance and Love." In *The Politics of Reality: Essays in Feminist Theory* by Marilyn Frye, 52–83. Trumansburg, NY: Crossing Press.

Gadamer, Hans-George. 1975. *Truth and Method*. Translated by William Glen-Doepel, edited by John Cumming and Garrett Barden. New York: Seabury Press.

Huizinga, Johan. 1968. *Homo Ludens: A Study of the Play-Element in Culture*. Translated by R. F. C. Hull. Buenos Aires: Emecé Editores.

Lorde, Audre. 1984a. "Eye to Eye: Black Women, Hatred, and Anger." In *Sister Outsider* by Audre Lorde, 145–175. Trumansburg, NY: Crossing Press.

Lorde, Audre. 1984b. "The Master's Tools Will Never Dismantle the Master's House," In *Sister Outsider* by Audre Lorde, 145–175. Trumansburg, NY: Crossing Press.

Wolff, Janet. 1992. "On the Road Again: Metaphors of Travel in Cultural Criticism." *Cultural Studies* 7 (2): 224–39.

6

Symptoms in Particular

Feminism and the Disordered Mind

Jennifer Radden

Fundamentally incompatible assumptions separate most feminist theorizing from influential explanatory models associated with medical psychiatry and cognitive psychology that portray disorder as emanating from the dysfunctional brain of each patient. For feminist theory, by contrast, any disorder afflicts a socially and culturally embedded subject, and thus is generated out of interplay between bodily, interpersonal, cultural, and environmental factors. After sketching these differences, I turn to the implications of the feminist analysis for how we think about psychiatric symptoms viewed as the voiced report of the sufferer. When not reduced to inessential, downstream, "symptomatic" effects of brain dysfunction, symptoms and symptom descriptions acquire a different prominence and status as salient and distinctive cases of situated, but vulnerable, knowing. Because of unresolved issues relating to testimonial competence, they also reveal unfinished business for accounts of epistemic justice. Most feminist theorizing was ahead of its time, I conclude. Yet further analysis is required once we turn our attention to symptoms in particular.

In the first section, medical and cognitivist conceptions of mind are noted briefly, with their associated explanations of mental disorder.[1] Challenges to such medical and cognitivist positions are introduced in the second section, including those arising from feminist theorizing about the "mind" or subject. The discussion adopts a revised ontology of psychiatric symptoms, at least as they indicate the mood disorders of depression and anxiety that are the most consistently attributed to, and diagnosed in, women. In the third section, the place of symptoms in relation to feminist theorizing about epistemic justice, and testimony is introduced.

Medico-Cognitivist Explanatory Models

By the middle decades of the twentieth century, medical models of disorder increasingly dominated psychiatry, psychiatric research, much philosophy of

Jennifer Radden, *Symptoms in Particular* In: *Feminist Philosophy of Mind*. Edited by: Keya Maitra and Jennifer McWeeny, Oxford University Press. © Oxford University Press 2022. DOI: 10.1093/oso/9780190867614.003.0007 psychiatry, and other theoretical writing.[2] On these accounts, the observable manifestations of mental disorder result from underlying dysfunction located within the individual's brain. Mental disorders are not merely disease-like, but true diseases, only distinguishable in insignificant ways from other, better-understood bodily conditions, whose observable signs and symptoms emanate from internal morbidity or dysfunction.

Cognitivism similarly directs itself toward the brain of the individual, this time through features of brain functioning sharing structural similarities with artificial intelligence. Its core assumptions are that cognitive processes and capacities depend on information processing; and that cognitive explanations are in some broad sense mechanistic (Von Eckardt 2012; Cratsley and Samuels 2013). At the center of the analysis is brain *functioning*, rather than the brain as an organ: in principle, computations can run on silicon-based hardware, and "nothing like a human body seems required for cognition," it has been pointed out (Gallagher 2005, 134). In recognition of their commonalities, and for brevity, these models from medicine and cognitivism will here be referred to as "medico-cognitivist." Of their many shared features, focus in the present chapter is on three weaknesses that are particularly highlighted by feminist theorizing: (1) the association of disorder with the individual's brain or brain functioning; (2) the analysis of symptoms as downstream effects of that brain or brain functioning; and (3) a conception of disorders as separable, discretely bounded entities analogous to bacterially caused diseases.

These medico-cognitivist paradigms may bear only indirectly on clinical practice, it is worth noting. The care of mental disorder exhibits many goals and approaches consistent with the attitudes of feminist care ethics. In attending to and addressing psychiatric symptoms, much treatment shows respect for the epistemic authority and self-narrative of the individual patient, a point to which we'll return in the third section of this chapter. Effective treatment and therapeutic goals are typically measured in terms of the interpersonal adjustment of a socially embedded, or relational, self (Frank and Frank 1993; Waring 2016; Tekin 2017). Moreover, unlike a technical expert delivering services to a client, the dyadic relationship between carer and patient is often assumed to be definitive of, and essential for, effective care and treatment (Frank and Frank 1993; Radden and Sadler 2010). In respects like these, feminism need have little quarrel with mental health *care*. While not unaffected by the explanatory models sketched above, much clinical practice proceeds at a considerable remove from, and often regardless of, them.

Challenges to Medico-Cognitivist Models

The presuppositions of the medical model, particularly, have been subject to insistent critique since the last decades of the twentieth century—critiques arising within feminist thought, and also independently of it. Largely taking place out-side of feminism, for example, were the antipsychiatry ideas of the 1960s and 1970s, whose particular target was mental illness and the institutions sur-rounding its treatment and care.[3] Similarly antithetical to the medical model and again adopted both within and beyond feminist thought are forms of social constructionism. According to feminist social constructionist accounts, asso-ciations that have allied the feminine with madness and a want of reason are the historical effects of misogyny, sexism, and oppressive power (Nissim-Sabat 2013). More generally, challenges to ideas making up medico-cognitivist models have come from every corner. Even in its earliest formulations, for example, cognitivism was criticized by the ecological positions emphasizing "the envi-ronment that the mind has been shaped to meet," over any theoretical models (Neisser 1976, 7–8). More recently, classical cognitivism has also been subject to revision. Embodied (or "situated") cognitive science recognizes the mind to be a system in which brain, body, and world are equally important elements (Gallagher 2011; Tschacher and Bergomi 2011; Bluhm et al. 2012).[4] And, in en-active cognition theory or "enactivism," cognition is achieved through feedback and flow between body, sensory processing, and affordances in the surrounding environment (Durt et al. 2017).

Any attempt to isolate feminist critiques of medico-cognitivism's disor-dered mind or subject from critiques arising within these concurrent streams (antipsychiatry, social constructionism, ecological and embodied, enactivist, or situated cognitivism), will have limited success: these challenges have been intermixed and mutually influential.

Among such challenges to medico-cognitivist paradigms, attacks on nat-uralism, metaphysical realism, and traditional epistemology have been more and less general, with many expressly directed toward mental disorder. For ex-ample, the view that, like "gender," "mental illness" is socially constructed and historically contingent (a position frequently accepted by feminists), remains quite compatible with the assumption that other scientific concepts might rest on a more enduring ontological footing.[5] Of course even over the specific case of mental illness, let alone over broader claims about objectivity, nature, and science, feminists have not spoken with one voice: their positions range from extreme social constructionism and postmodernism, to acceptance of classical realist assumptions.

As well as revising more fundamental concepts with implications for ideas about mental disorder, such as those of "subject," "person," "science," and "know-ledge," feminists directed particular attention to the meaning, classification, ex-planation, treatment, and care of such conditions. Feminist analyses of women and madness have a long and distinguished history that includes Charlotte Perkins Gilman's incendiary *Yellow Wallpaper* (2015) first published in 1892, together with work from the 1970s and 1980s like Phyllis Chessler's *Women and Madness* (1972). Ostensibly, analyses such as these are distinct from broader feminist theorizing about subjectivity, science, and epistemic justice, but one aim here is to elucidate links between these two bodies of writing.

Critiques of Freudian analyses of women were followed by emphasis on cases of women's enforced institutionalization, as well as more symbolic harms of disempowerment and silencing.[6] The cultural legacy of binaries assigning women and the feminine to illogic, emotionality, subjectivity, the bodily, and to madness itself, were also exposed (Lloyd 2004; Showalter 1985; S. Gilman 1985). And feminist thinkers have drawn attention to the medicalization of women's normal traits: to research neglect and distortion of gender-linked disorders such as depression and anxiety; to separate and unequal treatments offered women; to the mental health vulnerabilities associated with traditional women's roles and identities; and to diagnosis and treatment understood as tools of patriarchal social control (Russell 1995; Ussher 1991; Busfield 1986; Bluhm 2011). Their inquiries repeatedly take issue with traditional explanations of mental disorder in women, whether those explanations are derived from women's alleged psychological and affective nature, or invoke biological assumptions involving hormonal instabilities, reproductive cycles and life phases, or genetic predispositions (Bluhm 2011). Much of this early work focused on mood disorders, especially depression. *Women have been disproportionately diagnosed and treated as suffering mental disorder*, it was pointed out: *Why?*

The answers offered emphasize the ways patriarchal systems leave women vulnerable both to *actual disorder*, and to the diagnosis and treatment of misnamed "disorder."[7] Before reviewing such differing kinds of explanation, however, we need to consider the broader theorizing guiding them, by asking: What is the "mental" in feminist philosophy of mind?

Feminist accounts have generally been wary of strong mind-to-body reductionism, accepting that mental processes are distinguishable from, even if dependent on, physical processes.[8] But any robust dualism separating mind from body is also usually eschewed for its Cartesian taint. This has left "mind" a treacherous category, often avoided entirely, and thought best retired from use. The preferred targets of feminist analysis have been thicker entities than minds: selves, persons, and agents. And it is to them that we can most fruitfully turn as we seek implications about the special case of disordered "mentality."

Whichever category is employed, self, person, agent—or mind—feminist conceptual revisions and reconstructions consistently emphasize the features of *embodiment* and social and cultural *embeddedness*. In feminist and nonfeminist writing alike, the *disembodied* mind is widely deemed mistaken, even incoherent. Minds, like subjects, are necessarily embodied. The subject's embodiment is explained by feminists in a number of different ways. For example, the continuity of the first-person perspective provided by embodiment is *what makes us persons;* personal lives in this way "encompass" our organic lives (Baker 2000). Although Baker's philosophy of mind is not specifically directed toward mental illness, it is evident that, disordered or not, all mental and bodily processes are inextricably entwined.[9] And such embodiment is required for agency, the sense of identity and personhood in which we reflect about what we intend to do, and then act. Without embodiment, "practical identity," that is, oneself understood as a *doer*, and awareness of that status, would not be possible (Korsgaard 1989; Meyers 1997; Baker 2000). Agency is also linked to more political conceptions of autonomy in these analyses. As victims of patriarchal power, externally imposed and internalized social roles, and other evidence of system-wide gender bias, women have often been deprived of the possibility of exercising autonomy. Nonetheless, feminist theorists have stressed the social, relational, or intersubjective context even required for the development of a capacity for autonomy, including socialization that promotes self-reflection and other "autonomy competencies" (Friedman 1988, 39–40).[10]

Conceptions of selves, persons, and agents differ from one another in both emphasis and substance, but as *subjects*, selves, persons, and agents share the broad features identified in the following discussion, including the second feature of the self/person/agent: its status as relational, or socially embedded. And by rejecting the individualistic explanations presupposed by medico-cognitivist models of disorder, embeddedness serves as a corrective. Feminists emphasize the inherently social aspect of the subject, its nature, identity, and projects. The autonomous individual of traditional liberalism is rejected as neither realistic, nor desirable. At best there can be relational autonomy, and relational subjects, because the self/person/agent is said to be *constituted* in relation.[11] Social embeddedness also indicates a developmental psychology, carrying explanatory force. We are all products of social relationships, roles, and societal expectations. Persons are made, not born; they are "second persons," who have been "long enough dependent on others to acquire the essential arts of personhood" (Baier 1985, 84). These essential arts are acquired and shaped by social forces, many of them oppressive, due to stereotyped expectations about "what it is to be a female person" (Code 1987, 362). This theorizing has particular force here because of feminists' persistent emphasis on the inadequacies of explanations of women's madness based on features that are *inherently individualistic*—from the wandering womb of hysteria and the hormones of postpartum depression, to chemical imbalances, and epigenetic variations. Such idiopathic explanations must be misleadingly incomplete, at least with disorders affecting the self/person/agent (arguably, all disorders).

Feminist presuppositions about the embedded subject imply that the causal explanation of mental disorders cannot be solely understood in terms of features internal and distinctive to the individual sufferer, even if that sufferer is an indissoluble composite of "mind" and "body." For, in some quite real sense, the sufferer *is not an individual*. A kind of methodological individualism is often taken to at least dictate approaches to the *treatment* of disorder, if not to its nature. (The appropriate unit for treatment may actually be the entire family system, rather than the distressed individual within it, as some have thought.) And practical, as well as societal, demands similarly require that persons be accorded enduring and unitary identities (and held responsible accordingly, for example). But rather than isolated individuals, all subjects, including disordered ones, have identities embedded in the world of meanings, of shared, public, and interpersonal experience, and of social roles. For example, on a feminist analysis, the anorexia of a particular teenager is explained as much in terms of societal beauty and virtue norms and attitudes expressed by family and other institutions in her social world as by her individual attributes and eating behavior (Bordo 1993; Giordano 2005). Any exclusive emphasis on her individual attributes will be misplaced and misleading, providing an incomplete explanation of her disorder.

Given the nature of subjects, formed and constituted by their interpersonal, societal, and cultural environments, we cannot be content with the idiopathic causes of medico-cognitivist analyses. Whatever the causal explanation involved, it will be multifactorial, and complex. Feminists analyzing reductive explanations in biology were early alert to this sort of critique, recognizing a tendency to seek causes within the narrow system being studied, rather than the broader systems or levels within which that system occurs and, as a consequence, favoring genetic over environmental causes, including those that are social and cultural. And successful scientific explanation, Carla Fehr has demonstrated, can eschew the reduction of the objects of investigation to their smallest parts (Fehr 2004, 2008).

Medico-cognitivist explanations often support their tendency toward reductionism through an assumption: whatever environmental triggers may arise, every disorder's root cause lies with some underlying, biological vulnerability— whether as a dysfunctional system or a genetic propensity or risk factor. These presuppositions have been widely criticized, however, including by feminist philosophers of science and genetics, pointing out the dubious link between a particular genotype and its expression in a given phenotype (Fox Keller 2000; Spanier 1995; Hubbard 1990; Fausto-Sterling 1992). Such analyses emphasize systematic bias allowing researchers to disregard the context in which a phenomenon is found, and hence to value genetic and physiological over social and environmental causal factors. The prevailing, mistaken presupposition is methodologically individualistic: the critical causes of phenomena, toward which intervention should be directed, are *within* a person and *at the genetic level* (Scheman 1983, 1993; Fehr 2004). With regard to the connection between hormones and behavior so often cited in medico-cognitivist explanations of women's mood-related symptoms of depression and anxiety, a contrast has been drawn between a linear-hormonal model and one which is "interactionist." While not discounting genes or hormones, the interactionist model refuses to privilege those factors over what may be thought of—mistakenly—as more su- perficial, and secondary, environmental and social causes of behavior (Birke and Vines 1987).

These criticisms apply whether we are speaking of reductionist appeal to ge- netics, or to the reproductive phases of women's bodies claimed to predestine them to emotional and psychological vulnerability and madness. Today, the causes of mental disorder are regularly cited as biological states of brain chem- istry and neuronal function that are in turn reducible to genetic structures, even though no single genes have thus far been identified for any particular mental disorders, and the possibility of single-gene discoveries seems increasingly re- mote (Kendler 2013).

Genetic explanations of mental disorder have been subject to a range of meth- odological objections.[12] But important among them have been the distorting effects of medicine's exclusively idiopathic explanatory models, rejected by these feminist critiques of biological reductionism. Thus, the same failure to recog- nize a socially and culturally embedded subject has been echoed throughout the social sciences, as well as within philosophical method derived from phe- nomenological traditions. For example, recent work on mental disorder points to interactions among systemic causes eluding reduction to bodily or individual points of origin. In "ecosystemic" anthropological models, biological organisms are in constant, multilevel transaction through feedback loops with the social and cultural environment as much as with the physical one (Kirmeyer and Ryder 2016; Kirmeyer et al. 2016).

Feminist analyses of embedded subjects have seen no reason to single out mental disorders from other illnesses and disorders, it should be noted, and feminist bioethics has illustrated the way even conditions with entirely physical symptoms are best understood as occurring within a context that encompasses more than the afflicted body.[13] Yet because the symptoms of mental disorder are often problems *exclusively affecting social roles and functioning*, mental disorders depend on "culturally constructed institutions and forms of life" to a degree that may be seen to distinguish them (Kirmeyer et al. 2016, 6).

Added to the ecosystemic models of anthropology resting on many of the presuppositions of feminist theorizing are several revisions proposed within the philosophy of psychiatry.[14] One construes disorder in network terms, chal- lenging "common cause" analyses, by which each mental disorder comprises a symptom cluster brought about by some particular, distinctive underlying brain state on the model of bacterially caused diseases (Borsboom and Cramer 2013).

Within a network, internal causal relationships between separate symptoms can determine the characteristic profile of the disorder. Symptoms in the network form a self-sustaining, mutually reinforcing, relatively stable cluster, so that symptoms (of mood, thought, and habit) are indications of disorder when, because, and to the extent that the connected links and loops occur often enough to become entrenched (Kendler et al. 2011, 1147).

These recent findings and hypotheses from social science and contemporary philosophy of psychiatry direct us toward the observable manifestations of disorder—toward symptoms in particular. If, rather than understood as underlying, idiopathic dysfunction, mental disorders are collections of socially embedded, mutually reinforcing signs and symptoms sufficient to maintain clusters of traits in given individuals, and are the product of environment and social context as much as or more than any inherent common causes, then signs and symptoms call for further scrutiny. And that scrutiny invites application of feminist ideas about situated knowledge and epistemic injustice.

Symptoms, Ontology, and Epistemic Justice

Signs and symptoms form a major part of the available data for any model of mental disorder. As such, they are the diagnostic identities of such disorders: without independent verification and confirmation of the kind provided by the lab tests and scans employed elsewhere in medicine, signs and symptoms cannot be dispensed with for decisions about treatment and care. But as long as these observable indicators are construed as no more than downstream effects, theoretical attention to them will be limited and reluctant. Any expectation that organic causes of such effects will eventually be discovered leaves signs and symptoms somewhat stopgap, and perhaps temporary, features, suggesting that were lab tests or scans available, the patient's voiced complaint may be otiose. In the anthropological and network analyses described above, by contrast, symptoms descriptions offered by patients possess a different epistemic significance, apparently according mental disorder a different ontological status. Its signs and symptoms will not only be the disorder's diagnostic identity, but may be constitutive of it.

Whatever biology, neurology, or genetics might explain the phenomenon, and regardless of the bodily state of the individual, their subjective, discomforting, felt aspects of some conditions, such as depression and anxiety, are essential features. The subjective experience of distress and the extent of impairment of a person's day-to-day functioning are *intrinsic properties* of depression: conceptually, attributions of depression are made on the basis of "consequences of the syndrome as they manifest to the subject" (Rashed and Bingham 2014, 245). (How well the account applies to disorders with primarily behavioral symptoms such as addictions remains to be determined.)[15] A disorder's psychological symptoms may be inherent and constitutive, even if caused by biological or social factors— if not forever then at least as long as everyday and clinical intuitions concur over this status (Summers and Sinnott-Armstrong 2019).

Traditionally understood in medicine, the *sign* is observable by others or by instruments; the *symptom is the complaint or report proffered by the patient* in her own voice.[16] Although regularly disregarded in present-day medical and non-medical writing, this distinction between sign and symptom must be pertinent for feminist thought, with its stress on hearing the voices of the socially marginalized.[17] These voices provide an otherwise missing perspective necessary for complete, situated knowledge (Harding 2004). But it is not only in achieving situated knowledge that voiced symptoms are important; they also lie at the center of normative claims. Thus, in several different ways people's attempted testimony is silenced and violated when they speak from positions of societal oppression, it has been emphasized (Dotson 2011). Miranda Fricker writes about epistemic marginalization of individuals or groups whose experiences are ignored as unintelligible, or are misunderstood; in their exclusion from practices of meaning-making, they are the subjects of epistemic injustice (Fricker 2007).

This kind of epistemic injustice will affect the status of women patients recounting their symptoms.[18] Their words must be vulnerable to epistemic injustices such as Fricker and Dotson describe, even if, as we saw earlier, more sensitive listening occurs in the clinic than in many other places, and a finer-grained analysis recognizes the relative privilege enjoyed by some, such as the white, middle-class woman patient with secure citizenship, speaking in her native tongue (Code 1993; Garry 2011). The position of all women, as patients in the clinic as well as outside it, leaves their words vulnerable to dismissal, disregard, and misunderstanding.

Gender aside, every person diagnosed with and treated for mental disorder is subject to a heightened and distinctive form of epistemic jeopardy. Much of this jeopardy is attributable to stigmatizing attitudes. But also, these symptom descriptions contain an inherent ambiguity: cognitive disabilities involving comprehension, intelligibility, and reasoning—sometimes actually present—affect the status of all psychiatric patients as trustworthy and reliable narrators. Real or only, and mistakenly, suspected, and regardless of diagnosis, these attitudes leave the patient's account of her symptoms additionally vulnerable to misunderstanding, neglect, and injustice.

Voiced symptom descriptions viewed as testimony represent one form of such potential epistemic injustice. Any testimony must meet certain communicative norms. Cognitive disabilities, when in fact present, warrant some appropriately grounded expectations and doubts on the part of the listener. But these will be fused with what is likely stereotype-based biases predisposing observers to attribute lack of testimonial credibility. Thus, a recent attempt to consider delusional communications in light of Fricker's work points to three distinct ways in which epistemic injustice occurs: (1) the label "delusion" added to other factors may detract from the credibility accorded to the delusional claim (whether or not the labeling is accurate); (2) an independent attitude about the person's social undesirability will attribute delusional thought and irrationality when it is not present; and (3) impaired linguistic and communicative skills may lead to the unwarranted attribution of unintelligibility (Sanati and Kratsous 2015). Far-fetched assertions ("My husband meets with witches," or "I am 250 years of age") are examples, or the patently incomprehensible "word salads" and neologisms of formal thought disorder. These may be justifiably judged to lack *testimonial competence*, or *deserved* credibility.

Defined by Kristie Dotson, testimonial competence is "accurate intelligibility" and assertions that are "clearly comprehensible and defeasibly intelligible" (Dotson 2011, 245). Yet even restricting ourselves to syntactically acceptable statements that are intelligible, when and whether the patient's words indicate testimonial incompetence in being delusional, calls for conclusive, consensually agreed-upon analysis.

It is difficult to exaggerate this problem. The line between irrational claims and delusional ones is without precise boundaries (Bortolotti 2010; Radden 2011; Sanati and Kratsous 2015). In addition, the nature of delusions is itself contested. To cite only the most divergent hypotheses, one account allows some delusions at least to be meaningful, if obscure, communications, while on other accounts they are meaningless thought fragments, expressed through misleadingly unexceptional syntax.[19]

That close attention and clinical skill allow effective practitioners to regularly hear and understand the voices of patients is again worth acknowledging. But avoiding mistakes over testimonial competence ignores the more fundamental challenge raised by discordant hypotheses about the nature of delusional thought processes, which must affect the voices of all those suspected of mental disorder. We can illustrate this challenge using the common failure of many patients to acknowledge their condition as illness or dysfunction (their "lack of insight into illness," in the terminology of psychiatry). Some experts regard the patient's "There's nothing wrong with me" as an erroneous claim that, sharing a spectrum with self-deception and other forms of motivated irrationality, is potentially open to revision. Others analogize it to anosognosia, an indicator of neurological damage (Radden 2010).[20] On the first interpretation, the subject remains within the "space of reasons": it acknowledges the patient's potential as a knower capable of some agency in relation to her thought processes, some degree of reasons-responsiveness such that correction of the false or implausible opinion is allied to forms of rational persuasion employed with other instances of stubbornly maintained erroneous beliefs. Interpreted as anosognosia, by contrast—its proximate cause inner brain dysfunction—the patient's denial that she is ill leaves her as powerless to alter her erroneous convictions as she would be to *at will* directly alter her abnormal white cell count. Despite its misleading resemblance to more meaningful communications, her lack of insight on this view may be a sign, but it is not a symptom, of her disorder.

Problems thus remain. When and whether testimonial competence is present lies at the center of efforts to understand and give these symptom descriptions their due, as demanded by feminist approaches. If delusional reports are not actual symptoms, but merely signs, they will not exhibit the testimonial competence that is a precondition for vulnerability to the particular forms of epistemic injustice involving testimony. Without agreement over which voiced descriptions are actual symptoms, these normative assessments about justice cannot be made with any assurance. Moreover, as Eleanor Byrne has recognized, this may not be an all-or-nothing matter, and will likely require striking a balance between epistemic injustice and healthcare (Byrne 2020).

In conclusion: the kind of multicausal, interactionist explanatory analysis of mental disorder that can be traced to feminist theorizing is increasingly accepted today across the social sciences and philosophy. It is even acknowledged within psychiatry, network analyses illustrate, and in cognitivist theories of embodied and enactive cognition. Its increasing recognition confirms the force and viability of the feminist theorizing of the 1980s and 1990s.

These revisions were here shown to draw attention to a revised status for psychiatric symptoms. Rather than downstream effects of disorder, symptoms construed as the voiced descriptions of the patient's experience not only form the diagnostic identity of (at least some) disorders, they may be *constitutive* of the condition with which they are associated. As such, they are an important target of feminism's alertness to testimonial injustice. A revised conception of the self/person/agent may have allowed us to forge more appropriate explanatory models than those offered by medico-cognitivist paradigms. Still, the subject afflicted with mental disorder (or diagnosis) leaves us with remaining concerns, both epistemic and ethical, over women's mental disorders.

Notes

1. "Mental disorder" is used here to refer to responses judged apt for psychiatric diagnosis and care; "disordered mind" is attributed to the subject of those responses.
2. See Boorse (1975), Guze (1992), Murphy (2007).
3. Cohen and Timini (2008) is an example.

4. This departure from classical cognitivist assumptions and analogies returns us to the phenomenological work of thinkers such as Parnas and Sass (2008), Drayson (2009), Gallagher (2011), Stenghellini (2014), and Maiese (2016).

5. See essays in Garry and Pearsall (1996) and Antony and Witt (1993).

6. See Mitchell (1975), Meyers (1994, 1997), Gilbert and Gubar (1980), Bondi and Burman (2001), and Kristeva (1980, 1995).

7. Lugones, in this volume, illustrates the latter.

8. Essays in Antony and Witt (1993) and Atkins and Mackenzie (2010) are illustrative here.

9. As a requirement for the sense of self, embodied consciousness has recently been explored in relation to particular mental disturbances (Maiese 2016).

10. For more recent accounts of autonomy that acknowledge its intersecting social determinants, see Mackenzie and Stoljar (2000).

11. See Whitbeck (1992), Frye (1996), Ferguson (1996), Garry and Pearsall (1996), and Bayliss (2011).

12. Examples include Murphy and Stich (2000), Bolton (2008), and Varga (2012).

13. See, for example, Wolf (1996).

14. For a recent review, see Köhne (2020).

15. Depression and anxiety are the only disorders consistently shown to have higher incidence in women, so even if this analysis extends no farther, its significance for feminism is notable.

16. See King (1968).

17. *Hearing* includes an active role—providing "uptake" to the speaker (Potter 2003).

18. A more complete account would also include hermeneutical forms of epistemic injustice not dealt with here, but see Sanati and Kratsous (2015).

19. For these and other hypotheses, see Bortolotti (2010), Radden (2011), and Gerrans (2014).

20. See Amador and David (1998), Reimer (2010), Radden (2011), and Sanati and Kratsous (2015).

References

Amador, Xavier Francisco, and Anthony David. 1998. *Insight and Psychosis*. Oxford: Oxford University Press.

Antony, Louise, and Charlotte Witt, eds. 1993. *A Mind of One's Own: Feminist Essays on Reason and Objectivity*. Boulder, CO: Westview.

Atkins, Kim, and Catriona Mackenzie, eds. 2010. *Practical Identity and Narrative Agency*. London: Taylor & Francis.

Baier, Annette. 1985. *Postures of the Mind: Essays on Mind and Morals*. Minneapolis: University of Minnesota Press.

Baker, Lynne Rudder. 2000. *Persons and Bodies: A Constitution View*. Cambridge: Cambridge University Press.

Bayliss, Françoise. 2011. "The Self in Situ: A Relational Account of Personal Identity." In *Being Relational: Reflections on Relational Theory and Health Law*, edited by Jocelyn Downie and Jennifer J. Llewelyn, 109–131. Vancouver, BC: UBC Press.

Birke, Lydia, and Gail Vines. 1987. "Beyond Nature versus Nurture: Process and Biology in the Development of Gender." *Women's Studies International Forum* 10: 555–570.

Bluhm, Robyn. 2011. "Gender Differences in Depression: Explanations from Feminist Ethics." *International Journal of Feminist Approaches to Bioethics* 4 (1): 69–88.

Bluhm, Robyn, Anne Jaap Jacobson, and Heidi Lene Maibom, eds. 2012. *Neurofeminism: Issues at the Intersection of Feminist Theory and Cognitive Science.* New York: Palgrave Macmillan.

Bolton, Derek. 2008. *What Is Mental Disorder?* Oxford: Oxford University Press.

Bondi, Liz, and Erica Burman. 2001. "Women and Mental Health: A Feminist Review." *Feminist Review* 68: 6–33.

Boorse, Christopher. 1975. "On the Distinction between Disease and Illness." *Philosophy & Public Affairs* 5: 49–68.

Bordo, Susan. 1993. *Unbearable Weight: Feminism, Western Culture, and the Body.* Berkeley: University of California Press.

Borsboom, Denny, and Angélique O. J. Cramer. 2013. "Network Analysis: An Integrative Approach to the Structure of Psychopathology." *Annual Review of Psychopathy* 9: 91–121.

Bortolotti, Lisa. 2010. *Delusions and Other Irrational Beliefs.* Oxford: Oxford University Press.

Busfield, Joan. 1986. *Men, Women and Madness: Understanding Gender and Mental Disorder.* New York: New York University Press.

Byrne, Eleanor Alexandra. 2020. "Striking the Balance with Epistemic Injustice in Healthcare: The Case of Chronic Fatigue Syndrome / Myalgic Encephalomyelitis." *Medicine, Health Care and Philosophy* 23 (3): 371–379.

Chessler, Phyllis. 1972. *Women and Madness: A History of Women and the Psychiatric Profession.* New York: Doubleday.

Code, Lorraine. 1987. "Second Persons." *Canadian Journal of Philosophy* 17 (1), supplement: S357–S382.

Code, Lorraine. 1993. "Taking Subjectivity into Account." In *Feminist Epistemologies*, edited by Linda Alcoff and Elizabeth Potter, 15–48. New York: Routledge.

Cohen, Carl I., and Sami Timimi, eds. 2008. *Liberatory Psychiatry.* Cambridge: Cambridge University Press.

Cratsley, Kelso, and Richard Samuels. 2013. In *The Oxford Handbook of Philosophy and Psychiatry*, edited by K. W. M. Fulford, Martin Davies, Richard G.T. Gipps, George Graham, John Z. Sadler, Giovanni Stanghellini, and Tim Thornton, 413–433. Oxford: Oxford University Press.

Dotson, Kristie. 2011. "Tracking Epistemic Violence, Tracking Practices of Silencing." *Hypatia* 26 (2): 236–257.

Drayson, Zoe. 2009. "Embodied Cognitive Science and Its Implications for Psychopathology." *Philosophy, Psychiatry, & Psychology* 16 (4): 329–340.

Durt, Christoph, Thomas Fuchs, and Christian Tewes, eds. 2017. *Embodiment, Enaction and Culture: Investigating the Constitution of the Shared World.* Cambridge, MA: MIT Press.

Fausto-Sterling, Anne. 1992. *Myths of Gender: Biological Theories about Women and Men.* New York: Basic Books.

Fehr, Carla. 2004. "Feminism and Science: Mechanism without Reductionism." *NWSA Journal* 16 (1): 136–156.

Fehr, Carla. 2008. "Feminist Perspectives on the Philosophy of Biology." In *Oxford Handbook of the Philosophy of Biology*, edited by Michael Ruse, 570–594. Oxford: Oxford University Press.

Ferguson, Ann. 1996. "A Feminist Aspect Theory of the Self." In *Women, Knowledge, and Reality: Explorations in Feminist Philosophy*, edited by Ann Garry and Marilyn Pearsall, 93–107. 2nd ed. New York: Routledge.

Fox Keller, Evelyn. 2000. *The Century of the Gene*. Cambridge, MA: Harvard University Press.

Friedman, Marilyn. 1988. "Individuality without Individualism: Review of Janice Raymond's *A Passion for Friends*." *Hypatia* 3 (2): 131–137.

Frank, Jerome D., and Julia B. Frank. 1993. *Persuasion and Healing: A Comparative Study of Psychotherapy*. 3rd ed. Baltimore, MD: Johns Hopkins University Press.

Fricker, Miranda. 2007. *Epistemic Injustice: Power and the Ethics of Knowing*. New York: Oxford University Press.

Frye, Marilyn. 1996. "To See and Be Seen: The Politics of Reality." In *Women, Knowledge, and Reality: Explorations in Feminist Philosophy*, edited by Ann Garry and Marilyn Pearsall, 77–92. 2nd ed. New York: Routledge.

Gallagher, Shaun. 2005. *How the Body Shapes the Mind*. Oxford: Clarendon Press.

Gallagher, Shaun. 2011. "Interpretations of Embodied Cognition." In *The Implications of Embodiment: Cognition and Communication*, edited by W. Tschacher and C. Bergomi, 59–71. Exeter: Imprint Academic.

Garry, Ann. 2011. "Intersectionality, Metaphors, and the Multiplicity of Gender." *Hypatia* 26 (4): 826–849.

Garry, Ann, and Marilyn Pearsall, eds. 1996. *Women, Knowledge, and Reality: Explorations in Feminist Philosophy*. 2nd ed. New York: Routledge.

Gerrans, Phillip. 2014. *The Measure of Madness*. Cambridge, MA: MIT Press.

Gilbert, Sandra M., and Susan Gubar. 1980. *The Madwoman in the Attic: The Woman Writer and the Nineteenth-Century Literary Imagination*. New Haven: Yale University Press.

Gilman, Charlotte Perkins. 2015. *The Yellow Wallpaper*. London: Penguin.

Gilman, Sander. 1985. *Difference and Pathology: Stereotypes of Sexuality, Race, and Madness*. Ithaca: Cornell University Press.

Giordano, Simona. 2005. *Understanding Eating Disorders: Conceptual and Ethical Issues in the Treatment of Anorexia and Bulimia Nervosa*. Oxford: Oxford University Press.

Guze, Samuel B. 1992. *Why Psychiatry Is a Branch of Medicine*. Oxford: Oxford University Press.

Harding, Sandra. 2004. *The Feminist Standpoint Reader: Intellectual and Political Controversies*. London: Psychology Press.

Hubbard, Ruth. 1990. *The Politics of Women's Biology*. New Brunswick, NJ: Rutgers University Press.

Kendler, Kenneth S. 2013. "What Psychiatric Genetics Has Taught Us about the Nature of Psychiatric Illness and What Is Left to Learn." *Molecular Psychiatry* 18 (10): 1058–1066.

Kendler, Kenneth S., Peter Zachar, and Carl Craver. 2011. "What Kinds of Things Are Psychiatric Disorders?" *Psychological Medicine* 41 (6): 1143–1150.

King, Lester S. 1968. "Signs and Symptoms." *JAMA* 206 (5):1063–1065.

Kirmayer, Lawrence, Robert Lemelson, and Constance Cummings, eds. 2016. *Revisioning Psychiatry: Cultural Phenomenology, Critical Neuroscience, and Global Mental Health*. Cambridge: Cambridge University Press.

Kirmayer, Lawrence, and Andrew G. Ryder. 2016. "Culture and Psychopathology." *Current Opinion in Psychology* 8: 143–148.

Köhne, Annemarie. 2020. "The Relationalist Turn in Understanding Mental Disorders: From Essentialism to Embracing Dynamic and Complex Relations." *Philosophy, Psychiatry & Psychology* 27 (2): 119–140.

Korsgaard, Christine M. 1989. "Personal Identity and the Unity of Agency: A Kantian Response to Parfit." *Philosophy & Public Affairs* 18 (2): 101–132.

Kristeva, Julia. 1980. *Black Sun: Depression and Melancholia*. Translated by Leon S. Roudiez. New York: Columbia University Press.

Kristeva, Julia. 1995. *New Maladies of the Soul*. Translated by R. Guberman. New York: Columbia University Press.

Lloyd, Genevieve. 2004. *The Man of Reason: "Male" and "Female" in Western Philosophy*. 2nd ed. New York: Routledge.

Maiese, Michelle. 2016. *Embodied Selves and Divided Minds*. Oxford: Oxford University Press.

Mackenzie, Catriona, and Natalie Stoljar, eds. 2000. *Relational Autonomy: Feminist Perspectives on Autonomy, Agency, and the Social Self*. Oxford: Oxford University Press.

Meyers, Diana T. 1994. *Subjection & Subjectivity: Psychoanalytic Feminism & Moral Philosophy*. New York: Routledge.

Meyers, Diana. T., ed. 1997. *Feminists Rethink the Self*. Boulder, CO: Westview Press.

Mitchell, Juliet. 1975. *Psychoanalysis and Feminism*. Harmondsworth: Penguin.

Murphy, Dominic. 2007. *Psychiatry in the Scientific Image*. Cambridge, MA: MIT Press.

Murphy, Dominic, and Stephen Stich. 2000. "Darwin in the Madhouse: Evolutionary Psychology and the Classification of Mental Disorders." In *Evolution and the Human Mind: Modularity, Language and Meta-cognition*, edited by Peter Carruthers and Andrew Chamberlain, 62–92. Cambridge: Cambridge University Press.

Neisser, Ulrich. 1976. *Cognition and Reality: Principles and Implications of Cognitive Psychology*. San Francisco: W.H. Freeman.

Nissim-Sabat, Marilyn. 2013. "Race and Gender in Philosophy of Psychiatry: Science, Relativism, and Phenomenology." In *The Oxford Handbook of Philosophy and Psychiatry*, edited by K. W. M. Fulford, Martin Davies, Richard G. T. Gipps, George Graham, John Z. Sadler, Giovanni Stanghellini, and Tim Thornton, 139–158. Oxford: Oxford University Press.

Parnas, Josef, and Sass, Louis. 2008. "Varieties of Phenomenology: On Description, Understanding, and Explanation in Psychiatry." In *Philosophical Issues in Psychiatry: Explanation, Nosology and Phenomenology*, edited by Kenneth Kendler and Josef Parnas, 239–277. Baltimore, MD: Johns Hopkins University Press.

Potter, Nancy Niquist. 2003. "In the Spirit of Giving Uptake." *Philosophy, Psychiatry & Psychology* 10 (1): 33–35.

Radden, Jennifer. 2010. "Insightlessness, the Deflationary Turn." *Philosophy, Psychiatry & Psychology* 17 (1): 81–84.

Radden, Jennifer. 2011. *On Delusion*. London: Routledge.

Radden, Jennifer, and John Sadler. 2010. *The Virtuous Psychiatrist: Character Ethics for Psychiatric Practice*. Oxford: Oxford University Press.

Rashed, Mohammed, A., and Rachel Bingham. 2014. "Social Deviance and Mental Disorder." *Philosophy, Psychiatry & Psychology* 21: 243–255.

Reimer, Margot. 2010. "Treatment Adherence in the Absence of Insight: A Puzzle and Proposed Solution. *Philosophy, Psychiatry & Psychology* 17 (1): 65–75.

Russell, Denise. 1995. *Women, Madness and Medicine*. Cambridge, MA: Polity Press.

Sanati, Abdi, and Michalis Kyratsous. 2015. "Epistemic Injustice in Assessment of Delusions." *Journal of Evaluation in Clinical Practice* 21 (3): 479–485.

Scheman, Naomi. 1983. "Individualism and the Objects of Psychology." In *Discovering Reality: Feminist Perspectives on Epistemology, Metaphysics, Methodology and Philosophy of Science*, edited by Sandra Harding and Merrill B. Hintikka, 225–244. Dordrecht: Kluwer Academic.

Scheman, Naomi. 1993. *Engenderings: Constructions of Knowledge, Authority and Privilege*. New York: Routledge.

Showalter, Elaine. 1985. *The Female Malady: Women, Madness and English Culture, 1830–1980*. London: Virago.

Spanier, Bonnie. 1995. *Im/partial Science: Gender Ideology in Molecular Biology*. Bloomington: Indiana University Press.

Stenghellini, Giovanni. 2014. *Disembodied Spirits and Deanimated Bodies: The Psychopathology of Commonsense*. Oxford: Oxford University Press.

Summers, Jesse S., and Walter Sinnott-Armstrong. 2019. *Clean Hands: Philosophical Lessons from Scrupulosity*. Oxford: Oxford University Press.

Tekin, Şerife. 2017. "The Missing Self in Scientific Psychiatry." *Synthese* 196: 2197–2215.

Tschacher, Wolfgang, and Claudia Bergomi. 2011. "Cognitive Binding in Schizophrenia: Weakened Integration of Temporal Intersensory Information." *Schizophrenia Bulletin* 37 (2), supplement: S13–S22.

Ussher, Jane M. 1991. *Women's Madness: Misogyny or Mental Illness?* Amherst: University of Massachusetts Press.

Varga, Somogy. 2012. "Evolutionary Psychiatry and Depression: Testing Two Hypotheses." *Medicine, Health Care and Philosophy* 15 (1): 41–52.

Von Eckardt, Barbara. 2012. "The Representational Theory of Mind." In *The Cambridge Handbook of Cognitive Science*, edited by Keith Frankish and William Ramsey, 45–60. Cambridge: Cambridge University Press.

Waring, Duff. 2016. *The Healing Virtues: Character Ethics in Psychotherapy*. Oxford: Oxford University Press.

Whitbeck, Caroline. 1992. "A Different Reality: Feminist Ontology." In *Women, Knowledge, and Reality: Explorations in Feminist Philosophy*, edited by Ann Garry and Marilyn Pearsall, 51–76. New York: Routledge.

Wolf, Susan M., ed., 1996. *Feminism & Bioethics: Beyond Reproduction*. Oxford: Oxford University Press.

7

Passivity in Theories of the Agentic Self

Reflections on the Views of Soran Reader and Sarah Buss

Diana Tietjens Meyers

Reclaiming and revaluing features of human lives that have been ignored or devalued in traditional philosophy are among the prime projects of recent feminist philosophy.[1] By and large, this corrective trend proceeds by spotlighting ostensibly feminine attributes, questioning whether they deserve the neglect or disparagement they've received, and arguing that their value has been overlooked at least partly because of their association with femininity. Following on these lines of thought, feminist philosophers have moved to integrate these reclaimed values into philosophical conversations, and to show how including these values in our treatments of various topics enriches our understanding of them or obliges us to radically reframe them.

The best-known example of this reclamation and revaluation project is the centering of care work in moral and political philosophy. However, another reclamation and revaluation project is underway in discussions of emotion and autonomy. Feminist philosophers have been rethinking the interrelated contrasts between activity and passivity, on the one hand, and agency and vulnerability, on the other. Anticipating work in the philosophy of action, Martha Nussbaum argues for emotion's function as a gauge of value and its inextricability from neediness and vulnerability. Discomfort with the unavoidable neediness and vulnerability of human lives, she insists, does not excuse disregarding the vital role that emotion plays in alerting us to all sorts of goodness and badness (Nussbaum 2001, 11–13). In a similar vein, some philosophers of self and action, notably Soran Reader (2007) and Sarah Buss (2012), join Nussbaum in decrying the supposition that activity and passivity are separable and that agency and control are more essentially human than vulnerability and helplessness.

Today the gendered connotations of these dichotomies are obvious. Women are supposedly dependent, vulnerable, and passive, men supposedly independent, strong, and active. The evident falsity of these stereotypes gives feminists compelling reason to critique them. So it might come as a surprise that forty years ago Harry Frankfurt tabled the active/passive contrast as all but impossible to cogently explicate and proceeded to build his influential theory of

Diana Tietjens Meyers, *Passivity in Theories of the Agentic Self* In: *Feminist Philosophy of Mind.*
Edited by: Keya Maitra and Jennifer McWeeny, Oxford University Press. © Oxford University Press 2022.
DOI: 10.1093/oso/9780190867614.003.0008

agentic selfhood on the related but different distinction between internality and externality (Frankfurt 1998, 58–59). Although my views about the agentic self differ from his, I'm sure he was right to set aside the active/passive dichotomy and seek out alternative conceptual resources for theorizing autonomous subjects.

In keeping with this conviction, I am skeptical of current philosophical efforts to celebrate or otherwise salvage the reputation of passivity and vulnerability. I do not deny that vulnerability is a necessary consequence of our biological and psychosocial existence. Nor do I deny that it is a necessary concomitant of human agency or that human mastery is necessarily constrained. To deny these realities would be daft, and to denigrate them would be to denigrate the human condition. But, as I'll argue, Reader and Buss fasten so tenaciously on the ostensibly passive side of selfhood and agency that their views miss core features of human life. Not only are their conceptions of selfhood and agency distorted, but also their accounts misrepresent victims of wrongful, humanly inflicted suffering.

This chapter has two main parts. The first argues that Reader's contention that passivity is a necessary concomitant of activity and agency mistakes interactivity for passivity and falls into complicity with a malign stereotype of victims that relegates them to passivity and that prejudices their claims for justice. The second part takes up Buss's claim that autonomy is not premised on a special type of activity but rather on a special type of passivity. I argue that her account of autonomy overlooks the ways in which agentic subjects must exercise capacities in order to sustain minimal flourishing and that these oversights result in an unsatisfactory treatment of autonomy under oppression. Passivity is neither a feminine attribute that deserves reclamation nor a ground for accounts of victimhood that feminists should endorse.

The activity/passivity binary distracts Reader and Buss from key details concerning the phenomena they endeavor to analyze. As a result, they see passivity where I see various forms of interactivity and capacitation.[2] When I speak of interactivity, I mean to reference a wide variety of types of engagement with a person's social and material environment. Enculturation is a form of interactivity that takes place to a large extent at the subconscious level and relies partly on inborn mimetic capacities. Conversation is a form of interactivity that involves relatively effortless, localized overt movement but a lot of subpersonal interpretative processing and linguistic know-how. Playing tennis is a high-octane form of interactivity that requires extensive training and embodied skill. All forms of interactivity depend on corresponding forms of capacitation. Some, such as the mimetic and interpretative capacities mentioned above, can operate automatically without the agent's awareness. Others, such as talking or serving in a game of tennis, the agent deliberately mobilizes to respond to circumstances and take advantage of opportunities.

The target of my criticism in this chapter is passivity—a state in which one is controlled by external force, inert and uninvolved, or disposed to submit to another's will.[3] I'll argue that theories of the agentic self and autonomy would profit from jettisoning talk of passivity and replacing it with talk of interactivity and capacitation. Framing these topics in terms of interactivity and capacitation would underwrite a better understanding of what it is to be a victim and why it is possible for victims to be agents.

Reader's Reclamation of Passivity

Reader deplores the "agential bias" she detects in philosophical accounts of personhood (Reader 2007, 580). What she means is that philosophers err in excluding the "abject features of human life" from their understandings of personal identity and selfhood (Reader 2007, 579). In her view, suffering, weakness, vulnerability, constraint, and dependency are species of passivity and they are no less constitutive of who you are than acting, power, control, freedom, and independence. I grant that something like an agential bias distorts some philosophical accounts of the self and personal identity. However, I disagree that an agential bias is as prevalent as Reader believes it is, and I disagree that elevating the status of passivity or "patiency" is a viable remedy for whatever agential bias exists. My reasons for opposing Reader's strategy derive in part from the concerns we share about the objectification and denigration of victims of oppression and human rights abuse. Before I take up that issue, however, I need to raise some questions (1) about Reader's charge that an agentic bias skews philosophical theories of the person and (2) about her account of the role of patiency in the lives of persons.

Philosophical reflection on the relationships between agency and one kind of "patiency"—namely, vulnerability—dates back as far as ancient Greece. In acting for a reason, you risk misjudging what action best expresses your motivation, and you risk falling short of achieving your purpose. Thus you are vulnerable to failure—what Aristotle calls missing the mark (*Nicomachean Ethics* 1106b29–33). Another form of vulnerability is central to the liberal tradition of rights-based political theory as well as to contemporary human rights theory. Rights-bearers are individuals who are entitled to act as they choose within the bounds of their rights, but who are vulnerable to others' aggression or refusal to lend a hand. If their rightful agency is to be secured, institutionalized rights must protect their vulnerabilities. A number of contemporary philosophers of action focus attention on a third form of agentic vulnerability, namely, vulnerability to hostile social environments that prevent you from acquiring sufficient proficiency, self-regard, or psychological freedom to act autonomously.[4]

Conceptualizing the agentic subject as vulnerable is not new or philosophically peripheral. However, because these acknowledgments of agentic vulnerability treat vulnerabilities as hindrances to be overcome, and because they stop short of associating vulnerability with passivity, Reader might respond that they are infected with agential bias. I'll argue, however, that her arguments for introducing passivity into our conception of personhood are flawed.

Personhood as Patiency?

According to Reader, passivity is "necessarily presupposed by the 'positive' agential features"—action, capability, freedom, choice, rationality, and independence (Reader 2007, 588). Regarding action, Reader contends that all "doings involve sufferings," that "actions always have patients" (Reader 2007, 588). Her point seems to be that whenever you act, you affect someone or something else and in some small or large way yourself as well. This is true, yet it's not perspicuous to label all the ways in which persons can be affected "suffering" and to subsume suffering under the category of passivity. It is more apt to say that agents are receptive and responsive to neutral or positive stimuli, whereas they suffer and endure necessary pain and serious maltreatment. In either case, the concept of interactivity best captures the normal modality of agentic subjects.

When other people act in ways that harmlessly or beneficially affect you or that impose relatively mild or manageable types of harm on you, you *experience* these encounters. Far from passively undergoing what others do to you, you interact with them and process their inputs in myriad ways. Because your existing intellectual, affective, motivational, and valuational systems selectively assimilate or repudiate inputs, often modifying those inputs along the way, one upshot of this lifelong interactivity is the formation and refinement of your personal identity—the attributes that characterize you as a unique individual. Interactivity typifies most social experience. Since you do not passively suffer the effects of others' tolerably decent conduct,[5] it's misleading to maintain that activity can only take place in tandem with passivity. Later, I'll argue that it's also misleading to maintain that people necessarily suffer and endure severe abuse passively.

Reader regards incapacity as another neglected species of patiency (Reader 2007, 589). No one is endowed with every possible capability. So, possessing a particular set of capacities entails lacking others (Reader 2007, 589–590). Obviously she's right about this, but incapacities aren't a species of passivity. Although lacking a capacity entails not acting in arenas that expressly require it, lacking a capacity doesn't entail inertness or submission—that is, passivity. Spectating might be an option when participating isn't. Indeed, unless someone's incapacities interfere with living a satisfying life, philosophers typically celebrate the unique combinations of capacities and incapacities that characterize distinctive individual identities. Far from manifesting an agential bias by lamenting our incapacities, philosophers argue that we adapt to them through mutually beneficial social cooperation and coordination.

Reader might concede that incapacities are not a type of passivity, but she would reply that incapacities are not the only liabilities with which capabilities are conjoined. By exercising your capabilities in the service of malevolent purposes, for instance, you become vulnerable to charges of wrongdoing (Reader 2007, 590). I agree, but you may also exercise your capabilities in an exemplary manner in pursuit of lofty goals. In that case, it would be exceedingly odd to say that you become vulnerable to receiving the Nobel Peace Prize or some other award. That's because responsibility, whether for good or bad conduct, is not a species of passivity, nor is it a liability of agency. Taking responsibility and owning your actions are plainly forms of interactivity. That norms of engagement with others govern standing accused of wrongdoing as well as accepting credit or praise for meritorious conduct implies that these too are forms of interactivity.

Moreover, Margaret Walker points out that being accountable to others and having standing to call others to account signals full membership in a moral community (Walker 2014, 119). Although it follows that persons are "morally vulnerable" to powerful wrongdoers who may refuse to heed victims' accusations and demands for justice, Walker's call for reparations that affirm victims' status as full members of the moral community is not rooted in a noxious agential bias, but rather in a widely and properly shared understanding of the dignity of persons. Being deprived of this status is a grave sort of harm, a "moral wound" (Walker 2014, 120). Your dignity as a person rests on your entitlement to interact with others.

Reader holds that the passive side of freedom, choice, and rationality is constraint, necessity, and contingency. Your options are not unlimited; you don't always have more than one feasible choice; your deliberations aren't foolproof (Reader 2007, 590). Likewise, your independence is conditional on countless dependencies—including health, access to oxygen, nutrition, potable water, education, employment, and so on (Reader 2007, 591). To be sure, but locating these constraints, necessities, contingencies, and dependencies on the passive side of agency misses their significance for agentic subjects.

The situatedness of agentic subjects in a world that does not let them have everything they might want, including more complete knowledge of the contexts in which they must act, and in which they must rely on a vast array of social and material supports doesn't render them passive. On the contrary, this situatedness endlessly furnishes occasions for various kinds of interactivity. Indeed, it is because agentic subjects can make do with the givens of their lives and make use of the resources that they have at their disposal, that they are intelligent agents—not gods, not automatons.

It seems to me that what Reader is doing is cataloging the circumstances of respect for persons—that is, the ordinary conditions in which autonomous choice and action are possible and necessary. In framing my suggestion this way, I mean to allude to what John Rawls calls the circumstances of justice—the "normal conditions under which human cooperation is both possible and necessary" (Rawls 1971, 126). These circumstances aren't the positives and negatives of justice. They are the conditions that must obtain for instituting a system of justice to make sense as a desirable and practicable basis for social organization. Similarly, if we understand the imperfect workings of agentic subjects and the challenging contexts in which they must choose and act as preconditions for practices of respect for persons to make sense, the various dimensions of agency that Reader consigns to the realm of passivity are excellent candidates for inclusion in the circumstances of respect for persons.

Agentic subjects are equipped with limited epistemic, imaginative, and volitional powers and they inhabit complicated social, natural, and artifactual worlds. It is because of what they can accomplish despite the constraints and imponderables they face that respecting them is a desirable and practicable basis for interpersonal relations.

Protecting Victims by Revaluing Passivity?

One reason Reader advocates putting patiency on a par with agency is that she thinks that redeeming human patiency will rescue victims from objectification and scorn (Reader 2007, 595). Yet, real victims, whether female or male, don't always, even usually, fit the stereotype of victims as helpless, passive targets. If you need to be reduced to helplessness and passivity to count as a victim, Reader's reclamation strategy would exclude many victims of undeniably grievous wrongs.

Although Reader cites Susan Brison's groundbreaking book *Aftermath*, Brison's recounting of the sexual assault and attempted murder she survived does not support Reader's position. Far from collapsing into helpless passivity during the attack, she figures out her predicament, tries strategies of submission and fighting back, tells her assailant that she'll protect him by saying she'd been hit by a car, tells him he'll be punished more severely if he kills her, and finally plays dead to make him leave (Brison 2002, 88–89).[6] Like countless other victims, Brison was not reduced to an object except in the misogynistic fantasy life of her rapist and would-be killer.

I don't deny that villains sometimes succeed in reducing agentic subjects to helpless passivity. Some sexual assault victims freeze. Making a split-second judgment that neither defending yourself nor fleeing from your attacker will succeed, you seize up and dissociate from the abuse being inflicted on you.[7] Arguably, the freeze response is adaptive in situations in which you have no chance of fighting off or escaping from a grave threat, for freezing reduces your awareness of the fear and pain you are suffering. Yet, it seems to me that a distinctive kind of opprobrium attaches to crimes that de-agentify their victims. Consequently, valorizing a psychological mechanism designed to cope with such horrific attacks strikes me as defeatist, if not cynical.[8]

I agree with Reader that the "personal perspective of victims" is indispensable to theorizing the agentic subject (Reader 2007, 597). Although that perspective does entail respecting victims who freeze in the face of danger, it doesn't entail honoring passivity and inserting it into our concept of an agentic subject. Rather it entails that philosophers need to theorize how best to protect people from such egregious wrongs—what cultural and institutional measures would curtail them.

Reader's discussion of "enduring" violence indicates how she might rebut my view. She maintains that enduring violence is not action, does not show positive capability, is not chosen, and is not independent, but that it is difficult and courageous (Reader 2007, 597). Although you are passive, you are "fully present and alive" (Reader 2007, 598).[9] Thus she concludes that it's a mistake to think that undergoing harm "is somehow less personal, less expressive and determinative of me, than what I do of free rational choice" (Reader 2007, 600). I'm sure she's right to bind who you are to what you have been through, but not because passivity is inextricable from activity and hence constitutive of personal identity.

Enduring pain is not the same as going limp or numbing out. To endure pain, you must gird yourself to withstand what you are undergoing. What may appear to be passive submission from the outside is anything but from the perspective of the victim. The examples Reader invokes from Veena Das's work support this claim. In her studies of the survival strategies of Indian women from minority religious communities who had been subjected to multiple forms of violence, Das reports that some women spoke of "drinking all the pain" and "digesting the poison" (quoted in Reader 2007, 598). Reader comments that these women are enduring trauma by "metabolizing, neutralizing, containing, and living with it so that human life can continue" (Reader 2007, 598). Although their method of coping is obviously different from speaking out, accusing the perpetrators, and demanding that they be punished, it is certainly not passive.[10] Although it may not look as if they are doing anything, they are in fact inwardly contending with what they have been through.

Valuing patiency as much as agency finds passivity where it doesn't exist while eclipsing the agency of innumerable victims. In so doing, it disrespects them instead of securing their dignity. To spare victims the humiliation and marginalization they are commonly subjected to, we must critique the stereotype of the passive victim and promulgate a conception of victimhood that allows victims to be agents without sacrificing their standing as victims and their claim to redress (Meyers 2016).

Buss's Reclamation of Passivity

Buss also revalues passivity but in a different register. Whereas Reader claims that passivity is no less constitutive of personal identity and agentic selfhood than activity, Buss claims that a particular form of passivity is constitutive of character and personality and hence of autonomous action. Like Reader, Buss takes victims into account. However, Reader seeks to free victims from misplaced contempt and blame, whereas Buss seeks to explain how oppression compromises victims' agency. In order to understand Buss's treatment of victims, I first need to sketch her account of autonomy.

For Buss, autonomous action is action for which the agent is responsible (Buss 2012, 648). Thus she undertakes to explain what it is about an agent's participation in generating an action that confers responsibility. After rejecting explanations that rely on things that agents do, such as deliberating, identifying, or endorsing, Buss maintains that the role of the agentic subject in autonomous action cannot be an active one and must be a passive one. Autonomous action must be "self-determination in the passive mode" (Buss 2012, 657).

Autonomy in the Passive Mode?

According to Buss, "The distinguishing characteristic of autonomous action is that the agent forms her intention under the causal, nonrational influence of the *person she is* insofar as, in her agential capacity, she is a *representative of her species*" (Buss 2012, 680; emphasis added). Assuming, as is customary, that autonomy is self-governance, Buss unpacks this definition by furnishing an analysis of the self of self-governance or agentic self. Her account has two prongs: (1) a conception of an agent's practical identity—the "character condition," and (2) a normative constraint on the content of a representative of the human species' practical identity—the "human flourishing condition" (Buss 2012, 657–659). Together, these requirements clarify the sense in which autonomous action is a "more complete expression of the agent herself" (Buss 2012, 657).

To satisfy the character condition, an agentic subject must have a set of psychological traits that defines her character and personality—"the person she is" (Buss 2012, 658). These dispositions shape what an agent notices, how she interprets the information she gathers, and what she cares about. In turn they influence the formation of her value system, her interpersonal relationships, and her personal projects (Buss 2012, 657–658). Because these dispositions must be understood as purely causal, nonrational influences on an agentic subject's decision-making and intention-forming processes, the agentic subject is passive in relation to them (Buss 2012, 658). But such passivity is no obstacle to agency. On the contrary, when these psychological dispositions can properly be said to define who an individual is, and when they bring about her actions, her actions express her practical identity and are therefore autonomous.

Some possible sets of psychological dispositions cannot properly be said to define who an individual is and are therefore incompatible with autonomous agency. Sets that do not satisfy the human flourishing condition do not constitute agentic subjects—subjects who are capable of autonomous action.

Buss sets the bar for satisfying this condition at minimal flourishing, and she fleshes out this criterion negatively and positively. States of affairs that defeat the human flourishing condition bespeak pathology or induce pathology. They include being in extreme pain or fear; not having access to adequate and secure nutrition; being out of touch with reality; being cut off from positive sensations; and being constantly distracted (Buss 2012, 671, 673).[11] Such conditions thwart autonomy. Capacities that are conducive to meeting the human flourishing condition include being able to take care of yourself; being able to avoid serious legal troubles; and being able to maintain friendships (Buss 2012, 676). Whereas exercising these capacities promotes minimal flourishing and ensures autonomy, acting so as to undermine them precludes autonomy. Summing up her view, Buss observes, "A trait is disabling in the sense relevant to our assessment of autonomous agency if, when it is a stable disposition, it typically prevents members of the agent's species from satisfying one or more of their basic needs without exceptional effort" (Buss 2012, 672).

The human flourishing condition is crucial for autonomy in two respects. First, it determines whether or not an individual's settled psychological dispositions constitute an agentic self, a self that is representative of the human species and therefore capable of autonomous action (Buss 2012, 660). Second, when a psychological or physiological state motivates action that does not comport with an agent's settled psychological dispositions but that does comport with the human flourishing condition, her action is nevertheless autonomous (Buss 2012, 659).

Buss delineates two tiers of autonomy. On the principal tier, the agent's practical identity drives action, and the agentic subject is passive with respect to the dispositions that comprise her practical identity. This level takes seriously the familiar idea that autonomous agents are unique individuals whose autonomous actions express their unique identities. On the auxiliary tier, a motivation that all humans ought to have can give rise to conduct that is contrary to a particular individual's practical identity, yet autonomous. This backup conception is a sensible concession to the tensions within multidimensional practical identities; to the likelihood that no one's practical identity is well equipped to cope with every turn of events; and to the value of spontaneity. Here, the agentic subject's passivity in being governed by the disposition to sustain minimal flourishing comes to the fore. Freezing in response to an inescapable sexual assault would qualify as autonomous, it seems, provided that it reduced immediate suffering and subsequently conduced to minimal flourishing.

Recapping, Buss's passivity theory holds that agentic subjects needn't do anything to validate, own, or internalize their desires (Buss 2012, 678). All that matters is how a person's actions are caused. Actions that are caused by settled dispositions that promote minimal flourishing or by an inborn disposition to pursue minimal flourishing are autonomous. In my judgment, however, labeling this account "autonomy in the passive mode" is misleading. Against her contention that she is advocating a passivity account, I argue that she is presenting an interactive capacitation account and that the sense in which this type of account is passive is trivial.

Let's start with her character condition. It's clear that, for Buss, your practical identity serves as an interpretative system and as a motivational system. Since I've already argued that motivations aren't passively acquired, I'll now focus on the interpretative side. Like consolidating practical dispositions and commitments, construing situations is a type of interactivity. Your interpretative capacities strive to grasp what's going on, how it matters to you, and what options for action are available to you. Your circumstances do not impress a ready-made understanding on you as if your mind was a lump of wet clay. Rather, you must construct an understanding of your circumstances as Brison did when she came under attack.

Buss might respond that your interpretative system—your conceptual templates, inferential moves, affective feedback loops, and interactive gambits— functions causally to generate understandings of situations. But because causation plays a role in everything that happens at the macro level, it would be question-begging to infer that everything happens passively, for that inference would define activity out of existence by fiat. Worse, adopting this position would result in overlooking the intricacies, not to mention the vitality, of agentic selves.

Now consider the human flourishing condition. Buss identifies three capacities that contribute to satisfying this condition: (1) the capacity to care for yourself, (2) the capacity to stay out of trouble, and (3) the capacity to maintain friendships. Plainly these capacities are types of capacitation, and availing yourself of these capacities entails quite a lot of interactivity—noticing and acquiring needed goods and aid, noticing and avoiding potential dangers, and noticing associates' sensitivities and needs and considerately responding to them. This need for interactivity is hardly surprising because you can't maintain your health as a representative member of the human species passively. If Buss were to reply that the capacities that enable you to accomplish these aims operate causally cranking out health-preserving conduct, I would repeat that she is trivializing her affirmation of passivity by rendering it tautologous. In doing so, moreover, she would fail to capture the complex workings of agentic selves.

Buss's analysis of serious psychopathology's disastrous effects on autonomy implicitly supports my contention that hers is a capacitation account that requires much more interactivity than she acknowledges. Unlike agentic subjects, according to Buss, individuals afflicted by autonomy-disabling psychopathologies experience passivity intensely.[12] Although healthy agentic subjects are no less passive than unhealthy nonagentic subjects, healthy agentic subjects aren't aware of their passivity but unhealthy nonagentic subjects are acutely aware of theirs (Buss 2012, 684). This phenomenological difference together with the experience of mental disintegration that commonly accompanies psychopathology accounts for much of the suffering that victims of severe psychopathologies endure (Buss 2012, 685). Yet, according to Buss, their passivity isn't the problem, it's their suffering that's bad (Buss 2012, 684).

This strikes me as a very peculiar claim. As I argued a moment ago, there's a lot more capacitation and interactivity underwriting Buss's account of autonomy than she admits. If this is right, it's arguable that agentic subjects don't feel passive because they really aren't all that passive. In addition, as I argued in my discussion of Reader, we use the term "suffering" to signal that something bad is happening to someone and making her miserable. Thus, the grammar of suffering links suffering to the various harms that can befall sentient beings. If so, experiencing passivity because of grave mental illness causes suffering because passivity is bad for agentic subjects. If passivity really were as healthy and harmless as Buss makes it out to be, it wouldn't make sense that being aware of it would cause you to suffer. Buss might answer that agentic subjects are oblivious to their passivity—perhaps because they are endowed with a congenital illusion that they're exerting control over their conduct; perhaps because they are minimally flourishing and feel pretty good.[13] But if I'm right about all the capacitation and interactivity her passivity account conceals, this reply is irrelevant.

"Passive Autonomy" for Victims of Oppression?

In addition to victims of psychopathology, Buss considers victims of oppression. Many philosophers and activists contend that oppression adversely affects autonomy, and Buss offers an explanation of when oppression blocks autonomy and when it does not.

She approaches this problem by asking whether attributes instilled by a sexist upbringing—such as, a woman's self-inhibiting, subordination-perpetuating dispositions—should count as constitutive of her agentic self. Here's her answer:

> The issue is whether what is in her is internal to her identity as a representative human being—or whether, alternatively, it is an affliction or deformity of the psyche. (Buss 2012, 689)

Deciding this matter depends on whether or not the oppressed woman's character and personality traits obstruct minimal flourishing.[14] If they do, she is not a representative human being, and her actions are not autonomous. If they do not, she is autonomously embarked on the life prescribed for her by oppressive social norms and structures. This position is troubling in several ways.

First, Buss pegs minimal flourishing to being able to satisfy your basic needs without exceptional effort (Buss 2012, 672). But there's heated controversy about basic needs. Some philosophers maintain that a person's basic needs are satisfied if she has access to resources adequate for subsistence. Others propose more capacious understandings. A problem with resting a theory of autonomy on meeting basic needs is that it leaves questions concerning the autonomy of oppressed individuals unresolvable unless a consensus account of basic needs is in hand.

Moreover, a sensible assessment of the scope of basic needs may not correlate with intuitions about autonomy. Too meager a list of basic needs would yield an overinclusive assessment of the prevalence of autonomy and would overlook a lot of the damage to autonomy that oppression inflicts. If people are getting by, they'd be presumed to be autonomous. Too generous a list of basic needs would disrespect the agency of many victims of oppression. Enormous numbers of people aren't meeting some of these needs, so they wouldn't count as autonomous. Controversy over which needs are basic together with this potential for under- or overinclusive assessments of autonomy leaves the relations between autonomy and oppression opaque.

Second, Buss maintains that autonomy is a matter of degree. I agree with Buss that there are degrees of autonomy, but not with her explanation of them. According to Buss, there must be degrees of autonomy because there is no determinate point at which a character or personality trait becomes a symptom of pathology that disables autonomy (Buss 2012, 675).[15] Noting that people are often ambivalent about where to draw the line between pathology and health and that cultures draw the line differently, she appears to be saying that since we can't conclusively decide iffy cases, we should regard their autonomy as impaired but not eradicated. When in doubt, ascribe some autonomy but not full autonomy to an oppressed agent.

An illustration clarifies why I consider this account of degrees of autonomy makeshift. How might Buss analyze the legal quandaries that arise when victims of domestic violence kill their abusers while they are asleep or otherwise defenseless? She might hold that courts should punish these victims for the crime of cold-blooded murder on the grounds that they are representative members of the human species who pursued minimal flourishing by legally prohibited means. Yet, because this analysis is deplorably oblivious to what these women have suffered, Buss might seek out justifications for a more merciful approach. Reasoning that being subject to unpredictable, but frequent violence instills unhealthy personality traits that are incompatible with the human flourishing condition, she might hold that courts should decline to punish these victims and should instead refer them for psychiatric treatment. Supporting this second analysis, one study reports high rates of depression, PTSD, panic disorder, and other pathological conditions among women arrested for violence against their abusers (Stuart et al. 2006).

Yet, not all victims of domestic abuse develop diagnosable pathologies. In those cases, Buss might contend that courts should regard these victims' autonomy as impaired to some degree and should therefore exercise mercy, on the grounds that it's indeterminate whether these victims are in the grip of psychopathological traits or not. While leniency seems appropriate in cases in which the alleged perpetrator does not suffer from a diagnosable psychopathology but has endured severe abuse over an extended period of time, this justification for leniency makes no sense.

What is missing is a cogent explanation of what is interfering with these latter victims' autonomy. Asserting that someone's autonomy is impaired doesn't mean that the speaker isn't sure about the healthiness of the trait that brought about the individual's action. Rather, the speaker is pointing to something or other that's hindering the individual's autonomy but not completely nullifying it. Perhaps the anxiety induced by the intermittent, but severe violence made the victim desperate for surcease. Because her abuser kept a loaded gun at home, killing him offered the only readily available and sure to succeed route to surcease. Absent violence-induced desperation and a handy weapon, she would have acted differently. Buss's trouble pinpointing factors that diminish autonomy is evidence of a fundamental problem with her passivity-based theory. Conceiving agentic selves as functioning passively and sidelining the many ways in which they rely on capacities to interact with their surroundings in flourishing-compatible ways deprives Buss of a sufficiently rich conceptual toolkit to develop a tenable account of degrees of autonomy. Were she to embrace a capacitation account of autonomy, as I have argued she should, she would be in a position to notice the diverse forms of interactivity to which agentic capacities give rise, and she could watch for defects in the workings of those capacities or wrongful constraints imposed on their workings.[16] She could then point to these agentic privations to make sense of degrees of autonomy, and she could provide a more insightful treatment of the impact of oppression on agentic subjects.

I agree with Buss that autonomy isn't best explicated by picking out some kind of "super agency" (Buss 2012, 678). Where I disagree is that autonomy is some kind of passivity. In my view, autonomous action is best understood in terms of the outputs of a repertoire of capacities that enable agentic subjects to grasp situations, to envisage and evaluate options concordant with their practical identities, and to carry out the chosen option—that is, to interact with changing circumstances.

Passivity versus Capacitation and Interactivity?

The activity/passivity binary accurately represents very little in the lives of persons. It certainly doesn't capture gender or sexual difference, although it took centuries to debunk those associations.[17] Still, this pernicious dichotomy lingers in our colloquial and philosophical discourses as a nasty but somehow alluring conceptual trap. I've argued that it snares Reader and Buss. No one will be well served by a "balanced" view of the agentic subject larded with ostensibly passive features, nor by a passivity theory of the agential self that obscures the workings of agency—least of all victims of oppression and other unjustly inflicted harm.

Vulnerability to individual and institutional aggressors and to oppressive social structures is a fact of human life. Still, it's a mistake to think that there are unjust practices in relation to which autonomous agents are necessarily passive, helpless, or abject. Likewise, it's a mistake to expect judgments about the healthiness or unhealthiness of the attributes that such practices instill to resolve questions about victims' autonomy. What is missing in philosophical views that hold otherwise is an adequate appreciation of the nature and scope of human capacities to transform and individualize experience in medias res, capacities that are themselves amenable to cultivation and that vary from individual to individual, capacities that sustain interactivity and generate action. If anyone is tempted to doubt the authority of these capacities as manifestations of the agentic self, I would urge that David Velleman's claim that your understanding is inalienable insofar as you are an agent helps explain why this sort of objection isn't decisive (Velleman 2000, 137–138). I would amend his suggestion, however, and urge that agentic capacitation includes diverse intellectual, affective, and corporeal capacities that collaborate to constitute distinctive agentic subjects.

Notes

1. Thanks to members of New York SWIPshop for a lively, productive session on an earlier draft of this chapter. I'm also grateful to audiences at the 2016 Central APA, the University of Copenhagen, and Wesleyan University. Special thanks to the editors of this volume, Keya Maitra and Jennifer McWeeny, and to Amy Baehr, Nanette Funk, Serene Khader, Suzy Killmister, and Margaret Walker for helpful comments.

2. Precedents for my view include Taylor's dialogical account of the self and action and Gallagher's interaction theory of agency and social cognition (Taylor 1989, 1995; Gallagher 2003, 2007, 2008).

3. Curiously, the adjective "passive" commonly refers to motivations or behaviors that I would characterize as interactive. Passive aggression indirectly expresses hostility through uncooperative behavior, and passive resistance protests objectionable social policies or structural arrangements using nonviolent means.

4. See, for example, Meyers (1989), Benson (2000), Friedman (2003), Christman (2009), and Stoljar (2015).

5. Neither does your body passively suffer the effects of contact with the nonhuman environment unless your health is severely compromised.

6. For critique of objectification theories of womanhood and their failure to account for resistance, see Cahill (2011).

7. For discussion, of the fight/flight/freeze triad, see Seltzer (2015).

8. I set aside victims of terminal diseases, natural disasters, and accidents.

9. Note that Reader's claim that you are fully present and alive while enduring harm rules out the freeze response in which you dissociate from what's happening.

10. For an account of victims of oppression as resistant—that is, not passively subsumed by oppression—see Lugones (2003, 2006).

11. The percentage of the world's population that does not have access to adequate and secure nutrition is huge, and the implication that none of these people is autonomous and responsible for her actions is, to say the least, troubling.

12. Reader and Buss take contrasting views on suffering. Whereas Reader asserts that you can be "most yourself" while suffering, Buss asserts that suffering suppresses or distorts your practical identity.

13. In fact, there's a good deal of evidence that psychologically healthy individuals do tend to overestimate how much control they exert over the course of events. See, for example, Taylor and Brown (1988). However, this data doesn't support the conclusion that they are really passive and exert no control.

14. It's worth comparing Buss's position to Serene Khader's (2011). They agree that subminimal flourishing is a danger signal. However, Khader holds that subminimal flourishing justifies pursuing dialogical inquiry into whether or not a woman's seemingly adaptive preferences reflect her autonomous values and desires, whereas Buss holds that it justifies denying that she is autonomous.

15. She adds, "If someone resists the suggestion that her behavior is a symptom of an unhealthy mind, and if she takes this position despite acknowledging that the behavior tends to have a negative effect on her ability to take care of herself, steer clear

of the law, maintain friendships, and so on, then she is at least implicitly indicting the social 'order' to which she belongs" (Buss 2012, 676). This complicates her position by giving political struggle or an objectivist theory of health a role in her theory of self and action. Unfortunately, I don't have space to pursue this intriguing line of thought here.

16. It seems to me that Buss might have relied on her comments about the capacities necessary for human flourishing to develop an account of degrees of autonomy for mentally competent victims of domestic abuse who kill their abusers. Noting that domestic abuse puts the capacity to care for yourself at odds with the capacity to avoid legal trouble, she could have said that this conflict diminishes the degree of autonomy that victims of such abuse can achieve. I suppose she shuns this explanation because it highlights capacitation, thereby threatening her claim that autonomy is a form of passivity.

17. We now know that the vagina isn't a passive receptacle for the penis, nor is the ovum an inert cell patiently awaiting penetration by a spermatozoon.

References

Aristotle. 2012. *Aristotle's Nicomachean Ethics.* Translated and edited by Robert C. Bartlett and Susan D. Collins. Chicago: University of Chicago Press.

Benson, Paul. 2000. "Feeling Crazy: Self-Worth and the Social Character of Responsibility." In *Relational Autonomy: Feminist Perspectives on Autonomy, Agency, and the Social Self,* edited by Catriona Mackenzie and Natalie Stoljar, 72–93. New York: Oxford University Press.

Brison, Susan J. 2002. *Aftermath: Violence and the Remaking of a Self.* Princeton, NJ: Princeton University Press.

Buss, Sarah. 2012. "Autonomous Action: Self-Determination in the Passive Mode." *Ethics* 122 (4): 647–691.

Cahill, Ann J. 2011. "Sexual Violence and Objectification." In *Overcoming Objectification* by Ann J. Cahill, 127–142. New York: Routledge.

Christman, John. 2009. *The Politics of Persons.* Cambridge: Cambridge University Press.

Frankfurt, Harry. 1998. "Identification and Externality." In *The Importance of What We Care About,* 58–69. Cambridge: Cambridge University Press.

Friedman, Marilyn. 2003. *Autonomy, Gender, Politics.* New York: Oxford University Press.

Gallagher, Shaun. 2003. "Self-Narrative, Embodied Action, and Social Context." In *Between Suspicion and Sympathy: Paul Ricoeur's Unstable Equilibrium,* edited by Andrzej Wiercinski, 1–15. Toronto: Hermeneutics Press.

Gallagher, Shaun. 2007. "Moral Agency, Self-Consciousness, and Practical Wisdom." *Journal of Consciousness Studies* 14 (5–6): 199–223.

Gallagher, Shaun. 2008. "Inference or Interaction: Social Cognition without Precursors." *Philosophical Explorations* 11 (3): 163–174.

Khader, Serene. 2011. *Adaptive Preferences and Women's Empowerment.* New York: Oxford University Press.

Lugones, María. 2003. "Tactical Strategies of the Streetwalker / *Estrategias Tácticas de la Callejera.*" In *Pilgrimages/Peregrinajes: Theorizing Coalition against Multiple Oppressions* by María Lugones, 207–237. Lanham, MD: Rowman and Littlefield.

Lugones, María. 2006. "On Complex Communication." *Hypatia*. 21 (3): 75–85.

Meyers, Diana Tietjens. 1989. *Self, Society, and Personal Choice*. New York: Columbia University Press.

Meyers, Diana Tietjens. 2016. *Victims' Stories and the Advancement of Human Rights*. New York: Oxford University Press.

Nussbaum, Martha. 2001. *Upheavals of Thought: The Intelligence of Emotions*. Cambridge: Cambridge University Press.

Rawls, John. 1971. *A Theory of Justice*. Cambridge MA: Harvard University Press.

Reader, Soran. 2007, "The Other Side of Agency." *Philosophy* 82 (322): 579–604.

Seltzer, Leon F. 2015. "Trauma and the Freeze Response: Good, Bad, or Both?" *Psychology Today*. July 8. https://www.psychologytoday.com/blog/evolution-the-self/201507/tra uma-and-the-freeze-response-good-bad-or-both.

Stoljar. Natalie. 2015. "'Living Constantly at Tiptoe Stance': Social Scripts, Psychological Freedom, and Autonomy." In *Personal Autonomy and Social Oppression*, edited by Marina Oshana, 105–123. New York: Routledge.

Stuart, Gregory L., Todd M. Moore, Kristina Coop Gordon, Susan E. Ramsey, and Christopher W. Kahler. 2006. "Psychopathology in Women Arrested for Domestic Violence." *Journal of Interpersonal Violence* 21 (3): 376–389.

Taylor, Charles. 1989. *Sources of the Self*. Cambridge, MA: Harvard University Press.

Taylor, Charles. 1995. "To Follow a Rule." In *Philosophical Arguments*, 165–180. Cambridge, MA: Harvard University Press.

Taylor, Shelley E., and Jonathon D. Brown. 1988. "Illusion and Well-Being: A Social Psychological Perspective on Mental Health." *Psychological Bulletin* 103 (2): 193–210.

Velleman, J. David. 2000. *The Possibility of Practical Reason*. New York: Oxford University Press.

Walker, Margaret Urban. 2014. "Moral Vulnerability and the Task of Reparations." In *Vulnerability: New Essays in Ethics and Feminist Philosophy*, edited by Catriona Mackenzie, Wendy Rogers, and Susan Dodds, 110–133. New York: Oxford University Press.

8

The Question of Personal Identity

Susan James

A great deal of recent feminist work on philosophy of mind has been grounded on a central claim: that the key oppositions between body and mind, and between emotion and reason, are gendered.[1] While the mind and its capacity to reason are associated with masculinity, the body, together with our emotional sensibilities, is associated with the feminine. Evidence for this view comes from at least two sources. First, overtly sexist philosophers have in the past claimed that women are by nature less capable reasoners than men and are more prone to ground their judgments on their emotional responses. These authors have been repeatedly opposed by defenders of women, whether male or female. Second, feminists have explored ways in which gendered oppositions are at work even in the writings of philosophers who do not explicitly differentiate the mental capacities of men and women or connect women with the bodily work of reproduction and domestic labor. By studying the metaphorical structures of philosophical texts, looking at what may appear to be digressions from the main line of argument, and paying attention to examples, they have identified persistent patterns of association running through the history of philosophy. These patterns can fluctuate from century to century, from author to author, from work to work, and even from paragraph to paragraph, but they keep cropping up. They indicate that the terms associated with the feminine are persistently marginalized by comparison with those associated with masculinity, as when the rational powers of human beings are habitually regarded as more valuable than their emotional skills.[2]

In the light of this analysis, many feminists have worked to develop philosophical positions which do not devalue the symbolically feminine. They have done so by unsettling the hierarchical relations between mind and body, and between reason and emotion, approaching their task in various overlapping ways. Sometimes they have criticized existing, influential theories of body and mind; sometimes they have reconceptualized particular topics within the philosophy of mind; and sometimes they have drawn on the work of authors who have written "against the grain."[3]

Susan James, *The Question of Personal Identity* In: *Feminist Philosophy of Mind*. Edited by: Keya Maitra and Jennifer McWeeny, Oxford University Press. © Oxford University Press 2022. DOI: 10.1093/oso/9780190867614.003.0009

Personal Identity

Several of these themes can be traced in contemporary feminist writing about personal identity, which has tended to draw on the insights of psychoanalysis and postmodernism to explore the ways in which selves are embodied, discontinuous, malleable, and socially constructed.[4] At the same time, anglophone theorists of personal identity have continued to develop a conception of the self which revolves around a distinction between the psychological and the bodily, and a related notion of psychological continuity (Shoemaker 1984; Williams 1973; Parfit 1984; Lewis 1983). It is tempting to suppose that these two groups are addressing different questions: that feminists are for the most part interested in the variety of ways in which identity can be molded, lived, or transformed; and that theorists of personal identity are concerned with the prior question of what it is to have an identity at all. But this suggested division of labor is too simple. Feminist explorations of the self are, among other things, attempts to depart from the symbolically masculine character of much of philosophy, and their concern with embodiment, discontinuity, and social construction is driven by a desire to avoid reiterating the hierarchical oppositions between mind and body, reason and emotions. By embodying the self, they aim to undo the deeply rooted association between the self and the masculine mind; by emphasizing discontinuity, they aim to put pressure on the cultural alliance between unity and masculinity. From a feminist perspective, therefore, the continued dependence of personal identity theorists on various oppositions that feminist philosophy aims to dismantle is at least suspicious. In this chapter I shall explore some of the grounds for this suspicion, and suggest ways in which it is well-founded.

Contributors to the debate have found it helpful to distinguish two criteria for continuing personal identity—bodily continuity and psychological continuity—and in this way to separate body and mind. Among feminists, this sort of approach is widely regarded as worthy of scrutiny, as it is sometimes the prelude to an attempt to marginalize the body, and with it the symbolically feminine. In this particular case it is undoubtedly the prelude to a maneuver which reinforces the mind/body divide, namely the construction of thought experiments which press these two apart. In the last few years, a good deal of weight has been placed on imaginary examples which suggest that psychological as opposed to bodily continuity is what constitutes a person's survival. One kind of example, in particular, has been crucial in securing this view: the much-cited cases in which, by some means or other, one person's character and memories are transplanted into a second person's body (Shoemaker 1963; Williams 1973, 46–63).[5] Although other scenarios such as fission and fusion are also appealed to (Wiggins 1976; Parfit 1984), transplant cases are a crucial resource on which theorists of various persuasions rely, and are used to create a framework within which different accounts of survival can be discussed.

To make a case for the view that the debate about personal identity marginalizes the feminine, and is one of the ways in which philosophy privileges the symbolically masculine over its feminine counterpart, I shall concentrate on these examples. I shall try to show how imaginary examples of character transplant are used to sustain a symbolically masculine conception of personhood. I shall take up four points: one about the delineation of character; a narrower one about memory; a third about the role of the social world in sustaining identity; and a fourth about identity and male sexual power.

Delineation of Character

Imaginary cases in which one person's character is transplanted into another person's body generally assume that character has to be lodged in a material body of some sort. It may be a whole human body, a brain, or half a brain. The body in question may be inorganic, as when an imaginary machine stores the information from one brain and prints it off in another (Shoemaker 1984, 108–111). But in all these versions the body is thought of as a container or receptacle for character. The brain figures as a container in which a person's psychological states can be preserved, and the body figures as a more elaborate receptacle for the brain. Equally, a machine which copies the information from one brain and prints it into another is a receptacle for storing psychological states.

Several contributors to the literature on personal identity acknowledge that thinking of the body as a receptacle may be an excessive oversimplification, but brush this thought aside. In "The Self and the Future," for example, Bernard Williams notes that body swapping between people of different sexes may be hard to imagine, but comments, "Let us forget this" (Williams 1973, 46), so turning his back on a point he makes elsewhere, that it may be impossible for an emperor to express his personality when his body is that of a peasant (Williams 1973, 11–12). Other writers, such as Harold Noonan, note the problem, but bypass it by specifying that the bodies in question are either only numerically distinct, or extremely similar (Noonan 1989, 4). Any characteristics that might enable the body to disrupt the psychological continuity of the character transplanted into it are removed, with the result that bodies are regarded, for the purposes of the experiment, as uniform. They do of course differ in various ways, but these differences are held to be irrelevant.

Making the body anonymous in this way simultaneously affirms a particular view of what character is. The things that really matter about a person's character, the traits which constitute their psychological continuity, do not depend on their having a particular body, or a body with any particular properties. Anthony Quinton makes this point explicitly. "As things are," he writes, "characters can survive large and even emotionally disastrous alterations to the physical type of a person's body. . . . Courage, for example, can perfectly well persist even though the bodily conditions for its obvious manifestation do not" (Quinton 1975, 60). Courage, perhaps, but what about dexterity? Patience, perhaps, but what about delight in one's sexuality? (It would be interesting to consider whether all the traditional virtues can be construed as independent of the body in this way.) Quinton's argument exemplifies a tendency which runs through imagined cases of character transplant—a tendency to rely on a conception of character or psychological continuity which serves to emphasize, and even create, a division between the psychological and the bodily. Properties which do not fit neatly into the category of the psychological are held to be marginal or irrelevant to character. Then, if continuity of character is taken to be what matters in survival, merely bodily states become irrelevant to survival.

Memory

Partly because the states that contribute to psychological continuity are specified as states that are not bodily, theorists of personal identity are able to be both non-committal and inclusive about what exactly they are. Lewis, for example, regards this as a question of detail (Lewis 1983, 56), and Noonan claims that "in general *any* causal links between past factors and present psychological traits can be subsumed under the notion of psychological connectedness" (Noonan 1989, 13).[6] However, a central role is often given to memories as states which give us access to our pasts, and secure our sense of temporal continuity. How must memory be conceived if it is to fulfill this function, while leaving intact the division between body and character?

At least, I suggest, it must be a storehouse of recollections able to survive bodily vicissitudes. Take the case of Adam. Whatever happens to him—even if he has one of his ribs removed, even if his body changes beyond recognition, even if God refuses to recognize him—he will still be able to think of a sequence of things he did and things that happened to him as *his* actions and experiences. More particularly, changes in his body will not interfere with this capacity. For example, even when he is weak and wasted he remembers that he took the apple from Eve as a strong young man. Why, then, should this capacity not endure in the imaginary case where Adam's character is transplanted into a different body?

There are some obvious exceptions to the view that memory is unaffected by bodily vicissitudes. For instance, brain damage may make Adam amnesiac, and if his character is transplanted into a body with a damaged brain, it is not obvious that his memories will survive. A more interesting example is provided by cases of physical violation such as rape, other forms of torture, or malicious attack, which often have a profound impact on memory. In an illuminating paper, Susan Brison makes the point that experiences like these do not simply add to the victim's stock of memories, as a camera operator might shoot another few feet of film, nor are they safely lodged in the mind, as the camera operator might store the exposed film in a tin (Brison, this volume).[7] First, memories of trauma are in many cases closely tied to the body, indeed are *in* the body, and manifest themselves in physical states as much as in psychic ones. Here any neat separation between bodily states and memory as the bearer of psychological continuity seems to break down. To press a tasteless question, would a trauma victim retain her memories if her character were transplanted into a different body? Second, trauma destroys or alters existing memories, so that people who have been subjected to extended torture or deprivation lose conscious memories of their own pasts, and lose, too, the easy sense of continuity that memory is here supposed to provide. Their time scale may shrink so that their memories of their own experiences become mainly short-term ones. And the continuity of memory may be punctured and jumbled by uncontrollable, nightmarish recollections.[8]

If, as much discussion of personal identity assumes, memory is to be one of the guarantors of psychological continuity, and if psychological continuity is to be separable from bodily continuity, memory must be interpreted in a particular and selective way. Memories in the body have to be set aside in favor of those which appear to have no bodily aspects; and it has to be assumed that the impact of memory loss on other character traits is sufficiently limited for psychological continuity to survive. It is arguable that these are not very contentious assumptions. But they nevertheless help us to see that the division between body and character, around which imaginary transplant cases are organized, can only be sustained if the traits constituting character are laundered, and all traces of the body washed away. The purified conception of "the psychological" which emerges then appears as an unsullied self for which the body is simply a convenient receptacle.

Social Circumstances

The two steps we have examined—the expelling of everything bodily from the mind, and the simultaneous devaluation of the bodily—are familiar to feminists, many of whom have read them as an attempt to demarcate the masculine from the feminine and exclude the latter from philosophy. We can find further traces of this way of proceeding in discussions of personal identity if we focus on another curious feature of the persons around whom debate rages—their complete lack of any history or social context. As we have seen, the key question that concerns philosophers is what it takes for x at t_1 to survive at t_2. This assumes that we start out with a fully-fledged person, which is why I've called him Adam. And it assumes that in ordinary circumstances (if he doesn't die) he will survive until t_2. Philosophers who regard psychological continuity as what matters in survival thus assume that psychological continuity is a property of normal human beings.

To take it for granted that Adam at his creation is a person is to suppose that at that point he has both a body and a character—a suitably integrated set of memories, emotions, desires, and so on. The expectation that in normal circumstances he will survive to be expelled from Paradise has built into it the expectation that he possesses the means to maintain his character in some body or other, to satisfy the demands of psychological continuity. These are large assumptions which exclude a good deal. The first excludes the fact that character, in the sense of the ability to understand oneself as the subject of diverse psychological states, is not a birthright, but the fruit of a child's relations with the people who care for him or her. Theorists of personal identity appear to take a Lockean view of the genesis of character: once Adam is created, or once a baby reaches a certain stage, memory starts to roll and an integrated character develops. In doing so they exclude from consideration some of the ways in which the self is dependent on others, particularly on its mother figure. At the same time they make it unnecessary to consider whether features of the process by which the self is constituted may affect its subsequent continuity. The second assumption has complementary consequences: it brackets the question of whether the maintenance of psychological continuity also depends on social relations.

Particularly since Freud, writers have elaborated the view that a child's experiences are not initially integrated or continuous, and are not initially the experiences of an integrated self. The self for whom psychological continuity is a possibility has to be created through a series of interactions between the child, people around it, and the broader culture in which it lives. Equally, psychological continuity has to be sustained. Social circumstances may foster it; but where the recognition of others is withdrawn, our emotional investment in our memories and characters may be so weakened that we suffer a kind of depersonalization— an inability to feel that our experiences are our own, and a subsequent inability to integrate and order them. These finding have an impact on the personal identity theorist's assumption that bodily and psychological continuity are theoretically separable. They point to what is left out in the imaginary cases where it is assumed that psychological continuity would survive bodily transplant. Suppose we assume that psychological continuity does depend on the possession of a body image, and on an emotional investment in it. Is it now so obvious that the features of the body into which a character is transplanted are irrelevant to its survival? To dramatize the issue in a manner typical of this philosophical literature, what about a female fashion model whose character is transplanted into the body of a male garage mechanic? Might she not find it impossible to reconcile her body image with the body that had become hers, and suffer such a level of dislocation that she became unable to locate her experiences in that body? At the limit, might she not experience the depersonalization suffered by some psychotics, who lose interest in the whole body and do not invest any narcissistic libido in the body image? Their self-observations seem viewed from the perspective of the outsider and they display no interest in their own bodies (Grosz 1994, 76–77). Suppose, by contrast, we imagine a character whose body is transplanted into that of her identical twin. The point is that she remains psychologically continuous (if she does) because the body that is now hers has properties which make it possible for her to live in it as her own. Psychological continuity is not independent of the body. It is a feature of embodied selves.

If recognition makes a difference, the degree of a person's psychological continuity may also depend on social circumstances. To return to the case of the model, will her friends and lovers continue to recognize and affirm her? Will she be able to find anyone able to believe her story and hear her out? Anthony Quinton touches optimistically on the first point:

> In our general relations with other human beings their bodies are for the most part intrinsically unimportant. We use them as convenient recognition devices enabling us to locate the persisting characters and memory complexes ... which we love or like. It would be upsetting if a complex with which we were emotionally involved came to have a monstrous or repulsive physical appearance.... But that our concern and affection would follow the character and memory complex ... is surely clear. (Quinton 1975, 64)

Quinton is aware that this may not quite settle the argument, and addresses the looming objection that some personal relations, such as those "of a rather unmitigatedly sexual type" might not survive a change of body (Quinton 1975, 65). But here, too, he resolves the problem confidently:

> It can easily be shown that these objections are without substance. In the first place, even the most tired of entrepreneurs is going to take some note of the character and memories of the companion of his later nights at work. He will want her to be docile and quiet, perhaps, and to remember that he takes two parts of water to one of scotch, and no ice.... As a body she is simply an instrument of a particular type. (Quinton 1975, 65–66)

This solution to the problem employs the strategy we have already examined: it resolutely divides psychological properties from bodily ones and insists that the former are what matter in recognition. The wish to be loved for oneself alone and not for one's golden hair is simply granted. What this solution does not countenance, however, is the possibility that a person's ability to sustain psychological continuity may depend on other people recognizing and affirming the properties and potentialities of their embodied selves, and that where this possibility is removed, their psychological continuity may be damaged.

Marginalizing the Symbolically Feminine

We can now see more clearly that when personal identity theorists specify that characters are transplanted into bodies identical with the ones they had before, they are not introducing innocent simplifications. Instead, they are covering up and discounting ways in which psychological continuity is woven into the histories of our embodied selves. However, this is not the end of the matter. A theorist of personal identity may concede that psychological continuity has to be created, and that in extreme cases such as psychosis it can be destroyed. But he or she may nevertheless maintain that, in all ordinary cases, once psychological continuity is created, it survives. We see this, for example, in the testimony of the victims of extreme and extended trauma. While they may not remember much about their earlier lives, and may now lack well-defined characters, they identify with their past selves and speak about them in the first person (albeit sometimes rather oddly as when they say things like "I died there" or "I shall always miss myself as I was then"). We see it, too, in cases of physical mutilation where, although the body image usually takes some time to adjust, people do not lose all sense of who they are.[9] Only in pathological conditions such as psychosis and multiple personality does the self really fragment. So, putting these last cases aside, are we not right to posit a sense of psychological continuity which is independent of both bodily and social vicissitudes, or to imagine that this sense of continuity could survive if a character were transplanted from one body into another?

The arguments I have offered aim to show that, once we strip this imaginary situation of features which function to make it appear unproblematic, the kind of continuity that can be relied on is comparatively attenuated. All we are able to assume is that the transplanted character is able to locate its experiences in its new body, and that it remains sufficiently integrated to claim some memories as its own. We need not assume that it has much emotional investment in its memories. Nor need we assume much continuity of other character traits. Psychological continuity features here as a slender lifeline which enables the transplanted person to say to themselves "I know that such and such happened to me and that I am so and so" and just about believe it.

The personal identity theorist must be prepared to argue that this minimal level of continuity is sufficient to sustain the claim that we can fruitfully explore the question of what is involved in survival by playing off bodily and psychological continuity against one another. It seems to me, however, that the attractions of psychological continuity as a separable component of survival have been considerably reduced. Let me labor this point. Before, we were imagining that, transplanted into a new body, I would feel pretty much the same as I do now, would be able to continue the projects I have now, would be no less committed to my future than I am now, would have the memories and characteristics I now possess, and would retain the relations with other people that, so it seems to me, make life worth living. Now we imagine a situation in which it is much less clear what transplant will be like, and in which it may give rise to psychic and physical pain comparable, perhaps, to the pain of torture which looms so large in one of the problem cases constructed by Williams (Williams 1973, 48). I may lose many memories and character traits, so that my hold on my own past is tenuous and emotionally numbed, and my grasp of who I now am is fractured and confused. I may lose the affection and even recognition of the people who matter to me, and also the capacity to form new relationships. I may be unable to pursue my projects or embark on new ones, and may have very little emotional investment in the life I am living.

Some theorists of personal identity would, I suspect, insist that as long as there remains a thread of continuity between the pre- and post-transplant selves, we have a case for the conclusion that they are the same person. The barest "I" is enough to hold the self together and to underwrite an approach to the problem that separates psychological and bodily continuity. But in the light of the sorts of difficulties I have discussed it seems reasonable to ask: Why cling to this doctrine? Why deploy such resources of imagination to prize the bodily and the psychological apart? And why go to such lengths to protect psychological continuity from the effects of the body and the rest of the world?

At this point a reader might object that these questions misrepresent the current debate. Contemporary theorists of personal identity, it might be claimed, are by no means agreed that psychological continuity is essential, or even important, to personhood, and many of their accounts emphasize the centrality of the body. This is undoubtedly true. However, the approach I have been discussing is extremely influential, and continues to shape our understanding of what the problem of personal identity consists in.[10] As long as this much is conceded, the questions I have posed remain pertinent.

Feminists who have addressed these questions have frequently drawn on a conception of the self which is set over against, though not completely irreconcilable with, the view of personal identity we have been examining, insofar as it holds that there is an important aspect of the psyche, the unconscious, which this view neglects. To accept that the unconscious is at work when we philosophize is to accept that the psychological discontinuities so evident in pathological cases are present to some degree in all of us. Some aspects of the self are simply not picked up by accounts which emphasize psychological continuity, and the decision to discount these may itself have unconscious motivations. Taking the unconscious into account, then, feminist philosophers have explained the prominence of views which regard the body as unimportant to identity in various ways. Some have argued for the view that, in European culture, the mind is associated with masculinity and the body with femininity. One term can stand in for, or symbolize, the other. Philosophers (most of them men) have employed these associations. They have assumed (often unconsciously) that personal identity is male identity, and have developed accounts in which the symbolically masculine mind is given priority over the body (Lloyd 1984; Spelman 1982). Other writers have provided psychological explanations for this downgrading of the symbolically feminine. When male personal identity theorists construct imaginary examples which separate the bodily from the psychological, they resolve in fantasy the always-unresolved conflicts of the Oedipus complex—the separation of a male child from his mother figure, and his subsequent identification with his father. In establishing and maintaining a firm boundary between the maternal body and the paternal mind, they deny their own unconscious desire to be reunited with the mother figure. And in fixing on psychological continuity as the mark of identity, they construct a picture in which masculinity and selfhood coincide.[11] A further aspect of the transplant fantasy also serves to exclude the feminine. By positing fully-fledged persons whose history is irrelevant to the problem at hand, male philosophers imagine for themselves a condition of self-sufficiency, from which their indebtedness to a mother figure, or indeed to anyone else, is excluded.

These two types of explanation (one cultural, the other psychological) have a good deal in common. Both rest on the claim that philosophers (male and female) are themselves psychologically discontinuous, in the commonplace sense that their unconscious fears and desires play a part in determining the way they formulate and argue about problems, and the sorts of arguments they find persuasive, although this is not an aspect of their philosophizing over which they have conscious control. Moreover, both assume that particular associations at work in our culture continue to play a significant part in shaping our philosophical beliefs. According to the first kind of view, symbolic associations help to explain the fact that we privilege some terms over others. According to the second, these symbolic associations are themselves embedded in the psychological processes that form sexual identity.

Over the last two decades, feminist philosophers have amassed a range of evidence for both the explanatory hypotheses I have sketched. However, it remains to ask what internal support we can find for the view that theorists who equate personal identity with psychological continuity are upholding (however unconsciously) a masculine conception of identity. I have assumed, uncontentiously I hope, that we sometimes find clues to the unconscious in questions that hover round the margins of a text, so that when Williams or Noonan allows that transplant from one body into a very different one might be difficult, and then immediately put the problem aside, it is probably worth looking further.[12] I have also assumed—and Williams and Quinton make this explicit—that what they are putting aside here is the issue of sexual identity.[13] To return to the fantasy of character transplant, there are in principle a variety of ways of thinking about the case of a male character transplanted into a female body. Maybe it would be the ideal sex-change operation. Maybe it would condemn the resulting person to the unhappy condition of someone who desperately wants a sex-change operation. Maybe it would produce psychological breakdown. As we have seen, most writers block off exploration of lines of thought like these, which require us to think of the people concerned as embodied, in their investigations of personal identity. Why? Perhaps because they take it that the identity of a person is the identity of a male. Perhaps because an unconscious fear of jeopardizing their sexual identity prevents them from doing so, and helps to direct them toward an approach which brackets the body and concentrates on the mind.

It may be helpful to consider what kinds of criticism I have offered of the view that personal identity consists in psychological continuity. In the preceding sections of this chapter I have voiced some objections to this analysis which *can* be assessed independently of any claims about gender as arguments to the effect that authors who appeal to a particular kind of thought experiment rely on an inadequate conception of the self. Not only do the limitations of the conception they employ undermine the particular conclusions they draw from their thought experiments, but their very approach, which works with an oversimplified conception of memory, neglects the social construction of the self, and is insensitive to the ways in which selves are embodied. At the same time, however, I have claimed that the issue of gender is woven into arguments which rely on fantasies of brain transplant, and to bring this out I have asked what is going on when philosophers advance them. What is being said, explicitly and implicitly, and why? One of the things going on, so I have suggested, is that a symbolically masculine account of identity is being unselfconsciously articulated. A skeptically inclined reader may still wish to ask whether this diagnosis amounts to a criticism beyond those set out in the first part of the chapter. What is wrong with the symbolically masculine account, other than the fact that it suffers from the deficiencies just summarized?

To answer this question, it is helpful to distinguish the type of criticism which pinpoints a particular flaw in a position from the type which indicates the shortcomings of an approach. The diagnosis I have offered is of the latter kind. Its critical force rests on the assumptions that we are in search of philosophical interpretations that answer to our experience and acknowledge the complexity of our lives, and that, in the case of personal identity, part of this complexity lies in sexual identity. Theories which neglect or disavow sexual difference therefore cut themselves off from an important set of issues, and in doing so render themselves philosophically impoverished. To show how this occurs is not, of course, to specify what a feminist analysis of personal identity would be like, or to explore how a focus on sexual difference alters our understanding of the relation between personhood and embodiment, though many of the works cited throughout the chapter undertake these very tasks. My aim has been to articulate some of the features of an analytical approach to personal identity which leave feminist philosophers dissatisfied, and which explain the fact that their work has developed in different directions.

Identity and Social Power

The symbolic gendering of the opposition between body and mind, on which I have so far concentrated, has provided an exceptionally fruitful focus for feminist research. Nevertheless, it is important not to assume too readily that the body always figures as feminine and the mind as masculine, or to take it for granted that gender is exclusively associated with these terms.[14] Some theorists, I have been arguing, locate personal identity in a mind which they interpret as masculine; but there is also evidence that a man's continuing identity is sometimes implicitly understood to depend on his ability to control a woman. Here the issue is not how the "components" of a person are gendered, but how the relations between people of different sexes bear on the problem of identity. If social relations can secure or destroy continuing identity, as I suggested earlier on, they will provide another area in which identity and gender intertwine.

This motif is central to some works of literature. For example, in Janet Lewis's novella The Wife of Martin Guerre, Martin Guerre leaves his village and family and does not come back (Lewis 1977). Eight years later he returns—or rather, an impostor arrives, who slips into Guerre's place and takes up the life he had left behind. Some time goes by before Guerre's wife, tortured by the belief that the impostor is not her husband, and that she is an adulteress, confesses her suspicions, and the impostor is brought to trial. Just as judgment is about to be announced, the original Martin Guerre walks into the courtroom, and the impostor is punished with death.

In this narrative, it becomes important to establish the impostor's identity because he is usurping Guerre's sexual rights over his wife, or to put it another way, because Guerre has lost control over her. She is out of his control, and her independence of him is part of what threatens to obliterate Guerre's social identity, insofar as it is one of the conditions that allow the impostor to "become" him. The trial restores both Guerre's identity and sexual order.

We find the same link between identity and male sexual power in Honoré de Balzac's story about Colonel Chabert, who, when the tale begins, has been listed among the casualties of Napoleon's Russian Campaign (Balzac 1961). His name has appeared on the list of valiant heroes who sacrificed their lives for France, his wife has remarried, and his house has been sold. But in fact the Colonel has survived, and after several years returns to Paris, determined to reclaim his wife. Once again, loss of identity is linked to loss of control over a woman, and his desire to have his wife back is what drives the Colonel to explain his plight to a young lawyer, who takes up his case and tries to negotiate a settlement. In the course of the negotiations the Colonel comes to see that his wife is a ruthless and avaricious woman who will never return to him, and has never loved him anyway, and renounces his desire to reclaim her. But the recognition that he cannot possess her destroys him, and in the final scene the lawyer comes across him, unkempt and listless, sitting on a log beside the road staring vacantly into space. Here, loss of power over a woman is associated not just with loss of social identity but with psychological discontinuity. To be sure, Colonel Chabert is deprived of his social identity; but he loses more than this, and although the man sitting on the log may know who he is, his discontinuity with his past self prevents him from functioning.

When theorists of personal identity focus on psychological continuity as the stronghold of the self, and construe psychological continuity as independent of bodily continuity, they secure only a self which would in other circumstances be regarded as pathologically disturbed. This is, to be sure, a self of sorts, and one consonant with the problem "What is it to survive?" which already carries connotations of minimal continuity, of enduring against the odds and in the face of obstacles. Perhaps the question we should be addressing, then, is why the analytical philosophical tradition has been so concerned to explore and defend this minimal notion of survival, and hence personhood. Part of the explanation, I have suggested, lies in cultural constructions of masculinity and femininity which are at work in the unconscious, and consequently in philosophy. At the heart of identity lies the issue of sexual identity, and with it the desire of a male-dominated tradition to secure the masculinity of the subject and the subordination of women. This commonplace drama is played out in various philosophical arenas, but is worked through with particular intensity in the problem of identity itself.

Notes

1. This chapter was previously published in *The Cambridge Companion to Feminism in Philosophy*, edited by Miranda Fricker and Jennifer Hornsby, 29–48 (Cambridge: Cambridge University Press, 2000). It is reprinted here with abridgements and slight modifications with the permission of the author and press. Many helpful comments were made on an earlier draft of this chapter. I am grateful to the contributors to the conference "Feminism and the Philosophy of Mind" held at the University of London; to the Philosophy Department seminars at University College Dublin and at the University of York; and to John Dupré, Miranda Fricker, Jennifer Hornsby, Moira Gatens, Kathleen Lennon, Quentin Skinner, and Catherine Wilson.

2. See Merchant (1980), Spelman (1982), Lloyd (1984, 1993), Keller (1985), Irigaray (1985), Le Dœuff (1980), Chanter (1995), and Deutscher (1997).

3. Such reconceptualizations especially drawing on psychoanalytic theories include Mitchell (1974), Gallop (1982), Brennan (1989, 1992), Benjamin (1990), and Grosz (1994).

4. See, for example, Braidotti (1994), Butler (1990), Gatens (1996), Grosz (1994), and Young (1990).

5. For further discussion, see the articles collected in Noonan (1993).

6. See also Parfit (1984, 205).

7. The present section and the next are deeply indebted to Brison's chapter. For discussion of some closely related issues, see Campbell (1997, 51–62).

8. Writers on personal identity usually try to take account of the loops, breaks and fade-outs in our memories by emphasizing that psychological continuity requires only a sequence of overlapping sequences. Furthermore, it is added that where memory breaks down, other continuities such as those in a person's desires, intentions, or hopes can take over. However, Brison's discussion shows that trauma victims do not just lose their memories of past events or actions. They lose the pattern of memory in which their expectations, emotions, skills, desires, and so on are rooted, so that loss of memory is, in these cases, part of a broader destruction of character.

9. See, for example, the discussion of phantom limbs in Schilder (1978, 64).

10. With some exceptions—see, for example, the animalist views defended in Olson (1997) and Snowdon (1995)—even philosophers who do not regard psychological continuity as essential to personal identity continue to treat the body as a container for the mind.

11. There are several variants of this view. For discussion of Freud, see Mitchell (1974) and Gallop (1982); on object relations theory, see Benjamin (1990); and for the view that these patterns of development are to be explained by child-rearing practices, see Chodorow (1978).

12. For discussion of this view, see Le Dœuff (1980) and Deutscher (1997).

13. At the same time, they are implicitly putting aside other dimensions of identity, for instance racial identity, which may be intimately connected to the body.

14. For a particularly helpful discussion of these instabilities, see Deutscher (1997).

References

Balzac, Honoré de. 1961. *Le Colonel Chabert.* Edited by M. Didier. Paris: Société des textes français modernes.

Benjamin, Jessica. 1990. *The Bonds of Love: Psychoanalysis, Feminism and the Problem of Domination.* London: Virago.

Braidotti, Rosi. 1994. *Nomadic Subjects.* New York: Columbia University Press.

Brennan, Teresa, ed. 1989. *Between Feminism and Psychoanalysis.* London: Routledge.

Brennan, Teresa. 1992. *The Interpretation of the Flesh: Freud and Femininity.* Routledge: London.

Butler, Judith. 1990. *Gender Trouble: Feminism and Subversion of Identity.* London: Routledge.

Campbell, Sue. 1997. *Interpreting the Personal: Expression and the Formation of Feelings.* Ithaca: Cornell University Press.

Chanter, Tina. 1995. *Ethics of Eros: Irigaray's Rewriting of the Philosophers.* London: Routledge.

Chodorow, Nancy. 1978. *The Reproduction of Mothering.* Berkeley: University of California Press.

Deutscher, Penelope. 1997. *Yielding Gender: Feminism, Deconstruction and the History of Philosophy.* London: Routledge.

Gatens, Moira. 1996. *Imaginary Bodies.* London: Routledge.

Grosz, Elizabeth. 1994. *Volatile Bodies.* Bloomington: Indiana University Press.

Irigaray, Luce. 1985. *An Ethics of Sexual Difference.* Translated by Carolyn Burke and Gillian C. Gill. Ithaca: Cornell University Press.

Keller, Evelyn Fox. 1985. *Reflections on Gender and Science.* New Haven: Yale University Press.

Le Dœuff, Michèle. 1980. *The Philosophical Imaginary.* London: Athlone.

Lloyd, Genevieve. 1984. *The Man of Reason: "Male" and "Female" in Western Philosophy.* London: Methuen.

Lloyd, Genevieve. 1993. "Maleness, Metaphor and the 'Crisis' of Reason." In *A Mind of One's Own: Feminist Essays on Reason and Objectivity,* edited by Louise M. Antony and Charlotte Witt, 69–83. Boulder, CO: Westview Press.

Lewis, David. 1983. "Survival and Identity." In *Philosophical Papers, Volume 1* by David Lewis, 55–72. Oxford: Oxford University Press.

Lewis, Janet. 1977. *The Wife of Martin Guerre.* Harmondsworth: Penguin.

Merchant, Carolyn. 1980. *The Death of Nature: Women, Ecology and the Scientific Revolution.* San Francisco: Harper & Row.

Mitchell, Juliet. 1974. *Psychoanalysis and Feminism.* Harmondsworth: Penguin.

Noonan, Harold. 1989. *Personal Identity.* London: Routledge.

Olson, Eric. 1997. *The Human Animal: Personal Identity without Psychology.* Oxford: Oxford University Press.

Parfit, Derek. 1971. "Personal Identity." *Philosophical Review* 80 (1): 3–27.

Parfit, Derek. 1984. *Reasons and Persons.* Oxford: Clarendon Press.

Quinton, Anthony. 1975. "The Soul." In *Personal Identity,* edited by J. Perry, 53–72. Berkeley: University of California Press.

Schilder, Paul. 1978. *The Image and Appearance of the Human Body.* New York: International Universities Press.

Shoemaker, Sydney. 1963. *Self-Knowledge and Self-Identity*. Ithaca: Cornell University Press.

Shoemaker, Sydney. 1984. "Personal Identity: A Materialist View." In *Personal Identity* by Sydney Shoemaker and Richard Swinburne, 67–132. Oxford: Blackwell.

Snowdon, Paul. 1995. "Persons, Animals and Bodies." In *The Body and the Self*, edited by José Luis Bermudez, Naomi Eilan, and Anthony Marcel, 71–86. Cambridge, MA: MIT Press.

Spelman, Elizabeth. 1982. "Woman as Body: Ancient and Contemporary Views." *Feminist Studies* 8 (1): 109–31.

Wiggins, David. 1976. "Locke, Butler and the Stream of Consciousness: And Men as a Natural Kind." *Philosophy* 51 (196): 131–158.

Williams, Bernard. 1973. *Problems of the Self*. Cambridge: Cambridge University Press.

Young, Iris Marion. 1990. "Throwing Like a Girl: A Phenomenology of Feminine Body Comportment, Motility, and Spatiality." In *Throwing Like a Girl and Other Essays in Feminist Philosophy and Social Theory* by Iris Marion Young, 141–59. Bloomington: Indiana University Press.

PART III
NATURALISM AND NORMATIVITY

9

Sexual Ideology and Phenomenological Description

A Feminist Critique of Merleau-Ponty's *Phenomenology of Perception*

Judith Butler

Theories of sexuality which tend to impute natural ends to sexual desire are very often part of a more general discourse on the legitimate locations of gender and desire within a given social context.[1] The appeal to a natural desire and, as a corollary, a natural form of human sexual relationships is thus invariably normative, for those forms of desire and sexuality which fall outside the parameters of the natural model are understood as unnatural and, hence, without the legitimation that a natural and normative model confers. Although Maurice Merleau-Ponty does not write his theory of sexuality within an explicitly political framework, he nevertheless offers certain significant arguments against naturalistic accounts of sexuality that are useful to any explicit political effort to refute restrictively normative views of sexuality. In arguing that sexuality is coextensive with existence, that it is a mode of dramatizing and investigating a concrete historical situation, Merleau-Ponty appears to offer feminist theory a view of sexuality freed of naturalistic ideology, one which restores both the historical and volitional components of sexual experience and, consequently, opens the way for a fuller description of sexuality and sexual diversity.

In the section of Merleau-Ponty's *Phenomenology of Perception* entitled "The Body in Its Sexual Being," the body is termed a "historical idea" rather than "a natural species" (Merleau-Ponty 1962, 170). Significantly, Simone de Beauvoir takes up this claim in *The Second Sex*, quoting Merleau-Ponty to the effect that woman, like man, is a historical construction bearing no natural telos, a field of possibilities that are taken up and actualized in various distinctive ways (Beauvoir 1953, 38). To understand the construction of gender, it is not necessary to discover a normative model against which individual instances can be gauged, but, rather, to delimit the field of historical possibilities which constitute this gender, and to examine in detail the *acts* by which these possibilities are appropriated, dramatized, and ritualized. For Merleau-Ponty, the body is a "place of appropriation"

Judith Butler, *Sexual Ideology and Phenomenological Description* In: *Feminist Philosophy of Mind*.
Edited by: Keya Maitra and Jennifer McWeeny, Oxford University Press. © Oxford University Press 2022.
DOI: 10.1093/oso/9780190867614.003.0010

and a mechanism of "transformation" and "conversion," an essentially dramatic structure which can be "read" in terms of the more general life that it embodies. As a result, the body cannot be conceived of as a static or univocal fact of existence, but, rather, as a modality of existence, the "place" in which possibilities are realized and dramatized, the individualized appropriation of a more general historical experience.

And yet, the potential openness of Merleau-Ponty's theory of sexuality is deceptive. Despite his efforts to the contrary, Merleau-Ponty offers descriptions of sexuality which turn out to contain tacit normative assumptions about the heterosexual character of sexuality. Not only does he assume that sexual relations are heterosexual, but that the masculine sexuality is characterized by a disembodied gaze that subsequently defines its object as mere body. Indeed, as we shall see, Merleau-Ponty conceptualizes the sexual relation between men and women on the model of master and slave. And although he generally tends to discount natural structures of sexuality, he manages to reify cultural relations between the sexes on a different basis by calling them "essential" or "metaphysical." Hence, Merleau-Ponty's theory of sexuality and sexual relations at once liberates and forecloses the cultural possibility of benign sexual variation. Insofar as feminist theory seeks to dislodge sexuality from those reifying ideologies which freeze sexual relations into "natural" forms of domination, it has both something to gain and something to fear from Merleau-Ponty's theory of sexuality.

Merleau-Ponty's Criticisms of Reductive Psychology

In arguing that "sexuality is coextensive with existence," Merleau-Ponty refutes those theoretical efforts to isolate sexuality as a "drive" or a biological given of existence. Sexuality cannot be reduced to a specific set of drives or activities, but must be understood as subtending all our modes of engagement in the world. As an inexorable "aura" and "odor," sexuality is an essentially malleable quality, a mode of embodying a certain existential relation to the world, and the specific modality of dramatizing that relation in corporeal terms. According to Merleau-Ponty, there are two prominent theoretical attitudes toward sexuality which are fundamentally mistaken. The one regards sexuality as a composite set of drives which occupy some interior biological space and which, consequent to the emergence of these drives into conscious experience, become attached to representations. This contingent relation between drive and representation results in the figuration of drives as "blind" or motored by an internal teleology or naturalistic mechanism. The objects to which they become attached are only arbitrary foci for these drives, occasions or conditions for their release and gratification, and the entire life of the drive takes place within a solipsistic framework.

The other theory posits sexuality as an ideational layer which is projected onto the world, a representation which is associated with certain stimuli and which, through habit, we come to affirm as the proper domain of sexuality. In the first instance, the reality of sexuality resides in a set of drives which pre-exist their representation, and in the second case, the reality of sexuality is a production of representation, a habit of association, a mental construction. In both cases, we can see that there is no intentional relation between what is called a "drive" and its "representation." As intentional, the drive would be referential from the outset; it could only be understood in the context of its concrete actualization in the world, as a mode of expressing, dramatizing, and embodying an existential relation to the world. In the above two cases, however, sexuality is solipsistic rather than referential, a self-enclosed phenomenon which signals a rupture between sexuality and existence. As a drive, sexuality is "about" its own biological necessity, and as a representation, it is a mere construct which has no necessary relation to the world upon which it is imposed. For Merleau-Ponty, sexuality must be intentional in the sense that it modalizes a relationship between an embodied subject and a concrete situation: "bodily existence continually sets the prospect of living before me. . . . [M]y body . . . is also what opens me out upon the world and places me in a situation there" (Merleau-Ponty 1962, 165).

Written in 1945, *Phenomenology of Perception* offered an appraisal of psychoanalytic theory both appreciative and critical. On the one hand, Freud's contention that sexuality pervades mundane existence and structures human life from its inception is accepted and reformulated by Merleau-Ponty in the latter's claim that sexuality is coextensive with existence. And yet, in Merleau-Ponty's description of psychoanalysis, we can discern the terms of his own phenomenological revision of that method. Note in the following how Freud's theory of sexuality comes to serve the phenomenological and existential program:

> For Freud himself the sexual is not the genital, sexual life is not a mere effect of the processes having their seat in the genital organs, the libido is not an instinct, that is, an activity naturally directed towards definite ends, it is the general power, which the psychosomatic subject employs, of taking root in different settings, of establishing himself through different experiences. . . . It is what causes a man [*sic*] to have a history. In so far as a man's [*sic*] sexual history provides a key to his life, it is because in his sexuality is projected his manner of being towards the world, that is, towards time and other men [*sic*]. (Merleau-Ponty 1962, 158)

Merleau-Ponty's presumption that the Freudian libido is "not an instinct" does not take into account Freud's long-standing ambivalence toward a theory of instinctual sexuality, evident in the 1915 essay, "Instincts and Their

Vicissitudes" (1976), in *Beyond the Pleasure Principle* (1950), and in his later speculative writings (1961). Unclear, for instance, is how strictly Freud maintained the distinction between drive (*Trieb*) and instinct (*Instinkt*), and the extent to which drives are viewed as a necessary mythology or part of the framework of naturalistic ideology. Freud's theory of psychosexual development very often relies on a naturalistic theory of drives whereby the normal development of a sexual drive culminates in the restriction of erotogenic zones to the genital and the normative valorization of heterosexual coitus. Although complicated and varied in its methodological style, Freud's book *Three Essays on the Theory of Sexuality* nevertheless tends to subject the analysis of the body in situation to a description of the internal teleology of instincts which has both a natural and normal life of its own (Freud 1962).[2] Indeed, as a drive which develops along natural and normal lines, sexuality is figured as precisely the kind of naturalistic construction that Merleau-Ponty views as contrary to his intentional view. And as a "psychical representative of an endosomatic, continuously flowing source of stimulation," the sexual drive is precisely the kind of arbitrary construct that Merleau-Ponty also wants to repudiate (Freud 1962, 34).

But even more curious is Merleau-Ponty's attribution to Freud of a unified agent whose reflexive acts are manifest in his/her sexual life. In arguing that "the psychosomatic subject" takes root and establishes him/herself in different settings and situations, Merleau-Ponty glosses over the psychoanalytic critique of the conscious subject as a product of unconscious desires and the mechanism of repression. In effect, Merleau-Ponty assimilates the psychoanalytic subject to a reflexive Cartesian ego, a position that psychoanalytic theory sought to criticize as much more limited in its autonomy than rationalist philosophy had presumed.

In light of Merleau-Ponty's curious appropriation of psychoanalysis, it seems clear that he rejects any account of sexuality which relies upon causal factors understood to precede the concrete situation of the individual, whether those factors are natural or unconscious. Moreover, he refuses to accept any normative conception of sexuality such that particular social organizations of sexuality appear either more normal or more natural than others. We will later see, however, that while he does not assert such a telos, he nevertheless assumes one at various crucial points in the theory. Despite the alleged openness and malleability of sexuality in Merleau-Ponty's view, certain structures emerge as existential and metaphysical necessities which ultimately cast doubt upon Merleau-Ponty's nonnormative pretensions. Indeed, despite his trenchant critique of naturalistic accounts of sexuality, it becomes unclear whether Merleau-Ponty is himself wholly freed of naturalistic ideology.

The Constitution of Sexuality: Nature, History, and Existence

For Merleau-Ponty, the various expressions of human sexuality constitute possibilities arising from bodily existence in general; none can claim ontological priority over any other. Sexuality is discussed in general terms as a mode of situating oneself in terms of one's intersubjectivity. Little more is said, not because Merleau-Ponty thinks sexuality is abstract, but because the multifarious expressions of sexuality have only these expressive and intersubjective qualities in common. In its fundamental structure, sexuality is both reflexive and corporeal and signifies a relation between the embodied subject and others. The individual who is clinically considered asexual is misunderstood by the vocabulary that names him or her; "asexuality" reveals a definite sexual orientation, what Merleau-Ponty describes as "a way of life—an attitude of escapism and need of solitude—... a generalized expression of a certain state of sexuality.... [T]he fact remains that this existence is the act of taking up and making explicit a sexual situation" (Merleau-Ponty 1962, 169). On the other hand, sexuality is never experienced in a pure form such that a purely sexual state can be achieved: "Even if I become absorbed in the experience of my own body and in the solitude of sensations, I do not succeed in abolishing all reference of my life to a world. At every moment some intention springs afresh from me" (Merleau-Ponty 1962, 165).

As "a current of existence," sexuality has no necessary forms, but presents itself as having-to-be-formed. Sexuality is not a choice inasmuch as it is a necessary expression of bodily existence and the necessary medium of "choice." In opposition to Jean-Paul Sartre's claim in *Being and Nothingness* that the body represents a factic limitation to choice, the constraining material perspective, Merleau-Ponty argues that the body is itself a modality of reflexivity, a specifically corporeal agency. In this sense, then, sexuality cannot be said to "represent" existential choices which are themselves pre- or non-sexual, for sexuality is an irreducible modality of choice. And yet, Merleau-Ponty acknowledges that sexuality cannot be restricted to the various reflexive acts that it modalizes; sexuality is always there, as the medium for existential projects, as the ceaseless "current" of existence. Indeed, in the following, Merleau-Ponty appears to invest sexuality with powers that exceed those of the individual existence which gives it form:

> Why is our body for us the mirror of our being, unless it is a natural self, a current of given existence, with the result that we never know whether the forces that bear on us are its or ours—or with the result rather that they are never entirely either its or ours. There is no outstripping of sexuality any more than there is any sexuality enclosed within itself. (Merleau-Ponty 1962, 171)

This "natural" current is thus taken up through the concrete acts and gestures of embodied subjects and given concrete form, and this form thus becomes its specific historical expression. Thus, sexuality only becomes historical through individual acts of appropriation, "the permanent act[s] by which man [sic] takes up, for his own purposes, and makes his own a certain de facto situation" (Merleau-Ponty 1962, 172).

Here it is clear that while each individual confronts a natural sexuality and a concrete existential situation, that situation does not include the history of sexuality, the legacy of its conventions and taboos. It seems we must ask whether individuals do not confront a *sedimented* sexuality, and if so, are not the individual acts of appropriation less transformations of a natural sexuality into a historically specific sexuality than the transformation of past culture into present culture? It is unclear that we could ever confront a "natural" sexuality which was not already mediated by language and acculturation and, hence, it makes sense to ask whether the sexuality we do confront is always already partially formed. Merleau-Ponty is doubtless right in claiming that there is no outstripping sexuality, that it is there, always to be reckoned with in one way or another, but there seems no *prima facie* reason to assume that its inexorability is at once its naturalness. Perhaps it is simply the case that a specific formation of culturally constructed sexuality has come to *appear* as natural.

According to his own arguments, it would seem that Merleau-Ponty would discount the possibility of a subject in confrontation with a natural sexuality. In his words, "there is history only for a subject who lives through it, and a subject only insofar as he is historically situated" (Merleau-Ponty 1962, 173). Yet, to say that the subject is historically situated in a loose sense is to say only that the decisions a subject makes are delimited—not exclusively constituted—by a given set of historical possibilities. A stronger version of historical situatedness would locate history as the very condition for the constitution of the subject, not only as a set of external possibilities for choice. If this stronger version were accepted, Merleau-Ponty's above claim with regard to a natural sexuality would be reversed: individual existence does not bring natural sexuality into the historical world, but history provides the conditions for the conceptualization of the individual as such. Moreover, sexuality is itself formed through the sedimentation of the history of sexuality, and the embodied subject, rather than an existential constant, is itself partially constituted by the legacy of sexual relations which constitute its situation.

Merleau-Ponty's anthropological naiveté emerges in his view of how cultural conventions determine how the lived body is culturally reproduced. He distinguishes, mistakenly I believe, between biological subsistence and the domain of historical and cultural signification: " 'living' (*leben*) is a primary process from which, as a starting point, it becomes possible to 'live' (*erleben*) this or that

world, and we must eat and breathe before perceiving and awakening to relational living, belonging to colours and lights through sight, to sounds through
hearing, to the body of another through sexuality, before arriving at the life of
human relations" (Merleau-Ponty 1962, 160). When we consider, however, the
life of the infant as immediately bound up in a set of relationships whereby it
receives food, shelter, and warmth, it becomes impossible to separate the fact of
biological subsistence from the various ways in which that subsistence is admin-
istered and assured. Indeed, the very birth of the child is already a human relation, one of radical dependence, which takes place within a set of institutional
regulations and norms. In effect, it is unclear that there can be a state of sheer
subsistence divorced from a particular organization of human relationships.
Economic anthropologists have made the point various times that subsistence
is not prior to culture, that eating and sleeping and sexuality are inconceivable
apart from the various social forms through which these activities are ritualized
and regulated.

In accounting for the genesis of sexual desire, Merleau-Ponty once again
reverts to a naturalistic account which seems to contradict his own phenomenological procedure. In the following, he attributes the emergence of sexuality
to the purely organic function of the body: "there must be, immanent in sexual
life, some function which insures its emergence, and the normal extension of
sexuality must rest on internal powers of the organic subject. There must be Eros
or Libido which breathes life into an original world" (Merleau-Ponty 1962, 156).
Once again, it appears that sexuality emerges prior to the influence of historical and cultural factors. And yet, theorists such as Michel Foucault have argued
that cultural conventions dictate not only when sexuality becomes explicit, but
also in what form. What leads Merleau-Ponty, then, to safeguard this aspect of
sexuality as prior to culture and history? What dimensions of "natural" sexuality does Merleau-Ponty wish to preserve such that he is willing to contradict
his own methodology in the ways that he has? Although Merleau-Ponty is clearly
concerned with sexuality as the dramatic embodiment of existential themes, he
distinguishes between those existential themes that are purely individual, and
those that are shared and intersubjective. Indeed, it appears, for him, that sexuality dramatizes certain existential themes that are universal in character, and
which, we will see, dictate certain forms of domination between the sexes as
"natural" expressions of sexuality.

Misogyny as an Intrinsic Structure of Perception

Not only does Merleau-Ponty fail to acknowledge the extent to which sexuality is
culturally constructed, but his descriptions of the universal features of sexuality

reproduce certain cultural constructions of sexual normalcy. The case of the sexually disinterested Schneider is a rich example. In introducing the reader to Schneider, Merleau-Ponty refers to his "sexual incapacity," and throughout the discussion it is assumed that Schneider's state is abnormal. The evidence that Merleau-Ponty provides in support of this contention is considered to be obvious: "Obscene pictures, conversations on sexual topics, the sight of a body do not arouse desire in him" (Merleau-Ponty 1962, 155). One wonders what kind of cultural presumptions would make arousal in such contexts seem utterly normal. Certainly, these pictures, conversations, and perceptions already designate a concrete cultural situation, one in which the masculine subject is figured as viewer, and the yet unnamed feminine subject is the body to be seen.

In Merleau-Ponty's view, evidence of Schneider's "sexual inertia" is to be found in a general lack of sexual tenacity and willfulness. Deemed abnormal because he "no longer seeks sexual intercourse of his own accord," Schneider is subject to the clinical expectation that sexual intercourse is intrinsically desirable regardless of the concrete situation, the other person involved, the desires and actions of that other person. Assuming that certain acts necessitate a sexual response, Merleau-Ponty notes that Schneider "hardly ever kisses, and the kiss for him has no value as sexual stimulation. . . . If orgasm occurs first in the partner and she moves away, the half-fulfilled desire vanishes"; this gesture of deference signifies masculine "incapacity," as if the normal male would seek satisfaction regardless of the desires of his female partner (Merleau-Ponty 1962, 155).

Central to Merleau-Ponty's assessment of Schneider's sexuality as abnormal is the presumption that the decontextualized female body, the body alluded to in conversation, the anonymous body which passes by on the street, exudes a natural attraction. This is a body rendered irreal, the focus of solipsistic fantasy and projection; indeed, this is a body that does not *live*, but a frozen image which does not resist or interrupt the course of masculine desire through an unexpected assertion of life. How does this eroticization of the decontextualized body become reconciled with Merleau-Ponty's insistence that "what we try to possess is not just a body, but a body brought to life by consciousness" (Merleau-Ponty 1962, 167)?

Viewed as an expression of sexual ideology, *Phenomenology of Perception* reveals the cultural construction of the masculine subject as a strangely disembodied voyeur whose sexuality is strangely non-corporeal. Significant, I think, is the prevalence of visual metaphors in Merleau-Ponty's descriptions of normal sexuality. Erotic experience is almost never described as tactile or physical or even passionate.[3] Although Merleau-Ponty explains that "perception" for him signifies affective life in general, it appears that the meaning of perception occasionally reverts to its original denotation of sight. Indeed, it sometimes appears as if sexuality itself were reduced to the erotics of the gaze. Consider the following: "In the case of the normal subject, a body is not perceived merely as an object; this objective perception has within it a more intimate perception: the visible body is subtended by a sexual schema which is strictly individual, emphasizing the erogenous areas, outlining a sexual physiognomy, and eliciting the gestures of the masculine body which is itself integrated into this emotional totality" (Merleau-Ponty 1962, 156).

As Merleau-Ponty notes, the schema subtending the body emphasizes the erogenous zones, but it remains unclear whether the "erogenous areas" are erogenous to the perceiving subject or to the subject perceived. Perhaps it is significant that Merleau-Ponty fails to make the distinction, for as long as the erotic experience belongs exclusively to the perceiving subject, it is of no consequence whether the experience is shared by the subject perceived. The paragraph begins with the clear distinction between a perception which objectifies and decontextualizes the body and a perception which is "more intimate," which makes of the body more than "an object." The schema constitutes the intimate perception, and yet, as the schema unfolds, we realize that as a focusing on erogenous parts it consists in a further decontextualization and fragmentation of the perceived body. Indeed, the "intimate" perception further denies a world or context for this body, but reduces the body to its erogenous (to whom?) parts. Hence, the body is objectified more drastically by the sexual schema than by the objective perception.

Only at the close of the paragraph do we discover that the "normal subject" is male, and "the body" he perceives is female. Moreover, the sexual physiognomy of the female body "elicit[s] the gestures of the masculine body," as if the very existence of these attributes "provoked" or even necessitated certain kinds of sexual gestures on the part of the male. Here it seems that the masculine subject has not only projected his own desire onto the female body, but then has accepted that projection as the very structure of the body he perceives. Here the solipsistic circle of the masculine voyeur seems complete. That the masculine body is regarded as "integrated into this emotional totality" appears as a bizarre conclusion considering that his sole function has been to fulfill a spectatorial mode.

In contrast to this normal male subject is Schneider, for whom it is said "a woman's body has no particular essence." Nothing about the purely physical construction of the female body arouses Schneider: "It is, he says, predominantly character which makes a woman attractive, for physically they are all the same" (Merleau-Ponty 1962, 156). For Merleau-Ponty, the female body has an "essence" to be found in the "schema" that invariably elicits the gestures of masculine desire, and although he does not claim that this perception is conditioned by a natural or mechanistic causality, it appears to have the same necessity that such explanations usually afford. Indeed, it is difficult to understand how Merleau-Ponty, on other occasions in the text, makes general claims about bodies which starkly contradict his specific claims about women's bodies, unless by "the body" he means the male body, just as earlier the "normal subject" turned out to be male. At various points, he remarks that "bodily existence . . .is only the barest raw material of a genuine presence in the world," a "presence" which one might assume to be the origin of attractiveness, rather than the sexual schema taken alone (Merleau-Ponty 1962, 165). And rather than posit the body as containing an "essence," he remarks that "the body expresses existence" (Merleau-Ponty 1962, 166). To maintain, then, that the female body has an essence qua female and that this essence is to be found in the body contradicts his more general claim that "the body expresses total existence, not because it is an external accompaniment to that existence, but because existence comes to its own in the body" (Merleau-Ponty 1962, 166). And yet, female bodies appear to have an essence which is itself physical, and this essence designates the female body as an object rather than a subject of perception. Indeed, the female body is seemingly never a subject, but always denotes an always already fixed essence rather than an open existence. She is, in effect, already formed, while the male subject is in exclusive control of the constituting gaze. She is never seeing, always seen. If the female body denotes an essence, while bodies in general denote existence, then it appears that bodies in general must be male—and existence does not belong to women.

That Schneider finds only women with character arousing is taken as proof that he suffers from a sublimation of his true desires, that he has rationalized the object of his desire as a bearer of virtue. That Schneider conflates a moral and a sexual discourse is, for Merleau-Ponty, evidence of repression, and yet it may be that after all Schneider is more true to Merleau-Ponty's phenomenological account of bodily existence than Merleau-Ponty himself. By refusing to endow a woman with an essence, Schneider reaffirms the woman's body as an expression of existence, a "presence" in the world. Her body is not taken as a physical and interchangeable fact, but expressive of the life of consciousness. Hence, it appears that Schneider is a feminist of sorts, while Merleau-Ponty represents the cultural equation of normalcy with an objectifying masculine gaze and the corollary devaluation of moral concerns as evidence of pathology.

The Sexual Ideology of Master and Slave

The ideological character of *Phenomenology of Perception* is produced by the impossible project of maintaining an abstract subject even while describing concrete, lived experience. The subject appears immune from the historical experience that Merleau-Ponty describes, but then reveals itself in the course of the description as a concrete cultural subject, a masculine subject. Although

Merleau-Ponty intends to describe the universal structures of bodily exist-ence, the concrete examples he provides reveal the impossibility of that project. Moreover, the specific cultural organization of sexuality becomes reified through a description that claims universality. On the one hand, Merleau-Ponty wants sexuality to be intentional, in-the-world, referential, expressive of a concrete, ex-istential situation, and yet he offers a description of bodily experience clearly ab-stracted from the concrete diversity that exists. The effect of this abstraction is to codify and sanction one particular cultural organization of sexuality as legiti-mate. Hence, the promise of his phenomenological method to provide a nonnor-mative framework for the understanding of sexuality proves illusory.

Central to his argument is that sexuality instates us in a common world. The problem arises, however, when the common world he describes is a reification of a relation of domination between the sexes. Although he argues that sexuality makes us a part of a universal community, it becomes clear that this "univer-sality" characterizes a relationship of voyeurism and objectification, a nonrecip-rocal dialectic between men and women. In claiming that this universal dialectic is to be found in lived experience, Merleau-Ponty prefigures the analysis of lived experience, investing the body with an ahistorical structure which is in actu-ality profoundly historical in origin. Merleau-Ponty begins his explanation of this structure in the following way: "The intensity of sexual pleasure would not be sufficient to explain the place occupied by sexuality in human life or, for ex-ample, the phenomenon of eroticism, if sexual experience were not, as it were, an opportunity vouchsafed to all and always available, of acquainting oneself with the human lot in its most general aspects of autonomy and dependence" (Merleau-Ponty 1962, 167). The dynamics of autonomy and dependence char-acterize human life universally and "arise from the metaphysical structure of my body." Moreover, this dynamic is part of "a dialectic of the self and other which is that of master and slave: insofar as I have a body, I may be reduced to the status of an object beneath the gaze of another person, and no longer count as a person for him, or else I may become his master and, in my turn, look at *him*" (Merleau-Ponty 1962, 167).

Master-slave is thus a metaphysical dynamic insofar as a body is always an object for others inasmuch as it is perceived. Perception designates an affec-tive relation and, in the context of sexuality, signifies desire. Hence, a body is an object to the extent that it is desired, and is, in turn, a subject, inasmuch as it desires. Hence, being desired is equivalent to enslavement, and desiring is equivalent to mastering. Taken yet further, this dialectic suggests that the master, as the one who desires, is essentially without a body; indeed, it is a body which he desires to have. In other words, active desire is a way of dispensing with the existential problematic of being a body-object. In phenomenological terms, active desire is a flight from embodiment. The slave is thus designated as the body that the master lacks. And because the slave is a body-object, the slave is a body without desire. Hence, in this relationship, neither master nor slave constitutes a *desiring body*; the master is desire without a body, and the slave is a body without desire.

We can speculate yet further upon this "metaphysical" structure of bodily existence. The desire of the master must always be the desire to possess what he lacks, the body which he has denied and which the slave has come to *em*body. The slave, on the other hand, is not a person—a body expressive of consciousness—much less a person who desires. Whether or not the slave desires is irrelevant to the master, for his desire is self-sufficient; it posits the object of its desire and sustains it; his concern is not to *be* a body, but to have or possess the body as an object. But what does it mean to say that the master does not have a body? If the body is a "situation," the condition of perspective and the necessary mediation of a social existence, then the master has denied himself the condition for a genuine presence in the world and has become worldless. His desire is thus both an alienation of bodily existence and an effort to recapture the body from this self-imposed exile, not to be this body, but this time to possess and control it in order to nurse an illusion of transcendence. Desire thus signifies an effort at objectification and possession, the master's bizarre struggle with his own vulnerability and existence that requires the slave to be the body the master no longer wants to be. The slave must be the Other, the exact opposite of the Subject, but nevertheless remain his possession.

If the slave is a body without desire, the very identity of the slave forbids desire. Not only is the desire of the slave irrelevant to the master, but the emergence of the slave's desire would constitute a fatal contradiction in the slave's identity. Hence, the liberation of the slave would consist in the moment of desire, for desire would signal the advent of a subject, a body expressive of consciousness.

Although Merleau-Ponty does not equate the master with the male body or the slave with the female body, he does tend, as we have seen, to identify the female body with a sexual schema of a decontextualized and fragmented body. Read in light of Beauvoir's later claim in *The Second Sex*, that women are culturally constructed as the Other, reduced to their bodies and, further, to their sex, Merleau-Ponty's description of the "metaphysical" structure of bodily existence appears to encode and reify that specific cultural dynamic of heterosexual relations. Strangely enough, Merleau-Ponty's effort to describe lived experience appeals to an abstract metaphysical structure devoid of explicit cultural reference, and yet once this metaphysical structure is properly contextualized as the cultural construction of heterosexuality, we do, in fact, seem to be in the presence of a widely experienced phenomenon. In effect, *Phenomenology of Perception* makes gestures toward the description of an experience which it ultimately refuses to name. We are left with a metaphysical obfuscation of sexual experience, while the relations of domination and submission that we do live remain unacknowledged.

Toward a Phenomenological Feminism

In his incomplete and posthumously published *The Visible and the Invisible*, Merleau-Ponty criticizes Sartre for maintaining the subject-object distinction in his description of sexuality and bodily existence (Merleau-Ponty 1968). In the place of a social ontology of the look, Merleau-Ponty suggests an ontology of the tactile, a description of sensual life which would emphasize the interworld, that shared domain of the flesh which resists categorization in terms of subjects and objects. It may well be that by the time Merleau-Ponty undertook that study at the end of his life, he had achieved philosophical distance from the sexual Cartesianism of his phenomenological colleagues, and that the reification of voyeurism and objectification that we have witnessed would no longer conform to that later theory. At the time of *Phenomenology of Perception*, however, Merleau-Ponty accepts the distinction in a limited but consequential way. As a result, he accepts the dialectic of master and slave as an invariant dynamic of sexual life. Both "subject" and "object" are less givens of lived experience than metaphysical constructs that inform and obfuscate the theoretical "look" that constitutes sexuality as a theoretical object. Indeed, the greatest obfuscation consists in the claim that this constructed theoretical vocabulary renders lived experience transparent.

Merleau-Ponty's conception of the "subject" is additionally problematic in virtue of its abstract and anonymous status, as if the subject described were a universal subject or structured existing subjects universally. Devoid of a gender, this subject is presumed to characterize all genders. On the one hand, this presumption devalues gender as a relevant category in the description of lived bodily experience. On the other hand, inasmuch as the subject described resembles a culturally constructed male subject, it consecrates masculine identity as the model for the human subject, thereby devaluing, not gender, but women.

Merleau-Ponty's explicit avoidance of gender as a relevant concern in the description of lived experience, and his implicit universalization of the male subject, are aided by a methodology that fails to acknowledge the historicity of sexuality and of bodies. For a concrete description of lived experience, it seems crucial to ask *whose* sexuality and *whose* bodies are being described, for "sexuality" and "bodies" remain abstractions without first being situated in concrete social and cultural contexts. Moreover, Merleau-Ponty's willingness to describe a "natural sexuality" as a lived experience suggests a lamentable naiveté concerning the anthropological diversity of sexual expressions and the linguistic and psychosomatic origins of human sexuality. In the end, the version of "lived experience" commits the fallacy of misplaced concreteness, giving life to abstractions, and draining life from existing individuals in concrete contexts. What is the historical genesis of the "subject" that Merleau-Ponty accepts as an a priori feature of any description of sexuality? Does this "subject" not denote a given history of sexual relations which have produced this disembodied voyeur and his machinations of enslavement? What social context and specific history have given birth to this idea and its embodiment?

Merleau-Ponty's original intention to describe the body as an expressive and dramatic medium, the specifically corporeal locus of existential themes, becomes beleaguered by a conception of "existence" which prioritizes hypothetical natural and metaphysical structures over concrete historical and cultural realities. A feminist critique of Merleau-Ponty necessarily involves a deconstruction of these obfuscating and reifying structures to their concrete cultural origins, and an analysis of the ways in which Merleau-Ponty's text legitimates and universalizes structures of sexual oppression. On the other hand, a feminist appropriation of Merleau-Ponty is doubtless in order. If the body expresses and dramatizes existential themes, and these themes are gender-specific and fully historicized, then sexuality becomes a scene of cultural struggle, improvisation, and innovation, a domain in which the intimate and the political converge, and a dramatic opportunity for expression, analysis, and change. The terms of this inquiry, however, will not be found in the texts of Merleau-Ponty, but in the works of philosophical feminism to come.

Notes

1. This chapter was previously published in *The Thinking Muse: Feminism and Modern French Philosophy*, edited by Jeffner Allen and Iris Marion Young, pp. 85–100 (Bloomington, IN: Indiana University Press, 1989). It is reprinted here with permission of the author and editors.
2. See Freud (1962, 13–14): "We have been in the habit of regarding the connection between the sexual instinct and the sexual object as more intimate than it in fact is. Experience of the cases that are considered abnormal has shown us that in them the sexual instinct and the sexual object are soldered together—a fact which we have been in danger of overlooking in consequence of the uniformity of the normal picture, where the object appears to be part and parcel of the instinct." Not only is the instinct ontologically independent of the object, but it follows a development toward a reproductive telos whereby "the sexual object recedes into the background" (Freud 1962, 15). The normal development of this "instinct" dictates active sexual behavior for the male, and passive sexual behavior for the female with the consequence that the

reversal of roles signifies an abnormal sexuality, that is, one which has not developed according to the proper internal teleology (Freud 1962, 26). Sexuality which is not restricted to the erotogenic zones characterizes "obsessional neurosis" (Freud 1962, 35). The perversions thus characterize underdeveloped stages of instinctual development, and are in that sense "normal" inasmuch as those stages must be lived through. For Freud, however, they come to represent abnormalities when they are not relinquished in favor of heterosexual coitus. This link between normal sexuality and reproduction is recast in his theory of Eros in *Civilization and Its Discontents* (1961).

3. In *The Visible and the Invisible* (1968), Merleau-Ponty's posthumously published work, his discussion of sexuality focuses on tactile experience and marks a significant departure from the visual economy of *Phenomenology of Perception*.

References

Beauvoir, Simone de. 1953. *The Second Sex*. Translated by H. M. Parshley. New York: Vintage Books.

Freud, Sigmund. 1950. *Beyond the Pleasure Principle*. Translated by James Strachey. London: William Brown.

Freud, Sigmund. 1961. *Civilization and its Discontents*. Edited by Philip Rieff. New York: Macmillan.

Freud, Sigmund. 1962. *Three Essays on the Theory of Sexuality*. Translated by James Strachey. New York: Basic Books.

Freud, Sigmund. 1976. "Instincts and Their Vicissitudes." In *General Psychological Theory*, edited by Philip Rieff, 84–90. New York: Macmillan.

Merleau-Ponty, Maurice. 1962. *Phenomenology of Perception*. Translated by Colin Smith. New York: Routledge & Kegan Paul.

Merleau-Ponty, Maurice. 1968. *The Visible and the Invisible*. Translated by Alphonso Lingis. Evanston: Northwestern University Press.

10

Enactivism and Gender Performativity

Ashby Butnor and Matthew MacKenzie

The enactivist paradigm of embodied cognition represents a powerful alternative to Cartesian and cognitivist approaches in the philosophy of mind and the cognitive sciences. On this view, the body plays a constitutive role in the integrated functioning of perception, affect, and other cognitive processes. Moreover, cognition is understood to emerge from the ongoing interaction of an organism with its physical and (in the case of humans and many animals) social environment. Human mindedness, then, is fundamentally embodied, embedded, and intersubjective. In this chapter, we will extend the enactivist approach to examine the larger interpersonal and social contexts that frame embodied practices. Empathy, the embodied affective connectedness that serves as a basic connection between individuals, has been investigated within the enactive approach. However, the ways in which our intersubjective relationships are positioned within larger cultural and political frameworks has not received as much attention in the literature on embodied and embedded cognition. In order to get a fuller sense of how selves and worlds co-emerge and are co-constituted by this interrelationship, we need to examine the embeddedness of our embodied experience in various systems of meaning and forms of power.

Our enactive analysis of human sociality and meaning focuses on notions of identity, difference, and power, as discussed most thoroughly by feminist theorists, through the primary lens of gender. The enactive approach to embodied cognition already shares many of the long-standing themes and contentions of feminist theory. Like many feminist philosophers, the enactive approach criticizes mind-body dualisms, the separation of reason and emotion, and atomistic individualism, and emphasizes the deeply embodied, value-laden, and situated nature of human experience. We think the enactive approach in philosophy of mind and cognitive science provides further support for these core feminist themes, and it may open new avenues of inquiry and intervention related to them. Yet, while the enactive approach explicitly acknowledges the intersubjective, social, and cultural nature of human experience and cognition, its account of these dimensions remains underdeveloped. In particular, enactivism has not thematized the critical role of *power* in shaping and reshaping lifeworlds

Ashby Butnor and Matthew MacKenzie, *Enactivism and Gender Performativity* In: *Feminist Philosophy of Mind.*
Edited by: Keya Maitra and Jennifer McWeeny, Oxford University Press. © Oxford University Press 2022.
DOI: 10.1093/oso/9780190867614.003.0011

and the individuals that enact them. Here we must turn to the analyses of feminist theory to enrich and extend enactivism.

In so doing, we will first lay out the key components of an enactive theory of mind, including autonomy, sense-making, emergence, embodiment, and experience, as well as some distinct features of human experience, namely, value, affect, and sociality. After discussing how selves and worlds co-emerge and co-create meaning on a primitive level, we will apply these underlying mechanisms to explain larger and more complex social manifestations, specifically gender performance and its reproduction through time. By employing Judith Butler's notion of performativity, we will demonstrate how gender, as one marker of social identity and difference, emerges through similar processes, feedback loops, and relational domains of significance and valence that are at the heart of enactive theory.

While applying ideas from enactive theory to social identity and performance is interesting in its own right, we see further value in using these insights to shed light on how oppressive systems maintain and perpetuate themselves and, importantly, how they may be interrupted and revised. We argue that attention to the embodied, embedded, sense-making-and-maintaining interactions that partly constitute systems of oppression should be critically evaluated and assessed to understand their role in reproducing harm to both individuals and communities.

Fortunately, while our embodied ways of being in the world are always socially embedded, the particular nature of our various worlds is merely contingent. Thus, particular configurations of cultural worlds need not be seen as essential, necessary, or inevitable. Furthermore, it is not the case that individuals, as body-subjects, simply take the brunt of enforced social meanings. Rather, as work in embodied cognition amply supports, there is a reciprocal relationship between subject and world. Therefore, we have the capacity to revise social meanings and enact different kinds of worlds—worlds that are more conducive to individual and social flourishing, rather than harm and oppression. The goal of this chapter will be to bring feminist philosophy and the enactive approach into dialogue to highlight their explanatory and, perhaps, liberatory potentials.

The Enactive Approach

In *The Embodied Mind*, Francisco Varela, Evan Thompson, and Eleanor Rosch argue that cognition should be understood neither as the recovery of a pregiven outer world, nor the projection of a pregiven inner world, but rather as a form of embodied action (Varela et al. 1993, 172). By "embodied" they mean to highlight two points: "first, that cognition depends on the kinds of experience that come from having a body with various sensorimotor capacities, and second, that these individual sensorimotor capacities are themselves embedded in a more encompassing biological, psychological, and cultural context" (Varela et al. 1993, 173). By "action," they "mean to emphasize once again that sensory and motor processes, perception and action, are fundamentally inseparable in lived cognition. Indeed, the two are not merely contingently linked in individuals; they have also evolved together" (Varela et al. 1993, 173).

At the risk of oversimplification, we can say that there are five highly interconnected ideas at the core of enactivism: *autonomy, sense-making, emergence, embodiment*, and *experience* (Di Paolo et al. 2010, 37). First, on the enactivist view, living beings are self-organizing, autopoietic (self-making), and autonomous (self-individuating) systems. An autonomous system generates and maintains its identity through continuous matter-energy turnover and in precarious external conditions. More specifically, an autonomous system is characterized by organizational and operational closure. In organizational closure a system or process creates a boundary, which subsequently both constrains and enables the further operations of the system. For instance, at the cellular level, a self-organizing process of biochemical reactions produces a membrane that, in turn, constrains the process that created it (Weber and Varela 2002). The completion of this loop gives rise to a distinct biological entity that maintains its own boundary in its environment. Organizational closure, on this view, constitutes the system as a unity in its context. Living systems are also operationally closed in that "for any given process P that forms part of the system (1) we can find among its enabling conditions other processes that make up the system, and (2) we can find other processes in the system that depend on P" (Di Paolo et al. 2010, 38). That is, the internal processes of the system recursively depend on each other.

It is worth noting that the notion of autonomy central to enactivism is distinct from certain common metaphysical and ethical notions of autonomy. Metaphysically, the enactive account of biological autonomy does not entail— and indeed enactivism rejects—any strong notion of ontological independence. On the enactivist view, an organism is not a substance metaphysically independent of all other substances, but rather a thoroughly *relational* self-organizing *process*. Organisms are internally relational systems, and only emerge and maintain themselves in interdependence with a dynamic environment. Moreover, the notion of biological autonomy here is distinct from notions used in ethics. Yet, given the enactivist's fundamentally relational account of organism and agency and the commitment to the dynamic co-constitution of subject and world, the enactivist view looks incompatible with any notion of autonomy based on atomistic individualism. Indeed, while we cannot pursue the point here, the enactivist approach may be more in accord with feminist theories of relational autonomy (Mackenzie and Stoljar 2000).

In addition, cognitive systems display adaptive autonomy or adaptivity. All autopoietic systems are dynamically coupled to their environments. However, adaptive systems have the capacity to *regulate* their interactions with the environment. For instance, even single-celled organisms such as *E. coli* engage in positive and negative chemotaxis, that is, movement in response to chemical stimulus. The organism detects glucose and swims in the direction of its highest concentration. Likewise, it can swim away from noxious stimuli. The organizationally and operationally closed system here regulates its interaction with its environment.

The second core idea of the enactive approach is that adaptive autonomy is the root of cognition and cognition is sense-making. According to Thompson:

> Sense-making is threefold: (1) sensibility as openness to the environment (intentionality as openness); (2) significance as positive or negative valence of environmental conditions relative to the norms of the living being (intentionality as passive synthesis—passivity, receptivity, and affect); and (3) the direction or orientation the living being adopts in response to significance and valence (intentionality as protentional and teleological). (Thompson 2011, 119)

In its basic form, then, sense-making is a complex process in which these aspects are intertwined. During normal waking experience, we are open to the world through our senses in a general way and the sensory field is further structured by selective attention. For instance, one may be focused on a painting, while also being peripherally aware of background noise. The phenomena of which we are aware are often experienced as positively or negatively valenced. The background noise may be annoying, while the painting is beautiful. Further, as valenced, phenomena may call forth from us a certain orientation or action. The painting may elicit closer inspection or a change in vantage point, while the annoying sound may pull attention away from the painting. Fundamentally, the emergence of an autonomous organism entails the emergence of a field of possible interactions between that organism and the larger environment. Some interactions will allow the organism to continue and even thrive, while others can harm or kill it. Thus, the environment takes on significance and valence: some events are dangerous for the organism, some things are food, and so on. What *we* label the organism's physical surroundings becomes for *it* an environment, a relational domain of significance and valence.

Co-emergent with sentient and mobile beings is a sensorimotor world, which in turn shapes the ongoing dynamics, structure, and viability of the organism. To be alive is to come into being in the midst of this circular process. To remain alive entails making sense of (that is, acting appropriately in relation to) the significance and valence of one's world. The organism engages in sense-making at a variety of levels. First, the very sense of the world will be partly a function of the structure, capacities, and evolutionary history of the organism. Second, sense (significance and valence) is enacted and transformed through the organism's action in the world, for example, in exploration of the sensorimotor environment. Further, enactivists recognize the central importance of affect and emotion as forms of sense-making. Third, the organism makes sense of its world through viable conduct, which is arguably the most primitive form of circumspection or understanding. Overall, we can say that sense-making for the viable organism involves a form of experiential niche construction. That is, the organism *enacts a world* through ongoing adaptive interaction with a physical environment.

The third core idea of enactivism is emergence. Sentient beings are not understood as heteronomous, mechanical input-output systems, but rather as dynamic, autonomous systems that regulate their ongoing coupling with the environment. Autonomous systems, then, involve emergent processes. As Thompson describes, "An emergent process belongs to an ensemble or network of elements, arises spontaneously or self-organizes from the locally defined and globally constrained or controlled interactions of those elements, and does not belong to a single element" (Thompson 2007, 60). Emergent processes, and the systems in which they arise, exhibit two forms of determination. Local-to-global determination involves the emergence of novel macro-level processes and structures based on changes in the system components and relations. Global-to-local determination involves macro-level processes and structures constraining local interactions. Thus, self-organizing systems display circular causality: local interactions give rise to global patterns or order, while the global order constrains the local interactions (Haken 2004).

The type of self-production and self-maintenance found in living systems goes beyond the type of self-organization seen in nonliving systems. A Bénard cell, as a dissipative system, will display self-organization and self-maintenance to a degree, but the key boundary conditions that keep the system away from equilibrium are exogenous. In contrast, in truly autonomous systems, "the constraints that actually guide energy/matter flows from the environment through the constitutive processes of the system are endogenously created and maintained" (Ruiz-Mirazo and Moreno 2004, 238). Thus the degree of autonomy found in living beings is, according to the enactive approach, a form of dynamic co-emergence.

> Dynamic co-emergence best describes the sort of emergence we see in autonomy. In an autonomous system, the whole not only arises from the (organizational closure of the) parts, but the parts also arise from the whole. The whole is constituted by the relations of the parts, and the parts are constituted by the relations they bear to one another in the whole. Hence, the parts do not exist in advance, prior to the whole, as independent entities that retain their identity in

the whole. Rather, part and whole co-emerge and mutually specify each other. (Thompson 2007, 65)

The fourth core idea of the enactive approach is that cognition is fundamentally embodied. Cognition is sense-making, and sense-making is adaptive interaction between organism and environment. All of this is rooted in and depends on the integrated structures and capacities of the living body. As Ezequiel Di Paolo and Thompson put it, "Without a body, there cannot be sense-making. Moreover, sense-making is a bodily process of adaptive self-regulation. The link between the body and cognition is accordingly constitutive and not merely causal. To be a sense-maker is, among other things, to be autonomous and precarious, that is, is to be a body, in the precise sense of 'body' that the enactive approach indicates" (Di Paolo and Thompson 2014, 76). Organisms respond to the significance and valence of patterns in the environment, but these patterns only have the significance they do in relation to the needs and capacities of particular living bodies. The connection between embodiment as adaptive biological autonomy and cognition as sense-making is constitutive, not merely causal. On the enactive approach, "the body is the ultimate source of significance; embodiment means that mind is inherent in the precarious, active, normative, and worldful process of animation" (Di Paolo et al. 2010, 42). Further, as we discuss below, the human body is also a social and cultural body, and sense-making includes social, linguistic, and cultural dimensions.

The fifth and final core element of the enactive approach is the topical and methodological centrality of experience. Here, experience refers not to isolated qualia or phenomenal properties, but to the cognitive, conative, affective, and sensory aspects of sense-making *as lived through* by the subject. That is, experience is sense-making as lived. Recall that, on the enactive approach, the self-individuation of a living system entails the arising of a kind of interiority and perspective on the world. The biological system enacts a/its self. In enacting itself, it enacts its world. A world is a relational domain of significance, from the point of view of the organism and its needs and capacities. The ongoing enacting of self and world is sense-making and sense-making is necessarily lived through from the point of view of the organism. What it is like to adaptively engage the world of significance and valence just is the biological subject's experience. Thus, experience, on the enactive view is always first-personal—in the minimal sense of being lived through from a point of view—embodied, and interactive.

Yet, while constitutively first-personal, there is no assumption that phenomenal experience is intracranial. As Diego Cosmelli and Evan Thompson put it:

According to the "enactive" view of experience, consciousness is a life-regulation process of the body interacting with its environment. Perception, action, emotion, imagination, memory, dreaming—these are modes of self-regulation that depend directly on the living body and not just the brain. According to the enactive view, the body shouldn't be seen as a mere outside causal influence on an exclusively neuronal system for consciousness because the minimal requirements for consciousness include a living body, not just neuronal events in the skull. (Cosmelli and Thompson 2011, 164)

Hence, phenomenal consciousness is fundamentally an embodied, emergent biological capacity and process. Furthermore, experience is methodologically central to enactivism in two basic and interconnected ways. First, fidelity to the depth and complexity of lived experience serves as a fundamental constraint on the adequacy of enactivist accounts. Second, enactivism strives to integrate first-, second-, and third-person methods of inquiry into a more comprehensive account of life and mind. Hence, on this view, there can be no complete, nonexperiential (that is, purely third-person) account of life and mind.

The Social Dimension

Beyond the above core features, the enactive approach understands human experience as deeply value-laden, affective, and social. Sense-making is a constitutively evaluative process—it discloses the world and the organism's own interactions in terms of their significance and valence. "An organism's world," write Tom Froese and Ezequiel Di Paolo, "is primarily a context of significance in relation to that organism's particular manner of realizing and preserving its precarious identity" (Froese and Di Paolo 2009, 444). Further, the more flexibly adaptive the subject, the richer and more complex will be the value-dimension of her lifeworld. The valence landscape of the single-celled organism such as E. coli will be much simpler than that of the social primate like the bonobo. At the most basic level, "something acquires meaning for an organism to the extent that it relates (either positively or negatively) to the norm of the maintenance of the organism's integrity" (Thompson 2007, 70). For E. coli, the values may be simply metabolic and tied very closely to ongoing sensorimotor interaction with the environment. For the bonobo, the value landscape will be tied to its vastly more complex capacities for perception, action, emotion, and sociality. The key point here is that cognition (in the narrow sense) and evaluation, fact and value are deeply entangled on the enactive approach. The lifeworld is necessarily value-laden, and the value-dimension is neither simply recovered nor projected. Rather the value-dimension is both enacted and disclosed through sense-making.

Furthermore, the enactive approach sees human experience as fundamentally intersubjective and social. According to Thompson, the enactive account of human intersubjectivity rests on two central ideas.

> The first idea is that self and other enact each other reciprocally through empathy. One's consciousness of oneself as a bodily subject in the world presupposes a certain empathic understanding of self and other. The second idea is that human subjectivity emerges from developmental processes of enculturation and is configured by the distributed cognitive web of symbolic culture. For these reasons, human subjectivity is from the outset intersubjectivity, and no mind is an island. (Thompson 2007, 382–383)

The earliest forms of empathy can be seen in what developmental psychologists term "primary intersubjectivity" (Trevarthen 1979). Primary intersubjectivity involves sensorimotor capacities that enable relations and interactions with others (Gallagher 2012). These capacities, which are innate or early-developing, manifest in the ability to perceive another's feelings and intentions through their movements, facial expressions, gestures, and so on, and to respond with our own movements, expressions, and the like. Newborn infants, for instance, can perceive and imitate facial expressions, a capacity that is both sensory-motor and interpersonally interactive (Meltzoff and Moore 1977). At around two months, infants develop the ability to follow the gaze of another, sense what the other is looking at, and even anticipate the other's intentions (Baron-Cohen 1995). Primary intersubjectivity continues to develop so that, by the end of the first year of life, "infants have a non-mentalizing, perception-based, embodied and pragmatic grasp of the emotions and intentions of other persons" (Gallagher 2012, 197).

At around nine months, children begin to develop forms of secondary intersubjectivity. Through the development of joint attention, children are able to engage in triadic interaction between the child herself, another, and an object or event. Secondary intersubjectivity involves the development of two processes. As Gallagher summarizes:

> (1) They refer to others (in social referencing) and enter into joint actions where they learn how objects are used by using them and from seeing others use them, and they begin to co-constitute the meaning of the world through such interactions with others in a process of "participatory sense-making"; and
> (2) they build upon theses interactions to makes sense of the other's behavior in specific contexts. (Gallagher 2012, 197)

This transition from social interaction to participatory sense-making is central to the enactive understanding of full human sense-making. Participatory sense-making is "the coordination of intentional activity in interaction, whereby individual sense-making processes are affected and new domains of social sense-making can be generated that were not available to each individual on her own" (De Jaegher and Di Paolo 2007, 497). For instance, language learning and use open up a vast array of new modes of individual and social sense-making otherwise unavailable to us. The social and cultural dimensions of the human lifeworld are the product of participatory sense-making, and this sense-making is itself shaped by sociocultural structures. Thus, the social meanings of gender, race, sexual orientation, class, and so on are also co-enacted in and through embodied, perceptual, affective, and cognitive processes.

Gender Performance as Sense-Making

In accord with the central ideas of the enactive approach, social meaning is not just cognitive and symbolic, but always embodied, enacted, and affective as well. To date, the enactivist approach has not primarily been employed to investigate social meaning in terms of how sense-making emerges through powerful markers of identity and difference, such as race, class, sexual orientation, and gender. Like more simple forms of sense-making, these social categories are co-enacted in and through embodied, perceptual, affective, and cognitive processes and yet remain undertheorized as a significant co-emergent feature of human lifeworlds from an enactive approach. Our goal here, then, is to extend the insights of enactive theory to social identity, social practices, and social meanings to both highlight how these phenomena emerge through a complexity of interactions between selves and worlds, and demonstrate how we may conceptualize or, better, *enact* different and better selves and worlds.

According to the enactivist view, the lived body is metabolically, compositionally, and functionally *plastic*: "Both the nervous system and the body . . . can alter their structure and dynamics by incorporating (taking into themselves) processes, tools, and resources that go beyond what the biological body can metabolically generate (artificial organs and neural and sensorimotor prostheses)" (Thompson and Stapleton 2008, 28). But what about the incorporation of social and cultural forms? The process of enculturation in specific environments also involves a process of incorporation of the gendered (and raced, classed, sexed, etc.) behaviors that are being played out around us. As we perform and enact the social scripts of our historical situation, they in turn inscribe themselves upon our bodies and indeed become our lived experience of embodiment in the world. Significantly, this process of incorporation involves intersubjective resonance with other embodied persons in our environments. And it operates at both the primary and secondary levels of intersubjectivity. As Joan Mason-Grant explains:

> Other beings—human and nonhuman animals—are . . . part of our phenom-
> enological anatomy. We are involved in processes of mutual incorporation in
> which my corporeality in its functional telos is necessarily supplemented and
> extended through my relationship with others. As I spend time with someone
> I care about and come to know them intimately, I often incorporate their way of
> engaging the world, their mannerisms, their phrases, even their views, as they
> may incorporate mine, and our perception, judgment, and interactive know-
> how thereby transforms. (Mason-Grant 2004, 107)

This intersubjective incorporation begins with familial intimacy, but then extends beyond to freely chosen groups (such as friendships, social networks, or religious associations) and social identities, such as gender, race, class, ability, sexuality, and so on.

Gender provides a ready example of how social meanings are enacted in and through human bodies. Expressions of gendered meaning can range from styles of hair, dress, and comportment to familial roles, career tracks, and life aspirations depending on place and historical period. Gender performance can be understood as a multivalent form of participatory sense-making. Examples of gendered performance abound in everyday life—from the choice of outfit in the morning, to expectations of who will care for children, to how one sits on the subway on the way home from work—all express attitudes and expectations of typical gender categories. Gender, though, is not stable over time or across environments. Like other forms of sense-making, gender is neither the simple projection of a pregiven identity, nor the simple mirroring or recovery of external norms. Rather, it is an ongoing, embodied negotiation within and to the gendered social milieu. Even gender-nonconforming performances take place within a gendered space of meaning. In her theory of gender performativity, Judith Butler describes gender as "the stylized repetition of acts through time" (Butler 1988, 520). By renewing, revising, and consolidating a series of behaviors over time, the body becomes its gender (Butler 1988, 523). Hence, gender is not a stable social and cultural essence, but an emergent feature of humans engaging with their worlds of meaning and sense. We recognize gender via the perfor-mance of actions, gestures, costumes, mannerisms, and styles understood as appropriate (sensible) to a particular historical situation.

This understanding of gender allows us to see the co-creation and continuance of self, world, and meaning. While in some sense, "acts" may be individuated such that "one does one's body and, indeed, one does one's body differently from one's contemporaries and from one's embodied predecessors and successors," "acts" are always constrained by a historically proscribed set of action possibilities within the social milieu, the gendered structure of social affordances (Butler 1988, 521). Butler explains how the "gendered body acts its part in a culturally restricted corporeal space and enacts interpretations within confines of already existing directives" (Butler 1988, 526). In performing gender, we are in turn performing, instantiating, and enacting the gendered script that precedes us and yet requires our participation. Butler's theory of performativity models that of theatrical drama:

> The act that one does, the act that one performs, is, in a sense, an act that has been going on before one arrived on the scene. Hence, gender is an act which has been rehearsed, much as a script survives the particular actors who make use of it, but which requires individual actors in order to be actualized and reproduced as reality once again. (Butler 1988, 526)

This is not to say, however, that agency is lost and that the individual is a victim of an overwhelming tide of cultural meaning and predetermination. We are not, in Butler's words, "a lifeless recipient of wholly pre-given cultural relations" (Butler 1988, 526). We are not, in enactivist terms, merely heteronomous systems, but rather relationally autonomous systems enacting our identity in precarious conditions. While the environment limits sensible options, our enactment of proscribed choices comes to effect—that is, produce, constitute, and define—the environment.

> Subjective experience is not only structured by existing political arrangements, but effects and structures those arrangements in turn. Feminist theory has sought to understand the way in which systemic or pervasive political and cultural structures are enacted and reproduced through individual acts and practices, and how the analysis of ostensibly personal situations is clarified through situating the issues in a broader and shared cultural context. (Butler 1988, 522)

Hence, gender as a structuring feature of experience is shaped by value-laden individual acts of social expression. The gendered lifeworld, then, is not merely a pregiven domain, but one that is brought forth as a relational domain of significance and valence to the ongoing adaptive activity of gendered body-subjects.

Social Practices and Power

We instantiate social meaning through our reproduction of social scripts. To extend the enactivist approach to explain the emergence of social meaning, we could say that the interaction of selves and worlds results in a process of coordi-nated sense-making. However, to speak in terms of "participatory" sense-making here may now give the impression that we intentionally and autonomously create or choose together the social worlds in which we live. Rather, our participation is always constrained by both the kinds of environments into which we are born and the process of enculturation that shapes our early lives and very sense of self in these worlds. In situations of substantial power disparities within com-munities, our social positioning greatly determines the extent to which we are able to "participate" in the constitution of worlds by limiting opportunities and affordances for well-being. A question remains regarding the extent to which we are capable of actively rewriting oppressive social scripts, and how, given the often unconscious embodiment of meaning, this could effectively take place.

If enactivism is to be a valuable theory to explain human action, we must con-sider the fact that the lifeworld of social relations does not exist on politically or ethically benign terrain. Butler describes gender identity as a "performative accomplishment compelled by social sanction and taboo" (Butler 1988, 520). In the process of "becoming a woman" (à la Beauvoir), one must "compel the body to conform to an historical idea of 'woman,' to induce the body to become a cultural sign to materialize oneself in obedience to an historically delimited possibility, and to do this as a sustained and repeated corporeal project" (Butler 1988, 522). However, Butler dismisses this as a project through which one can autonomously exercise her will. Rather, gender (or raced, classed, able-bodied, etc.) performance is better understood as a *strategy*, an attempt at viable conduct in precarious conditions, which "better suggests the situation of duress under which gender performance always and variously occurs. Hence, as a strategy of survival, gender is a performance with clearly punitive consequences" (Butler 1988, 522). While gender is not at all stable as a category of immutable or essen-tialist meaning, it nevertheless exists as a "*regulatory* fiction" that dictates sen-sible behavior and identity as well as social punishments and rewards based on our performances of it. If we analyze worlds in terms of structures of significance, valence, and affordance (Gibson 1979), we can see that the regulatory fictions of gender operate like attractors in the dynamical structure of the social milieu. As nutritive chemicals attract *E. coli*, the gendered lifeworld *pulls* us toward certain normative constructions of gender.

Though gender exists as an emergent feature of social and cultural envir-onments that lacks any essentialist foundations, its regulatory strength is not to be underestimated. Indeed, while we cannot fully develop it here, a feminist-enactivist account of power will take as a central theme the power to structure and restructure lifeworlds. That is, power in part operates by shaping and constraining the landscape of significance, valence, and affordance that constitutes the lived worlds of subjects. Gendered systems of power fundamentally structure the opportunities for perceiving, feeling, and acting—the very *sense*—of human lifeworlds and the body-subjects that co-constitute them. Just as an organism exercises its autonomy within "precarious conditions" that can result in life or death, so too do individual persons make gendered decisions that have real consequences for their survival, or, minimally, their degree of flourishing, in environments that hold tightly to their gendered norms. This is demonstrated by examples of how people who have expressed nonconforming gender behavior have suffered harm, such as ridicule, social ostracism, loss of family, cultural exclusion, and even death, for choosing to transgress gendered expectations.

One difficulty for challenging these social practices and inscribing more liberatory practices is simply the difficulty of recognizing and interrupting our ingrained behaviors. Social performances are often tacit and rarely serve as objects of conscious reflection. As Mason-Grant explains, "As familiarity grows, self-consciousness recedes" (Mason-Grant 2004, 107). Indeed, this receding seems to be a basic feature of incorporation. Evan Thompson and Mog Stapleton point out that "environmental resources that are incorporated gain this transparency. They are no longer experienced as objects; rather the world is experienced through them" (Thompson and Stapleton 2008, 29). This notion of familiarity or transparency implies a level of skill or comfort in navigating a given environment. However, this ease will vary considerably depending upon one's social positioning. Social practices that are taken to be neutral, socially unproblematic, and appropriate tend to be distributed along predictable axes of power, such as those occupied by members of traditionally powerful gender, race, and class groups. In Mason-Grant's words, "Privilege enables persons to live their lives as socially unproblematic—as morally neutral, normal, average, unremarkable—and to experience their agency as a 'natural' attribute rather than produced" (Mason-Grant 2004, 112). Predictably, embodied practices that are deemed problematic, incite suspicion, or indicate inferiority are likely those exhibited by members of less powerfully positioned genders, races, classes, and sexualities within a given environment.

As María Lugones demonstrates, there can certainly exist a plurality of different "worlds," or social environments, through which we travel and within which we feel different levels of ease. When one is confident and "at ease in a 'world,'" one may "know all the norms that there are to be followed . . . know all the words that there are to be spoken . . . know all the moves" (Lugones, this volume, 115). However, "There are 'worlds' we enter at our own risk, 'worlds' that have agon, conquest, and arrogance as the main ingredients in their ethos. These are 'worlds' that we enter out of necessity" (Lugones, this volume, 120). Within these hostile worlds, we are not at ease and we have not perfected—due to limitations placed on access to such power—the social know-how that enables such familiarity and viable conduct. The lives of those who fail to live up to the social norms and expectations are much more difficult and are often marked by domination, Lugones remarks. The affordance structure of their physical and social environments presents myriad obstacles to the exercise of agency and opportunities to flourish.

A difficulty for underprivileged members of society is the embodiment of their very own oppression—that is, the re-enactment of oppressive scripts that continue to maintain the behaviors, attitudes, and expectations that limit one's opportunities. Diana Tietjens Meyers points out the possibility of a disconnect opening in our mind-body-world enactment when the embodied values of a society may be enacted despite *rational* rejection of said values, or disvalues (Meyers 2004). Even though one may cognitively resist oppression, embodiment may betray this belief by enacting oppressive practices. There are a number of examples of this disconnect in our "psycho-corporeal identity" in contemporary feminist theory:

(1) Iris Marion Young observes that one can see *embodied racism* in individuals who profess racial equality and yet "enact bigotry" in the presence of people of color "by becoming jittery or by keeping their distance." (Young 1990, 141–142)

(2) Sandra Bartky points to women's *embodied inferiority*: "By satisfying feminine body norms, women homogenize their own looks, constrict their own agency, and deprive themselves of the individuality and freedom that full persons should enjoy." (Bartky 1990, 71–74)

(3) Lugones shows how we may *enact stereotypes* of ourselves when we enter hostile "worlds": "I may not accept [a given stereotype] as an account of myself, a construction of myself. And yet, I may be *animating* such a construction." She continues, "indeed those who are oppressed animate oppressive constructions of themselves in the 'worlds' of their oppressors." (Lugones, this volume, 113–114, 122n.5)

In each case, women who believe in their own and others' equality, strength, autonomy, or playfulness may actually embody self-loathing, inequality, and prejudice. This disconnect is a resultant feature of limited agency in participatory sense-making in a given environment or "world." In these cases, despite a reflective and conscious endorsement of a particular set of beliefs and values, one's embodied comportment—demonstrative of histories of interaction in a particular world of meaning—continue to enact the disvalues of the environment. This in turn negatively informs self-identity, self-understanding, and intersubjective relationships, though sometimes in ways that are not transparent, that is, invisible, to most.

Though typically experienced as disturbing and emotionally taxing, such tensions create the possibility for radical transformation. It may be extremely difficult if not impossible for one who is "at ease" or privileged in an environment to notice problems brought forth by power differentials without advanced powers of empathetic perception. However, for those who experience "outlaw emotions," fissures in psycho-corporeal identity, or breaks in narrative construction, obstacles to well-being are readily apparent—affectively if not consciously (Jaggar 1989). These emotional responses to embodied situatedness may be the key to ignite catalysts for change and provoke movements for social justice.

The resonance of enactivism and feminist theory is apparent in the realization that embodied selves, worlds, and meaning co-emerge through their interaction with one another. This dynamic co-emergence is fundamentally embodied, enactive, embedded, and affective. It is the product of the sense-making of living body-subjects, and living body-subjects are themselves constituted in and through their physical and social environments. As such, many aspects of our particular worlds of sense are merely contingent and, hence, open for change and revision. As just one example, we have discussed how gender is merely an emergent feature of the interactions of individuals in worlds of sense and is constituted by the repetition of acts available within a particular historical and social milieu. Despite the naturalizing tendency to correlate sex and gender, there is nothing essential to our gender constructions and nothing holding social norms in place other than our policing of their performances. As Butler describes, "Discrete genders are part of what 'humanizes' individuals within contemporary culture. . . . Because there is neither an 'essence' that gender expresses or externalizes nor an objective ideal to which gender aspires, and because gender is not a fact, the various acts of gender create the idea of gender, and without those acts, there would be no gender at all" (Butler 1999, 178).

A reclamation of embodiment and subjectivity involves changing the social landscape—including harmful values, enforced embodied practices, and incorporated oppressions—that produce damaged subjects. While we typically consider social change in terms of a modification of law or social policies, this method is limited if not also accompanied by a concurrent change in embodied attitudes and practices. In line with Meyers, we argue that "corporeally attuned strategies are pivotal to emancipatory transformation" (Meyers 2004, 86). This focus on corporeally attuned strategies, or, in the words of enactivism, embodied and embedded strategies, is bolstered by our cross-disciplinary analysis. The enactivist analysis enables us to articulate forms of liberation from oppressive sociocultural patterns in ways that go beyond merely envisioning such possibilities to actualizing them. Social change needs also to be enacted at the ground level—in the embodied values, affective engagements, and activities we assume.

Thus, recognizing the extent to which social meaning and value are encoded in the body, that is, the way (even social) sense-making is constitutively embodied, can contribute to the emergence of new domains of truly participatory sense-making and flourishing.

References

Baron-Cohen, Simon. 1995. *Mindblindness: An Essay on Autism and Theory of Mind*. Cambridge, MA: MIT Press.

Bartky, Sandra. 1990. "Foucault, Femininity, and the Modernization of Patriarchal Power." In *Femininity and Domination: Studies in the Phenomenology of Oppression* by Sandra Bartky, 63–82. New York: Routledge.

Butler, Judith. 1988. "Performative Acts and Gender Constitution: An Essay in Phenomenology and Feminist Theory." *Theatre Journal* 40 (4): 519–531.

Butler, Judith. 1999. *Gender Trouble: Feminism and the Subversion of Identity*. 2nd ed. New York: Routledge.

Cosmelli, Diego, and Evan Thompson. 2011. "Brain in a Vat or Body in a World? Brainbound versus Enactive Views of Experience." *Philosophical Topics* 29 (1): 163–180.

De Jaegher, Hanne, and Ezequiel Di Paolo. 2007. "Participatory Sense-Making." *Phenomenology and the Cognitive Sciences* 6 (4): 485–507.

Di Paolo, Ezequiel, Marieke Rohde, and Hanne De Jaegher. 2010. "Horizons for the Enactive Mind: Values, Social Interaction, and Play." In *Enaction: Toward a New Paradigm for Cognitive Science*, edited by John Stewart, Olivier Gapenne, and Ezequiel Di Paolo, 32–87. Cambridge, MA: MIT Press.

Di Paolo, Ezequiel, and Evan Thompson. 2014. "The Enactive Approach." In *The Routledge Handbook of Embodied Cognition*, edited by Lawrence Shapiro, 68–78. London: Routledge.

Froese, Tom, and Ezequiel Di Paolo. 2009. "Sociality and the Life–Mind Continuity Thesis." *Phenomenology and the Cognitive Sciences* 8 (4): 439–463.

Gallagher, Shaun. 2012. *Phenomenology*. New York: Palgrave Macmillan.

Gibson, James. 1979. *The Ecological Approach to Visual Perception*. Boston: Houghton Mifflin.

Haken, Hermann. 2004. *Synergetics: Introduction and Advanced Topics*. Berlin: Springer.

Jaggar, Alison M. 1989. "Love and Knowledge: Emotion in Feminist Epistemology." *Inquiry: An Interdisciplinary Journal of Philosophy* 32 (2): 151–176.

Mackenzie, Catriona, and Natalie Stoljar. 2000. *Relational Autonomy: Feminist Perspectives on Autonomy, Agency, and the Social Self*. New York: Oxford University Press.

Mason-Grant, Joan. 2004. *Pornography Embodied: From Speech to Sexual Practice*. Lanham, MD: Rowman & Littlefield.

Meltzoff, Andrew, and M. K. Moore. 1977. "Imitation of Facial and Manual Gestures by Human Neonates." *Science* 198 (4312): 75–78.

Meyers, Diana Tietjens. 2004. "The Personal, the Political, and Psycho-Corporeal Agency." In *Being Yourself: Essays on Identity, Action, and Social Life* by Diana Tietjens Meyers, 77–94. Lanham, MD: Rowman & Littlefield.

Ruiz-Mirazo, Kepa, and Alvaro Moreno. 2004. "Basic Autonomy as a Fundamental Step in the Synthesis of Life." *Artificial Life* 10 (3): 235–259.

Thompson, Evan. 2007. *Mind in Life: Biology, Phenomenology and the Sciences of Mind.* Cambridge, MA: Harvard University Press.

Thompson, Evan. 2011. "Living Ways of Sense Making." *Philosophy Today* 55, supplement: S114–S123.

Thompson, Evan, and Mog Stapleton. 2008. "Making Sense of Sense-Making: Reflections on Enactive and Extended Mind Theories." *Topoi* 28 (1): 23–30.

Trevarthen, Colwyn. 1979. "Communication and Cooperation in Early Infancy: A Description of Primary Intersubjectivity." In *Before Speech*, edited by M. Bullowa, 321–347. Cambridge: Cambridge University Press.

Varela, Francisco, Evan Thompson, and Eleanor Rosch. 1993. *The Embodied Mind: Cognitive Science and Human Experience.* Cambridge, MA: MIT Press.

Weber, Andreas, and Francisco Varela. 2002. "Life after Kant: Natural Purposes and the Autopoietic Foundations of Biological Individuality." *Phenomenology and the Cognitive Sciences* 1 (2): 97–125.

Young, Iris Marion. 1990. *Justice and the Politics of Difference.* Princeton: Princeton University Press.

11

Norms and Neuroscience

The Case of Borderline Personality Disorder

Anne J. Jacobson

In a recent retelling of an Aboriginal story, a creature emerges from a swamp without any idea of what it is (Wagner and Brooks 1977). A platypus tells it that it is a bunyip, but learning the word does not go far to answer the creature's questions about itself. The bunyip then discovers a scientist, a very busy one, who without looking tells it that bunyips do not exist. Depression ensues until the bunyip discovers another one just like it.

The bunyip's encounter with the scientist might seem to capture a common fear that many feminists have felt about the scientific gaze, a gaze still typically male. Far from an insightful examination of how women function, the male scientist may take himself as the model of the healthy human being, and then find healthy women do not exist (Potter 2009; Wirth-Cauchon 2001). Such a picture of scientific psychology and psychiatry is of course an exaggeration, but there is enough in it to lead many to expect a discussion of "borderline personality disorder" from a neuroscientific perspective is hardly likely to get much right.

The work in this chapter is motivated by a different set of expectations. Many of us are unlike the bunyip in that descriptions of us are plentiful. Far from passing through our environment scarcely described, many of us are told almost continuously what we are, what we are doing, and why we are doing it. And, of course, what we should be doing. These views may come both through explicit theories and by seeming common sense, where the latter may encode partial and questionable views developed over a century or even over millennia. Cognitive neuroscience (CNS) is introducing alternatives to these views. Supposed common sense on a wide range of topics is being challenged. The result is potentially very liberating in allowing us to consider anew the nature of human thought and action.

From the point of view of feminist philosophy, neuroscience itself, however, has a challenge to meet, in addition to any raised by specific topics involving particular mental characteristics. Neural systems appear to be socially isolated items hidden inside our bodies. The picture of mental activity as separable from embodied activity is itself the product of a view that has appealed to many as mere

Anne J. Jacobson, *Norms and Neuroscience* In: *Feminist Philosophy of Mind*. Edited by: Keya Maitra and Jennifer McWeeny, Oxford University Press. © Oxford University Press 2022. DOI: 10.1093/oso/9780190867614.003.0012 common sense; it is also enshrined in a great deal of philosophical theory largely inherited from Descartes. Opposition to this view has a number of sources, but feminist philosophy is clearly one of them.

The challenges CNS presents both to prevailing theories and to common sense are relatively easy to describe. To situate such views within the picture of mentality as embodied, including socially embodied, is a harder task. We will try to go some distance with it. The account we arrive at places normativity at the center of cognitive ontology, and it does so in a way that connects the ontology with social facts. There will not be the space to investigate all the implications of the emerging view, but there are connected theses both in my own work, referenced elsewhere in this chapter, and in that of a number of other feminist writers, such as those appearing in *Mattering: Feminism, Science, and Materialism* (Pitts-Taylor 2016).

Borderline Personality Disorder and Its Problems

We will discuss some major problems arising from the notion of borderline personality disorder (BPD). The syndrome itself is problematic, as we are about to see. Accordingly, we will use it principally as an example to discuss how neuroscience can challenge a widespread interpretation of personality traits. If the neuroscience we will look at is correct, then this chapter does have genuinely enlightening things to say about the disorder. At the same time, we need to recognize that some excellent theoreticians have doubts about the validity of the categorization.

Thus, though there is considerable agreement about what should be said to be its major behavioral characteristics, very serious issues have been raised about BPD's legitimacy as a psychopathological category.[1] (I think the three most important concerns about it are: (a) the category pathologizes characteristics that are really just socially acquired ways of negotiating one's way through a limited set of alternatives; (b) the category takes a possibly illusory idea of male excellence and labels as ill those who do not present themselves as answering to it; (c) BPD sufferers are actually difficult people and the use of the category reflects a pervasive discomfort with difficult women.

We will start with behavior thought to typify BPD. BPD can involve relatively unusual behaviors, some of which look very much like tantrums directed to someone who is hardly deserving of such treatment. Consider this example involving a psychiatrist who accompanied her patient to a meeting about the results of removing cancerous material:

> That day I went into the ob-gyn's office with her and sat across from the doctor who reported great news that the patient was cancer-free. . . . Out in the hallway . . . my patient yelled and cried.

"You colluded with her! I can't believe how you doctors were so self-satisfied. You didn't even consider me. You and that doctor talked down to me like I was a moron!"

... "I hate you both!" she screamed and ran down the hall. I dashed after her, calling her name, but she jumped into an elevator and ran off. (Berman 2014)

Theorists, social critics, and psychotherapists who write about BPD tend to agree that it is typified by a number of features, including some or all of the following: an unstable sense of self; a deficit in empathy; a fear of abandonment and an inability to sustain relationships; risk taking and self-harming; splitting or successively idealizing and damning individuals. There are sometimes differences in emphasis, with the fragility in self accorded predominance in some accounts and the destructiveness of relationships emphasized in others. These two may be closely related, given the hypothesis we will see from CNS. Being unable to share a social reality with others may have a profound effect on one's sense of self.

The internet in fact has many descriptions of BPD. The National Institute of Mental Health provides us with a more fleshed-out list of symptoms in the following:

People with borderline personality disorder may experience extreme mood swings and can display uncertainty about who they are. As a result, their interests and values can change rapidly. Other symptoms include:
Frantic efforts to avoid real or imagined abandonment
  A pattern of intense and unstable relationships with family, friends, and loved ones, often swinging from extreme closeness and love (idealization) to extreme dislike or anger (devaluation)
  Distorted and unstable self-image or sense of self
  Impulsive and often dangerous behaviors, such as spending sprees, unsafe sex, substance abuse, reckless driving, and binge eating
  Recurring suicidal behaviors or threats or self-harming behavior, such as cutting
  Intense and highly changeable moods, with each episode lasting from a few hours to a few days
  Chronic feelings of emptiness
  Inappropriate, intense anger or problems controlling anger
  Having stress-related paranoid thoughts
  Having severe dissociative symptoms, such as feeling cut off from oneself, observing oneself from outside the body, or losing touch with reality
  Seemingly ordinary events may trigger symptoms. For example, people with borderline personality disorder may feel angry and distressed over minor

separations—such as vacations, business trips, or sudden changes of
plans—from people to whom they feel close. (National Institute of Mental
Health 2017)

From a feminist point of view, the typifying traits we have just seen can also easily
appear to be derived from a set of behaviors that many women, at least in the
West, arrive at as the best of a very narrow set of options allowed to them through
the restrictions of their society.[2] In an environment where a women's capacity
to rationally select among options is denigrated or denied, an emotional out-
burst may remain as the most effective instrument to influence others. When a
woman's worth, including her very livelihood, depends on her relationships with
others, abandonment may indeed be greatly feared. Accordingly, a feminist may
well approach the use of BPD as a diagnosis with the expectation that it reflects
not some well-grounded individual psychopathology but rather the negative
results of following the choices more or less forced on women.

We can add into the picture a commonly believed view of women failing to fit
a male model of stoic independence and cohesion. There has been quite a large
popular literature recently that has sought to ground the difference between men
and women in a difference between their brains (Brizendine 2006; Schulz 2005).
The differences in gender traits, however, are the ones which were accepted before much in brain science was generally available. Accordingly, men are stoic,
unemotional, analytic, ready to judge and punish others in terms of their adherence to the society's rules. Women, on the other hand, are emotional, helpful,
empathetic creatures who have scattered attention.

A similar picture can also be found in more professional literature. As in the
Gilligan-Kolhberg disagreement, men are often said to be interested in justice
and rules, while women's empathetic concern for caring for people keeps them
more focused on relationships with others (Gilligan 1982). According to one
major way of drawing the contrast, men are systematizers, capable of concen-
trating on one topic, but women tend not to have the capacity for a narrow focus
(Baron-Cohen 2004).

Another but perhaps related problem arises when the BPD person enters
the clinical, diagnostic setting. Such settings can have features that are very dis-
tressing to clients with BPD. Susan Nyquist Potter gives an interesting account of
how a standard approach in much psychotherapy can provide an anger-inducing
failure to recognize a client's authenticity (Potter 2009). The negative demanding
reactions of someone with BPD in such cases may in fact be quite close to a response from someone without that syndrome. The BPD patient, however, often
arouses very negative responses from therapists in such situations. Studies have
found that clinicians tend to impute the ability to have self-control to BPD
patients in comparison with clients with other diagnoses and, then, blame them

for their behavior. Correspondingly, clinicians are less likely to be empathetic. A patient may be difficult at the outset, but she may also become even more "difficult" in response to the reception she is getting.

The history of European society's treatment of difficult women is not fortunate. Both witches and hysterics can be seen as earlier examples of recipients of the very adverse treatment difficult women can receive. We may indeed find the foundations of psychiatry emerging with the institutionalizing of hysterics (Gunn and Potter 2015).

From what we have seen, today's BPD sufferer may differ from others in ways significantly brought about by differences in environment. Those who object to the BPD label on feminist social constructionist grounds may be starting from just this point of view. A social constructionist account of some phenomenon holds it is created by society and culture, as opposed to occurring independently of the specifics of a culture's beliefs and evaluations. It is important that social constructionist accounts may vary according to whether they attribute any causally basic neural similarity beyond the behavioral syndrome created by society (Haslanger 2012). In any case, a feminist version of the view will tend both to be concerned with the effects of being labeled in terms of the phenomenon and to emphasize the power relations involved in using the labels.

Accordingly, a feminist may well approach the use of BPD as a diagnosis with the expectation that it reflects not some well-grounded individual psychopathology but rather the negative results of following the choices more or less forced on women. And added to this is the failure of women to adopt a male display of independence and cohesion. We might, then, think that the unattractiveness of BPD is really in the eye of the beholder; as such, it is evidence of a social creation.

Recent neuroscience, however, has provided an explanatory account of BPD that challenges aspects of what we have just seen. One thing it does is to locate a fundamental aspect of the disorder in the workings of the brain. As such, it places BPD at the biologically grounded end of the socially constructed spectrum. Much in the clinical attitudes toward and treatment of BPD may be the product of social values, but there is significantly more to it than just that.[3]

A Neuroscientific Approach

Feminist theorizing has historically displayed some antipathy toward CNS. In large part this was due to the quite early claims that investigating the brain showed why patriarchal divisions of labor were good and natural. Given that the distinctions between men and women we saw above are often said now to be the result of neurophysiological differences, this is a matter of important and continuing disagreement (Bluhm, Jacobson, and Maibom 2012; Fine 2010, 2005, 2017). In addition, CNS has been seen as offering reductive explanations that dehumanize human characteristics. Nonetheless, there are also now attempts to re-understand a feminist, materialist perspective that engenders a more positive approach to much in neuroscience (Pitts-Taylor 2016). Accordingly, this chapter provides a place for human values in determining the ontology of neuroscience; the resulting view is quite different from the more traditional twentieth-century approaches.

The woman in the episode described near the opening of the previous section seems highly sensitive to slights. At the same time, we might well think that she cannot fully comprehend how hurtful her reaction to the therapist would have been. But in fact CNS reverses this story (King-Casas et al. 2008; Kagel and Roth 2015). What we are learning is that those with BPD are deeply incapable of establishing the cooperative relationships so many of us can easily do. And this incapacity is due to a failure in a region of the brain.

In the relevant research, subjects were asked to participate in a well-studied "trust game" (Berg et al. 1995). A "trustee" and an "investor" successively give each other some money. Success depends on trust and cooperation, including being able to repair the trust if broken. The BPD subjects in particular could not repair broken cooperation; very significantly, they could not read the signals that the trustee sent to indicate mistakes on their part, while the trustees failed to be able to form an adequate picture of the BPD subject's thought processes.

The fundamental explanation of the failures comes from fMRI scans that reveal an asymmetrical reaction in one brain region, the anterior insula. The research we are looking at indicates the insula is involved in reactions to norm violations, both when the subject violates a norm and when the subject is the target of a norm violation. According to the readings of the fMRI scans, the BPD subjects were registering when they were violating norms, but they did not experience the norm-violating negativity directed at them (King-Casas et al. 2008). This result is contrary to what clinicians and others ordinarily think is going on with BPD subjects. That is the idea that BPD subjects are vulnerable people with challenged egos who fly off the handle when they perceive a slight. It is much more accurate to say that BPD subjects do not perceive slights. Rather, the source of irritation must be something else, such as their sense that they are in an unintelligible situation.

This research can provide a systematic understanding of the concept of BPD by our employing a rich account of concepts that enables us to articulate a structure for our concept of borderline personality disorder. The account, sometimes called "the theory account" (Machery 2009; Murphy 2002), takes concepts of kinds to refer both to recognition conditions and to an underlying metaphysically necessary cause of such conditions, or its essence. In such a case, the essence

of the illness is internal and asocial. But psychological illnesses are also importantly connected to aspects of the society in which their sufferers occur (Davies
2016). On such an account, BPD is not and cannot be purely dispositional.
Without any manifestations, there is no BPD.

Let us stress that human interests in BPD go vastly beyond anything like neural
conditions. BPD is in many ways a social phenomenon. Nonetheless, attending
to the neural basis of BPD means we need to revise our understanding of BPD.
Many have found it obvious that BPD reactions are overreactions to slights. It
may be more accurately thought of as a manifestation of a failure to understand
the social situation. But what we have missed out on previously goes beyond this
gap in our understanding. That is, we have missed out on the consequences of the
failure of the BPD sufferer to register negative reactions from others. That failure
means they do not share at all fully in the social reality of others and that they are,
or should be, themselves an enigma to those interacting with them.

Philosophical Objections

We will look at a particularly important objection to taking asymmetrical
reactions of the insula to constitute a metaphysically necessary cause of the observable symptoms of BPD. This objection comes from the insistence on a per-
sonal/subpersonal distinction. Jennifer Hornsby and Daniel C. Dennett are early
advocates of it (Hornsby 2000; Dennett 1969; Drayson 2014).

The personal/subpersonal distinction is sometimes presented as just the observation that properties of a whole person cannot be attributed to a proper
part of the person. For example, Jones believes, but Jones's brain does not believe, even if Jones's brain's activity is thought to be the main site of belief-related
neural activity. There are, however, too many cases where part-whole boundaries
are not respected in the attribution of properties. Thus, if one says one is in pain,
the question "Where does it hurt?" is an invitation to locate the pain in a part of
the person even though being in pain is attributed to the person. In addition,
for a number of theorists, psychological states are to be understood in terms of
brain mechanisms, where descriptions of the contribution of the parts are very
important to our understanding of the grounding of the states. For such theories,
descriptions of the mechanisms can provide a complete characterization of the
psychological state. Hence, insisting on the distinction begs the question about
such theories.

A more seemingly solid version of the objection starts by saying that personal-
level properties are often normative (Thornton 2013). But the level of neural facts
investigated by CNS is not normative, it is maintained, and so it cannot be ground

or be essential to personal facts. Similarly, normative personal-level properties cannot be (partially) constitutive of most neural reactions, and vice versa.

We can see embodied mind theorists as developing another version of the argument from the personal/subpersonal distinction. For them the problem is that subpersonal causal relationships are not going to add up to some personal-level phenomenon. I think we can agree in part with this point. For example, one needs far more than asymmetrical activity in the insula to get the chaotic relationships borderline persons characteristically have. But just as the biological importance and the social implications of the existence of a human fetus do *not* show it cannot be characterized on a cellular level, so it seems right to say that the consequences of the asymmetrical activity do not show that the essence of BPD cannot be a neural condition.

Normativity and Neuroscience

The question of levels and reduction is often envisaged as involving levels where, as in Hume's world, one little thing happens after another. The little things may be at the atomic or neural level, but on this picture, the explanatory aim is to uncover regularities and the laws that express them. A normatively neutral description in terms of mechanisms is presumably also possible (Chirimuuta 2014; Craver and Darden 2013; Craver 2007). Instead of one little thing happening after another, we have little things interacting with other little things, or parts of them. Instead of laws, we have algorithms for interactions. Whether or not such a picture fits physics, it drastically mischaracterizes CNS. CNS has an explanatory task that is quite different. To see this, we can look at a norm-neutral model of a cognitive neuroscientific explanation:

> But one sort of understanding that cognitive scientists are often interested in achieving is analogous to the understanding that one would have of a clock if one could identify each of its functional parts (its springs and cogwheels, its pendulum, and so on), and the way in which all these parts interact to bring it about that the clock has a reliable disposition to tell the correct time....
>
> An analogous understanding of how a computer works would involve an understanding of the structure of its electrical circuits and of the logical structure of its programming code. If this is the sort of understanding that cognitive science is particularly interested in, that would help to explain why cognitive scientists are so interested in actually trying to *build* machines that can do some of the things that minds can do. (Wedgwood 2006, 311)

It is important to see, nonetheless, that this description does not fit the goals of CNS as actually practiced, and that it should not be true of it. CNS in general does not aim simply to describe the mechanism of some subset of a kind of object. Rather, it aims to describe what it is for objects of the kind to work well. Similarly, a medical textbook may describe the internal workings of a kidney, but it will be a well-functioning kidney that is connected to other organs in the body.

The idea that examining the internal workings of a clock will help us understand how it has the disposition to tell time has two large problems on its surface. First of all, a clock ticking over may not have that disposition. Perhaps it runs fast or slow, or perhaps its running is irregular or intermittent or both. Second, if you decouple the watch from its environment and take it to another time zone, it can stop telling the correct time without any internal change.

The clock example illustrates a major difference between typical philosophical aims and those of CNS. Philosophy is often interested in where the line between, for example, seeing and not seeing is drawn. CNS, in contrast, is interested in what it is to see well. The central task of CNS, as P. Read Montague and Steven R. Quartz have pointed out, is to explain how a creature solves the problems posed by its niche (Montague and Quartz 1999). Thus a neuroscientist looking at the organs we employ in cognitive activities is looking at those organs' functions and how they perform those functions. Performing their functions well will be part of what it is for the organism to solve the problems posed by its niche.

So far we have a good argument for locating normativity in neuroscientific explanations; neuroscience aims to describe what it is to function well. Still, one might argue that this normativity is eliminable. We can just naturalize "function" and so eliminate the normativity.

A discussion of naturalizing will take us on quite a detour. So here it will have to suffice to challenge a major component of the majority of attempts to naturalize functions. The outstanding naturalizing account for functions is the selected effect account. On this view, functions of objects or traits are selected by evolution. Functioning well is just then functioning as a trait or thing is selected to function. And "selected" here may just mean that it is that functioning that contributed to the trait or organism increasing its presence in a relevant population. For this view, we can think of the items as having numerical success, which is to be understood in factual terms as increasing its representation.

There is a problem with this view, however. The problem is that there are ways of functioning that have come on the scene too recently for evolutionary success to explain their presence. Among the late arrivers are ballet dancing, driving at night, and reading.

Can the idea of a derived function developed by Ruth Garrett Millikan bring such items under the "selected for" label (1984)? On this account, a function is derived from a primary, selected function if it is necessary in a context to realize the primary function. There is a problem applying this solution to all the cases just mentioned. In particular, reading requires, among other things, a rewiring effected by cultural demands that creates new, nonevolved functions. Culture changes the brain's functions, as we are about to see.

Recent research on reading shows the unlikeliness of explaining reading ability as a selected effect rather than a cultural object; learning to read involves very substantially changing the inherited brain:

> From a basic research point of view, working with illiterate people is also very rewarding. Writing is a very recent cultural invention if we look at the evolutionary history of our species. The first proper scripts were invented less than 6000 years ago. That means there is no reading area or reading network that could be specified in our genes. Looking at how cultural inventions change brain function and structures helps us to understand how the brain works on a fundamental level.
>
> . . . We found the expected changes in the cortex but we also observed that the learning process leads to a reorganization that extends to deep brain structures in the thalamus and the brainstem. The relatively young phenomenon of human literacy therefore changes brain regions that are very old in evolutionary terms and already core parts of mice and other mammalian brains.
>
> . . . These deep structures in the thalamus and brainstem help our visual cortex to filter important information from the flood of visual input even before we consciously perceive it. Interestingly, it seems that the more the signal timings between the two brain regions are aligned, the better the reading capabilities. (Skeide et al. 2017)

Learning to read progressively alters the ancient structure of the brain. Neither the results needed for reading nor the original structures are or were selected by evolution.

I have maintained that CNS's interest in functioning is principally an interest in functioning well. We still, however, lack an account of how to characterize what functioning well amounts to. In addition, we need to situate BPD in this latter part of our discussion.

If evolution does not give us the sense of "well-functioning," what does? Let us start with ourselves and our judgments. Even the slightest knowledge of early medicine reveals that the human species has long had complaints about bodily functioning and symptoms of malfunctioning. We may quite dislike the way things are going in some part of our body, or we may be quite pleased with other areas. Certainly our understanding of the facts of well and poor functioning has changed greatly, but it seems highly likely that well and poor functioning are to be understood largely in terms of our interests. Some of these interests will be so closely tied to our survival that they may be hard to see as simply interests. Nonetheless, our evaluations of things like the reading abilities of people with mild dyslexia, along with the social abilities of people on the autism spectrum disorder, start to look like simply agreed-upon interests, as many disability theorists have argued (Barnes 2016).

Our account here comes close to a development of an account initially proposed by Robert Cummins that draws on the idea that the function of some trait is a matter of its causal contribution to the larger system of which it is a part (1975). On the initial version a trait or thing will end up with a very large array of functions, since it will be part of multiple systems. A more recent defense holds that the effects that it is a thing's function to produce are the effects for the system that we are interested in. In this version, the account ceases to naturalize functions, since "our interests" bring in both perspective and normativity. They are a matter of what we think is important. Nonetheless, the account seems to fit well with the conclusions our investigation has revealed.

When we see BPD as a disability, we can be reminded that a number of cultural factors help shape the problematic positions its sufferers occupy. Our culture disdains difficult women, while many standard therapeutic features may make the situation BPD patients encounter at least unfriendly. In addition, our culture may encourage in women features that make them very prone to possessing characteristics of BPD sufferers. However, there is a very serious underlying problem that recent work in CNS has brought out. This is a failure to be able to establish cooperative relationships. In social creatures such as ourselves, this ability is close to the core abilities required for anything we might count as fitness.

As we can see from the place of BPD as a disability, CNS may not solve all the problems feminist theorists find in a classification of mental syndromes. What was initially claimed for it has nonetheless been shown true: CNS can show up new ways of thinking about the human mind that challenge approaches coming from a mixture of supposed common sense and early psychological theorizing, ones which are the product of and serve the aims of nonfeminist approaches. At the very least, this feature of CNS can support feminist theorists in questioning patriarchal views of women. It also opens up a harder task: discovering news ways of thinking about ourselves.

Notes

1. See, for example, Wirth-Cauchon (2001), Friedel (2004), Sharp and Sieswerda (2013), and Gunn and Potter (2015).
2. Until recently there has been wide agreement that a large majority of those diagnosed with BPD are women; the figure is put at 75%–90%. This view may, however, reflect more accurately the fact that women are disproportionately more likely to be diagnosed as having BPD (Sansone and Sansone 2011).
3. The discussion in this chapter principally concerns CNS's ability to introduce new and possibly empirically more adequate accounts of various psychological traits. There are a number of other examples where CNS makes available new interpretations. These include the perception of affordances, our imitative capacities, and some types of implicit bias. One consequence of this focus is that the discussion is orthogonal to other recent considerations about normativity and mental illnesses, where the emphasis is much more about whether psychopathological categories have scientific validity. The interested reader can find an overview of this debate and an excellent bibliography in Varga (2017).

References

Barnes, Elizabeth. 2016. *The Minority Body: A Theory of Disability*. Oxford: Oxford University Press.

Baron-Cohen, Simon. 2004. *The Essential Difference: Male and Female Brains and the Truth about Autism*. New York: Basic Books.

Berg, Joyce, John Dickhaut, and Kevin McCabe. 1995. "Trust, Reciprocity, and Social History." *Games and Economic Behavior* 10 (1): 122–142.

Bluhm, Robyn, Anne Jaap Jacobson, and Heidi Lene Maibom. 2012. *Neurofeminism: Issues at the Intersection of Feminist Theory and Cognitive Science*. New York: Palgrave Macmillan.

Brizendine, Louann. 2006. *The Female Brain*. New York: Morgan Road Books.

Berman, Carol W. 2014. "9 Tips on How to Recognize Someone with Borderline Personality Disorder." April 28. https://www.huffpost.com/entry/9-tips-on-how-to-recogniz_b_5224432.

Chirimuuta, Mazviita. 2014. "Minimal Models and Canonical Neural Computations: The Distinctness of Computational Explanation in Neuroscience." *Synthese* 191 (2): 127–153.

Craver, Carl F. 2007. *Explaining the Brain: Mechanisms and the Mosaic Unity of Neuroscience*. Oxford: Oxford University Press.

Craver, Carl F., and Lindley Darden. 2013. *In Search of Mechanisms: Discoveries across the Life Sciences*. Chicago: University of Chicago Press.

Cummins, Robert. 1975. "Functional Analysis." *Journal of Philosophy* 72 (20): 741–765.

Davies, Will. 2016. "Externalist Psychiatry." *Analysis* 76 (3): 290–296.

Dennett, Daniel C. 1969. *Content and Consciousness*. London: Routledge and Kegan Paul.

Drayson, Zoe. 2014. "The Personal/Subpersonal Distinction." *Philosophy Compass* 9 (5): 338–346.

Fine, Cordelia. 2005. *A Mind of Its Own: How Your Brain Distorts and Deceives*. Crows Nest, New South Wales: Allen & Unwin.

Fine, Cordelia. 2010. *Delusions of Gender: How Our Minds, Society, and Neurosexism Create Difference*. New York: Norton.

Fine, Cordelia. 2017. *Testosterone Rex: Myths of Sex, Science, and Society*. New York: Norton.

Friedel, Robert O. 2004. *Borderline Personality Disorder Demystified*. New York: Da Capo Press.

Gilligan, Carol. 1982. *In a Different Voice: Psychological Theory and Women's Development*. Cambridge, MA: Harvard University Press.

Gunn, Jacqueline Simon, and Brent Potter. 2015. *Borderline Personality Disorder: New Perspectives on a Stigmatizing and Overused Diagnosis*. Santa Barbara: Praeger.

Haslanger, Sally. 2012. *Resisting Reality: Social Construction and Social Critique*. New York: Oxford University Press.

Hornsby, Jennifer. 2000. "Personal and Sub-personal: A Defence of Dennett's Early Distinction." *Philosophical Explorations* 3 (1): 6–24.

Kagel, John H., and Alvin E. Roth, eds. 2015. *The Handbook of Experimental Economics*. Vol. 2. Princeton, NJ: Princeton University Press.

King-Casas, Brooks, Carla Sharp, Laura Lomax-Bream, Terry Lohrenz, Peter Fonagy, and P. Read Montague. 2008. "The Rupture and Repair of Cooperation in Borderline Personality Disorder." *Science* 321 (5890): 806–810.

Machery, Edouard. 2009. *Doing without Concepts*. New York: Oxford University Press.

Millikan, Ruth Garrett. 1984. *Language, Thought, and Other Biological Categories: New Foundations for Realism*. Cambridge, MA: MIT Press.

Montague, P. Read, and Steven R. Quartz. 1999. "Computational Approaches to Neural Reward and Development." *Mental Retardation And Developmental Disabilities Research Reviews* 5 (1): 86–99.

Murphy, Gregory L. 2002. *The Big Book of Concepts*. Cambridge, MA: MIT Press.

National Institute of Mental Health. 2017. "Borderline Personality Disorder." https://www.nimh.nih.gov/health/topics/borderline-personality-disorder/index.shtml.

Pitts-Taylor, Victoria. 2016. *Mattering: Feminism, Science, and Materialism*. New York: New York University Press.

Potter, Nancy Nyquist. 2009. *Mapping the Edges and the In-Between: A Critical Analysis of Borderline Personality Disorder*. Oxford: Oxford University Press.

Sansone Randy A., and Lori A. Sansone. 2011. "Gender Patterns in Borderline Personality Disorder." *Innovations in Clinical Neuroscience* 8 (5): 16–20.

Schulz, Mona Lisa. 2005. *The New Feminine Brain: How Women Can Develop Their Inner Strengths, Genius, and Intuition*. New York: Free Press.

Sharp, Carla, and Simkje Sieswerda. 2013. "The Social-Cognitive Basis of Borderline and Antisocial Personality Disorder: Introduction." *Journal of Personality Disorders* 27 (1): 1–2.

Skeide, Michael A., Uttam Kumar, Ramesh K. Mishra, Viveka N. Tripathi, Anupam Guleria, Jay P. Singh, Frank Eisner, and Falk Huettig. 2017. "Learning to Read Alters Cortico-Subcortical Cross-Talk in the Visual System of Illiterates." *Science Advances* 3 (5): 1–7.

Thornton, Tim, 2013. "Clinical Judgment, Tacit Knowledge, and Recognition in Psychiatric Diagnosis." In *Oxford Handbook of Philosophy and Psychiatry*, edited by K. W. M. Fulford, Martin Davies, Richard G. T. Gipps, George Graham, John Z. Sadler, Giovanni Stanghellini, and Tim Thornton, 1047–1062. Oxford: Oxford University Press.

Varga, Somogy. 2017. "Mental Disorder between Naturalism and Normativism." *Philosophy Compass* 12 (6): 1–9.

Wagner, Jenny, and Ron Brooks. 1977. *The Bunyip of Berkeley's Creek*. Scarsdale, NY: Bradbury Press.

Wedgwood, Ralph. 2006. "The Internal and External Components of Cognition." In *Contemporary Debates in Cognitive Science*, edited by Robert J. Stainton, 307–325. Malden, MA: Blackwell.

Wirth-Cauchon, Janet. 2001. *Women and Borderline Personality Disorder: Symptoms and Stories*. New Brunswick, NJ: Rutgers University Press.

12

Embodiments of Sex and Gender

The Metaphors of Speaking Surfaces

Gabrielle Benette Jackson

Within feminist theory, embodiments of sex and gender may be explained differently, depending on whether one takes a social constructivist or phenomenological approach. My aim in this chapter is to show that specific recurring
metaphors, used within both strains of feminist theorizing, carry an undue ideological weight. Time and again, we find sex and gender symbolically carved onto
the surfaces of bodies that figuratively speak a hegemonic text. I call these "the
metaphors of speaking surfaces." I argue that these metaphors imply a conceptual
dichotomy wherein sex and gender are *either* the product of self-willed personal
choice *or* the consequence of social forces imposed onto the individual from the
outside. This either/or has been forcefully criticized in philosophy of mind and
phenomenology, and even targeted specifically on feminist grounds, as being
unable to capture the lived experience of agency. And yet it is found in feminist
theorizing about sex and gender, inadvertently let in through the metaphorics
of speaking surfaces, sometimes in the work of the very same theorists who dis-
parage this dichotomy in their other writings. Because metaphors shape and
influence our thinking, deploying a poorly chosen one can obscure the phenomenon it is meant to illuminate, and we set out trying to understand the wrong,
because displaced, thing. I contend that the metaphors of speaking surfaces have
this distorting effect in many feminist accounts of the embodiments of sex and
gender, and should be abandoned.

In this chapter, I have three goals. First, I must show that these metaphors
are the guiding metaphors within this important thread of feminist theorizing—
as expressed in the works of Susan Bordo, Elizabeth Grosz, and Judith
Butler. This is the exegetical project I take up in the first two sections of the
chapter: "Embodiments of Sex and Gender" and "Metaphors of Speaking
Surfaces." My second goal is to argue that the metaphors of speaking surfaces
rest on a questionable dichotomy: that the sexed and gendered body is *either* internally chosen *or* externally constituted. I take this up in the third and fourth
sections of the chapter: "Interlude on Metaphors" and "Critique of Speaking
Surfaces." Having identified these metaphors and drawn out their problematic

Gabrielle Benette Jackson, *Embodiments of Sex and Gender* In: *Feminist Philosophy of Mind.*
Edited by: Keya Maitra and Jennifer McWeeny, Oxford University Press. © Oxford University Press 2022.
DOI: 10.1093/oso/9780190867614.003.0013

consequences, I suggest a way to bypass both, which involves the project of producing precise descriptions of the iterated patterns of bodily behaviors that constitute sex and gender—to theorize sexed and gendered bodies, literally, as they are. This is the topic of the fifth section of the chapter: "Bodily Agency."

Embodiments of Sex and Gender

To claim that sex and gender are *socially constructed* is to reject the view there are innate or essential, fixed or inevitable traits determining what it is to be a boy or girl, a woman or man, masculine or feminine, male or female.[1] Instead, social constructivists argue that the biological, physiological, behavioral, and psychological characteristics associated with these categories—the basis upon which we often identify and distinguish women from men, males from females—are produced by the social forces of history, society, ideology, and culture. Importantly, these dynamics have the added effect of managing the power relations among the genders and sexes—maintaining or even augmenting the status quo of who has authority over whom, how this control is enforced, and in which spheres of life that influence can be exerted. For those who believe in social construction, the apparent reality of gender and sex is made and remade through material practices, discourses, and power.

To offer a *phenomenological* analysis of sex and gender is to start from a different point—treating a woman or man, or a male or female, as modes of being in the world that, while not fundamental in themselves, are fundamentally manifest in and through bodies. Phenomenologists disclose the patterns of bodily behavior that produce sex and gender. When those practices are found to be constraining, repressive, or oppressive, phenomenologists propose paths to liberation by imagining how those performances might be reformed—a phenomenological exercise put to feminist goals.

When the social constructivist and the phenomenologist focus their analyses on bodily practices, they find that the embodiments of sex and gender are sometimes achieved by *explicit decisions* on the part of the individual, as would be familiar to anyone who has thought about whether to have children or breastfeed (in public), what constitutes the best exercised body, what is appropriate work attire or handshake firmness, whether an exchange at the office amounts to sexual harassment, or what constitutes consent in a sexual encounter—and then to act on those deliberations. These accounts of sexed and gendered embodiments remind us of how we choose to conform to gendered roles or sexed types, perhaps giving us an opportunity to decide whether to go on with those practices. Here one also finds analyses of bodily practices that question or subvert normative iterations of sex and gender—for example, as in Beauvoir's descriptions in *The*

Second Sex of the lesbian and the liberated woman (Beauvoir 2011); discussions of drag in Butler's early work (Butler 1990); Anne Fausto-Sterling's presentation of the five sexes (Fausto-Sterling 1993); bell hooks's accounts of black and brown female embodiments (hooks 1982); Mary Russo's history of the female grotesque (Russo 1994); Kathy Davis's interest in radical body art (Davis 1997); Nancy Mair's writing on disabled embodiment (Mair 1997); and in the many writings on androgynous, genderqueer, and trans identities. In these works, subversion is achieved through an act of concerted imagination, envisioning how the current situation might be different, and then making it so, in practice.

And yet the embodiments of sex and gender are just as often *tacitly manifested* through gestures and manners that have been drilled down, hidden, and obscured by their location in the background of everyday life. Both the social constructivist and phenomenologist contribute to our understanding of these tacit manifestations of sex and gender, too. The emergence of sex and gender can be surprisingly commonplace: for example, in Beauvoir's descriptions of the girl, the married woman, and the mother (Beauvoir 2011); in Iris Marion Young's account of athletic comportment ("throwing like a girl") (Young 2005); and Linda Alcoff's discussions of gender and race (Alcoff 2006). It emerges in everyday practices: learned patterns of speech (like *vocal fry* and *up-speak*), customs (crossing one's legs, smiling at strangers), and even seemingly trivial habits, as where one's hand automatically reaches to button one's shirt (if it is a woman's shirt, the buttons are on the right). In the case of tacit manifestations of sex and gender, we do not realize the ways we enact these norms until we see them written out before us—enunciated in those careful descriptions of everyday gestures and manners—at which point we can entertain whether they help us abide, or keep us from flourishing.

In feminist theorizing about embodiment, the relationship between social constructivism and phenomenology is not a straightforward one. Many theorists believe that these orientations can be quite distinct, as the explanations offered do tend to diverge: with sex and gender either constructed through power relations or expressed in bodily movements.[2] And yet for both approaches, what is under investigation is the same: the embodiments of gendered roles or sexed types. And so is their goal: to understand the ways in which gendered roles and sexed types are manifest in and through bodily practices, as possible objects of biopower, by individual choices, and through the comportments of everyday life.

Metaphors of Speaking Surfaces

What exactly is the relation between the norms of gender and sex and bodily practices? Looking at both the social constructivist and phenomenological literature, words like "produce," "generate," "manifest," and "constitute" are repeatedly used. But how do feminists of embodiment theorize these terms? How exactly are norms built into, or through, the body? When I looked deeper into those texts for answers, I was surprised by what I found: *metaphors*. And very particular metaphors at that.

Women's bodies are "sites" where norms of femininity are "made explicit"; the "surface" of the body "signifies" conventions by being "etched" or "inscribed" or "written" upon; and even when the woman does not literally speak, the norms figuratively "speak" for her or are "read" off her body.[3] In my best approximation of a survey, I have identified two related lines of metaphors:

(1) *Bodies as Texts or Scripts*: on this version of the metaphor, gender and sex are "texts" that bodies involuntarily "speak" (as in "narrate") and what they "say" is "I am a woman" or "I am a man," "I am female" or "I am male."

(2) *Bodies as Surfaces or Sites*: on this version of the metaphor, gender and sex are "etched" or "inscribed" or "written" on bodies that are "viewed" or "read," and what they "express" is "this is a woman" or "that is a man," "this is female" or "that is male."

You can pick up book after book, I would suggest, and find these metaphors of "speaking surfaces" in some form—as in, for instance, Carrie Noland's book, *Agency and Embodiment*, where she writes that "it is now time to explore how the body might speak to us—not beyond but through cultural frames" (Noland 2009, 11); or Janet Wolf's words in *Feminine Sentences*, "the body [is] a privileged site of political intervention, precisely because it is the site of repression and possession" (Wolf 1990, 122); in Helena Michie's claim in *Flesh Made Word* that "[the word] 'women,' with verbs of passive alliance, remain inscribed in a patriarchical grammar" (Michie 1987, 96). And one may remember Monique Wittig's claim in "The Mark of Gender" that "language casts sheaves of reality upon the social body, stamping it and violently shaping it" (Wittig 1985, 4). A whole collection of authors who readily reach for these metaphors can be found in Katie Conboy, Nadia Medina, and Sarah Stanbury's 1997 edited volume entitled, not surprisingly, *Writing on the Body*.

While, as I say, metaphors of speaking surfaces crop up again and again in feminist texts, it is sometimes hard to say whether the authors who use them are truly theoretically committed to these metaphors, or whether it is a mere matter of style.[4] I will now present three major authors in whose works the metaphorics of speaking surfaces are used deliberately and repeatedly, with velocity: Susan Bordo (social constructivist), Elizabeth Grosz (phenomenologist), and Judith Butler (at times, both).

For Susan Bordo, in her excellent book *Unbearable Weight*, about female body image and its disorders, the body is entirely a surface or site for writing, until the moment that the written-upon woman begins to suffer and explode into overaction—at which point the body "speaks," even if the "words" are not the woman's own.

According to Bordo, young women learn to embody both the feminine and masculine values of their time. But because these values are deeply incompatible (because they are defined in opposition to one another, Bordo observes), in certain women, for undetermined reasons, normal bodily practices collapse into the pathological. Bordo writes that "the bodies of disordered women in this way offer themselves as an aggressively graphic text for the interpreter—a text that insists, actually demands, that it be read as a cultural statement, a statement about gender" (Bordo 1993, 169). The interpreter seems to be anyone who notices the pathological phenomenon, like Bordo herself. In a major statement, she writes:

> In hysteria, agoraphobia and anorexia, then, the woman's body may be viewed as a surface on which conventional constructions of femininity are exposed starkly to view, through their inscription in extreme or hyperliteral form. They are written, of course, in language of horrible suffering. It is as though these bodies are speaking to us. (Bordo 1993, 174–175)

But here, finally, in suffering, it is *as if* the woman's agency comes into play—along with a particular idea of speaking, as "shouting"—and thus giving a fake or illusory feeling of power:

> The language of femininity, when pushed to excess—when shouted and asserted, when disruptive and demanding—deconstructs into its opposite and makes available to the woman an illusory experience of power previously forbidden to her in virtue of her gender. (Bordo 1993, 179)

For Bordo, the norms of femininity are "written" on the women's body, like them or not. And when the woman finally "reads" them aloud, as revealed by her bodily behaviors, her "assertions" turn out to be only simulacra of language, because they are understood only through the skein of her pathology. For example, when the anorexic starves away her breasts, her body "says," "I don't want breasts," which her doctor "hears" as "I have a pathological relationship to my body, and therefore to my gender." There can be no uptake, as she intends. Likewise, the anorexic's ability to control her appetite, or to limit her caloric intake, her capacity to harm those who care about her, or to garner the concern of medical professionals—these powers exist only within the circumscribed, institutionalized context of her disorder. She lacks real power.

Elizabeth Grosz's metaphorics work differently from Bordo's. In her remarkable books *Volatile Bodies* and *Space, Time and Perversion*, Grosz too begins with the image of bodies as "inscribed surfaces." But she does not see the creation of the sexed and gendered body through a turn to "speech." Instead, she adds a dimension that analogizes corporeal modification of the physical body to a kind of textual engraving:

> This analogy between the body and a text remains a close one: the tools of body engraving—social, surgical, epistemic, disciplinary—all mark, indeed constitute, bodies in culturally specific ways; the writing instruments—the pen, stylus, spur, laser beam, clothing, diet, exercise—function to incise the body's blank page. (Grosz 1995, 117)

Already Grosz's preferred metaphor is that of the body as inscribed or carved, which creates the effect of depth (however shallow) on what otherwise would be a smooth surface. In her work we also find references to a Möbius strip (Grosz 1994, 36; Grosz 1995, 183) and intercalated surfaces that fold back onto themselves (Grosz 1993, 45–46).[5] Grosz's construal of enfolding-the-body's-inscribed-upon-page never overcomes the dichotomy of inside versus outside. Instead she imagines an increasingly folded, padded, and textured surface, which produces the illusion of interior. On her view, "the body is seen as a purely surface phenomenon, a complex, multifaceted surface folded back on itself, exhibiting a certain torsion but nevertheless a flat plane whose incision or inscription produces the (illusion or effect of) depth and interiority" (Grosz 1995, 116). For Grosz, the body manifests sex and gender by being "carved upon"—a decorated exterior that, because twisted and folded onto itself, creates the (false) impression of an interior. But no matter how many times you pleat, wrap, gather, or crumple a page, it is still a "surface." And without "depth," everything is external.

Finally, there is Judith Butler. In many of her works, she seems to prepare us for a more complex, less metaphorically determined description of bodily practices that produce gender and sex. Butler announces, "gender operates as an act of cultural inscription . . . and yet gender is not written on the body as the torturing instrument of writing in Kafka's 'In The Penal Colony' inscribes itself unintelligibly on the flesh of the accused" (Butler 1990, 146). Butler seems genuinely to be moving away from the metaphorics of text, speech, and writing. She adopts ideas from Beauvoir and Maurice Merleau-Ponty: "gender is instituted through the stylization of the body and, hence, must be understood as the mundane way in which bodily gestures, movements, and enactments of various kinds constitute [this] illusion" (Butler 1988, 519). In *Gender Trouble*, she expands this assertion, adding a bit of Michel Foucault to boot: "[Gender is] a set of repeated acts within a highly rigid regulatory frame that congeal over time to produce the appearance of substance, of a natural sort of being" (Butler 1990, 33). Even in other works, Butler is clear that gender and sex are exercises of bodily skill: "a purposive and appropriative set of acts, the acquisition of a skill" (Butler 1986, 36); and once more, "a project, a skill, a pursuit, an enterprise, even an industry" (Butler 1989, 256). So far, so good.

And yet, in her key moments, and in some of her most famous further steps, Butler abandons the possibly rich investigation into how bodily skills "produce," "constitute," or "institute" gender and sex. Instead, she reaches for the metaphorics of language, albeit Austinian ordinary language, but to language nonetheless, offering "performative utterances" (namely, "performativity") as her preferred metaphor for the bodily practices under scrutiny (Butler 1988, 1993). In explaining why she adopts this metaphor, Butler writes that "'performative' itself carries the double-meaning of 'dramatic' and 'non-referential'" (Butler 1988, 522). The gendered and sexed body is "dramatic" in the sense that it is played to an audience in a public space and "non-referential" because it is doing (as opposed to describing) something with words. Patterns of bodily behavior perform sex and gender in the same way that saying "I thee wed" in the right circumstances performs marriage. Thus, for Butler, the gendered and sexed body is performative not because it is nonlinguistic, but precisely because *it speaks*—in the sense given by ordinary language philosophy. In *Undoing Gender*, Butler finally admits that, "every time I try to write about the body, the writing ends up being about language" (Butler 2004a, 198). We are thrown back into the metaphors of speaking surfaces in characterizing the embodiments of gender and sex.

Interlude on Metaphors

A possible concern I must acknowledge before continuing is this: why do these *metaphors* matter so much, since they are, after all, not *explanations*? This is quite true. Metaphors are not explanations. But they do play an important role in our understanding. Metaphors are found explicitly in art and literature, for certain. And they actively operate in other areas, too—for example, in analogical reasoning, concept formation, model building, perspective taking, and so forth. An impressive amount of scholarship and debate turns on what metaphors are, how they work, and what they do.[6] All seem to agree that we run into trouble, however, when we misuse metaphors. What kind of trouble, exactly?

You could propose *a danger of substitution for explanations*: in some cases one finds that, if we are not careful, a nicely chosen metaphor can give the illusion of an explanation. For instance, "the war on drugs" is a metaphor that is too often taken literally, as a war (with a real enemy) requiring militarization, leading to the misdirected marshaling of attention and resources. But this is just sloppiness on our part. And I don't think this is what is being done with the metaphors of speaking surfaces.

The real hazard is that metaphors have the potential *to model phenomena inaccurately*: a framing that then makes us look for the wrong kinds of explanation, or explanations for the wrong—because now slightly displaced—phenomena. Once this happens, we are too much misled to remember our original query, and the details we fight hard to fill in about those phenomena are simply for things that do not exist.

For instance, visual metaphors are found everywhere in philosophical writing. Consider Thomas Nagel's contribution: "the view from nowhere" (Nagel 1986). We know full well that, taken literally, the view from nowhere is no view at all. It is a metaphor for objectivity. For Nagel, an objective account is one that does not privilege any one point of view. In a succinct statement, Nagel explains, "the less it depends on specific subjective capacities—the more objective it is" (Nagel 1986, 5). The experiences of subjects, the perspectives of individual people, and the standpoints of political groups cannot be objective because they necessarily, essentially involve points of view. Not that points of view do not matter; for Nagel, they are inescapable. In reviewing *The View from Nowhere*, Bernard Williams sums up Nagel's view elegantly, if not vertiginously: "experience or thought is had from a certain point of view: the objective account is an account *of* that point of view which is not itself given *from* that point of view" (Williams 1986, 5).

And here is where we get into the misuse of metaphors—of potentially modeling target phenomena incorrectly. Continuing with the example of "the view from nowhere," at the interface of philosophy of mind and feminism, we find a host of feminists who argue that "the view from nowhere" models objectivity incorrectly, even dangerously. For example, Catherine MacKinnon claims that this kind of objectivity is objectifying because it offers (in disguise) an omnipresent male gaze as the view from nowhere (MacKinnon 1983). Donna Haraway calls the view from nowhere "an illusion, a god trick" that allows us to not be answerable for what we see (Haraway 1988, 583). And Sandra Harding argues that "strong objectivity" actually requires privileging certain (subaltern) standpoints over other (hegemonic) ones (Harding 1993).[7] My point is that if "the view from nowhere" is a poorly chosen metaphor, modeling objectivity incorrectly (and I am not saying whether it is), then contorting ourselves to understand Nagel's puzzle of "viewing the inside from the outside" is wasted intellectual energy at best, and counterproductive to feminism at worst. The metaphors we use do matter.

Again, my concern is not with mistaking metaphors for explanations. I have to believe feminists are not making this error—that they do not think women are literal texts to be read, or actual surfaces on which to write. And I should state here, too, that my concern is not with metaphors containing implicit marks of patriarchy (of course, we should always be vigilant). Rather, my real worry is about incorrectly modeling, and therefore misunderstanding, the embodiments of sex and gender. That is, the metaphors of speaking surfaces may classify sex and gender in a way that obscures a deeper, or at least different, analysis. Whether social constructivist or phenomenological, feminists who address issues of sexed and gendered embodiments rightly say, "Note the implications of patriarchy on your bodies!" I would add, now, notice the implications of the metaphors offered by these feminists.

Critique of Speaking Surfaces

By assuming the metaphors of speaking surfaces, feminists of embodiment are displacing the target phenomena—the embodiments of sex and gender—and thereby committing themselves to a misleading either/or. Specifically, they preserve the idea of bodily practices as controlled *either internally or externally*, an assertion of an exclusive disjunction. They seem to reason that if gender and sex do not emanate from "the inside" of the animate individual—from a deep, core, existential part of oneself, an innate spring of will, which authentically expresses these traits—then gender and sex must be surface phenomena imposed from "the outside"—by external historical, societal, ideological, or cultural forces. For feminists of embodiment, overcoming the traditional oppressive story of an internal source of gender and sex (*bursting forth, from the inside*) involves constituting sexed and gendered bodily practices externally (*pressing down, from the outside*). We see their commitment to this reversal through the metaphors of speaking surfaces: of bodies, ventriloquized by social forces, speaking or shouting their gender and sex, of social forces writing or carving the body into scripted gendered and sexed forms, publicly performed for the masses. Bordo, Grosz, and Butler each have slightly different ways of doing this.

Bordo claims that gender and sex are pressed onto the body from the outside, leaving the host few resources with which to object, in rare cases, a turn toward pathology. In her words, "a steady motif in the feminist literature on female disorder is that of pathology as embodied protest—unconscious, inchoate, and counterproductive protest without an effective language, voice, or politics, but protest nonetheless" (Bordo 1993, 175). Here we might think that Bordo is moving beyond metaphor by introducing embodied protest. Refusing to eat or to digest, the symptoms of hysteria, frigidity, or generally garnering attention out of concern rather than admiration—these seem like rebellions against the impossible norms of sexed and gendered embodiment. But, looking more closely, we realize this is not an explanation of the structure of female disorder, it is just another metaphor—*pathology as embodied protest*. And an equivocal one at that—it is unclear what notion of pathology is supposed to emerge from this comparison. Insofar as embodied protest is "unconscious, inchoate, and counterproductive protest without an effective language, voice, or politics," what does it have in common with familiar forms of protest—how could it be "protest nonetheless" (Bordo 1993, 175)? And on behalf of whom exactly, or what, is this protest carried out? Bordo leads us away, rather than toward, answers. Upon reflection, pathology as embodied protest does not even seem like a good metaphor for the phenomenon Bordo so carefully, and concretely, describes. Because we are the ones who "view" the norms "inscribed" on the female patient, her body can "speak" and "protest," but she cannot. She lacks genuine power. On her account, the agent has disappeared.

Relatedly, Grosz relies on the distinction between inside and outside, even as she focuses on enfolded surfaces. She writes that the body is "an open materiality, a set of (possibly infinite) tendencies and potentialities which may be developed" (Grosz 1994, 190). When it comes to constructing gendered and sexed bodies, however, "these are not individually or consciously chosen, nor are they amenable to will or intentionality: they are more like bodily styles, habits, practices" (Grosz 1994, 190). Here Grosz makes the interesting claim that the body is equipped for a set of (possibly infinite) modes of life, and that the body is ushered, through habit, into a set of (decidedly finite) gendered forms and sexed types. But, in limiting the ways this development occurs, she too commits herself to the dogma of either inside or outside. For Grosz, habits are not manifestations of individual conscious choice, will, or intentionality. How could they be, inscribed as they are onto an interior-less, albeit enfolded, surface? Grosz leaves us no choice: styles are taught, habits are imposed, practices carve into the body from the outside. Once again, agency vanishes.

Butler makes a comparable move. Her early view that sex and gender are patterns of repetitive bodily acts relies heavily on a phenomenologically rich notion of action, including its "wider political and social structures" (Butler 1988, 523). She is explicit that "the body is *not passively scripted with cultural codes*, as if it were a lifeless recipient of wholly pre-given cultural relations" (Butler 1988, 526; emphasis added). And her notion of gender as a "pre-reflective choice" strikes an auspicious tone:

> The choice to assume a certain kind of body, to live or wear one's body a certain way, implies a world of already established corporeal styles. To choose a gender is to interpret received gender norms in a way that reproduces and organizes

them anew. Less a radical act of creation, gender is a tacit project to renew a cultural history in one's own corporeal terms. (Butler 2004b, 26)

But in key moments like these, we find Butler advancing the metaphor of bodies that *perform* cultural codes. Where we might have hoped to find *action*, we find instead *actors*. She writes, "just as a script may be enacted in various ways, and just as the play requires both text and interpretation, so the gendered body acts its part in a culturally restricted corporeal space" (Butler 1988, 526). The collective historical, societal, ideological, or cultural elements are, once again, the scripts that construct norms from outside. For Butler, the sexed and gendered body is not written upon or inscribed, *it is scripted*, delivering ("once more, with feeling") the lines of a text that the agent did not write herself. If there is agency on Butler's view, then it is the highly circumscribed agency of an actor performing a play.

To be absolutely clear, the problem with these analyses of sex and gender, which I am not the first to identify, is the apparent evaporation of individual agency. This is, in part, what critiques by Simone de Beauvior (2009), Sandra Bartky (1990), Toril Moi (1999), Iris Marion Young (2005), even Judith Butler herself (1988), and other phenomenologically oriented feminists are aiming at—that accounts of social construction run the risk of sacrificing the *lived experience* of women for an increasingly abstract tale of sex and gender. Upon taking agency out of the picture, but without introducing some revised notion of action (or alternative to it), the patterns of bodily behavior that constitute gender and sex come to be no different than biological mechanism (for example, the so-called female brain). It hardly matters whether these processes reside literally inside or outside the skin; they will still be *external to the agent herself*, and in particular, outside any lived experience, for her, of action. To put it another way, even if we grant that the norms of gender and sex are formed by social forces operating outside of the gendered and sexed body, they still must be embodied—that is, lived by someone who experiences her body as gendered or sexed—otherwise these norms would have no meaning. And yet they do. Gender and sex are meaningful to us because we live them, as both extensions of and impediments to our agency—empowering, alienating, frustrating, liberating, oppressive.

At this point, however, we should not be tempted to reinstate the idea that sex and gender emanate from the inside just to capture the lived experiences of those who embody them—to make the pendulum swing back once more. The phenomenologist is in trouble, too. I suspect this is a source of the anxiety articulated by the social constructivists, who see problems with phenomenological accounts of sex and gender that refocus on experience, because experience (though now lived) is still understood as internal, private, privileged, and ultimately incorrigible. And experience, so understood, would seem to evade the scope of social construction.

Bodily Agency

How does one overcome the false dichotomy of either internal or external in explaining the embodiments of sex and gender? I want to suggest something that all involved parties acknowledge, while still seeming to miss the deeper point. A third term is required. What must be theorized is neither body practice nor lived experience but instead *bodily agency*. Allow me to explain.

One central idea behind the mid-twentieth-century reorientation toward the body in Western philosophy—as found in phenomenology, behaviorism, and pragmatism—is that the body *itself* can manifest agency, without being the instrument of a self-enclosed conscious will or the product of sociohistorical institutions.[8] In my own research, I call this notion "bodily agency" (Jackson 2018). Similar views can be found in the feminist literature as well, notably in the work of Sara Heinämaa (2003).[9] It involves the idea that particular kinds of bodily behavior—like skills and habits—comprise a metastable unity of solicitation and projection. That is, bodily agency involves the dynamic looping of two processes: the body entertaining certain patterns of behaviors called for by a situation *while at the same time* the body conjuring a situation that calls for certain patterns of behaviors.[10] Bodily agency finds a dynamic balance being pulled and resisting the social milieu, within one and the same action. In instances where there is just an internal intention to behave, or where only social forces control behavior, there is no bodily agency of the sort I am describing *because* these instances preserve the internal *versus* external dichotomy that the notion of bodily agency is meant to overcome.

I want to say that the embodiments of sex and gender are not created from the outside by writing, inscribing, or performing a script—as in Bordo's "writing the female body," Grosz's "corporeal inscription," or Butler's "performance of a normative script." But they are certainly not generated by the springing forth of some eternal femininity or masculinity, some innate maleness or femaleness—from the inside. Instead, they are enacted through bodily agency. The bodily practices that comprise gender and sex feel like doings, not happenings, experienceable through the body, but also within the realm of volition, even if they are proffered by culture. And the reason is, I am hypothesizing, because the bodily practices that constitute gender and sex involve a double process—the power to project and the power to be solicited—that is united in and through the body. Social norms might circumscribe the limits for manifesting female or male, man or woman. But these norms are nothing more than bodily solicitations that must be taken up by an agent. They must be enacted, not in the sense of choosing to act, or even in the Butlerian sense of performing a script, but in the sense of the body's projecting an existing social milieu, and, when revolution is possible, conjuring a new one. And while the feminists I have discussed here may well agree with this view, their choices of metaphors work against it—insofar as sex and gender are carved, inscribed, read, and scripted, the bodies that manifest them can only be surfaces without depth, mere bodies without agency of their own.

Feminists of embodiment embrace the idea that gendered and sexed bodies are shaped by the social forces of history, society, ideology, and culture. But how exactly do these social forces form bodily behavior into regular arrangements that follow in discernible sequences, creating the conspicuous affinities that are intelligible as feminine or masculine, female or male?

I have argued that in the place of an answer to this question, currently, there are metaphors, and that the metaphors of speaking surfaces preferred by feminists of embodiment are linked to an unfortunate dichotomy of internal choice *versus* external control. In order to bring the experience of agency back into the picture, I insist that the metaphors of speaking surfaces, and the binarism they rely on, should be abandoned. What is needed is an account of bodily agency, a personal-level phenomenon, where the powers of history and culture press bodies into gendered roles and sexed types *and* bodies respond by accepting or rejecting these demands, by uniting the elements of bodily solicitation and bodily projection.

It might come to seem, at this point, that I am endorsing a departure from metaphor in favor of precise descriptions of embodied practices, from which the structures of sex and gender may be revealed. This is true. But because metaphors help us to understand complex phenomena that we cannot grasp directly—expanding our cognitive perspectives, enhancing our expressive resources, and in some rare cases enabling the discovery of new properties—their pragmatic value should not be ignored. Thus, there are questions that my proposal raises but does not answer: What is it like to conform to or deviate from the norms of sex and gender, such that we understand (explicitly or tacitly) where we are in relation to them? How are those experiences different from, say, discovering the optimal distance from which to view a painting or finding a compassionate response to a partner in crisis? How do we experience the judgments of others in our conformation or deviation from sexed and gendered norms, and how do they nudge our practices? How do sexed and gendered embodiments create distinctions among people? In answering these questions, we may still need the figurative resources of bodily agency—for example, the *blind* habits, the *tangled* practices, the *revolutionary* improvisations; even the important notion of the *background* is, to some degree, metaphorical.

Perhaps, then, I am not advocating a complete move away from metaphors. But I do recommend that we first try to understand what sexed and gendered embodiments are really like, in greater detail, to uncover any logics or structures that may underlie, connect, or distinguish them, before once again resorting to metaphorical abstractions.

Notes

1. Sex and gender are normative categories that have been complicated in recent decades. In this chapter, I use terms like "masculine" and "feminine," "female" and "male," but I do not believe they designate natural (or even social) kinds.
2. The edited volume *Differences: Rereading Beauvoir and Irigaray* explores the similarities and differences of these approaches to embodiment (Parker and van Leeuwen 2018).
3. These metaphors already exist, for example, in the works of Friedrich Nietzsche, Franz Kafka, and Michel Foucault, as when Foucault writes, "the body is the inscribed surface of events" (Foucault 1984, 83). For my purposes here, I am less interested in the ultimate origin of these metaphors than I am in their current use and mobilization in feminist thought.
4. I have discovered two authors—Margaret McLaren (2002) and Pippa Brush (1998)— who acknowledge the prevalence the metaphors of speaking surfaces, although these theorists embrace the metaphors without much concern.
5. Grosz discusses "enfolding" primarily as a development of ideas from Maurice Merleau-Ponty's essay "The Intertwining—the Chiasm" (published as the climactic chapter in *The Visible and the Invisible* [Merleau-Ponty 1964]). But she does so with some trepidation. Merleau-Ponty's oeuvre is controversial in feminist theory, being criticized for, among other things, assuming he was theorizing all bodies when in fact he may have been theorizing masculine conceptions of male bodies (see Butler, this volume; Irigaray 1993; Grosz 1993; Le Dœuff 2003).
6. See, for example, Black (1962), Davidson (1978), Lakoff and Johnson (1980), Kittay (1987), Grice (1989), Derrida (1982), Ricoeur (1993).
7. Debates about source and value of visual metaphors generally form a fascinating category of feminist critique. See Mulvey (1975), Keller and Grontkowski (1983), and Code (1991). Other curious examples of visual symbolism that have been subject to scrutiny are these: the mind *as* camera obscura, seeing *as* believing, bias *as* blind spot, the (male) gaze *as* penetrating.
8. For an example from phenomenology, Edmund Husserl and Merleau-Ponty; from behaviorism, Ludwig Wittgenstein and Gilbert Ryle; from pragmatism, John Dewey.
9. See also Burke (2013), Stoller (2014), and Weiss (2002).
10. Both Grosz and Butler come close to capturing this metastable unity. They each recognize the aspect of bodily agency associated with *solicitation*. But I can find no place where the feature of bodily agency associated with *projection* fits into their picture of gendered roles and sexed types.

References

Alcoff, Linda Martín. 2006. *Visible Identities, Race, Gender, and the Self*. New York: Oxford University Press.

Bartky, Sandra Lee. 1990. *Femininity and Domination*. New York: Routledge.

Beauvoir, Simone de. 2011. *The Second Sex*. Translated by Constance Borde and Sheila Malovany-Chevallier. New York: Vintage Books.

Black, Max. 1962. *Models and Metaphors*. Ithaca: Cornell University Press.

Bordo, Susan. 1993. *Unbearable Weight: Feminism, Western Culture, and the Body*. Berkeley: University of California Press.

Brush, Pippa. 1998. "Metaphors of Inscription." *Feminist Review* 58: 22–43.

Burke, Megan. 2013. "Anonymous Temporality and Gender: Rereading Merleau-Ponty." *philoSOPHIA* 3 (2): 138–157.

Butler, Judith. 1986. "Sex and Gender in Beauvoir's *Second Sex*." *Yale French Studies* 72: 35–50.

Butler, Judith. 1988. "Performative Acts and Gender Constitution." *Theatre Journal* 40 (4): 519–531.

Butler, Judith. 1989. "Gendering the Body: Beauvoir's Political Contribution." In *Women, Knowledge, and Reality: Explorations in Feminist Philosophy*, edited by Ann Garry and Marilyn Pearsall, 253–262. Boston: Unwin Hyman.

Butler, Judith. 1990. *Gender Trouble*. New York: Routledge.

Butler, Judith. 2004a. *Undoing Gender*. New York: Routledge.

Butler, Judith. 2004b. "Variations on Sex and Gender: Beauvoir, Wittig, and Foucault." In *The Judith Butler Reader*, edited by Sara Sahil, 21–28. Malden, MA: Blackwell.

Code, Lorraine. 1991. *What Can She Know?* Ithaca: Cornell University Press.

Conboy, Katie, Nadia Medina, and Sarah Stanbury. 1997. "Introduction." In *Writing on the Body*, edited by Katie Conboy, Nadia Medina, and Sarah Stanbury, 1–13. New York: Columbia University Press.

Davidson, Donald. 1978. "What Metaphors Mean." *Critical Inquiry* 5 (1): 31–47.

Davis, Kathy. 1997. "'My Body Is My Art': Cosmetic Surgery as Feminist Utopia?" In *Embodied Practices: Feminist Perspectives on the Body*, edited by Kathy Davis, 168–181. London: Sage Press.

Derrida, Jacques. 1982. "White Mythology: Metaphor in the Text of Philosophy." In *Margins of Philosophy*, translated by Alan Bass, 207–272. Chicago: University of Chicago Press.

Fausto-Sterling, Anne. 1993. "The Five Sexes: Why Male and Female Are Not Enough." *The Sciences* 33 (2): 20–24.

Foucault, Michel. 1984. "Nietzsche, Genealogy, and History." In *The Foucault Reader*, edited by Paul Rabinow, 76–100. New York: Pantheon.

Grice, Paul. 1989. "Logic and Conversation." In *Studies in the Way of Words* by Paul Grice, 22–40. Cambridge, MA: Harvard University Press.

Grosz, Elizabeth. 1993. "Merleau-Ponty and Irigaray in the Flesh." *Thesis Eleven* 36: 37–59.

Grosz, Elizabeth. 1994. *Volatile Bodies*. Bloomington: Indiana University Press.

Grosz, Elizabeth. 1995. *Space, Time and Perversion*. New York: Routledge.

Haraway, Donna. 1988. "Situated Knowledges: The Science Question in Feminism and the Privilege of Partial Perspective." *Feminist Studies* 14 (3): 575–599.

Harding, Sandra. 1993. "Rethinking Standpoint Epistemology." In *Feminist Epistemologies*, edited by Linda Alcoff and Elizabeth Potter, 49–82. New York: Routledge.

Heinämaa, Sara. 2003. *Toward a Phenomenology of Sexual Difference: Husserl, Merleau-Ponty, Beauvoir*. New York: Rowman & Littlefield.

hooks, bell. 1982. *Ain't I a Woman: Black Women and Feminism*. Boston: South End Press.

Irigaray, Luce. 1993. *An Ethics of Sexual Difference*. Translated by Carolyn Burke and Gillian Gill. Ithaca: Cornell University Press.

Jackson, Gabrielle. 2018. "Maurice Merleau-Ponty's Concept of Motor Intentionality." *European Journal of Philosophy* 26 (2): 763–817.

Keller, Evelyn Fox, and Christine Grontkowski. 1983. "The Mind's Eye." In *Discovering Reality: Feminist Perspectives on Epistemology, Metaphysics, Methodology, and Philosophy of Science*, edited by Sandra Harding and Merrill B. Hintikka, 207–224. Boston: Kluwer Academic Publishers.

Kittay, Eva. 1987. *Metaphor*. New York: Oxford University Press.

Lakoff, George, and Mark Johnson. 1980. *Metaphors We Live By*. Chicago: University of Chicago Press.

Le Dœuff, Michèle. 2003. *The Sex of Knowing*. Translated by Kathryn Hamer and Lorraine Code. New York: Routledge.

MacKinnon, Catharine. 1983. "Feminism, Marxism, Method and the State." *Signs* 8 (4): 635–658.

McLaren, Margaret. 2002. *Feminism, Foucault, and Embodied Subjectivity*. Albany: State University of New York Press.

Merleau-Ponty, Maurice. 1968. *The Visible and the Invisible*. Translated by Alphonso Lingis. Evanston: Northwestern University Press.

Michie, Helena. 1987. *Flesh Made Word*. New York: Oxford University Press.

Moi, Toril. 1999. *What Is a Woman? and Other Essays*. New York: Oxford University Press.

Mulvey, Laura. 1975. "Visual Pleasure and Narrative Cinema." *Screen* 16 (3): 6–18.

Nagel, Thomas. 1986. *The View from Nowhere*. New York: Oxford University Press.

Noland, Carrie. 2009. *Agency and Embodiment*. Cambridge, MA: Harvard University Press.

Parker, Emily Anne, and Anne van Leeuwen. 2018. "Introduction." In *Differences: Rereading Beauvoir and Irigaray*, edited by Emily Anne Parker and Anne van Leeuwen, 1–20. New York: Oxford University Press.

Ricoeur, Paul. 1993. *The Rule of Metaphor*. Translated by Robert Czerny with Kathleen McLaughlin and John Costello, SJ. Toronto: University of Toronto Press.

Russo, Marry. 1994. *The Female Grotesque*. New York: Routledge Press.

Stoller, Sylvia. 2014. "The Indeterminable Gender." *Janus Head* 13 (1): 17–33.

Weiss, Gail. 2002. "The Anonymous Intentions of Transactional Bodies." *Hypatia* 17 (4): 187–200.

Williams, Bernard. 1986. "A Passion for the Beyond: Review of *The View from Nowhere* by Thomas Nagel." *London Review of Books* 8 (14): 5–6.

Wittig, Monique. 1985. "The Mark of Gender." *Feminist Issues* 5: 3–12.

Wolf, Janet. 1990. *Feminine Sentences*. Berkeley: University of California Press.

Young, Iris Marion. 2005. *On Female Body Experience: "Throwing Like a Girl" and Other Essays*. New York: Oxford University Press.

PART IV
BODY AND MIND

13

Against Physicalism

Naomi Scheman

> When I do not see plurality stressed in the very structure of a theory,
> I know that I will have to do lots of acrobatics—like a contortionist or
> tight-rope walker—to have this theory speak to me without allowing
> the theory to distort me in my complexity.
>
> —María Lugones[1]

For most contemporary analytic philosophers, the physical sciences are the lodestone both for epistemology and for ontology; other ways of knowing and other ways of saying what there is have somehow to be squared with what physics might come to say.[2] In the philosophy of mind, central problems arise from the difficulties in accounting for the phenomena of consciousness (in Thomas Nagel's terms "what it's like to be" a subject of experience), and from the apparent intractability (compared, say, to chemistry or even biology) of psychological explanations. This sense that—both ontologically and epistemologically—something distinctively mental would be unaccounted for, after physics had accounted for everything it could, has often been taken to motivate dualism: the mental is left over after the physical is accounted for just as (though, of course, not nearly so unproblematically) the forks are left over after the spoons are accounted for.

Feminists have been critical of dualism in part for its implicit if not explicit privileging of the mind over the body and for the misunderstanding of each that results from their being prised apart. Such criticisms remain apt, as Susan James argues, even in relation to accounts that, while metaphysically nondualist, nonetheless continue to prise the mental apart from the physical, by abstracting such phenomena as memory from their attachment to (better: their realization in) specific, socially embedded bodies (James, this volume). But if dualism has been unappealing to feminists, its usual alternative—physicalism—has seemed to many an unpalatable alternative, in large measure because the sort of attention to bodies that, for example, James encourages is not the attention of the scientist to an object of study, but the attention of a subject to her or his own experience, as well as the attention of diversely engaged others.[3]

Naomi Scheman, *Against Physicalism* In: *Feminist Philosophy of Mind*. Edited by: Keya Maitra and Jennifer McWeeny, Oxford University Press. © Oxford University Press 2022. DOI: 10.1093/oso/9780190867614.003.0014

Feminists' work on topics such as the emotions, the nature of the self and of personal identity, and the relations between minds and bodies can seem irrelevant to the issues that concern physicalists: the starting points, the puzzles and perplexities that call for theorizing, seem quite different. I want to argue that the appearance of irrelevance is misleading: while it is true that feminist theorists are asking different questions and thereby avoiding direct answers to the questions posed in the literature around physicalism, the reorientation of attention characteristic of the feminist questions usefully reframes the problems that vex that literature—problems of accounting for ourselves as physical beings in the world. In particular, what comes to be crucial in accounting for psychological explanation are the ways in which such explanations are irreducibly *social*, a "problem" to which dualism is an entirely irrelevant response. Understanding our emotions, beliefs, attitudes, desires, intentions, and the like (including how it is that they can cause and be caused by happenings in the physical world) is akin to understanding families, universities, wars, elections, economies, and religious schisms: positing some special sort of substance out of which such things are made would hardly help, nor does it seem metaphysically spooky that there is no way, even in principle, of specifying, on the level of physics, just what they *are* made of. (The university buildings count, but what about the dirt on their floors? If we count the faculty, do we count the food in their stomachs?)

Consider the performance of a piece of music. There is nothing going on *in addition to* the physical movements of the bodies of the members of the orchestra, but there is no way, appealing just to physics, to specify which of those movements are parts of the complex event that is the performance and which are not. What is and is not part of the event has to do with what sort of thing a performance is, what norms and expectations determine what its parts are. For example, the first violinist's coughing is not typically part of the performance, but it certainly can be—if, for example, it's written into the score. When it comes to identifying the performance as a cause, there are two very different possibilities. To say, for example, that the performance caused a crack in the ceiling is to say that there are physical events more or less loosely associated with the performance that caused the cracking, but the performance per se is not among them (that certain sounds are part of the performance is irrelevant to whether they contributed to causing the crack). If, by contrast, as with the premiere in Paris of Stravinsky's *Le Sacre du printemps,* the performance caused a riot, its being a musical performance (something about which the audience had certain expectations) is crucial: in this case the performance per se was the cause, but not as a physical event, since it is not one. To say that a performance is not a physical event is not to embrace some odd form of dualism; it is to acknowledge that, from the perspective of physics, the performance is not a particular complex event—one whose (physical) cause and effects we can inquire into—but rather an inchoate jumble of events. Performances are "socially constructed," meaning that their integrity as particulars is dependent on sets of social practices that make them meaningful wholes.

It is not, of course, at all clear how to relate social explanations to physical ones: the relationships between the social and physical sciences are deeply vexed. But the problems are importantly different from those that have engaged the philosophy of mind, less likely to provoke the a prioristic metaphysical demands that characterize the discussions of physicalism, however empirical those discussions are meant to be. What I want to suggest is this: in explaining ourselves to ourselves and to each other we allude to such things as beliefs, intentions, emotions, desires and attitudes. Physicalism consists in the claim (specified and argued for in a wide range of very different ways) that, insofar as these explanations are true, the events, states, and processes to which they refer must be identical with or somehow dependent upon or determined by events, states, and processes in or of the body of the person to whom they are attributed. Such a claim is neither required for nor supported by empirical research that shows how it is that, for example, emotional responses are related to changes in brain chemistry. Surely how we act and feel has enormously to do with what goes on in our bodies, but recognizing that fact no more supports the claims of physicalists than recognizing the importance of physiology to the carrying out of the actions that constitute a performance or a riot would support the claim that physiology explains why the premiere of *Le Sacre du printemps* caused a riot. The performance as such does not survive abstraction from social context, and neither do its causal powers: its "realness" and its causal efficacy are dependent in part on its being the socially meaningful type of thing that it is. Similarly, I will argue, beliefs, desires, emotions, and other phenomena of our mental lives are the particulars that they are because they are socially meaningful, and when they figure as those particulars in causal accounts, neither those accounts nor the phenomena that figure in them survive abstraction from social context.

Most of those working in the philosophy of mind today subscribe to one or another of the dizzyingly many varieties of physicalism. They share a demand for the mental to be composed of, or determined by, the physical—however differently they work out the details—in some way that attributes to mental phenomena not only continuity with the physical but also the sort of reality that the physical is presumed to have, including independence from our practices of noticing and naming. The failure of such independence, the possibility that much of what we talk about when we talk about our mental lives—our beliefs, emotions, desires, attitudes, intentions, and such—does not exist as determinate physical "somethings," is thought to undermine the possibility of taking such talk seriously, of taking it to be part of a true account of what there is in the world. It is here that feminist discussions both in the philosophy of mind and in seemingly remote areas can shed light, since they lead us to see the importance and the possibility of holding on *both* to the idea that our mental lives are constituted in part by the ways we collectively talk and think about them, *and* to the idea that such talking and thinking are not arbitrary and that the realm of the mental is no less real for being in this sense "made up."

Disputes among feminist theorists frequently take the following form: theorists of type A argue against the appeal to absolute standards of truth or rightness that exist in abstraction from our lives and practices, on the grounds that such appeals reflect a suspicion of plurality and diversity and a disdain for that which is local, particular, contextual, contingent, embedded, and embodied; while theorists of type B argue for the importance of standards of truth or rightness that are independent of what people happen to do or say, on the grounds that what most people happen to do and say—expert discourses and common sense alike—is prone to sexist and other forms of bias, and that we need a more compelling response than simply that we don't like it. Thus arise the debates between universalists and particularists in ethics, essentialists and social constructionists in gender and sexuality theory, empiricists and postmodernists in philosophy of science, objectivists and relativists in epistemology. The tendentious nature of all those labels reflects the divisiveness of the disputes, a divisiveness that obscures the fact that for many of us the disputes are internal to any position we might occupy. They are, I want to suggest, better thought of as necessary tensions, as reminders of the theoretical and political importance *both* of attention to diversity and particularity *and* of nonarbitrary, rationally defensible justification.[4]

One way of characterizing the disputes is as between the suspicion of and the demand for some special kind of thing, which answers to our needs precisely by being independent of them, by being what it is—Reality or the Good, the essence of something or the measure of an argument—no matter what we might think or do. Such disputes are not, of course, peculiar to feminist theory: they are arguably at the heart of the problems of modern philosophy, where, however, they tend to be treated as purely intellectual puzzles. In their feminist articulations, they reanimate the very practical urgency that gave birth to them—in the turmoil of early modernity, out of the need to ground the claims to truth and rightness being made by upstart rebels against the prevailing standards of a theocratic and aristocratic social order. As part of those struggles it was necessary to articulate new conceptions of the nature of persons and their states, the subject matter of the philosophy of mind. Feminist perspectives at this late stage of modernity throw into relief the historical specificity of those projects of articulation—for example, the field-defining epic struggle between the self as subject of inner experience, abstracted from the surrounding world (even, supposedly, from its own body), and the body as object of scientific scrutiny.

Feminist perspectives shift attention to understanding persons as both bodily and social, and knowledge as interpersonal and interactive. Physicalism then appears not so much false as empty: ontologically, it puzzles over how to establish a relationship—whether of identity or of some form of supervenience—between what ought not to have been analytically distinguished in the first place; and epistemologically, it concedes to (a philosopher's fantasy of) physics a dominating role even over explanatory schemes explicitly being argued to be nonreducible to it. To reject physicalism is not, as Wittgenstein says, to deny anything—not anything, that is, by way of actual investigation into or explanation of how our experienced lives are shaped by our being the bodies that we are. What is denied is the demand that such explanations have either to underwrite or to supplant the accounts of those lives that rest on appeal to the social practices and norms that make us the persons that we are.

The Demands of Physicalism

Jennifer Hornsby, in a series of articles going back to 1980 and collected in her book *Simple Mindedness*, argues against the ontological foundations of physicalist theses. One of the central targets of these arguments is what she identifies as "mereological conceptions" of the objects in an ontology, according to which relatively big objects can be identified with the unique "fusion" of the smaller objects—their parts—which make them up (Hornsby 1997, 48–49). John Dupré similarly identifies mereological conceptions as at the heart of what he finds problematic about physicalism (or any requirement of a unified account of diverse phenomena) (Dupré 1993, 91–94). Both these authors see themselves as blocking at some very early stage a frequently unvoiced argumentative move that not only licenses a range of diverse positions but frames the arguments between them. Such a move, if noticed at all, can seem obvious, unavoidable: avoiding it can seem like being committed to something like a soul, a mysterious addition to the physical stuff that constitutes the goings-on in and of our bodies (Dupré 1993, 90; Hornsby 1997, 12).

Supervenience theses most explicitly mobilize this picture, since, unlike other physicalist theses, they typically are mute about actual explanation and insistent on what are taken to be the requirements on the possibility of any explanations at all. Consider the following:

> We think of the world around us not as a mere assemblage of objects, events, and facts, but as constituting a system, something that shows structure, and whose constituents are connected with one another in significant ways. . . . Central to this idea of interconnectedness of things is a notion of dependence

(or its converse, determination): things are connected with one another in that whether something exists, or what properties it has, is dependent on, or determined by, what other things exist and what kinds of things they are. . . . Activities like explanation, prediction, and control would make little sense for a world devoid of such connections. The idea that "real connections" exist and the idea that the world is intelligible and controllable are arguably an equivalent idea. (Kim 1993, 53)

This paragraph is the start of an essay in which Jaegwon Kim lays out a range of supervenience theses. He goes on to argue for the strongest among them, on the grounds that only it can meet the demands he lays out here. The demands themselves, however, are widely accepted among physicalists, including those who believe they can be met by some form of nonreductive supervenience, much weaker than the reductionism Kim promotes. The paragraph perfectly accomplishes the slide from saying something quite ordinary to being in the grip of a picture, one that leads us to lay down requirements on what the world, or our accounts of the world, *must* be like.[5] The argument is a transcendental one: given that explanation is possible, what *must* be the case? The appeal is to (what is taken to be) explanation *per se*, not to the details of particular explanations or explanatory practices. Later in the same essay, in fact, Kim explicitly argues for the importance of separating metaphysical from epistemological considerations: the mental can be said to be determined by the physical whether or not we ever could be in a position to provide the explanations that determinacy underwrites (Kim 1993, 175–176) The picture (and on this point there is wide agreement with Kim) is that physicalism provides the ontological grounds for the possibility of mental explanations, however autonomous or irreducible such explanations might be argued to be.

A linchpin of Kim's arguments to the conclusion that attempts at nonreductive supervenience are doomed is what he calls the principle of "causal closure": "If we trace the causal ancestry of a physical event, we need never go outside the physical domain" (Kim 1993, 280). Davidson and Fodor, among many others, explicitly commit themselves to essentially this principle (though they disagree with Kim as to its consequences), and it is one Hornsby and Dupré, among others, have challenged. I am persuaded by those challenges, but want, for the purpose of this chapter, largely to bracket that issue and focus instead on the question of ontology. In the passage quoted from Kim, he refers repeatedly to "things," as in "things that happen," and at the start of the passage he refers to "objects, events, and facts." For his argument to work, such "things" need to be related in ways that exhibit structure: they depend on and determine each other; their "real connections" are what make the world intelligible.[6] One of my central arguments is that taking commonsense psychology seriously is to be committed *not* to a theoretically vexing ontology of objects (mental events, states, and processes), but rather to practices, explanation among them, and to the nuances of our lives as shaped and made intelligible through those practices.

For Kim, as for some others, notably Davidson, the "things" in question are preeminently events, and there are long arguments between them and others as to what it is that events are. Beyond those arguments lies an even murkier ontological swamp—the "states and processes" that usually get appended to the list of mental phenomena. Any physicalist theory is going to have to say something about the ontology of swamp-dwellers—something that provides a way, in theory at least, of individuating the contents of the swamp independently of the norm-laden, interpretive social practices that characterize commonsense psychology. Those "things" have to be individuated in ways that suit their role in the properly physical causal accounts in which they are thought to have to figure if common sense is to be scientifically vindicated. Issues about individuation often slip by, as "the initial move in the conjuring trick," the assumption that mental events, states, and processes are particulars whose nature can be investigated: we can ask what *they* are, whether *they* are identical with or constituted by physical events, states, and processes, and how *they* enter into causal relationships.

When Robert Wilson, in a careful and detailed account of individualism in the philosophy of mind, says that anti-individualist arguments have concerned taxonomic rather than instantial individuation, he is, I think, right. Wilson suggests that one cannot ask whether A is the same as B (a question of instantial individuation) without asking what sorts of things A and B are taken to be (a taxonomic question) (Wilson 1995, 21–25). Davidson's anomalous monism exploits the idea that the framework of space-time can provide for material objects, and the framework of causation can provide for events, a way of individuating that doesn't depend on any *finer* taxonomizing (Davidson 1980). That solution is, however, ultimately question-begging in its assumption that, in particular in the case of events, the presumptively closed and complete system of physical causation individuates all the events that there are.[7] As my example of the performance was meant to suggest, this assumption is deeply problematic, amounting to what Davidson and other nonreductive physicalists are committed to denying—that the explanatory system within which the performance exists as a particular complex event (in terms of which we can make sense of what's part of it and what isn't) can ultimately be reduced to (or otherwise explicated in terms of) physics. If it can't be—if, in general, the discourses with respect to which we understand performances, or our mental lives, can't be systematically connected to physics—then the objects that are constituted in its terms will not be *any* sorts of physical objects, since, with respect to physics, they will have the status not of complex objects but of incoherent jumbles or heaps—certainly not the sorts of things to enter as particulars into nomological causal relationships.

The Useful Vacuity of Global Supervenience

Global supervenience, which is frequently criticized as both excessively permissive and explanatorily opaque, has a role for theorists like Dupré and Hornsby in making the point that the denial of the existence of immaterial stuff does not commit one to physicalism. As such it is proffered not as a positive thesis but as a way of granting the falsehood of dualism and of articulating the minimal truth of physicalism (so minimal as not to count as physicalism on the terms of most physicalists). Thus Dupré says: "if one removed from the universe all the physical entities . . . there would be nothing left" (Dupré 1993, 91). Global supervenience has been formalized by John Haugeland, though that is not his term for it. (He calls it "weak supervenience," which for most authors in this terminologically confusing literature refers to something quite else, involving a different parameter of variation among theses from the one that concerns me here.) Haugeland's formulation (replacing his use of "weakly" with "globally") is "K *globally supervenes on* L (relative to W) just in case any two worlds in W discernible with K are discernible with L." (K and L are languages, W is a set of possible worlds. For present purposes let L be the language of microphysics and K be the language of commonsense psychology) (Haugeland 1982, 97).

Global supervenience captures the idea that if anything happens at all, something has to happen on the level of microphysics. If everywhere and for all of time all the microparticles (or whatever microphysics turns out to be about) were exactly as they in fact are, then nothing *else* could be any different. What is important to note is just how weak this thesis is. It does not imply token identities. (Haugeland in fact proposes it explicitly as an alternative to token identities, which, he argues, fail for cases far less complex than the mental.) Nor does it imply that supervening (mental) events are "determined by" or "dependent upon" physical events—an implication that is crucial for what most theorists want out of a supervenience principle and partly definitive of what is meant by "physicalism."

The point of calling global supervenience "global" is to stress (what "serious" supervenience theorists find problematic) that there need be no spatial or temporal contiguity between a difference on the supervening level and a difference in the supervenience base. A difference in my mental state need not be correlated with a difference in my body or in anything near or causally connected to my body, nor must there be a physically describable difference simultaneous with or prior to the mental difference.[8] All that matters is that there be some difference, even if far away and long ago or even yet to come. Such laxity is frequently expressed as a (supposed) reductio: Post calls it ARFL, the "argument from licentiousness" (Post 1995, 76). But whether such laxness counts for or against global supervenience ought to depend on what sorts of connections one thinks there actually are. It is a feature, for example, of many of our ordinary psychological terms that whether they truly apply can be a genuinely open question with respect to everything, known or unknown, in the present or the past, but become retroactively settled by something in the future.

It is, of course, precisely features of commonsense psychology such as this that many psychologists and philosophers of psychology will want to "clean up," in part by imposing constraints on what can belong in the supervenience base. But such constraints have nothing to do with avoiding substance dualism and ought to reflect, rather than dictate, ordinary judgments of explanatory adequacy. One may, for example, believe that the best (most explanatory, most nearly true) accounts of love include this feature: that ascriptions of it remain, up to a certain point (as Aristotle argued for happiness) hostage to the future. Up to that point it can be indeterminate, to be settled by how things go on, whether or not one's feelings are really love. And if one thinks that, then one will, for reasons having to do with explanatory adequacy, reject a restriction of the supervenience base to the present and past. A common move at this point is to posit some state that, it is claimed, does supervene on the person's current physical state—as, for example, the notion of narrow content was developed to try to deal with arguments about the nonindividualist nature of propositional attitudes. But if, as I will argue below, our beliefs, attitudes, desires, and so on are explanatory—have the causes and effects that they do—in virtue of their being socially meaningful, then such posits will lose their point, which is precisely their supposed explanatory role.

Thus, the "licentiousness" that physicalists deplore in global supervenience— the fact that it licenses neither token identities nor theses of determination or dependency—is part of its appeal, not because anything goes, but because the question of what goes and what doesn't cannot, and should not, be settled *a priori*. Kim charges adherents to global supervenience with accepting it as "a mere article of faith seriously lacking in motivation both evidentially and explanatorily" (Kim 1993, 159); but as I am appealing to it, it no more requires either evidence or explanatory usefulness than does my nonbelief in imperceptible and causally inert fairies. The work that appears to be done by physicalist theses—including reductionism, eliminativism, functionalism, and token identity theses—is actually done by complex and diverse explanations, including explanations that may be locally reductive. We may in particular areas have well-founded expectations for one or another sort of explanation, but those expectations do not rest on, nor are the successes explained by or evidence for, any metaphysical theses such as physicalism in any of its forms. The unmotivated act of faith is, thus, on the part of the physicalists, who not only have boundless and groundless faith in the explanatory powers of some unimaginably remote Future Physics, but who are

willing to sacrifice common sense (as well as real science) on its altar, placing ontological requirements on the objects of explanation in advance of working out
what those explanations are.

Taking Explanation Seriously

If we actually look at psychological explanations—in particular, if we attend
to the aspects of those explanations that lead functionalists and Davidsonian
anomalous monists, among others, to reject the reductionism of type-
identity theories—we find that the phenomena that give such explanations
their explanatory force cannot be identified with, or be determined by, particular physical phenomena, for two general, related sorts of reasons. First,
the anomalousness of psychological explanations entails that the phenomena
that figure in them cannot be presumed to satisfy the constraints on being a
physical particular, and will, in fact, typically fairly obviously *fail* to satisfy
such constraints, however loosely conceived. And second, in many cases in
which psychological explanations *can* be seen to rest in some sense on physical goings-on, such "supervenience" is on happenings that are sufficiently
scattered and remote in space and time as to defeat any general, substantive
claim of determining supervenience. The irreducibility of psychological explanation is inherited by psychological ontology: we have no grip on what
the phenomena of psychology are other than whatever they have to be for
psychological explanations to be true.[9] In general, our ordinary explanations
of human action, thought, and feeling appeal to social practices and norms;
and there is no reason to require, and much reason to deny, that our *best*
explanations will be compatible with an ontology whose objects' individuation is independent of the social and the normative.

I want to urge an understanding of socially constructed phenomena that has
close connections with understandings, such as those of John Dupré (1993),
Ian Hacking (1986, 1992), and Michael Root (1993, 149–172; 2000), of socially
constructed kinds.[10] Such kinds can figure in explanation, even causal explanation. Consider:

(1) Q: Why didn't Alex get a heart attack when she was younger?
     A: Because she's a woman.
(2) Q: Why didn't Alex become CEO of the corporation?
     A: Because she's a woman.
(3) Q: Why does Alex use the toilet marked with a stick figure with a triangle
     in its middle?
     A: Because she's a woman.

In the first exchange, referring to Alex's being a woman points in the direction of some physiological property that accounts for her having been less at risk of a heart attack. "Woman" need not be a biologically real kind; gender can be (as many feminist theorists have argued) socially constructed, perhaps to be distinguished from sex, which some have argued *is* biologically real. The explanation works by gesturing toward something both causally related to the risk of heart attacks and typically true of those in the social category "woman," though by no means true of all women (like, for example, the currently suspected property in question, namely, the presence of relatively high levels of estrogen). The answer in the second exchange is explanatory, by contrast, because of the social significance of the category "woman"; thus, it might function as a cautionary admonition to a biological male contemplating sex change. Not only does this explanation give us no reason to attribute biological reality to the category "woman," but any biological category that might be proposed would inevitably lead to a "cleaning up" around the edges that would hurt rather than help explanations such as this one (whereas explanations like the first, while useful as they stand, would be helped by replacing the social category with the relevant biological one, if any). The third exchange is explanatory in a rather different sense. It notes a connection between gender and segregated public toilets, and what exactly is being explained is a matter of what the questioner can be presumed not to know or to understand: it might, for example, explicate the meaning of the international sign for "women's toilet," or it might be a reply, albeit a somewhat impatient one, to someone who finds Alex's womanhood questionable, perhaps because, unlike the stick figure, Alex does not wear skirts.

Mental phenomena can be real in the same sort of way. Through our social practices we interpret as meaningful bits of experience that may well be related in significant, nonsocial ways (as people who share a race or a gender will typically be similar or otherwise related in many nonsocial ways). But those relationships are not such as to constitute particular entities of any sort. That constitution is done by our finding and acting on patterns of salience, interpreting ourselves and each other, and having and acting on expectations formed in the light of those interpretations. As feminists have argued, for example, not just anyone can be angry at any time, since part of what constitutes the pattern that counts as anger has to do with who you are and whom you might be thought to be angry at, about what, and so on (Frye 1983; Scheman 1993). It was easier not to notice this fact when theorizing was in the hands of those who were less likely to run up against the limits of intelligibility and who, when they did, had little reason to see their failure to make sense as anything other than an idiosyncratic glitch. (Similarly, noticing the social constructedness of gender was greatly helped by the experiences of those, such as transsexuals, whose identities were, according to the biologically naturalized view of gender, literally impossible.)

Consider the following explanations:

(1a) Q: Why did her blood pressure shoot up?
      A: It must have been because she got angry.
(2a) Q: Why did he fire her?
      A: It must have been because she got angry.
(3a) Q: Why do they think she hates men?
      A: It must be because she got angry.

The first and second examples offer causal explanations and would seem to call for an account of her getting angry that indicates how it can cause something in her body, or some piece of his behavior. By analogy with the first set of examples, however, neither 1a nor 2a supports the idea that her getting angry is (or supervenes on or is determined by) some particular physical event(s). In 1a we can adequately account for the explanatoriness of A while taking anger to be a socially salient pattern of behavior, thoughts, and bodily feelings—once we note that the feelings typical of getting angry are correlated with sorts of bodily tension that can cause a rise in blood pressure. Particular emotions are more or less closely associated with bodily feeling (anger more closely than happiness, less closely than rage), and the nature of such associations is one of the ways in which cultures differ in their emotional repertoires, explanations, and styles.[11] What is important to note—just as with explaining the ceiling crack by blaming the performance or explaining Alex's lesser vulnerability to heart attack by her being a woman—is that as we move toward the more physically explanatory, getting angry per se drops out; what matters is the tension, not what the tension means.

In 2a, by contrast, her getting angry (that it's angry that she got) does not drop out of the explanation—any more than the performance drops out of the explanation of the riot or Alex's being a woman drops out of the explanation of her not being promoted. He fired her because of what he took anger to mean and because of his views about its (in)appropriateness for a woman. In Davidsonian terms, we can put the point by saying that the anomalousness of psychological explanation is inherited by psychological ontology. The normative, interpretive element in psychological explanation enters into the construction of psychological phenomena. No more physicalistically respectable phenomenon could play the causal role getting angry plays in this explanation (as getting tense plays such a role in 1a), since abstracting from the social constructedness means abstracting from the context-specific, normatively laden nature of (her) anger, and hence from precisely what makes an appeal to it explanatory.

The third example would not usually be regarded as offering a causal explanation: rather, getting angry (at something like that) is taken by A to be part of what it is to be a feminist. Furthermore, we can argue over whether to count whatever she said and did as anger, as well as whether to count her anger as marking her as a feminist. The patterns we note as salient and what we take them to signify are matters for real dispute, as real and as resolvable as are disputes over causal explanations; and we need an account of emotions and other psychological phenomena that makes such disputes intelligible.

One might ask at this point whether we, the serious participants in the discursive practices of commonsense psychology, are ontologically committed to such things as beliefs, desires, attitudes, intentions, and emotions. Yes and no. No—if by "ontological commitment" you mean, as Quine meant, that the phenomena in question need to be in the domain over which range the bound variables of a well-regimented theory that we regard as (approximately) true. There is no particular reason to believe (and some good reason to doubt) that the explanatory practices of commonsense psychology will (or should) ever be so regimented. Nor is there reason to think that anything is to be gained by insisting on the role of specifically nominalized explanations: on "her anger" rather than "she was angry," on "his belief" rather than "he believes," on "her arrogance" rather than "she's talking arrogantly." But yes—if what's at stake (and I do think this is what matters more) is the possibility of objective, true accounts of ourselves and each other, accounts that we can intelligibly challenge and revise, justify and rebut, accounts that actually explain. That sort of commitment requires not theoretical regimentation but seriousness about our roles and stakes in the practices that construct the phenomena to which we are committed.

Thus, far from urging with respect to commonsense psychology something analogous to Moore's "Defence of Common Sense" with respect to physical objects, I am arguing that attention to our practices is needed precisely because what we are presumed to have in common, what "we" do or say is, from a feminist perspective, far from unproblematic. "The common woman," the poet Judy Grahn told us in the 1970s, "is as common as the best of bread / and will rise . . . I swear it to you on my common / woman's / head" (Grahn 1973, stanza VII). Feminist writers, artists, and theorists have often valorized common women's lives, including the knowledge that emerges from hands-on engagement with the messiness of daily life, in contrast to the idealizations of science. When we want to urge experts to take us and our concerns seriously, common sense is what is "ours," not "theirs." But appeal to what "we" are supposed have in common, to what "everyone" knows or values, can prove notoriously uncongenial to feminists and our allies. Many of us stand condemned by common sense: our lives are variously immoral, foolish, obscene, misguided, or impossible. Expert discourses of various sorts can offer real or imagined refuge from those condemnations: we may feel on firmer ground casting our lot with "them" than with an "us" that places us on the margins or beyond the pale. We may, for example, be confident that science will reveal the unnaturalness of heterosexist construals of sexuality or the ungroundedness of presumptions of male superiority.

When, however, María Lugones writes about the tyranny of common sense, as the expression of what the comfortable can presume to be obvious, in contrast to the improvisations of those she calls "streetwalkers," she is articulating a perspective from which science and common sense are, as they are for many philosophers, continuous, one the disciplined extension of the other, both grounded in what we all are presumed to have and to know in common and which, she argues, actually excludes many from the realm of sense-making (Lugones 2003). Such are the ambiguous resonances of the word that one could even say that being "common" (not, as some would say, "our kind of person") is one way of being excluded from the commons, the space of commonality. The exclusion Lugones describes—from the easy truths of common sense, what all "right-thinking" people know—is the epistemic analogue of the ejection of homeless people from the public library.

Once we acknowledge the ways in which, in Lugones's terms, we "make each other up," set the terms in which we will be intelligible, mark out the patterns of salience that construct the phenomena of mentality, we can ask about who "we" are, how and why we do what we do, who reaps the benefits and bears the burdens of the practices that give our lives the shapes they have, and who has what sort of power when it comes to issues such as these. These are questions that redirect our attention away from what is presumed to lie under and to underwrite the truths of common sense, and toward the practices through which such truths are constructed.

Notes

1. Lugones (1991, 44).
2. This chapter was previously published in *The Cambridge Companion to Feminism in Philosophy*, ed. Miranda Fricker and Jennifer Hornsby, 49–67 (Cambridge: Cambridge University Press, 2000). It is reprinted here with abridgements and slight modifications with the permission of the author and press. I would like to thank David Golumbia and Lisa Banks for first encouraging me to reenter the philosophy of mind fray; Ernie Lepore for his criticisms of an earlier (1983) paper and for (only partially heeded) advice on updating it; and Louise Antony, Richard Boyd, and especially Georges Rey for pushing me to explain why I professed to believe things that sounded completely crazy. I have presented versions of the present chapter at the University of Toronto, University of London (where John Dupré was my commentator) and Gothenburg and Umeå Universities, and was greatly helped by the discussions, as I was by Michael Root's and Georges Rey's careful critical readings of an earlier draft (though Rey, in

particular, may wish to dispute any influence on the current version) and by long conversations with Hornsby, Dupré, and Miranda Fricker.

3. On feminist accounts of the specifically social nature of the self, see, for example, among philosophers in the analytic tradition, Baier (1985b), Friedman (1991), and Lugones (this volume, 1991).

4. On the recasting of the central schisms between feminists as fruitful tensions, see Snitow (1989, 205–224).

5. On the laying down of requirements, see Diamond (1991). On the slide into the problematically philosophical, see Goldfarb (1983).

6. Here I don't take exception to Kim's use of "things" per se. I myself use "phenomena" in a way that won't stand up to heavy ontological scrutiny. For the use of "phenomena" as an ontologically neutral umbrella term, see Rey (1997, 13 n. 4). My own use is even more neutral than his, since he claims neutrality only with respect to the *sort* of phenomenon in question (event, state, process, etc.), whereas I intend to be neutral on the prior question of ontological commitment.

7. For Davidson's argument that this is the case, see Davidson (1980, 180). For a similar argument to mine against the idea that token identities can survive the demise of any theory connecting types, see Putnam (1979). Putnam recognized, as Davidson has not, that views about the holistic, normative nature of psychological explanation are incompatible with taking such explanations to be *about* things whose existence as particulars is independent of the practices that ground the explanations.

8. Thus, the insights of Tyler Burge, Hilary Putnam, and others about the social nature of the content of propositional attitudes go much deeper than is usually presumed and cannot, for example, be met by appeals to narrow content.

9. The parallel to Quine's famous dictum "To be is to be the value of a variable" is, of course, intentional. I would argue, however, that psychological explanation cannot be sufficiently regimented to meet Quinean standards for ontological commitment, and that, in fact, there is no good reason to commit ourselves to any particular *ontology* for the mental at all, which is not to say that we don't have good grounds for committing ourselves to the possibility of objectively true psychological explanations.

10. Root (2000) develops an account of what he calls "real social kinds," whose realness consists in the ways in which systematic social practices make all those things (typically, people) that fall within the kind interchangeable. He argues that social kinds are relative to times and places, reflecting the variability of the relevant social practices: if, for example, race or gender is real here and now, it is because we make it so.

11. Bodily goings-on are taken to be differently significant, to form a more or less central part of patterns that are emotions, in different cultures. See, for example, Rosaldo (1989).

References

Baier, Annette. 1985. *Postures of the Mind*. London: Methuen.
Davidson, Donald. 1980. "The Individuation of Events." In *Essays on Actions and Events* by Donald Davidson, 163–180. Oxford: Oxford University Press.

Diamond, Cora. 1991. "Introduction II: Wittgenstein and Metaphysics." In *The Realistic Spirit: Wittgenstein, Philosophy, and the Mind* by Cora Diamond, 13–38. Cambridge, MA: MIT Press.

Dupré, John. 1993. *The Disorder of Things: Metaphysical Foundations of the Disunity of Science*. Cambridge, MA: Harvard University Press.

Friedman, Marilyn. 1991. "The Social Self and the Partiality Debates." In *Feminist Ethics*, edited by Claudia Card, 161–179. Lawrence: University of Kansas Press.

Frye, Marilyn. 1983. "A Note on Anger." In *Politics of Reality: Essays in Feminist Theory* by Marilyne Frye, 84–94. Trumansburg, NY: Crossing Press.

Goldfarb, Warren. 1983. "I Want You to Bring Me a Slab: Remarks on the Opening Sections of the *Philosophical Investigations*." *Synthese* 56 (3): 265–282.

Grahn, Judy. 1973. "The Common Woman Poems." In *Rising Tides: Twentieth Century American Women Poets*, edited by Laura Chester and Sharon Barba, 280–288. New York: Pocket Books.

Hacking, Ian. 1986. "Making Up People." In *Reconstructing Individualism*, edited by Thomas C. Heller, Morton Sosna, and David E. Wellbery, 222–236. Palo Alto: Stanford University Press.

Hacking, Ian. 1992. "World-Making by Kind-Making: Child Abuse for Example." In *How Classification Works: Nelson Goodman and the Social Sciences*, edited by Mary Douglas and David Hull, 180–238. Edinburgh: Edinburgh University Press.

Haugeland, John. 1982. "Weak Supervenience." *American Philosophical Quarterly* 19 (1): 93–103.

Hornsby, Jennifer. 1997. *Simple Mindedness: In Defense of Naive Naturalism in the Philosophy of Mind*. Cambridge, MA: Harvard University Press.

Kim, Jaegwon. 1993. *Supervenience and Mind: Selected Philosophical Essays*. Cambridge: Cambridge University Press.

Lugones, María. 1991. "On the Logic of Pluralist Feminism." In *Feminist Ethics*, edited by Claudia Card, 35–44. Lawrence: University of Kansas Press.

Lugones, María. 2003. "Tactical Strategies of the Streetwalker/ *Estrategias Tácticas de la Callejera*." In *Pilgrimages/Peregrinajes: Theorizing Coalition against Multiple Oppressions* by María Lugones, 207–237. Lanham, MD: Rowman & Littlefield.

Post, John F. 1995. "'Global' Supervenient Determination: Too Permissive?" In *Supervenience: New Essays*, edited by Elias E. Savellos and Ümit D. Yalçin, 73–100. Cambridge: Cambridge University Press.

Putnam, Hilary. 1979. "Reflections on Goodman's *Ways of Worldmaking*." *Journal of Philosophy* 76 (11): 603–618.

Rey, Georges. 1997. *Contemporary Philosophy of Mind*. Oxford: Blackwell.

Root, Michael. 1993. *Philosophy of Social Science: The Methods, Ideals, and Politics of Social Inquiry*. Oxford: Blackwell.

Root, Michael. 2000. "How We Divide the World." *Philosophy of Science* 67 (3), supplement: S628–S639.

Rosaldo, Renato. 1989. "Grief and a Headhunter's Rage." In *Culture and Truth: The Remaking of Social Analysis* by Rosaldo Renato, 1–21. Boston: Beacon Press.

Scheman, Naomi. 1993. "Anger and the Politics of Naming." In *Engenderings: Constructions of Knowledge, Authority, and Privilege* by Naomi Scheman, 22–35. New York: Routledge.

Snitow, Ann. 1989. "Pages from a Gender Diary: Basic Divisions in Feminism." *Dissent* 36: 205–24.

Wilson, Robert A. 1995. *Cartesian Psychology and Physical Minds: Individualism and the Sciences of the Mind*. Cambridge: Cambridge University Press.

14

Why Feminists Should Be Materialists and Vice Versa

Paula Droege

For most of my scholarly life, philosophy of mind and feminism have been separate and distinct pursuits.[1] It is time for this to change. As a feminist, I am committed to the investigation of factors contributing to inequality. Since belief systems are one of the most pernicious sources of inequality due to the way they justify and perpetuate the status quo, we need to understand the material basis of beliefs and values in order to appreciate the constraints and possibilities for change. A clearer sense of the way real, biologically evolved minds negotiate their physical and social environments can deepen our sense of connection to the world and to one another.[2]

As a materialist, I am committed to an explanation of mental phenomena in physical terms. At one time in analytic philosophy that commitment entailed logical arguments about the reduction of folk psychology to physics. In the first section, I distinguish between this restrictive physicalism and a broader materialist account of the dynamic relations among mind, body, and environment. This empirically based, interdisciplinary approach to explanation demands engagement with the world in a way that is distinctively feminist. Feminist practices include a focus on process, dialogue, collaboration, and other epistemic skills to consider the perspective of others. We need these practices to understand and appreciate the value of alternative methodologies. Materialists also need feminism to interrogate the social and political forces that structure our work. The sorts of questions we ask, the way questions are formulated, and the way evidence is gathered in support of answers are all shaped by assumptions about what and who is valuable. In the second section, I show how interdisciplinary research on fish consciousness demonstrates the epistemic and ethical value of feminist methods. I consider the liberatory praxis of these methods to be fundamentally feminist, even when the researchers utilizing them do not identify their approach with the label "feminist." The effective results of these practices in the interdisciplinary investigation of fish minds is a strong argument for the inclusion of feminist critique and methodology in philosophy of mind. Feminism

Paula Droege, *Why Feminists Should Be Materialists and Vice Versa* In: *Feminist Philosophy of Mind.*
Edited by: Keya Maitra and Jennifer McWeeny, Oxford University Press. © Oxford University Press 2022.
DOI: 10.1093/oso/9780190867614.003.0015

provides materialists with alternative ways of thinking and methods for investigating the nature of mind.

Why Feminists Should Be Materialists

At the outset, a word about terminology is in order. "Materialism" in feminist theory is usually cashed in terms of some version of Marxism. Like Darwin, Marx was prescient in recognizing that minds are shaped by physical interactions. Yet traditional Marxist analysis focuses too narrowly on material relations of production to offer a general theory of mind. As I use the term, "materialism" refers to accounts of mental processes in terms of natural, physical relations. Materialist theories explain how the mind could be produced by brains and bodies operating in the world. Next, I discuss a reductive version of materialism, standardly called "physicalism." On this more restrictive account, the items and laws of fundamental physics specify all mental states and their causal powers. I will argue for a nonreductive account of materialism and show how it escapes earlier feminist criticisms of physicalism.

Not Your Father's Physicalism

In "Against Physicalism," Naomi Scheman presents an argument that targets both physicalism and the broader form of materialism that I advocate. Since the terms are often used interchangeably, one reason for using "physicalism" to refer just to reductive materialism is to separate what is right in Scheman's objections from what is wrong about a wholesale rejection of physical causal explanation in philosophy of mind. According to Scheman, physicalism is empty: ontologically, mind and body "ought not to have been analytically distinguished in the first place," and epistemically, psychological explanation is social and so cannot be reduced to the terms of physics (Scheman, this volume, 243). These two dimensions of the argument are interrelated, so it can be tricky to tease them apart.

Beginning with the epistemological claim, Scheman is certainly correct to object to the physicalist claim that beliefs, desires, and values can be entirely explained in terms of the causal relations of physics. My belief that raising the minimum wage would help alleviate poverty is structured by concepts that have no analogues in physical theory. Just think about what in the world could serve as the physical instantiation of "minimum wage." Like the "average family," the term does not refer to anything describable using the language of atoms, vectors, and such. The physical structures that constitute my belief are, as Scheman puts it, "incoherent jumbles or heaps—certainly not the sorts of things to enter as particulars into nomological causal relationships" (Scheman, this volume, 245). An explanation of my belief requires an examination of my upbringing and experiences as well as consideration of my other beliefs. In the minimum wage example, concepts are essentially social, but the point applies to more mundane beliefs such as the belief that apples are delicious. What items I consider to be "apples" and "delicious" depends on how my mind has come to organize the world as a result of positive and negative interactions with fruit and other tasty things. My English linguistic community also shaped the way I sort things into categories. A good explanation should also be able to predict the sort of actions that would follow from my belief that apples are delicious, such as the inclination to eat one when hungry. Yet even a perfect understanding of the quantum processes that subserve mental states would be unable to determine the content of my belief, much less predict action, unless the belief is first individuated *as* the belief it is.

Neuroscientists often fail to recognize this crucial point when they make claims about the ability of brain imaging machines to "read minds" (Smith 2013). Images of the brain can only be interpreted as representing an object or a face as a consequence of previously correlating that specific brain activity with objects and faces. To interpret a brain image as representing an emotion, such as fear, requires subjective report to identify the relevant brain processes (Popper 2013). Any ability of a machine to read minds depends on first making the text legible, and that depends on an understanding of the relations among brain, mind, and world. In other words, a belief is a meaningful object only at the psychological level of explanation.

The importance of the psychological (and social) in understanding the physical does not mean, however, that "our mental lives . . . can't be systematically connected to physics" (Scheman, this volume, 245). Physics is systematically connected to chemistry, which is systematically connected to biology, which is systematically connected to neuropsychology. There is value in articulating these connections, in seeing the forces operative at different levels of explanation. While Scheman is right to object to physicalist arguments that the ontological dependence of the mind on the body rules out psychological explanation, she commits an equivalent mistake when she rules out the potential contribution of physical causal explanation.[3] Nonreductive materialists offer an account of levels of explanation that preserves a role for social relations in individuating belief content yet remaining committed to the material constitution of mental states and processes (Baker 2009).

The larger worry that seems to motivate Scheman's opposition to physicalism is that grounding the reality of the mental in the physical puts socially constituted structures at risk of elimination or devaluation. We will be inclined to look for structures that fit neatly into a physical causal system and fail to recognize the forces operating at a higher level of explanation. In her example of the explanation of a rise in blood pressure as a result of getting angry, Scheman argues that the socially salient fact of anger drops out when the physical connection between bodily stress and blood pressure become the focus. According to Scheman, we need to reject physicalism in order to preserve the value of social and psychological explanation:

> In general, our ordinary explanations of human action, thought, and feeling appeal to social practices and norms; and there is no reason to require, and much reason to deny, that our *best* explanations will be compatible with an ontology whose objects' individuation is independent of the social and the normative. (Scheman, this volume, 248)

I think Scheman is right to worry about the tendency to privilege physical explanation over other forms of explanation. This worry applies both to the reductive physicalism she targets and to the broader form of materialism I recommend. The gendered hierarchy of knowledge subordinates domains such as social theory to domains coded as masculine, such as physical theory (Anderson 1995). Testosterone makes men aggressive, rather than a normative masculinity that encourages violence and abuse. Poor diet explains poverty, rather than the reverse. Physical explanations such as these are tempting, because they offer the possibility of simple solutions. A tweak of the genes or the biochemistry is far less costly and disruptive to those in power than restructuring the social system to teach men better self-control or eliminate wealth inequality. Feminists have reason to be careful that social and political explanations are not eclipsed when a physical account appears.

Nonetheless, we can maintain our epistemic vigilance without sacrificing metaphysical explanation in the way Scheman argues:

> One of my central arguments is that taking commonsense psychology seriously is to be committed *not* to a theoretically vexing ontology of objects (mental events, states, and processes), but rather to practices, explanation among them, and to the nuances of our lives as shaped and made intelligible through those practices. (Scheman, this volume, 244–245)

The suggestion here is that attention to ontology distracts from understanding social relations. This move is problematic because practices, including explanation, cannot be fully understood without an ontology of the physical world. To think otherwise is to accept the same picture Scheman finds faulty: that physical causation is essentially independent from social forces.

Take, for example, the theoretically vexing ontology of sex differences. Longtime feminist dogma drew a sharp distinction between sex and gender. Sex is biological and irrelevant except in the way that social forces gender bodies as feminine and masculine. There were certainly some important theoretical benefits to this move. By ignoring the physical and focusing on the social, feminists usefully revealed the disciplinary practices that train bodies to perform gender (Butler 2006). At the same time, however, the split between sex and gender obscured the complex interactions between biological and social forces that are now being explored by feminist scientists. As one example, Anne Fausto-Sterling offers a detailed account of the ways biological differences like intersex resist social construction into a neat gender binary (Fausto-Sterling 2012). Social theory is indispensable in its ability to identify power hierarchies and their influence on our observation of and theories about sex differences. Nonetheless, explanation is limited without an ontology of the physical forces at play in our interactions with the world and one another.

Toward a Feminist Materialism

A distinctively feminist materialism suggests we reconceive the physical world as imbricated in while remaining autonomous from the social world. Rather than focus feminism exclusively on social practices, we should construct a materialism that demonstrates the dynamic interaction among social, environmental, mental, and biological processes. Adherents of this view, called "new materialism," advocate a picture of physical causation as indeterminate, constantly in flux, and potentially both disruptive and supportive of human projects.

This new picture of the physical world departs from the clockwork machine envisioned by Isaac Newton. While a classical calculus regulates interactions between middle-sized objects like billiard balls, items at both the quantum scale and the astrophysical scale fail to fit the neat patterns of Newton's laws. So long as they are described within an appropriate frame, causal processes are perfectly predictable. Objects in motion tend to stay in motion; force is equal to mass times acceleration. Complications arise when factors outside the frame are involved. Subatomic particles spin out of grasp; planets cycle in nonlinear rotation.

Biology likewise resists the regimentation of law-based causation. Formulas for deriving effect from cause are less useful than explanations that identify patterns and mechanisms. Things become exponentially more complicated as psychology, meteorology, and sociology introduce causal factors such as emotion, climate, and familial bonds into the explanatory mix. In this picture of a multifaceted, dynamically changing world, materialism is not adequately described in terms of simple, unexceptioned causal laws. Consequently, the idea that a pill or snip of the genetic code will solve anyone's problems misrepresents the complexity of physical systems.

Samantha Frost describes the liberating potential of materialism in terms of the openness to resources beyond the subjective and historical. Humans are neither Cartesian minds operating in a disembodied realm of reason, nor simply products of Marxist praxis whereby our actions in the world condition our nature. By recognizing that the material world has "its own impetus and trajectory," we can "explore how the forces of matter and the processes of organic life contribute to the play of power or provide elements or modes of resistance to it" (Frost 2011, 70). Feminists who eschew the material world deprive themselves of its explanatory power as well as its inherent tendency to change and adapt.

As the unrelenting forces of climate change demonstrate, natural processes operate outside the constraints of political and economic hegemony. Climate deniers can prevent appropriate response, but they cannot stop the earthquakes, arctic melt, or drought by sheer political will. The material world exhibits a kind of agency, a capacity to act independently of human intention in unexpected and transformative ways. Of course, climate change itself was caused by human projects, so the independence exhibited by natural processes is additive to rather than exclusive of human agency. The forces of nature act in response to human action, and humans act in response to the forces of nature. As Frost puts it:

> New materialists push feminists to relinquish the unidirectional model of causation in which *either* culture *or* biology is determinative and instead to adopt a model in which causation is conceived as complex, recursive, and multi-linear. (Frost 2011, 71)

Adopting this interactive model of causation requires a reconception of traditional ideas about free will and determinism (Droege 2010; Roskies 2006). Agency is not a matter of a conscious mind deciding to act in the absence of physical causation. Instead, what is critical to robust agency is a capacity for control of action in a way that is appropriate for the proper functioning of the system. An advantage of this description is that it is expansive enough to cover ecosystems, yet it can be tailored to the specific needs and abilities of humans. Ecosystems control action by responding adaptively to achieve homeostasis. For humans, biological responsiveness is conditioned by cognitive processes and social influences.

So, though I endorse the new materialist ascription of agency to natural processes, I do not agree with those who believe agency requires a mind. In my view, a mind is a physical system that serves the function of representing the world, including various states of itself. Ecosystems do not survive by virtue of representational states, so they have no mind. Nonetheless, ecosystems act in ways to preserve themselves, to adapt to changing conditions.

One of the appealing features of new materialism is the way agency is prior to and an ontological ground for mental attributes such as a sense of self. In "Feminism, Materialism, and Freedom," Elizabeth Grosz argues that reconfiguring concepts of agency can make them "ontological conditions rather than moral ideals" (Grosz 2010, 139). Feminist arguments for rights and recognition, while necessary to open up a space of action free from oppressive structures, fail to articulate a positive account of how to use that freedom. The assumption is that removal of restraints will allow a person to pursue her "real" interests and values, as if a true person exists separate from social shaping. Such an idea runs counter to both feminist and materialist conceptions of a self formed through its interactions with the social and physical environment.

Given this relational view of the self, the release from restraint is only liberatory if action in the future differs from the past. As Grosz argues, a future-oriented conception of freedom is needed to describe how a person can change herself through her actions:

> The question of freedom for women, or for any oppressed social group, is never simply a question of expanding the range of available options so much as it is about transforming the quality and activity of the subjects who choose and who make themselves through how and what they do. (Grosz 2010, 151)

A subject acts in the world in ways that conform to or violate her sense of herself. Actions that violate a subject's sense of herself prompt change, whereas actions that express her self are free. In contrast to the standard formulation, acts are not entirely free or entirely determined, freedom is the degree to which an action expresses the self. Further, the self is not a static metaphysical substance, on this view, but a dynamically evolving constellation of physical and mental states. So an action that is consonant with my self today may be discordant with my self in the future and vice versa.

Memory is a central component in the human capacity to transform ourselves. Actions with negative consequences are remembered, and the self is refigured to avoid repeating the error. Even actions we do not cause must be somehow incorporated into the story we tell ourselves about ourselves. In this ongoing process of action and interpretation, a self is formed and reformed over time.

> Freedom is thus not primarily a capacity of mind but of body: it is linked to the body's capacity for movement, and thus its multiple possibilities of action. Freedom is not an accomplishment granted by the grace or good will of

the other but is attained only through the struggle with matter, the struggle of
bodies to become more than they are, a struggle that occurs not only on the
level of the individual but of the species. (Grosz 2010, 152)

This reconfigured materialism is not only compatible with freedom, but is, as
Grosz proposed, the ontological condition for freedom. Feminists should be
materialists, because our engagement with the material world shapes who we are
and holds the promise of what we can become. Consider, for instance, the ways
implicit bias functions to reproduce racism. Research in cognitive psychology
demonstrates that most people unconsciously associate white faces with positive attributes and black faces with negative attributes (Banaji and Greenwald
2013). These biases are formed by interacting with a racist culture, and they
shape how we act in the world—whom we trust or fear, whom we love or hate.
By understanding how implicit biases are formed and reinforced, it is possible to
act in ways that can reshape bias. We can restructure physical environments to
encourage diversity; develop media to undermine stereotypes, and personally
work to develop friendships that cross familiar boundaries of race. While these
recommendations are not new and are consistent with the sort of social construction theory advocated by Scheman, the empirical grounding in cognitive
psychology gives them additional force (Devine et al. 2012). Tools for assessing
the extent of bias and efforts in remediation are based in materialist theories of
habit formation and perception. Far from distracting feminists from the social
practices that structure action, materialism places those practices within a causal
network open to multiple points of pressure. Issues of racism and sexism are no
longer only social/political issues on which opinions and values differ; the material basis of attitudes makes them real in a way that can motivate change. A feminism that utilizes the full range of pressure points is best suited to shaping a
future empowering to women.

Why Materialists Should Be Feminists

If the foregoing argument is accepted, feminists should be materialists, but why
should materialists be feminists? Naturalized epistemologists long ago argued
against the positivist idea that social and political values can be separated from
metaphysical facts. Yet there persists a masculinist tendency in analytic philosophy of mind to privilege logical analysis and neuroscientific data in isolation from their connections to issues of ethics and justice. This myopia is both
unsustainable and oppressive. Contemporary research on the mind demands
interdisciplinary investigation, and its empirical and theoretical results have immediate and far-reaching consequences. Materialists no longer have the luxury

of fantasizing about possible worlds. The real world requires answers to real questions about the nature of the mind.

Before her untimely death, I spent several years collaborating with a cognitive ethologist, Victoria Braithwaite, to find an answer to the very pressing question of animal consciousness. As a result of this collaboration I have learned a great deal about animals, and also the practices and values of animal researchers. My impression is that the field of animal cognition is significantly less patriarchal than philosophy, yet research in animal cognition is not published as "feminist." This situation raises some provocative issues about what exactly feminism is and what value it contributes to theorizing about the mind.

In this section I propose two ways that feminist theory is useful to the development of a materialist theory of mind:

(1) Feminist epistemology offers insight into engaging across disciplines.
(2) Feminist theory questions assumptions about the nature of minds that are based on a history of unequal power relations.

I will show how these features of feminist theory are advantageous in addressing the question of animal consciousness, and also how the values of feminism arise organically when one adopts a naturalist perspective on reality. Consequently, feminist praxis proves to be the best method for interdisciplinary research on the mind, even when it is not conducted under the label "feminism."[4] This last point will bring us full circle back to the reasons why feminists should be materialists.

Feminism and Interdisciplinary Research

Let me begin with a description of the current debate about animal consciousness. The philosophical problem was laid out by Thomas Nagel in his famous rhetorical question: "What is it like to be a bat?" (Nagel 1974). The answer is supposed to be that we have no idea and *cannot possibly* have an idea about what it is like to be a bat, because we don't share the conceptual structure of a bat. Unless you *are* a bat, you cannot understand the conscious experience of a bat.

While Nagel's mysterianism about consciousness has given way to philosophical and neuropsychological theories of consciousness for humans, many still think that we cannot possibly have an idea about the consciousness of animals because they cannot tell us what their experience is like. The driving assumption is that we can solve the problem of consciousness for humans to the extent that we are very much like one another. If your brain is similar to mine and you say similar things about your experience as I say about mine, then we can conclude that we share similar sorts of conscious experience. I will come back to the problems with this argument from analogy in the next section. For now I just want to point out that the analogy breaks down with animals at the very beginning—with their failure to report about their experiences.

Curiously, at about the same time that Nagel published his musings about bat consciousness, bat researcher Donald Griffin published *The Question of Animal Awareness* where he argues that animals are indeed conscious (Griffin 1976). Griffin's book, along with work by others published about the same time, began the field of *cognitive ethology*, which is the study of how minds evolve as a function of behavior. The field is deeply and essentially interdisciplinary as it requires expertise in at least psychology, biology, physiology, and paleontology.

To this list we should add philosophy and feminism. The contribution philosophers can make to this research is to help organize concepts and relations in order to better identify the targets for explanation. This work is especially important in consciousness research because the concepts are all fairly muddled. There is disagreement across the board on whether self-consciousness is necessary to consciousness, whether representations are involved and if so how, whether unconscious mental states exist, and so on. Different philosophical theories yield different answers to the question of whether animals are conscious, so it is important to have some idea about what exactly the claim is when one claims to show that animals are conscious.

Feminists can help researchers from these various different fields learn to talk to one another. In particular, work done by multicultural feminists addresses the challenges and possibilities of communicating across differing worldviews (hooks 2015; Lugones, this volume; 2003). It takes time to learn the language of another field and to find value in the knowledge and practices that another person brings to a problem. Because interdisciplinary research runs counter to the hierarchical, individualist structure of academic rewards, participants need skills for developing collaborations and encouragement for tackling its challenges.

Feminist practices such as a focus on process rather than product and dialogue rather than debate facilitate an open-ended approach that can expand thinking beyond disciplinary borders. By asking the process question of *how* we know rather than the product question of *what* we know, feminist epistemologists draw attention to the situatedness of participants within their fields and their ways of knowing (Harding 1991; Tuana 2013). Recognition of different standards of evidence and forms of reasoning are essential to collaborative research. Likewise, effective collaboration depends on eschewing the adversary method that dominates philosophy. As Janice Moulton argues, philosophers problematically assume that "the only, or at any rate, the best, way of evaluating work in philosophy is to subject it to the strongest or most extreme opposition"

(Moulton 2013).[5] This oppositional stance fails to acknowledge the importance of shared beliefs and values in the pursuit of truth. We need to agree minimally on the question to be investigated and the results that would count as a solution. Moreover, the emphasis on a winning argument comes at the expense of other epistemic goals such as fitting together beliefs into a coherent and useful pattern.

Even where the benefits of interdisciplinary research are obvious to participants, the lack of structural support in terms of grants, publication, and promotion can undermine commitment. A feminist critique of the power relations that reinforce existing research paradigms can galvanize group members to resist the status quo. Recognition of the power of a creative, collaborative effort inspires the development of new structures, such as the revaluation of publication in interdisciplinary journals, a push for more interdisciplinary grant awards, the acceptance of promotion letters from outside a researcher's home discipline, and so forth (Fehr 2011; Stewart 2009; Bronstein 2003).

Happily, some of these changes are taking place; however, the changes are rarely based on feminist arguments or undertaken by people who think of themselves as feminists. This raises the question of whether this work is, in fact, feminist, and the prior question of what it is for materialism to be feminist. At its core, feminism works to include the voices of women in accounts of their experience and location (Lugones and Spelman 1983; Butnor and McWeeny 2014). The principal goal for feminism is to find a way to end the subordination of women while recognizing differences between women and men, and among women. Methods for achieving this goal require foremost a respect for the beliefs and values that structure different views. In tackling the problem of animal consciousness, cognitive ethologists have adopted similar methods. Whether to call their efforts "feminist" may seem a matter of semantics, and as such a reason not to apply a political label to practices that are not conducted under that label.

But there is a deeper, substantive issue about the sort of practices that are both epistemically effective and socially just. To say that cognitive ethology is *already* feminist is to say that practices designed to recognize value in another's knowledge and experience are liberating. By advocating that cognitive ethology include feminism, I am proposing that the field can benefit from a better understanding of the values it already promotes for epistemic reasons. More to the point of this book, I maintain that philosophy of mind would benefit from *both* cognitive ethology and feminism.

As noted in the beginning of this section, philosophy of mind continues to be dominated by masculinist values. Logical analysis is prized over explanation that incorporates other forms of reasoning based on empirical evidence and hermeneutic interpretation.[6] Where data do appear, fields such as neuroscience and psychophysics are more likely to be represented than behavioral or social research. Though Nagel asked what it is like to be a bat, it was Kathleen Akins who took that question seriously and presented a beautiful interdisciplinary answer (Akins 1993). By combining insights from vision science, biology, and behavioral psychology, Akins described how much we *can* actually know about what it is like to be a bat from the bat's perspective.

Assumptions about the Nature of Mind

So, one reason materialists should be feminists is that the process of interdisciplinary work will be more effective if everyone develops feminist epistemic practices. The second reason materialists should be feminists is to rethink problematic assumptions that are the legacy of a male-dominated history in philosophy of mind. Assumptions about the nature of the mind have been developed by privileged, educated, adult men reflecting on their own minds. Descartes's dualism and his skeptical rationalism epitomize the theoretical mistakes that result from this disengaged, disembodied perspective (Bordo 1999). But even contemporary, enactivist philosophers can suffer from self-oriented modes of thought produced by privilege. Alva Noë begins his recent book with the "everyday experience" of coming to appreciate unfamiliar art (Noë 2012). While this sort of experience is fascinating and worthy of philosophical examination, it is hardly everyday.

Regarding animals, the experience is entirely foreign. Art may not be entirely foreign to animals (there are the elephants that paint portraits), but coming to appreciate an unfamiliar style probably is. By starting theory from a perspective that excludes the possibility of participation from other species, either the theory will rule out the possibility that they are conscious or it will simply fail to address the question.

Beginning with an examination of relatively simple animals such as fish, on the other hand, addresses several important questions. For one, fish exemplify the weakness of the argument from analogy. Nagel thought bats were alien, but now most consciousness researchers agree that the neurophysiology and behavior of mammals are clear evidence of consciousness (Low et al. 2012). Much less is known about the neural structure of fish, and what we do know speaks to a very different functional architecture (Braithwaite 2010).

Working with fish also demands attention to environmental pressures and evolutionary history. The wide variety of fish species exhibits an equally wide variety of cognitive capacities. A fish species that evolved in a relatively safe, nutrient-rich environment does not exhibit the same foraging skills or escape behavior as a fish species that evolved in a more stressful environment. Cognitive differences can also be found in members of the same species that live in different ecological niches. For example, three-spined stickleback fish raised in a pond navigate using landmark cues, whereas when the same fish are raised in a river they use water flow direction to navigate (Braithwaite and Girvan 2003).

Good experimental work in fish cognition requires adopting the perspective of the animal in order to determine how it solves the challenges that arise in its particular environment. Rather than drawing analogies from human experience to fish experience, we need to enter the world of the fish. In philosophy, rather than theorizing about the necessary and sufficient conditions for consciousness across possible worlds, we need to decenter logical reasoning and focus instead on function, evolutionary continuity, and interdependence.

In my work on animal consciousness, I find myself using all of the skills I have learned in feminist epistemology. In thinking about other beings, it is important to avoid both *assimilation*, the assumption that others are just like me, and *exoticization*, the assumption that others are nothing like me (Narayan 1998). I need to *decenter my knowledge and values* in order to be open to understanding another's way of being and acting in the world (Saul 2003). Finally, thinking about *who benefits* from various assumptions about the criteria for consciousness reveals the political interests that often motivate oppressive structures (Harding 1991).

With fish, the tendency toward *exoticization* is particularly strong. Fish are different: they don't breathe air, they don't walk, they don't communicate through facial expressions (outside of Disney movies). A recent argument maintains that fish cannot possibly feel pain because pain requires a cortex and fish have no cortex (Key 2016). There can hardly be a clearer example of exoticization. Human pain defines the nature of pain, so an animal that fails to satisfy the human-defined standard does not feel pain. This move effectively puts fish outside the circle of ethical concern. Not only are fish incapable of Kantian self-legislation, they are not even due utilitarian consideration. The other extreme of *assimilation* is no better. Relevant differences among animals and their various behavioral repertoires need to be delineated. No one-size-fits-all test of consciousness will be adequate to determine how different minds navigate different environments.

I have argued that a theory of consciousness grounded in evolutionary function can articulate a definition of consciousness that accounts for key features of human phenomenology and opens the way to scientific investigation of animal consciousness (Droege and Braithwaite 2014). When consciousness is defined in terms of function, evidence that animal minds fulfill that function is evidence that they are conscious. There is good evidence that many fish exhibit the behavioral flexibility that I believe requires consciousness. This prospect raises concerns about the welfare of fish in the aquaculture and fishing industries. While the consciousness of fish is not in itself an argument against raising or hunting fish for food—we raise and hunt mammals which are widely acknowledged to be conscious—it is an argument for practices that minimize their pain. Some groups have been responsive to this argument and have developed methods to kill fish as swiftly and painlessly as possible (Athrappully 2013).

So, on the issue of animal welfare, we again find researchers at the forefront who do not think of themselves as feminist, yet they embody the values and practices advocated by feminist epistemology and feminist ethics. I am convinced that a naturalist approach to knowledge gathering produces both the most effective scientific results *and* the most socially just methodology as research and industry collaborate to develop best practices for animal welfare.

In sum, materialists need feminists to gain a critical perspective on current practices and assumptions. Particularly in the case of animal consciousness, traditional philosophical methods of detached reflection fail to address the fundamental question: What is it like to be a fish? The best animal researchers have engaged that question and adopted the perspective of fish to better understand their needs and capacities. A more explicit feminist approach can only aid these researchers in articulating effective arguments in favor of a naturalized and humane animal research program.

There remains the significant problem of how exactly materialists could incorporate feminist methodology. A first step in philosophy of mind would be to include feminist epistemology in research and pedagogy. In other words, materialist philosophers should be feminist philosophers. We can also encourage better feminist praxis by breaking down the institutional barriers to interdisciplinary work. This step is important, because no one can master the knowledge and practices of all the relevant disciplines needed to understand the mind. Perhaps the most important intervention, then, is to increase the number of feminist administrators to advocate for collaborative research.

At root, the argument that materialists should be feminists rests on the same reasons that feminists should be materialists. Feminist materialism offers greater explanatory power, more effective epistemic practices, better tools for interdisciplinary engagement, and multifaceted resources for scientific investigation and political intervention. A dynamic, interactive materialism offers feminists a conception of agency that avoids the strictures of reductionism and determinism as well as the empty promise of rights in the absence of the material conditions for action. Feminist epistemology and ethics offer materialists an understanding of the value in recognizing divergent perspectives and methods for developing theory that incorporates insights from multiple points of view. Feminist materialism balances the drive toward truth grounded in a complex and shifting reality with a recognition that our tools of inquiry are shaped by a particular social and political position. Consequently, our theories about the nature of the mind and the remedy for injustice should be integrated into a single approach that acknowledges the full range of connections among mind and body, social and physical world.

Notes

1. This chapter benefited enormously from the generous comments by Keya Maitra and Jennifer McWeeny. I am also grateful for the feedback on an earlier version of the second section, presented at the FEMMSS6 conference.
2. Even evidence that suggests disconnection, such as research revealing implicit racial bias, is more effectively confronted when better understood.
3. On the mind-body problem and psychological explanation, see Kim (2005).
4. Thanks to Mariana Ortega (in conversation) for helping me to articulate the value of feminist praxis whether or not it is recognized as such.
5. Moulton also points out that the adversary method must be deductive, which is obviously at odds with predominantly inductive reasoning in the sciences.
6. Analytic philosophy of mind is becoming more open to empirical evidence. Though phenomenology takes hermeneutical interpretation to be essential to its methodology, its tradition is more resistant to evidence from other disciplines such as neuroscience and biology. To the extent that standards are changing in these traditions, I endorse this movement.

References

Akins, Kathleen A. 1993. "A Bat without Qualities?" In *Consciousness: Psychological and Philosophical Essays*, edited by Martin Davies and Glyn W. Humphreys, 258–273. Oxford: Basil Blackwell.

Anderson, Elizabeth. 1995. "Feminist Epistemology: An Interpretation and a Defense." *Hypatia* 10 (3): 50–84.

Athrappully, Naveen. 2013. "New Zealand Teaches World How to Fish." *Epoch Times*. October 26. https://www.theepochtimes.com/new-zealand-teaches-world-how-to-fish_330039.html.

Baker, Lynne Rudder. 2009. "Non-reductive Materialism." In *The Oxford Handbook of Philosophy of Mind*, edited by Ansgar Beckermann, Brian P. McLaughlin, and Sven Walter, 109–127. Oxford: Oxford University Press.

Banaji, Mahzarin R., and Anthony G. Greenwald. 2013. *Blindspot: Hidden Biases of Good People*. New York: Delacorte Press.

Bordo, Susan, ed. 1999. *Feminist Interpretations of René Descartes*. University Park: Penn State University Press.

Braithwaite, Victoria A. 2010. *Do Fish Feel Pain?* Oxford: Oxford University Press.

Braithwaite, Victoria A., and J. R. Girvan. 2003. "Use of Water Flow Direction to Provide Spatial Information in a Small-Scale Orientation Task." *Journal of Fish Biology* 63 : 74–83.

Bronstein, Laura R. 2003. "A Model for Interdisciplinary Collaboration." *Social Work* 48 (3): 297–306.

Butler, Judith. 2006. *Gender Trouble: Feminism and the Subversion of Identity*. Classics edition. New York: Routledge.

Butnor, Ashby, and Jennifer McWeeny. 2014. "Feminist Comparative Methodology: Performing Philosophy Differently." In *Asian and Feminist Philosophies in Dialogue:*

Liberating Traditions, edited by Jennifer McWeeny and Ashby Butnor, 1–21. New York: Columbia University Press.

Devine, Patricia G., Patrick S. Forscher, Anthony J. Austin, and William T. L. Cox. 2012. "Long-Term Reduction in Implicit Race Bias: A Prejudice Habit-Breaking Intervention." *Journal of Experimental Social Psychology* 48 (6): 1267–1278.

Droege, Paula. 2010. "The Role of Unconsciousness in Free Will." *Journal of Consciousness Studies* 17 (5–6): 55–70.

Droege, Paula, and Victoria A. Braithwaite. 2014. "A Framework for Investigating Animal Consciousness." In *Ethical Issues in Behavioral Neuroscience*, edited by Grace Lee, Judy Illes, and Frauke Ohl, 79–98. Berlin: Springer.

Fausto-Sterling, Anne. 2012. *Sex/Gender: Biology in a Social World*. New York: Routledge.

Fehr, Carla. 2011. "What Is in It for Me? The Benefits of Diversity in Scientific Communities." In *Feminist Epistemology and Philosophy of Science*, edited by Heidi E. Grasswick, 133–155. Dordrecht: Springer.

Frost, Samantha. 2011. "The Implications of the New Materialisms for Feminist Epistemology." In *Feminist Epistemology and Philosophy of Science*, edited by Heidi E. Grasswick, 69–83. Dordrecht: Springer.

Griffin, Donald R. 1976. *The Question of Animal Awareness: Evolutionary Continuity of Mental Experience*. New York: Rockefeller University Press.

Grosz, Elizabeth. 2010. "Feminism, Materialism, and Freedom." In *New Materialisms: Ontology, Agency, and Politics*, edited by Diana Coole and Samantha Frost, 139–157. Durham, NC: Duke University Press.

Harding, Sandra. 1991. *Whose Science? Whose Knowledge? Thinking from Women's Lives*. Ithaca: Cornell University Press.

hooks, bell. 2015. *Yearning: Race, Gender, and Cultural Politics*. New York: Routledge.

Kim, Jaegwon. 2005. *Physicalism or Something Near Enough*. Princeton, NJ: Princeton University Press.

Key, Brian. 2016. "Why Fish Do Not Feel Pain." *Animal Sentience* 1 (3): 1–33.

Low, Philip, Jaak Panksepp, Diana Reiss, David Edelman, Bruno Van Swinderen, and Christof Koch. 2012. "Cambridge Declaration on Consciousness." July 7. https://fcmconference.org/img/CambridgeDeclarationOnConsciousness.pdf.

Lugones, María. 2003. *Pilgrimages/Peregrinajes: Theorizing Coalition against Multiple Oppressions*. Lanham, MD: Rowman & Littlefield.

Lugones, María, and Elizabeth V. Spelman. 1983. "Have We Got a Theory for You! Feminist Theory, Cultural Imperialism and the Demand for 'the Woman's Voice.'" *Women's Studies International Forum* 6 (6): 573–581.

Moulton, Janice. 2013. "A Paradigm of Philosophy: The Adversary Method." In *Just Methods: An Interdisciplinary Feminist Reader*, edited by Alison M. Jaggar, 13–21. Boulder: Paradigm Publishers.

Nagel, Thomas. 1974. "What Is It like to Be a Bat?" *Philosophical Review* 83 (4): 435–450.

Narayan, Uma. 1998. "Essence of Culture and a Sense of History: A Feminist Critique of Cultural Essentialism." *Hypatia* 13 (2): 86–106.

Noë, Alva. 2012. *Varieties of Presence*. Cambridge, MA: Harvard University Press.

Popper, Ben. 2013. "For the First Time, Scientists Can Identify Your Emotions Based on Brain Activity." *The Verge*. June 19. https://www.theverge.com/2013/6/19/4445684/brain--scan-fmri-identify-emotion.

Roskies, Adina. 2006. "Neuroscientific Challenges to Free Will and Responsibility." *Trends in Cognitive Sciences* 10 (9): 419–423.

Saul, Jennifer Mather. 2003. *Feminism: Issues & Arguments*. Oxford: Oxford University Press.

Smith, Kerri. 2013. "Brain Decoding: Reading Minds." *Nature News* 502 (7472): 428.

Stewart, Abigail. 2009. "What Might Be Learned from Recent Efforts in the Natural Sciences?" *APA Newsletter on Feminism and Philosophy* 8 (2): 16–19.

Tuana, Nancy. 2013. "Revaluing Science: Starting from the Practices of Women." In *Just Methods: An Interdisciplinary Feminist Reader*, edited by Alison M. Jaggar, 257–267. Boulder: Paradigm Publishers.

15

Which Bodies Have Minds?

Feminism, Panpsychism, and the Attribution Question

Jennifer McWeeny

Mental attribution is a social and political issue as much as it is an epistemological and metaphysical one.[1] Feminist philosophers, decolonial theorists, philosophers of race, and other critical social theorists have examined how systems of domination perpetuate themselves by denying minds and mental capacities to particular kinds of bodies, including those of women, Black people, people of color, Jews, the working classes, people with disabilities, and non-human animals. Philosophers of mind who do not also engage these literatures have pursued the question of which bodies have minds abstractly by comparison, analyzing the concepts of "mind" and "matter" that would allow the two to interact, specifying the necessary and sufficient conditions that a body would need to meet if it were to have a mind, and invoking thought experiments about the conceivability of zombies and other imagined bodies to illustrate relationships between the mental and the physical.

During the twentieth century, philosophers primarily approached mental attribution from an epistemological angle through the problem of other minds. Although the majority of this literature looks at how we come to attribute minds and mental states to other individuals or other species, recent work has considered the problem of other minds in terms of social categories, noting ways that minds and mental states are differentially recognized across people of different genders, races, classes, and abilities (Taylor 2015; Tullman 2019; Jones, this volume).

The twenty-first century has brought with it an ontological turn in the question of mental attribution that stretches beyond the traditional epistemological interpretation. Rather than focus on the possibility of knowing minds besides our own, a number of research programs challenge conventional understandings of the metaphysical relationship between mindedness and materiality by reimagining ontologies of the human, animal, vegetable, and mineral domains, as well as the purported boundaries among them. For example, artificial intelligence researchers consider whether computers have consciousness; feminist new materialists and posthumanists emphasize the agency of the environment;

Jennifer McWeeny, *Which Bodies Have Minds?* In: *Feminist Philosophy of Mind.* Edited by: Keya Maitra and Jennifer McWeeny, Oxford University Press. © Oxford University Press 2022. DOI: 10.1093/oso/9780190867614.003.0016

Black studies scholars examine links between attributions of irrationality/ hypermateriality and the dehumanization of Black people, colonized peoples, and others; and panpsychists argue that particles such as electrons and quarks are experiential in nature.

Such projects reframe the classic metaphysical problem of how the mind interacts with the body in terms of the attribution question: Which bodies have minds?[2] At the same time that upending general assumptions about who (or what) is minded has opened a variety of present-day theoretical orientations or revived historically marginalized ones, we lack a method for positively identifying the precise range of bodies or types of bodies to which minds are attributed according to each of these views, as well as the notion of "mind" that is consistent with a view's "attribution pattern." An *attribution pattern* is a theory's answer to the attribution question. Absent this precision, theories that derive their explanatory and liberatory potentials from the radical suggestion that we must reconceive status quo ontologies of the human, animal, machine, and environment risk working against their own aims.

This chapter develops a metaphysical framework for asking and answering the attribution question by bringing together two bodies of literature that are traditionally kept separate, but whose joint consideration promises to advance conversations in both areas and beyond: critical analyses of mental attribution practices from feminist philosophy, decolonial studies, and philosophy of race and theories of panpsychism from the philosophy of mind.[3]

Attending to the ways that critical social theories describe the mental attribution and disattribution of bodies belonging to people who have been subject to various, intersecting oppressions illuminates three different categories of attribution experiences: (1) "immanence" and "nonbeing," (2) "dehumanization," and (3) "objectification" and "hypermateriality."[4] The differences among these experiences suggest that the metaphysics of mental attribution is not merely about (1) whether a body (or set of bodies) is classified as minded or mindless, but also involves (2) the strength or amount of mentality/kind of mind and (3) the understanding of mental constitution (including causation) that is attributed to each minded body (or set of bodies). This schema leads us to identify three components of an attribution pattern, which we will respectively refer to as the *ratio component*, the *comparison component*, and the *constitution component*.

Theories of panpsychism are especially useful for thinking through the metaphysics of mental attribution because their insistence on the ubiquity of mentality requires us to consider mental attribution on a cosmic scale in all ontological domains at the same time. Accounts of panpsychism from the philosophy of mind thus provide ready examples of attribution patterns that map mindedness within the set of all bodies that exist. This chapter examines the opposing attribution patterns of two types of physicalist panpsychism: Russellian physicalist panpsychism, espoused by David J. Chalmers, Galen Strawson, and others, and Cavendishian physicalist panpsychism, developed by Margaret Cavendish from 1652 to 1668.[5] *Russellian panpsychism* employs a "selective" or "exclusive" pattern that attributes minds to a select set of bodies, attributes more mentality to some minded bodies than others, and understands mental constitution in the mechanistic terms of Newtonian physics. *Cavendishian panpsychism* entails an "unrestricted" or "inclusive" pattern that attributes a mind to all bodies, sees each mind as just as mental as every other, and understands mental constitution in organicist terms that exceed explanation by Newtonian physics. These contrary metaphysical positions serve as the endpoints for a spectrum of attribution patterns whose exclusivity or inclusivity falls somewhere between these two.

The first section of the chapter provides an overview of the similarities and differences between Russellian and Cavendishian panpsychisms. The second, third, and fourth sections respectively describe the ratio, comparison, and constitution components of mental attribution with reference to the three categories of experiences discussed in critical social theories: immanence and nonbeing, dehumanization, and objectification and hypermateriality. Each of these sections then shows how Russellian and Cavendishian panpsychisms in turn embody a selective and unrestricted approach to each component. The fifth section mobilizes the opposing patterns of the two panpsychisms to generate a taxonomy of mental attribution that promises to inspire fresh theories of mind and liberatory configurations of the social.

Russellian and Cavendishian Panpsychisms

A given theory about the nature of reality is properly labeled "panpsychism" if it holds that *mentality is ubiquitous in nature*. This definition encompasses different types of theories that vary from one another in regard to how "mentality" is understood. "Mentality" could signify consciousness, experientiality, sensation, perception, self-awareness, subjectivity, intelligence, intentionality, feeling, thought, agency, or some other mental characteristic (or combination of characteristics). Not all panpsychists believe that the presence of "mentality" entails the presence of "mind"; as this reasoning goes, a body could be made of "experiential" or "mental" stuff without being conscious or having a mind insofar as mindedness (and/or consciousness) requires being a subject with a point of view (Nagel 2016, 194; Strawson 2017, 381).

Physicalist panpsychism combines a belief that everything is physical with the belief that mentality is ubiquitous. Physicalist panpsychists therefore understand mentality as fundamentally physical and the physical as fundamentally mental (at least in part). Both Russellian and Cavendishian panpsychisms are physicalist panpsychisms that adopt a "dual-perspective" view of matter that distinguishes between its *behavior* or structure and its *nature*. Russellian panpsychism builds from Bertrand Russell's belief that physics tells us what matter does, but not what it is; we have access to the former through empirical observation, but the intrinsic constitution of matter is largely unknown to us (Russell 2014, 384). Russellian panpsychists reason that mentality is part of the unknown intrinsic nature of matter; specifically, they believe that at least some of the properties that play microphysical roles such as the mass role (for example, "resisting accelera-tion, attracting other masses") are experiential (Chalmers 2017a, 181; 2017b, 26; Strawson 2017, 381–382; Goff 2019, 130–138).

Cavendish anticipates Russell's distinction between the structure and nature of matter by several centuries with her own distinction between matter's "effective parts" and "constitutive ingredients" (Cavendish 2001, 25–27).[6] *Effective parts* are individuated physical bodies, such as trees, rocks, hands, humans, horses, fish, hearts, blood cells, and so on. These parts of nature are, as Cavendish's mon-iker implies, merely the *effects* of matter's intrinsic constitution; they are not "the ingredients of which nature is made up" that are the origin of nature's motions, actions, and forms (Cavendish 2001, 25). Although Cavendish maintains that the nature of matter cannot be known through empirical observation, she believes we can use reason to construct hypotheses about matter's constitutive ingredients that correspond with different *roles* or *functions* that matter plays (Cavendish 2001, 99).[7] Using this method, Cavendish concludes that matter must be fundamentally mental (that is, rational, sensitive, and perceptive) such that matter cannot exist without mind and vice versa.

Despite sharing the same basic metaphysical commitments (physicalism, pan-psychism, and a dual-perspective view of matter), Russellian and Cavendishian panpsychisms require very different patterns of mental attribution. The differ-ence stems from the different ways that they conceive of the relationship between minds and bodies. Contrary to Russellian panpsychists, Cavendish denies that minds are the types of things that can be (a) variably or contingently attributed among bodies, (b) attributed in degrees of mentality with some bodies having more or less than others, and (c) understood entirely according to the terms of Newtonian physics. Disagreements on these points result in a selective attribu-tion pattern in the former case and an unrestricted pattern in the latter. Let us now take each of these issues in turn.

The Ratio Component: Equal or Unequal Attribution?

Feminist philosophers, philosophers of race, critical phenomenologists, and other social theorists have described a number of experiences that are associated with the differential attribution of minds to bodies according to sex, race, class, and other social categories. The first of these involve experiencing one's body (and one's self) as that which is treated as if it lacks a mind in any meaningful sense of the term. Two such experiences include Simone de Beauvoir's account of *species immanence* and Frantz Fanon's description of *racial nonbeing*, which are respectively linked to women's bodies and Black bodies. Both experiences are connected to the practice of denying minds to some types of bodies while simultaneously attributing minds to other types (White men's bodies, for example), thus establishing an unequal ratio of bodies to minds in the social order.

In *The Second Sex*, Beauvoir argues that sexist oppression employs a conception of woman that equates femininity with an overdetermined body and an underdetermined mind. Man "considers woman's body an obstacle, a prison, burdened by everything that particularizes it" and suggests that, as a result, woman "thinks with her hormones" (Beauvoir 2010, 5). Embedded in these social meanings, woman experiences herself in terms of immanence; her body is a means to carry out the mechanisms of species survival regardless of her own individual will (Beauvoir 2010, 39–44). Indeed, she is "the most deeply alienated of all the female mammals" due to her social context (Beauvoir 2010, 44). By contrast, social meanings encourage man to experience himself in terms of the transcendent activity of consciousness, and to "[forget] that his anatomy also includes hormones and testicles" (Beauvoir 2010, 5). Woman is thus not attributed a mind in any meaningful sense of the term because her hormones and uterus stand in for her brain, operating in the service of the species often against her personal desires. Her mindlessness warrants external control and direction; sexist society expects her to offer her body as a vehicle for someone else's desires in institutions such as heterosexuality, marriage, and motherhood—as a sexual, domestic, or reproductive machine. Alternatively, a man's mind fulfills his desires through women's bodies, extending his volition and subjectivity to bodies that are not his own. In sum, sexism requires woman to be a body without a mind (immanence) and man to be a mind that is not necessarily tied to his body (transcendence).[8]

Although different from the experience of species immanence, the phenomenon of racial nonbeing is also tied to a logic that denies minds to certain types of bodies while attributing minds to other types. Describing his experience of being a Black body in a racist and White supremacist social order, Fanon distinguishes between "a feeling of inferiority" and "a feeling of not existing" (Fanon 2008, 118). Lewis Gordon, Sylvia Wynter, and others connect this feeling of nonexistence with White people failing to recognize that Black people have minds, desires, and experiential interiority. As Gordon explains, antiblack racism "demands [that] the black body . . . be a body without a perspective" (Gordon 1999, 102). Conversely, antiblack racism understands White bodies as sources of an outward perspective that does not see its own body being seen by others in the third person (Gordon 1999, 103). The experience of racial nonbeing is related to this practice of withholding minds from Black bodies and withholding bodies from White minds whenever White supremacy is furthered by this arrangement.[9] Wynter likens Fanon's experience of racial nonbeing to Haitian Vodunist descriptions of "being transformed into a zombie," which is a process that creates a body without a soul, personality, or will (Wynter 2001, 33). In both cases (racism and zombification), the threat of losing one's perspective and one's self, of being determined from the outside, ironically works to regulate behavior and discipline bodies into specified social functions (Wynter 2001, 34).

These accounts of species immanence and racial nonbeing point to the first and most basic component of a mental attribution pattern, namely, the ratio of minded to mindless bodies that is consistent with a given conception of mind. Imagine a metaphysical map that has a point for each body that presently exists. The ratio component of mental attribution designates the proportion of these points that have minds. Physicalist panpsychisms, which would not permit a mind to exist without a body (but may permit a body to exist without a mind), illustrate this component with two categories of responses:

(1) Of all the bodies that exist, each and every body has a mind (or mentality). (ratio of bodies to minds: 1:1)
(2) Of all the bodies that exist, some bodies have minds (or mentality) and some do not. (ratio of bodies to minds: >1:1)

Option 1 represents *equal attribution* because the ratio of minds to bodies is equal: it attributes a mind to each and every body. Option 2 is indicative of *unequal attribution* because there are more bodies than minds: only some bodies in the set are attributed minds.[10]

Insofar as we understand "panpsychism" according to the standard interpretation of the term, namely, that all things have mind, we might assume that any physicalist panpsychism must subscribe to equal attribution. However, this assumption does not apply to the contemporary landscape in the philosophy of mind, where the most popular versions of panpsychism uphold an unequal attribution ratio, generally allowing for a wide swath of bodies that lack minds (or mentality). We can make sense of a panpsychism that recognizes mindless bodies in nature by appealing to the dual-perspective view of matter embraced by Russellian panpsychisms. A Russellian panpsychist affirms the presence of mentality at the level of matter's intrinsic constitution while denying the presence of mind (or mentality) of certain macro-level bodies. Strawson, for instance, emphatically refuses the suggestion that tables, forks, and similarly inert objects are conscious even though he maintains that the nature of the matter of which they are made is "entirely experiential" (Strawson 2017, 381). As he explains, "the natural distinction [between the conscious and the nonconscious] is entirely valid in its everyday deployment: tables and chairs and trains are not conscious" (Strawson 2017, 381). Thomas Nagel and Chalmers likewise refrain from attributing minds to certain physical bodies, such as rocks, lakes, blood cells, and the Eiffel Tower (Nagel 2016, 194–195; Chalmers 2017b, 19).

Despite also assuming a dual-perspective view of matter, Cavendishian panpsychism draws a different conclusion in regard to the necessity of the relationship between minds and bodies. Mind, on Cavendish's view, is a body's capacity to perceive those entities with which it is in material proximity, to know its place in this nexus of relationships, and to respond accordingly but not necessarily mechanistically. Cavendish reasons that nature would not be what it is, exhibiting change, variety, and interactions among bodies, if each and every one of these bodies were not fundamentally perceptive. She explains:

> Perception is an exterior knowledge of foreign parts and actions; and there can be no commerce or intercourse, nor no variety of figures and actions; no productions, dissolutions, changes, and the like, without perception: for how shall parts work and act, without having some knowledge or perception of each other? (Cavendish 2001, 15)

Cavendish therefore insists that "it is not only the five organs in an animal, but every part and particle of his body, that has peculiar knowledge and perception" (Cavendish 2001, 140). Because bodies are necessarily extended and located in space and time such that no entity can occupy the same place as another physically and historically, there is never an exact similarity or repetition of form or position among distinct bodies, and, thus, there is never an exact repetition between perspectives. Nature therefore consists in "infinite particulars" (Cavendish 2001, 102). Mindedness takes an infinite variety of forms that corresponds to each particular, from a membrane perceiving which particles to let across and which to block, to a bee pollinating the yellow flower and not the pink one, to humans reflecting on their existential situation. Cavendishian panpsychism therefore upholds an equal attribution ratio that sees each and every body from particle, lodestone, or tree to honeybee, horse, or human as a mind of its own.

Beauvoir's and Fanon's descriptions of species immanence and racial nonbeing have led us to identify the ratio component of a mental attribution pattern. Considering possible answers to the ratio component reveals that Russellian panpsychism advances an unequal ratio of bodies to minds, while Cavendishian panpsychism entails an equal one. This discrepancy reflects their disagreement about whether minds are the types of things that can be contingently attributed to bodies, with Russellian panpsychists taking the affirmative position and

Cavendish maintaining that bodies are necessarily minded. The second component of mental attribution is about whether minds are the types of things that come in degrees (or whose mentality can otherwise be ordered hierarchically), with some minds attributed more or less mentality than others depending on the bodies with which they are associated.

The Comparison Component: Attribution by Kind or Degree?

Immanence and nonbeing are not the only experiences that critical social theorists connect with practices of mental attribution. Aníbal Quinajo and María Lugones describe a specific kind of *dehumanization* tied to colonized peoples in the Americas that construes their bodies as animal and bestial, and that therefore designates their minds as less rational than those of the colonizers. Frantz Fanon and Sylvia Wynter evoke a similar, but also different, sense of *dehumanization* in their critiques of biological conceptions of the human that position White people as the most evolved of all and consequently deem the minds of Black people as less rational and less human. Whereas immanence and nonbeing have to do with being denied a mind altogether, dehumanization in both of these accounts involves one's body being marked as having less of a mind (or less mentality) than other bodies in the social sphere.[11]

Feminists and critical social theorists have long noted connections between systems of domination and the hierarchical ranking of minds according to sex, race, class, nationality, and other bodily categories. These arrangements are fueled by a notion of the human that understands full humanity in terms of full mentality, and that in turn understands full mentality in terms of Whiteness, maleness, able-bodiedness, the possession of wealth, and European cultural practices. In his study of the colonization of Latin America, Quijano explains that "from the Eurocentric perspective, certain races are condemned as inferior for not being rational subjects. They are objects of study, consequently bodies closer to nature" (Quijano 2000, 555). Lugones expands upon Quijano's account by attending to the relationship between coloniality and modern concepts of gender and heterosexuality. While the minds of White European women were believed to mirror their fragile bodies and thus were thought of as weaker than those of White European men (but still human), the minds of the colonized were seen as lesser than the colonizers' minds for a different reason: colonized people were viewed as laborers and resources and so their bodies were not gendered in human terms (Lugones 2007, 202–203). As Lugones explains, "The behaviors of the colonized and their personalities/souls were judged as bestial and thus non-gendered, promiscuous, grotesquely sexual, and sinful. . . . Hermaphrodites, sodomites, viragos, and the colonized were all understood to be aberrations of male perfection" (Lugones 2010, 743). For both Quijano and Lugones, dehumanization accompanies attributions of being *more* "primitive," "animal," and agendered and thus *less* mental, rational, and human.

Fanon's and Wynter's conceptions of dehumanization underscore the role of scales of biological and psychological development in establishing White supremacist notions of the human. Fanon recounts how, upon moving from Martinique to France, he learned the racializing logic that "the more the black Antillean assimilates the French language, the whiter he gets—i.e., the closer he comes to becoming a true human being" (Fanon 2008, 2). Substituting the language of the colonized with the settler's language is part of the dehumanizing process that "turns [the native] into an animal" (Fanon 1963, 42). This linguistic spectrum from least White to most White takes hold in European culture through psychological theories that "represent the black man as the missing link in the slow evolution from ape to man" (Fanon 2008, 1). In Wynter's terms, this aspect of racism has "'totemized' being fully human (i.e. the ostensibly farthest from the primates and thereby the most highly evolved)" (Wynter 2001, 35).[12] Such models encourage White men and others who purportedly occupy the superlative points on the spectrum to experience their minds *and bodies* as representative of the "fullness and genericity of being human" insofar as they compare them with the presumed deficient mentality associated with the bodies of Black people, women, and people of color (Wynter 2001, 40).[13]

These descriptions of dehumanization point to a second component of mental attribution that overlays the ratio component. After the ratio component circumscribes the set of bodies that have minds, *the comparison component* indicates how much or how little mentality to attribute to each of these minded bodies in comparison with the others. An approach to the comparison component that entails that the minds (or mental states) of some bodies display more mentality than those of other bodies is appropriately labeled *degree attribution*. Contrary to degree attribution, *kind attribution* holds that any one mind (or mental state) is *just as mental* (or conscious, experiential, and so on) *as* any other; minds are different from one another in kind and not in their comparative strengths of mentality (or mindedness). Both degree and kind attribution can be applied to differences between individual bodies or to differences between groups and categories of bodies.

On the surface, panpsychism (and specifically physicalist panpsychism) does not seem predisposed to one mode of comparison over another when it comes to mental attribution. However, in their attempts to describe the mentality of the fundamental constituents of reality such as electrons and quarks and to accommodate the ideas of "biologically evolved experientiality" and evolutionary complexity, most contemporary panpsychists appeal to degree attribution (Strawson 2020, 320).[14] As Philip Goff explains:

> Human beings have a very rich and complex experience; horses less so; mice less so again. . . . [T]his continuum of consciousness fading while never quite turning off carries into inorganic matter, with fundamental particles having almost unimaginably simple forms of experience to reflect their incredibly simple nature. This is what panpsychists believe. (Goff 2020)

Goff's description applies well to the Russellian panpsychisms espoused by Nagel, Chalmers, Strawson, and Luke Roelofs, who respectively characterize the mentality of the fundamental constituents of reality as "less subjective," "much simpler," "primitive," and "rudimentary" in comparison with that of conscious organisms (Nagel 2016, 194; Chalmers 2017b, 24–25; Strawson 2020, 323; Roelofs 2019, 78). This model is also at play in William Seager's emergentist panpsychism, which "reflects . . . the growth of mentality in correlation with the increasing complexity of physical systems" (Seager 2017, 234). Contemporary panpsychists likely conceive of this degree scale in terms of species-types or entity-types rather than individuals, and would not rank members of the same species or particle-type as having more or less of a mind than others of that same type. They may also pursue a "threshold" approach that attributes mind and mental phenomena such as consciousness, subjectivity, concept formation, representation, and agency not in stronger or weaker concentrations at each and every degree, but only once a specific degree of evolutionary or physiolog-ical complexity is achieved. In this case, degree attribution yields hierarchical differences in qualities or kinds of minds.

Cavendishian panpsychism rejects the idea that mentality and mindedness come in degrees, whether comparing individual bodies or species categories. Minds are *not* like shades of blue; they are not the sorts of thing that can be more or less concentrated, diluted, faded, developed, simple, complex, and evolved. According to Cavendish's ontology, a honeybee's perception of the world does not amount to a *lesser* (or greater) mentality than human perception; it is in-stead a *different* mental capacity suited to the distinctive corporeality ("figure") and unique relational location (perspective) of the bee vis-à-vis other bodies. Cavendish explains:

> We cannot say a bird is a more perfect figure than a beast, or a beast a more perfect figure than a fish, or worms; neither can we say man is a more perfect figure than any of the rest of the animals: the like of vegetables, minerals, and elements; for every several sort has as perfect a figure as another, according to the nature and propriety of its own kind or sort. . . . [F]or there is no such thing

as most or least perfect, because *there is no most nor least in nature*. (Cavendish 2001, 204; emphasis added)

There is no most nor least in nature because nature consists in an infinite variety of corporeal forms that embody infinite perceptive, sensitive, and epistemic capacities. The strength of perception and sensation does not augment or diminish as physical complexity does; it changes in kind. It is not the type (or arrangement or complexity) of a body that makes a mind, but the bare presence of a body of any sort because a body—*any* body—is a perspective, that is, a unique manner of perceiving, sensing, and knowing the world. Nature's radical variety of bodies amounts to a radical variety of minds, with each body being just as minded as any other.

Critical social theorists' descriptions of the relationship between dehumanization and mental attribution highlights how mental attribution is not merely about recognizing bodies as minded or mindless. Mental attribution also involves attributing more, less, or equal mentality (or mindedness) to some bodies in comparison with others. Russellian and Cavendishian panpsychisms exemplify different approaches to the comparison component. The former sees mental attribution as a matter of degree depending on the body type with which it is associated, while the latter insists that each body and body type is just as mental as every other. This difference reflects different understandings of what makes a mind, which in turn reflects different conceptions of the physical employed in different physicalist panpsychisms. The third component of mental attribution focuses on how mental constitution (including causation) is understood in relation to physical or bodily constitution (including causation).

The Constitution Component: Attributing Organicist or Mechanistic Minds?

Many social theorists have criticized the tendency to think about the constitution of minds in the same ways that we think about the constitution of objects, machines, and matter. Ecofeminists Carolyn Merchant and Val Plumwood have observed that the bodies of laborers, women, colonized peoples, nonhuman animals, and the environment are readily *objectified* in a global, capitalist economy; the minds that are attributed to them can be manipulated by external forces, substituted for one another, and reduced to the operation of their parts.[15] More recently, Black feminist theorists analyze the ways that Black femininity figures in social imaginaries as a *hypermateriality* that enables the reduction and appropriation of Black women's minds and bodies. Both phenomena connect practices of mental attribution to mental constitution: objectification and hypermateriality involve one's body being attributed a mind whose constitution is equated with a physical constitution that operates according to Newtonian mechanics.

Merchant's poignant phrase "the death of nature" refers to the historical transition from animist, organicist, and vitalist conceptions of matter as living, moving, and internally motivated to the Newtonian paradigm that sees matter as a collection of dead particles acted on by external forces (Merchant 1980, 193). In the seventeenth century and beyond, the mechanistic idea that bodies are "passively determined vehicles of larger forces" facilitated the growing capitalist economy and its joint need to dominate nature and laborers in a social world that was becoming more egalitarian (Plumwood 1993, 122; Merchant 1980, 194, 287). Knowing how to manipulate matter by developing products and technologies was a way of gaining social and economic power. In this context, conceiving of certain categories of bodies as closer to nature than others implied that the minds associated with these bodies were more "material"—more like objects than subjects, and thus more in need of direction and domination. As Merchant explains, "Nature, women, blacks, and wage laborers were set on a new status as 'natural' and human resources for the modern world system" (Merchant 1980, 288). Plumwood associates this "stripping out of agency" with "a particular atomistic account of causation which later became enshrined in Newtonian physics" (Plumwood 1993, 125). Not all minds, however, were attributed an atomistic constitution governed by Newtonian causation. The minds attributed to the bodies of wealthy White male Europeans were understood to consist of a nonextended, immaterial substance that would render them free, unique, and irreducible to the workings of matter, or, at the very least, less susceptible to dictates of their material bodies (Quijano 2000, 555).

Also concerned with relationships between mental attribution and ideas about physical constitution, Black feminist theorists have described and resisted the ways that the Black female body is viewed as the limit case of materiality with reference to concepts and metaphors from physics, including those of the black hole, dark matter, chaos, sublimation, superposition, the void, the plenum, determinacy, universality, and causality. For example, Denise Ferreira da Silva connects the devaluation of Black lives to the ways that the materiality of blackness is conceived in modern thought. Black lives exist in the social imaginary as "content without form, or *materia prima*—that which has no value because it exists (as ∞) without form" (Ferreira da Silva 2017, 9). The infinity and indeterminacy of Black materiality does not register in a modern world that links moral value with the operations of universal reason, Newtonian causality, and self-determination. Ferreira da Silva reveals a logic that interprets differences in economic status between White Europeans and colonized and enslaved peoples as "the effects of particular bodily arrangements, which are established as the causes for particular mental (moral and intellectual) traits, which are themselves expressed in the social configurations found across the globe" (Ferreira da Silva 2017, 8). This etiology that grounds differences in the social order in mental differences, which are in turn traced to differences in bodily constitution, generates the category of blackness as a justification and obfuscation of violence perpetrated through slavery, colonialism, and capitalism. And yet, because it is imagined as a hypermateriality that exceeds the modern values of determinacy and efficient causality, blackness also exposes this hidden racial violence and calls for liberatory physics and ontologies. As an act of resistance against the view that would understand the constitution of Black women's minds in Newtonian terms as the effects of their physical parts and causes of their social status, Black feminist scholars invoke the image of "Black (w)holes," an irreducible perspective that founds Black feminist creativity and potential (Hammonds 1994; Bradley 2016). Zakkiyah Iman Jackson suggests that such metaphors "alert us to and perform a critique of *the logic* of microfundamentalism," a metaphysical view that reduces mind and world to the predictable behavior of fundamental particles (Jackson 2018, 638).

These descriptions of objectification and hypermateriality show how ideas about what a mind is made of come to bear on the type of mind and mental capacities attributed to certain bodies. Janine Jones explains, "Excess and/or hypercorporeality indicates that a mind has failed to set limits and order on its body: it is, par excellence, a nonrational mind" (Jones, this volume, 87). Unlike their engagements with the ratio and comparison components of mental attribution, contemporary panpsychists have discussed mental constitution extensively, focusing on two aspects specifically: (1) whether the experiences of macrolevel bodies are grounded in the experiences of microphysical entities, and (2) whether the experiences of microphysical entities combine to form the experiences of macrolevel bodies (Chalmers 2017a). The current discussion adds a third consideration that derives from critical social theorists' analyses of mental attribution and is especially relevant to physicalist panpsychisms: (3) whether mental constitution is conceived entirely in the terms of a Newtonian conception of the physical. Although the label "mechanistic" can be interpreted in a number of ways, when we refer to *mechanistic attribution* we mean to indicate the practice of attributing to a body a mind with an atomistic, Newtonian constitution, which understands minds as the types of things that can be summed and/or decomposed and explained entirely by a causality amenable to classical mechanics. On the contrary, *organicist attribution* is the practice of attributing to a body a mind with an irreducible constitution that cannot be composed or decomposed according to smaller parts and whose causality is at least partly explained by a non-Newtonian mechanics. Notably, organicist attribution does not entail a rejection of physics, nor does it necessarily deny Newtonian views of *bodily* constitution. According to this definition, Niels Bohr's description of the metaphysical implications of quantum phenomena such as nonlocality and complementary is consistent with organicist ideas of mental constitution: recognizing these phenomena leads to "the necessity of a final renunciation of the classical ideal of causality and a radical revision of our attitude toward the problem of physical reality" (Bohr 1935, 697).

The distinction between mechanistic and organicist attribution calls for panpsychists to be more explicit about how they understand the relationships between empirical findings in physics, metaphysical views about bodily constitution, and metaphysical views about mental constitution. Russellian panpsychists favor mechanistic attribution; they reason that if minds are physical, and the physical consists of particles governed by efficient causality, then mental constitution must also be atomistic and causal in the same way that bodily constitution is atomistic and causal. Russellian panpsychism entails that microexperiences (the experiences of microphysical particles such as quarks and electrons) combine to form macroexperiences (the experiences of humans, horses, and other organisms). Its proponents believe that minds are the types of things that can be composed or decomposed. Moreover, Chalmers maintains that "microphenomenal properties . . . play the most fundamental causal roles in physics" (Chalmers 2017b, 29; 2017a, 181). He suggests that macroexperience inherits causal relevance from microexperience in the same manner that a billiard ball inherits causal relevance from its constituting particles; insofar as the one constitutes the other, causal relevance can transfer between them (Chalmers 2017b, 29). To the extent that Russellian panpsychists challenge the atomistic interpretation of the physical or understand the causality of experiences as partially recalcitrant to the terms Newtonian mechanics, they will lean away from a mechanistic notion of mental attribution. Roelofs, for example, admits that it may turn out that the world is "infinitely divisible, displaying no identifiable 'basic parts,'" but he nonetheless insists that we should operate according to a Newtonian model that recognizes the ontological independence of cells, molecules, and atoms (Roelofs 2019, 77).

Whereas the imagination of contemporary physicalist panpsychists is necessarily influenced by the dominance and pervasiveness of Newtonian conceptions of the physical, Cavendish's position as Newton's contemporary who published her major works in natural philosophy before he published his renders her views especially useful for envisioning a non-Newtonian materialist panpsychism. Cavendish rejects the idea that the intrinsic nature of matter consists in microphysical entities. Atomism and materialism are incompatible on Cavendish's view because all material bodies are divisible, no matter how small or large (Cavendish 2001, 125). She criticizes atomistic philosophers for "[making] an universal cause, of a particular effect: for no particular part or action [effective part], can be prime in nature, or a fundamental principle of other creatures or actions" (Cavendish 2001, 113). Instead, Cavendish imagines matter's intrinsic constitution as a plenum that is constantly in motion—a nondiscrete field whose infinite, particular motions at the intrinsic level are the cause and basis of nature's *effects*, that is, the individuated bodies and minds that we encounter at the level of experience.[16] Because each body/perspective/mind is a result of the collective, relational motions and actions of the material plenum, a human's experience is no more grounded in the experiences of fundamental particles than it is in those of whales or honeybees. Cavendish writes:

> Those parts that are composed into the figure of an animal, make perceptions proper to that which figures corporeal, interior, natural motions; but, if they be dissolved from the animal figure, and composed into vegetables, they make such perceptions as are proper for vegetables; and being again dissolved and composed into minerals, they make perceptions proper to minerals, etc. so that no part is tied or bound to one particular kind of perception, no more than it is bound to one particular kind of figure. (Cavendish 2001, 166)

In other words, minds are not the types of things that combine or decompose; *they transform*. When the corporeal shape of a body is augmented or reduced, its perspective is not augmented or reduced accordingly. Instead, each new corporeal configuration instantiates *a new kind of mind* that is likewise non-composable and irreducible. While the causality implicated by classical mechanics may well apply to the effective parts of matter (including atoms and particles), the causalities that operate at the level of matter's constitutive ingredients and underlie mental causation require a different physics that treats matter *as a whole*, which fills all space and therefore lacks individuation and position, but is nonetheless in motion (Cavendish 1664, 98–100).[17] Cavendishian panpsychism is therefore illustrative of organicist attribution that sees mental constitution as irreducible and mental causation as an entangled, holistic causation different from the interactions of individuated bodies. Cavendish's metaphysics is thus aptly described as a "carnal monadology" where the constitution of matter as a nondiscrete field does the harmonizing work among infinite particular perspectives that God performs in a Leibnizian universe.[18]

Analyses of objectification and hypermateriality by Merchant, Plumwood, Ferreira da Silva, Jackson, and other feminist theorists reveal an intimacy between understandings of mental constitution and mental attribution. In the social order, minds with constitutions amenable to the workings of Newtonian mechanics are attributed to certain bodies, while minds with irreducible constitutions are attributed to others. We gain a clearer picture of the difference between Newtonian and non-Newtonian approaches to mental attribution by studying the different ways that Russellian and Cavendishian panpsychisms imagine the intrinsic nature of matter. On the one hand, Russellian panpsychism takes a mechanistic approach to mental attribution that understands mental constitution in terms of Newtonian atomism and Newtonian causality. On the other hand, Cavendishian panpsychism's organicist attribution insists upon the irreducibility of minds and admits of mental causality that exceeds Newtonian causality.

A Taxonomy of Mental Attribution Patterns

Examining critical social theorist's analyses of mental attribution in regard to the bodies of women, Black people, colonized peoples, laborers, and others led us to identify three metaphysical components of mental attribution: the ratio component, the comparison component, and the constitution component. We then turned to examples of physicalist panpsychisms to illustrate at least two different ways of approaching each respective component: equal and unequal ratios, kind and degree comparisons, and mechanistic and organicist constitutions. Russellian panpsychism exhibits a *selective pattern* that attributes minds to some bodies (unequal), designates comparatively more (or less) mentality to certain of these (degree), and explains mental constitution in the atomistic, causal terms of Newtonian mechanics (mechanistic). Alternatively, Cavendishian panpsychism is consistent with an *unrestricted pattern* that attributes a mind to each and every body (equal), maintains that any one mind is just as mental as any other (kind), and understands minds as fundamental in themselves and in excess of the workings of Newtonian causality (organicist).

The opposing patterns consistent with Russellian and Cavendishian panpsychisms establish two endpoints that frame a spectrum of answers to the attribution question—Which bodies have minds?—from the most selective mental attribution pattern to the least selective. Adding up the possible combinations of approaches to the ratio, constitution, and comparison components yields eight possible attribution patterns that could be entailed by a given theory of mind:

Unequal Attribution Patterns	Equal Attribution Patterns
(a) unequal degree mechanistic (UDM)	(e) equal degree mechanistic (EDM)
(b) unequal kind mechanistic (UKM)	(f) equal kind mechanistic (EKM)
(c) unequal degree organicist (UDO)	(g) equal degree organicist (EDO)
(d) unequal kind organicist (UKO)	(h) equal kind organicist (EKO)

The attribution patterns of Russellian and Cavendishian panpsychisms are respectively represented by the extremes: types (a) and (h). We could expand this arrangement further to twenty-four types of attribution patterns if we also factored in three basic metaphysical positions: materialism, idealism, and dualism.

This taxonomy of mental attribution patterns is a tool that promises to advance and expand theories of panpsychism, critical social theories, and views about the mind generally. In the first place, it reveals that most contemporary panpsychisms are not as radical about attribution as their name implies. Insofar as panpsychism's potential to address long-standing problems in the philosophy of mind, such as the mind-body problem and the problem of consciousness, lies in its radical and economical approach to mental attribution, panpsychisms that embrace selective attribution patterns are likely to walk back this advantage. Selective patterns often reflect ontotheologic residues from the Cartesian context that birthed the problems in the first place, such as a belief in a contingent connection between mind and body or a mechanistic interpretation of matter. Moreover, seeking alternatives to dominant attribution patterns led to the recovery of an unrestricted physicalist panpsychism from the history of philosophy that can be weighed against contemporary views. To borrow a quip from Strawson, Cavendishian physicalist panpsychism is really realistic about panpsychism; it is *real panpsychism*—panpsychism that attributes a complete mind to each and every body, all the way down and in between.

Thinking in terms of the metaphysics of attribution patterns can expand critical social theories because an attribution pattern considers mental attribution in human, animal, vegetable, and mineral domains at the same time, and thus draws our attention to the ways that ideas about one category of bodies are related to practices of mental attribution that are applied to other categories. This taxonomy also highlights how the different components of a mental attribution pattern can work together to maintain systems of domination. Fanon expresses this synergy when he writes, "So they were countering my irrationality with rationality [unequal attribution], my rationality with the 'true rationality' [degree attribution]. I couldn't hope to win" (Fanon 2008, 111). In addition, recognizing the different components of mental attribution and the different ways that they can be combined to form an attribution pattern enables feminists and other critical social theorists to make fine-grained phenomenological distinctions between different experiences of oppression and resistance. According to the views discussed in this chapter, the experience of immanence is not the same as hypermateriality in part because they involve different components of mental attribution, and experiences of objectification that go by the same name can be distinguished based on the different practices of mental attribution that comprise them. The metaphysics of mental attribution can thus support critical social theorists in retaining phenomenological specificity in their analyses by situating experiences within their descriptive, personal, and ontological contexts so that the heterogeneity of our resistances is not erased and the freedom of some beings is not imagined in ways that entrench the oppression of others. Although the taxonomy of mental attribution patterns developed here is a tool that can be applied to different problems and literatures, its purpose is to generate more theoretical contextualization, precision, and specificity, as well as inter- and intradisciplinary dialogues and collaborations.

Beyond feminism and panpsychism, it is likely that the attribution question and this taxonomy of possible answers will inspire fresh thinking about our conceptions of the relationship between mind and body and their role in establishing ontologies of the human, animal, machine, and environment that organize the social sphere. Attending to the patterns of mental attribution at stake in twenty-first-century research programs such as artificial intelligence, new materialisms, assemblage theory, environmental studies, panpsychism, and others is a way of making explicit metaphysical and political commitments so that they can be subjects of conversation, debate, and critique. Most important, the attribution question spurs us to revise our "imaginative picture[s] of matter [and mind]" in ways that lead to greater theoretical innovation and liberatory potential (Russell 2014, 382). Collectively imagining metaphysical pictures that challenge conventional ways of thinking can help us "break away from the enclosures of modern thought" that limit both the explanatory capacities of our theories and the social and practical possibilities of our lives (Ferreira da Silva 2017, 1).

This chapter has posed the question of mental attribution in metaphysical terms: *Which bodies have minds?* The attribution question is not orthogonal to the question that has historically been at the heart of philosophy of mind: *What is the mind?* On the contrary, views about who (or what) has a mind entail views about whether minds are the types of things that can exist without bodies, be more or less mental, compose and decompose into simpler or more complex minds, and operate according to a causality explained by Newtonian mechanics.

Metaphysical contemplation is neither apolitical nor ahistorical, nor is it a practice that is inconsequential to the social and political possibilities of beings who inhabit a world structured by multiple, intersecting oppressions. Readers who have been trained to cleanly separate fact from value, the descriptive from the normative, objective from subjective, exteriority from interiority, and the metaphysical from the social may be inclined to resist the complexity of the attribution question by appealing to philosophical divisions of labor that mirror these separations. But twenty-first-century life frustrates such divisions at every turn with its landscapes of conscious objects and objectified humans, global flows of knowledge and capital, and diverse social movements that illuminate and inspire liberatory ways of thinking, living, and being. Different from the individualist epistemological problem of other minds, the attribution question calls us to situate accounts of what the mind is and how minds and bodies interact in terms of a broader social, political, economic, and relational nexus that is invested in particular patterns of attributing and disattributing minds (and mentality) to certain categories of bodies. Here we find that not all views of mind are equal when it comes to explaining mental phenomena, nor are all conceptions of mind equally egalitarian when it comes to instantiating liberatory configurations of the social. The task of a feminist philosophy of mind is to hold both desiderata at the same time.

Notes

1. This chapter benefited greatly from conversations with Janine Jones, Keya Maitra, Jay Garfield, Matt MacKenzie, and Anand Vaidya.
2. See also Harfouch (2018), who shows how Immanuel Kant's association of certain psychological characteristics with bodies of certain races is central to the historical development of the mind-body problem in the philosophy of mind.
3. This chapter resists the disciplinary habit of thinking of these areas as mutually exclusive. Many feminist philosophers are also decolonial theorists, many philosophers of race are also philosophers of mind, and so on.
4. Different theorists, writing from different contexts, often describe these experiences differently even if they call them by the same name. My interpretations of the experiences of mental attribution and disattribution discussed in this chapter are linked to contexts developed by the critical social theorists cited here and cannot necessarily be transposed to others.
5. For overviews of Cavendish's philosophy, see Cunning (2016) and Boyle (2018).
6. That contemporary philosophers of mind working to articulate a viable form of physicalist panpsychism have looked to Leibniz, Spinoza, and Russell rather than Cavendish is both curious and unfortunate, given that her panpsychism possesses the desirable elements of the men's systems but has the added virtue of being materialist already (not to mention that it predates the others).
7. Cavendish recognizes three ingredients: rational, sensitive, and inanimate matter. Each ingredient tends toward a different respective *effect*, such as structural integrity, swiftness, slowness, perception, or sensation. However, thinking of these types of matter as spatially distinct "parts" would be incorrect because matter's ingredients are "completely blended" in the sense that one cannot exist independently of the others (Cavendish 2001, 16, 24, 34–35; 1996, 252). The Stoic view that matter has both active and passive principles that are completely mixed in nature has obvious parallels in Cavendish's system, as does the concept of *pneuma*, a creative, moving fire that is present in all things, albeit with three varying degrees of intensity: *hexis, physis, and psyche*. See O'Neill (2001, xxi–xxxii).
8. The applicability of Beauvoir's phenomenological descriptions of immanence and transcendence to social locations and bodies that are not White, bourgeois, and European is widely debated. See, for example, Jones (2019).

9. Cf. Harfouch, who defines racial nonbeing as a "mind-body union without reason" (2018, xiii).

10. For simplicity's sake, I will not take up the fascinating possibilities that no bodies are attributed minds (0:≥1) and that bodies can be attributed more than one mind (1:>1).

11. Cf. Mikkola, who understands dehumanization differently (2016, 146–185).

12. For more on the relationships among the concept of race, racism, and evolutionary theory, see Gould (1981) and Zack (2002).

13. See also Taylor (2015).

14. Many philosophers of mind would dispute the ideas that evolutionary adaptation yields degree scales and/or is teleological. See, for example, Millikan (1984).

15. Cf. Cahill, who emphasizes the difference between objectification and derivitization (2011).

16. Cavendishian panpsychism is not cosmopsychism because the nondiscrete plenum lacks an individuated body and thus a mind: "nature is not a deity" (Cavendish 2001, 13). Cf. Itay (2015).

17. On Cavendish's views of causality and freedom, see Detlefsen (2007). Although this remains to be argued, I believe Cavendish's materialist panpsychism is compatible with quantum holism. Her view anticipates, for example, that of David Bohm, who recognizes two distinct "orders" of reality (Bohm and Hiley 1993, 9).

18. For more on "carnal monadology," see McWeeny (2019, 133).

References

Beauvoir, Simone de. 2010. *The Second Sex*. Translated by Constance Borde and Sheila Malovany-Chevallier. New York: Alfred A. Knopf.

Bohm, David, and Basil J. Hiley. 1993. *The Undivided Universe: An Ontological Interpretation of Quantum Theory*. London: Routledge.

Bohr, Niels. 1935. "Can Quantum-Mechanical Description of Reality Be Considered Complete?" *Physical Review* 48: 696–702.

Boyle, Deborah. 2018. *The Well-Ordered Universe: The Philosophy of Margaret Cavendish*. New York: Oxford University Press.

Bradley, Rizvana. 2016. "Living in the Absence of a Body: The (Sus)stain of Black Female (W)holeness." *Rhizomes: Cultural Studies in Emerging Knowledge* 29. http://www.rhizo mes.net/issue29/bradley/index.html.

Cahill, Ann J. 2011. *Overcoming Objectification: A Carnal Ethics*. New York: Routledge.

Cavendish, Margaret. 1664. *Philosophical Letters, or Modest Reflections upon Some Opinions in Natural Philosophy*. London: Early English Books Online.

Cavendish, Margaret. 1996. *Grounds of Natural Philosophy*. West Cornwall, CT: Locust Hill Press.

Cavendish, Margaret. 2001. *Observations upon Experimental Philosophy*. Edited by Eileen O'Neill. New York: Cambridge University Press.

Chalmers, David J. 2017a. "The Combination Problem for Panpsychism." In *Panpsychism: Contemporary Perspectives*, edited by Godehard Brüntrup and Ludwig Jaskolla, 179–214. New York: Oxford University Press.

Chalmers, David J. 2017b. "Panpsychism and Panprotopsychism." In *Panpsychism: Contemporary Perspectives*, edited by Godehard Brüntrup and Ludwig Jaskolla, 19–47. New York: Oxford University Press.

Cunning, David. 2016. *Cavendish*. New York: Routledge.

Detlefsen, Karen. 2007. "Reason and Freedom: Margaret Cavendish on the Order and Disorder of Nature." *Archiv für Geschichte der Philosophie* 89 (2): 157–191.

Fanon, Frantz. 1963. *The Wretched of the Earth*. Translated by Constance Farrington. New York: Grove Press.

Fanon, Frantz. 2008. *Black Skin, White Masks*. Translated by Charles Lam Markmann. New York: Grove Press.

Ferreira da Silva, Denise. 2017. "1 (life) ÷ 0 (blackness) = ∞ − ∞ or ∞ / ∞: On Matter beyond the Equation of Value." *e-flux journal* 79: 1–11.

Goff, Philip. 2019. *Galileo's Error: Foundations for a New Science of Consciousness*. New York: Vintage Books.

Goff, Philip. 2020. "Does Consciousness Pervade the Universe? Philosopher Philip Goff Answers Questions about 'Panpsychism.'" Interviewed by Garrett Cook. *Scientific American*. January 14. https://www.scientificamerican.com/article/does-consciousness-pervade-the-universe/

Gordon, Lewis R. 1999. *Bad Faith and Antiblack Racism*. New York: Humanity Books.

Gould, Stephen Jay. 1981. *The Mismeasure of Man*. New York: Norton.

Hammonds, Evelyn. 1994. "Black (W)holes and the Geometry of Black Female Sexuality." *differences* 6 (2–3): 126–145.

Harfouch, John. 2018. *Another Mind-Body Problem: A History of Racial Non-being*. Albany: State University of New York Press.

Itay, Shani. 2015. "Cosmopsychism: A Holistic Approach to the Metaphysics of Experience." *Philosophical Papers* 44 (3): 389–437.

Jackson, Zakiyyah Iman. 2018. "'Theorizing in a Void': Sublimity, Matter, and Physics in Black Feminist Poetics." *South Atlantic Quarterly* 117 (3): 617–648.

Jones, Janine. 2020. "When Black Female Presence in Beauvoir's *L'Invitée* Is (Seemingly) Not Invited to *The Second Sex*." *Simone de Beauvoir Studies* 30 (1): 87–109.

Lugones, María. 2007. "Heterosexualism and the Modern/Colonial Gender System." *Hypatia* 22 (1): 186–209.

Lugones, María. 2010. "Toward a Decolonial Feminism." *Hypatia* 25 (4): 742–759.

McWeeny, Jennifer. 2019. "The Panpsychism Question in Merleau-Ponty's Ontology." In *Merleau-Ponty and Contemporary Philosophy*, edited by Emmanuel Alloa, Frank Chouraqui, and Rajiv Kaushik, 121–144. Albany: State University of New York Press.

Merchant, Carolyn. 1980. *The Death of Nature: Women, Ecology, and the Scientific Revolution*. New York: Harper & Row.

Mikkola, Mari. 2016. *The Wrong of Injustice: Dehumanization and Its Role in Feminist Philosophy*. New York: Oxford University Press.

Millikan, Ruth Garrett. 1984. *Language, Thought, and Other Biological Categories: New Foundations for Realism*. Cambridge, MA: MIT Press.

Nagel, Thomas. 2016. "Panpsychism." In *Mortal Questions*, 181–195. Cambridge: Cambridge University Press.

O'Neill, Eileen. 2001. "Introduction." In *Observations upon Experimental Philosophy* by Margaret Cavendish, x–xxxvi. Cambridge: Cambridge University Press.

Plumwood, Val. 1993. *Feminism and the Mastery of Nature*. New York: Routledge.

Quijano, Aníbal. 2000. "Coloniality of Power, Eurocentricism, and Latin America." *Nepantla: Views from the South* 1 (3): 533–580.

Roelofs, Luke. 2019. *Combining Minds: How to Think about Composite Subjectivity.* New York: Oxford University Press.

Russell, Bertrand. 2014. *The Analysis of Matter.* Mansfield Center, CT: Martino.

Strawson, Galen. 2017. "Physicalist Panpsychism." In *Blackwell Companion to Consciousness,* edited by Susan Schneider and Max Velmans, 374–390. 2nd ed. Malden, MA: John Wiley & Sons.

Strawson, Galen. 2020. "What Does Physical Mean? A Prologomenon to Physicalist Panpsychism." In *Routledge Handbook of Panpsychism,* edited by William Seager, 317–339. New York: Routledge.

Taylor, Ashley. 2015. "The Discourse of Pathology: Reproducing the Able Mind through Bodies of Color." *Hypatia* 30 (1): 181–198.

Tullman, Katherine. 2019. "The Problem of Other Minds: What Problem? Whose Mind?" *Metaphilosophy* 50 (5): 708–728.

Wynter, Sylvia. 2001. "Towards the Sociogenic Principle: Fanon, Identity, the Puzzle of Conscious Experience, and What It Is Like to Be 'Black.' " In *National Identities and Sociopolitical Changes in Latin America,* ed. Mercedes F. Durán-Cogan and Antonio Gómez-Moriana, 30–66. New York: Routledge.

Zack, Naomi. 2002. *Philosophy of Science and Race.* New York: Routledge.

16

Sexual Orientations

The Desire View

E. Díaz-León

Talk about sexual orientations is widespread in our society and our culture: it occurs in the media, in political debates, in religion, in the natural and social sciences, and in fiction.[1] But very few analytic philosophers have paid attention to questions about the nature of sexual orientation, such as what sexual orientations are, what "sexual orientation" means, and whether sexual orientations really exist. Some important exceptions include Edward Stein (1999), Cheshire Calhoun (2002), William Wilkerson (2013), and Robin Dembroff (2016).

In this chapter, I examine four main theories about the nature of sexual orientations that are available in the recent and growing literature on this topic, including behaviorism, ideal and ordinary versions of dispositionalism, structuralism, and views according to which sexual orientations are mental states such as sexual desires. I discuss several objections to these views, and I will develop and defend a new version of the view that characterizes sexual orientations in terms of sexual desires.

Before we start, it will be useful to clarify the methodology that we are going to use, that is, we should get clearer about what questions are our main focus here, and what methods are the most useful for approaching those questions. Following Sally Haslanger and others, I will distinguish between two different projects in philosophy (Haslanger 2006). On the one hand, we have the *descriptive* project, which seeks to reveal the concept we actually use, that is, the ordinary concept associated with the corresponding term, which is known as the "operative concept." On the other hand, we have the *ameliorative* or *conceptual engineering* project, which seeks to reveal the concept that we ought to use given certain purposes, that is, the concept that would best serve certain aims and goals, which may or may not correspond to the operative concept. This is known as the "target concept." My ultimate aim in this project is to reveal the target concept, that is, the concept of sexual orientation that would best serve the aims and goals of sexual orientation talk. But in order to know which concept we ought to use, it will be useful to know first which concept we are actually using. In the first part of the chapter, I will focus on the descriptive project, which in my view is a

E. Díaz-León, *Sexual Orientations* In: *Feminist Philosophy of Mind*. Edited by: Keya Maitra and Jennifer McWeeny, Oxford University Press. © Oxford University Press 2022. DOI: 10.1093/oso/9780190867614.003.0017

necessary step in the search for the target concept, and, in the second part of the chapter (the fifth section), I will make some preliminary remarks concerning the ameliorative project, which I hope to be able to develop fully in the future.

Dembroff also makes clear that the ultimate goal of their project is to reveal a concept of sexual orientation that can satisfy certain political aims (Dembroff 2016). In particular, Dembroff argues that our target concept of sexual orientation should be as close as possible to the original concept in order to facilitate communication, but it may depart in some ways from the ordinary concept in order to fulfill some other political aims. We should also distinguish between the *property* that the concept of sexual orientation picks out (which we can initially characterize as the property of being attracted to people of one's same or different sex or gender), and the *extension* of this property, that is, the entities or groups that satisfy that property (for example, the group of men who are attracted to men, the group of women who are attracted to women, and so on).

The Sex/Gender Distinction

On a preliminary characterization, sexual orientation has to do with the sex and/ or gender of the people one is sexually attracted to. Therefore, in order to have a clear characterization of sexual orientation, it would be useful to have a working characterization of "sex" and "gender."

According to a standard conception, "sex" refers to biological or anatomical features, whereas "gender" refers to social or cultural features. In this way, *being male* and *being female* are two types of sex, whereas *being a man* and *being a woman* are two types of gender. The crucial question for our purposes here is the following: Should we characterize sexual orientations in terms of attraction to people of a certain sex, or of a certain gender, or both? In order to answer this question, we would need to answer a prior, difficult question: What is "sex" and what is "gender"?

Both Stein and Dembroff aim to be neutral regarding the nature of sex and gender in their characterizations of sexual orientation. For example, Stein says: "To leave these various issues unresolved, I use the term sex-gender to encompass both sex and gender as standardly used. Sex-gender includes all the characteristics (biological, psychological, cultural, etc.) that are supposed to distinguish males/men from females/women" (Stein 1999, 33). That is, he introduces a new notion by stipulation, namely, "sex-gender," which is supposed to refer to the combination of all markers of biological sex plus all the markers of gender (independently of whether the connection between them turns out to be biologically constrained or socially constructed). Similarly, Dembroff claims:

An account of sexual orientation should be sensitive to the fact that individuals
may be sexually attracted to persons with various sex/gender combinations. . . .
I purposively build this flexibility into my account in order to construct a concept of sexual orientation (and of its taxonomy) that can be structurally preserved even when the number or understanding of recognized sex and gender
categories undergoes shift. (Dembroff 2016, 10–11)

That is to say, not only do we want a characterization of sexual orientation that
has a placeholder for different notions of gender and/or sex, as Stein suggests, but
we should also allow the possibility that people can be attracted to individuals
with several sex/gender combinations. In this way, Dembroff extends the scope
of Stein's neutral characterization (and allows that sex and gender might turn out
to be distinct kinds). Appeals to "sex-gender" in the characterizations of sexual
orientation that follow should be understood in this spirit.

Behaviorism and Dispositionalism about Sexual Orientation

According to behaviorism, "a person's sexual orientation is determined solely
by their observable sexual behavior" (Dembroff 2016, 12). Both Dembroff
(2016) and Stein (1999) argue that behaviorism does not seem to capture our
ordinary notion of sexual orientation. The main problem has to do with the idea
that there can be individuals who engage in behaviors that do not express their
sexual desires. For example, we can think of individuals who repress their sexual
orientations so that they do not act on their real sexual desires, or do not even
realize that they have those desires (that is, these individuals could be ignorant
of, or mistaken about, their own sexual desires). On the other hand, we could
have individuals who engage in some behaviors because of coercion or societal
pressures, not in virtue of their sexual desires. Finally, we can have cases of individuals who have chosen to be celibate for personal or religious reasons but can
be said to have a sexual orientation. Intuitively, these seem to be cases where
someone's behavior does not express their "true" sexual orientation. Therefore,
sexual orientation cannot consist merely in their sexual behavior.

Given the problems facing behaviorism, it seems more plausible to say that
someone's sexual orientation does not consist in the behaviors she actually
engages in, but rather in the behaviors she is *disposed* to engage in, that is to say,
in the behaviors she would engage in, given certain manifesting conditions. As
Dembroff puts it, "dispositionalism," as a general view, is the view that "a person's
sexual orientation is determined solely by what sex[es] and gender[s] of persons
S is disposed to sexually engage under certain stimulating circumstances" (2016,
13). Stein characterizes dispositionalism as follows:

According to [the dispositional view], a person's sexual orientation is based on his or her sexual desires and fantasies and the sexual behavior he or she is disposed to engage in under ideal conditions. If a person has sexual desires and fantasies about having sex primarily with people of the same sex-gender and is inclined under ideal circumstances to engage in sexual acts primarily with such people, then that person is homosexual. Conditions are ideal if there are no forces to prevent or discourage a person from acting on his or her desires, that is, when there is sexual freedom and a variety of appealing sexual partners available. (Stein 1999, 45)

The crucial question in order to properly characterize dispositionalism is how to characterize the relevant manifesting conditions. That is, not any disposition to have sex with women, say, will entail that a person is attracted to women. The relevant, sexual-orientation-determining dispositions will be only those that are expressed in the relevant manifesting conditions. But how could we identify those?

Dembroff interprets Stein's position in terms of the manifesting conditions being *ideal* conditions, that is, ideal circumstances where there are no forces preventing someone from acting on her desires. More precisely, Dembroff characterizes Stein's ideal version of the dispositional view in the following way:

Ideal dispositionalism: A person's sexual orientation is determined solely by what sex[es] and gender[s] of persons S is disposed to sexually engage under ideal conditions. (Dembroff 2016, 14)

Dembroff's main worry regarding ideal dispositionalism is that it is difficult to characterize ideal conditions in a way that is free from counterexamples but is not completely vacuous.[2] For example, the following would be a trivial characterization of the manifesting conditions that define "flammability": the match has the disposition to light if and only if, if the match were struck, the match would light unless it didn't light (Dembroff 2016, 15).

In response to this problem, Sungho Choi argues that we should examine the purposes behind our ordinary concept of a given disposition (such as flammability), and this will reveal what manifesting conditions are conceptually connected to that disposition (Choi 2008). Drawing on Choi's suggestion, Dembroff proposes the following characterization of manifesting conditions:

In the case of sexual orientation . . . the manifesting conditions for the behavioral dispositions relevant to determining sexual orientation must be understood within the framework of the purposes behind the everyday operative concept of sexual orientation. . . . These purposes determine the "ordinary" conditions under which the term is applied. (Choi 2016, 16)

That is, in order to characterize the manifesting conditions that are relevant for sexual orientations, Dembroff believes that we should take into consideration the purposes of our ordinary concept of sexual orientation. Why do we ascribe sexual orientations? Answering this question will be illuminating for discerning the relevant manifesting conditions that should appear in a characterization of the relevant dispositions that determine someone's sexual orientation. Dembroff calls this version of dispositionalism, based on Choi's account of dispositions, "ordinary dispositionalism." According to Dembroff, reflecting on the ordinary application conditions of our concept of sexual orientation reveals the following conceptual constraints:

(1) The operative concept assumes attraction to persons of a certain sex or gender (at least partially) *because* they are that sex and/or gender.
(2) The operative concept assumes attraction to certain persons while having a reasonable diversity of potential sexual partners.
(3) The operative concept assumes that one is willing and able to sexually engage with other persons. (Dembroff 2016, 17)

In this way, Dembroff clarifies the manifesting conditions for the relevant behavioral dispositions that determine our sexual orientations. Moreover, Dembroff emphasizes that a characterization of sexual orientation should appeal to different possible combinations of sex and/or gender. They thus arrive at the following characterization of ordinary dispositionalism about sexual orientations:

Bidimensional dispositionalism: A person S's sexual orientation is grounded in S's dispositions to engage in sexual behaviors under the ordinary condition[s] for these dispositions, and which sexual orientation S has is grounded in what sex[es] and gender[s] of persons S is disposed to sexually engage under these conditions. (Dembroff 2016, 18)

The ordinary conditions for the relevant dispositions are given by conditions (1)–(3) (or whatever turns out to be the right account of the ordinary conditions for the application of the concept of sexual orientation). This version of the dispositional view is known as "bidimensional dispositionalism" (BD) since it appeals to two dimensions of attraction, namely, the sex(es) and the gender(s) of the person(s) the subject is attracted to (which may be distinct or not). As Dembroff says:

BD understands sexual orientation solely in terms of the sex[es] and gender[s] of the persons one is disposed to sexually engage, without reference to the sex or gender of the person so disposed. . . . It also removes the connotation that "sexual orientation" is what distinguishes (e.g.) the so-called "straight" and "queer" communities. I believe that this is a socially and politically beneficial result. (Dembroff 2016, 19)

In the next section, I will discuss some objections to this view, understood as a descriptive account of the ordinary concept of sexual orientation. In the final section, I also raise some worries for this view insofar as it aims to contribute to the ameliorative project. I will argue that this concept does not satisfy some moral and political aims that a revised concept of sexual orientation should satisfy.

Objections to Bidimensional Dispositionalism

I will introduce two counterexamples that show that the bidimensional dispositional account offered by Dembroff cannot capture the ordinary concept of sexual orientation. Thinking about these objections will lead us to a new version of the dispositional account of the ordinary concept of sexual orientation.

Alicia is a bisexual woman who has decided to be in a long-term monogamous relationship with her male partner. Being monogamous is a central feature of her character, and therefore it seems plausible to assume that in all the relevant close possible worlds, she would not have sex with people, including other women, other than her male partner. That is to say, in all those possible worlds that are relevantly similar to the actual one, she is also similar regarding this central aspect of her personality, namely, she is in a monogamous relationship with her male partner. In all of these possible worlds, she satisfies the relevant manifesting conditions according to Dembroff's constraints above, that is, she is willing to have sex and she has a reasonable diversity of potential sexual partners available, but her behavior in those worlds still does not seem to fully capture her sexual desires, since she is not disposed to have sex with anyone other than her male partner. My conjecture is that it seems intuitive to say that this person is sexually attracted to both men and women, given the content of her sexual desires, even if she does not engage in sexual activities with women in any of the relevant possible worlds. Therefore, it's not clear that bidimensional dispositionalism can capture Alicia's sexual orientation in the ordinary sense of this notion, that is, the sexual orientation that ordinary speakers would attribute to her.

Perhaps it could be argued that we should also take into account possible worlds where she is single, or she has a female partner, or she doesn't want to be monogamous. But then we should include these conditions in order to define manifesting circumstances. Perhaps, though, this point contradicts the letter of Dembroff's account but not its spirit, since this seems to follow Choi's suggestion that we should focus on our ordinary concept of a certain disposition in order to figure out the relevant manifesting conditions. It could thus be argued that the counterexample just helps us to further develop the relevant manifesting conditions. However, the problem for Dembroff's version of dispositionalism goes deeper than this. In what follows, I will present a second counterexample that shows that there is a dilemma for bidimensional dispositionalism here, and that it seems that no version of the dispositional account of sexual orientations that attempts to characterize them in terms of *behavioral* dispositions could satisfy both horns of the dilemma at the same time.

Cary is a man who identifies as being attracted mostly to women but is such that in close possible worlds he wants to experiment and engages in some sporadic sexual activities with men. Intuitively, this person would be classified as heterosexual in the actual world, or so I would want to argue. But it's not clear that Dembroff's account can capture this intuition. According to the example, in those close possible worlds where Cary engages in some sexual activities with men, the relevant manifesting conditions are satisfied, that is, the subject has a reasonable diversity of potential partners available and willingness to engage in sex, and so on. But we would still say, intuitively, that this person is heterosexual, even if he is disposed to have sex with men in some close possible worlds.

The main worry for bidimensional dispositionalism can be put in the form of a dilemma: if we understand the account loosely enough, then we can count possible worlds where Alicia is not monogamous and has sex with women as being relevant for determining her sexual orientation, and then the account would rightly capture the intuition that she is bisexual. But if we take this approach, then there seems to be no way of ruling out possible worlds where Cary feels like experimenting and has sex with some men, so the account could not capture the intuition that Cary is heterosexual. On the other hand, if we understand the relevant manifesting conditions more narrowly, and restrict the possible worlds to those where Cary doesn't feel like experimenting with men, then we should also restrict the possible worlds to those where Alicia is in a monogamous relationship with her male partner, but then Alicia would count as heterosexual, not bisexual. In sum, I don't see any way of modifying the account so that it can accommodate both counterexamples at the same time.

At this point, some readers might have the feeling of déjà vu: this dialectical situation seems familiar. It is similar to problems encountered by philosophical behaviorism about the mental, defended by Gilbert Ryle and others in the first half of the twentieth century (Ryle 1949). Let me briefly summarize a story familiar to anyone who has taken an introductory course in philosophy of mind: classical behaviorism about the mental attempted to define mental states in terms of a subject's *actual* behavior, or somewhat more nuanced, in terms of our *dispositions* to behave in certain ways, given certain inputs. But this project was doomed to fail. As most philosophers of mind in the second half of the twentieth century would agree, we cannot define a mental state M in terms of certain behavior B given circumstances C, because there is no determinate behavior that a subject undergoing M would manifest, given circumstances C, *independently of other mental states*. That is, we cannot explicate a mental state in terms of the connection of that mental state with some inputs (perceptual inputs, for example) and some outputs (behavioral outputs), in the absence of other mental states. We can only formulate conditionals like the following: "If subject S is in mental state M, and mental states $m_1, m_2, m_3 \ldots m_n$, and there is input X, then S will do A." The additional mental states are ineliminable, or so it has been argued.[3]

Likewise, it seems contrary to our intuitions to define someone's sexual orientation *just* in terms of the behavior she would engage in, given such and such circumstances, because it seems that the behavior she would engage in, given those circumstances, essentially depends on what other mental states she has (for instance, whether she wants to be monogamous, or whether she feels like experimenting, and so on). That is to say, two subjects with the same sexual orientations but different mental states could engage in different sexual behaviors in the same manifesting circumstances. Moreover, two subjects with different sexual orientations could engage in the same sexual behavior in the same manifesting circumstances insofar as they possess different mental states.

This similarity between the problems for (dispositional) behaviorism about the mental and bidimensional dispositionalism about sexual orientations gives us some indirect evidence that perhaps we have similar problems here because in both cases we are trying to define *mental states* in terms of behavioral dispositions. These problems for the dispositional account of sexual orientations provide some indirect motivation for the view that sexual orientations are identical to certain mental states, and if so, it would not be surprising that we cannot define them just in terms of the disposition to engage in certain behaviors given certain inputs, *independently of other mental states*, since this is a worry for any attempt to analyze mental states in terms of behavioral dispositions more generally. In the following section, I develop in more detail the view that sexual orientations are identical to mental states.

The Desire View

Recall Stein's formulation of dispositionalism: "According to [the dispositional view], a person's sexual orientation is based on his or her *sexual desires and fantasies and* the sexual behavior he or she is disposed to engage in under ideal conditions" (Stein 1999, 45; emphasis added). As we can see, Stein wants to characterize sexual orientation in terms of behavioral dispositions *and* sexual desires and fantasies. My claim is that these sexual desires and fantasies cannot be reduced to the sexual behavior someone is disposed to engage in under ideal conditions, independently of other mental states that she has.

Here I want to discuss the following conjecture: we could understand sexual orientations in terms of *sexual preferences*, where a sexual preference is understood as a complex mental state. In this section, I will explain how I understand preferences in general, and sexual preferences in particular.

Preferences are dispositional mental states. In particular, I understand preferences as *dispositions to instantiate certain desires and feelings*. The central question for our purposes is: How can we characterize *sexual* preferences? I suggest that we can understand a sexual preference in terms of the dispositions to have *sexual desires* under the relevant manifesting conditions (as opposed to the dispositions to engage in certain kind of sexual behaviors). Therefore, my suggestion is that we characterize sexual orientation in terms of sexual preference, and sexual preference in terms of a disposition to have sexual desires of certain kinds, given certain manifesting conditions. We can call my proposed view of sexual orientations "the desire view," which we can characterize a bit more precisely in terms of a new version of dispositionalism:

> *Dispositionalism**: A person S's sexual orientation is determined by the sex[es] and/or the gender[s] of persons for whom S is disposed to have sexual desires, under the relevant manifesting conditions.

A remaining question in order to flesh out this account is: What is *sexual desire*? According to a standard conception of desires, a desire is a propositional attitude of the form "subject S bears the attitude of desiring toward proposition p." Therefore, a *sexual* desire could be understood in terms of the desire that certain propositions about sexual activities be the case, such as the proposition that S has sex with some men (or some women), or men (or women) in general. But some problems arise: this formulation doesn't seem to capture our ordinary concept of sexual desire. For instance, S might have the desire to have sex with a certain person in order to get paid, or to win a bet, or in order to cheer them up, and so on, but intuitively S still bears the attitude of desiring to the proposition that S has sex with such and such, even if this is not motivated by sexual arousal in those cases. Therefore, having a propositional attitude of the form "S desires that S has sex with such and such" is not sufficient for instantiating *sexual* desire in the relevant sense. What is missing is the connection with some specifically *sexual experiences*, such as sexual arousal and sexual pleasure. Stein provides a formulation along these lines:

> A desire is sexual to the extent that it involves (in the appropriate way) the arousal of the person who has the desire. . . . By arousal, I do not mean the various physiological manifestations of arousal . . . but the psychological state of being aroused. (Stein 1999, 69)

This seems very plausible to me: sexual desire is a mental state that is somehow connected with some experiences such as sexual arousal (which is typically correlated with the physiological state of arousal but is not identical to it).

In my view, we should distinguish between *standing* mental states such as beliefs or desires, which are dispositional and are not always manifested; and *occurring* mental states, which enter into the stream of consciousness during a certain interval of time and are necessarily conscious and manifested. It seems intuitive to say that sexual desire is a *standing* mental state (for example, someone could be attracted to another person, say her partner or her lover, during a long period of time, and this does not mean that she is experiencing arousal during the whole period), whereas sexual arousal per se is an *occurring* mental state, because it is necessarily conscious. On the other hand, a person can be said to have sexual desires for women, or for men, even when she is not conscious of it, for instance when she is dreamlessly sleeping or suffering excruciating pain, and so on.

Following Stein, I will distinguish between the experience of sexual arousal as an occurring mental state, and the *physiological* state of sexual arousal. (We can similarly distinguish between the mental state of pain and the physiological state of tissue damage, or the experience of orgasm and the physiological state of orgasm.) A crucial question remains: What is the relation between sexual desire and the experience of sexual arousal? As we have seen, if we understand sexual desires as standing mental states, then they do not necessarily involve the experience of sexual arousal at all times, but there is still a connection. Here I want to suggest the following hybrid view of sexual desires for men and/or women (or the relevant sex/gender combination):

> *Hybrid View*: A sexual desire (for men and/or women, or people of certain sex and/or gender) involves the combination of a propositional attitude (of the form "S bears the relation of desiring toward proposition p") plus a disposition to be sexually aroused by, or sexually attracted to, men and/or women.[4]

In my view, it can be useful to distinguish between an intentional and a causal reading of this characterization of sexual desire. According to the *causal reading*, S experiences sexual attraction that is caused by (the perception of, or interaction with) people of certain sex(es) or gender(s); whereas according to the *intentional reading*, S experiences sexual attraction toward people of certain sex(es) or gender(s) because they are represented as having certain sex(es) or gender(s). The intentional interpretation assumes that the relevant mental state is accompanied by a *representation* of certain people as having a certain sex or gender (which could be false). Arguably, this representation could have *conceptual content*, as in the case of beliefs or thoughts, or *nonconceptual content*, as in the case of perceptual experiences or mental imagery. I am sympathetic to the intentional reading, but, for our purposes here, I will leave this qualification open.

An interesting question that I have left out so far is how my account would deal with the cases of Alicia and Cary above. In the case of Alicia, it is clear my account would predict that she is attracted to both men and women, since she is disposed to have desires for both men and women. The case of Cary is a bit more complicated: it seems that he is also disposed to experience sexual arousal with respect to both men and women in the relevant possible worlds, but we wanted to save the intuition that he is heterosexual. In my view, we could argue that Cary lacks the dispositions to have sexual desires for men in the relevant manifesting conditions, since he is not disposed to experience sexual arousal with respect to men in the relevant conditions, even if he has the propositional attitude to have sex with men in some contexts (because he wants to experiment), so he wouldn't count as bisexual on my account, which seems to be the right result.

It could be argued that sexual desire does not need to involve a propositional attitude of this form, since, for instance, a celibate person S does not seem to have the propositional attitude of desiring that S has sex with anyone, although she can have sexual desires for men or for women. Moreover, a monogamous bisexual person whose partner is a man, say, could have sexual desires for women even if she does not seem to have the attitude of desiring that she has sex with women, given that she is monogamous. In response, I would argue that these subjects *do* have these propositional attitudes, but they also have propositional attitudes with the opposite content, so that they have contradictory attitudes (even if, all things considered, the desire not to have sex with such and such people trumps the desire to have sex with some people). In my view, the cases of the celibate person and the monogamous person are different from the case of an asexual person, who does not seem to have the attitude of desiring that she has sex with anyone at all (or at least not in virtue of her sexual desires: she might have the desire to have sex with some people in virtue of her desire to make money or to cheer someone up). On the other hand, the mere feeling of sexual arousal does not seem sufficient to capture the ordinary notion of sexual desire: someone could be sexually aroused by different people, but this does not seem sufficient to say that this person is attracted to, or has desires for, such and such people, in the absence of a propositional attitude with the appropriate content.

To sum up: in this section I have provided an account of the ordinary concept of sexual orientation in terms of S's sexual preferences, and I have characterized sexual preference in terms of S's dispositions to instantiate certain sexual desires in certain manifesting conditions. Furthermore, I have characterized the relevant sexual desires as complex mental states composed of a propositional attitude of the form "S desires that S has sex with such and such people" plus the disposition to instantiate certain sexual experiences *about* certain kinds of people (or *caused* by certain kinds of people).

The Ameliorative Project: In Search of the Target Concept

As we have seen, Dembroff's proposed concept of sexual orientation can do a lot of explanatory work, and can satisfy several important political desiderata. But in my view it fails to satisfy an important desideratum, namely, it does not provide categories that capture the similarity between those people who identify as male/men and are attracted to other males/men, and those who identify as female/women and are attracted to other females/women. And I believe that it is politically useful to have concepts that make this similarity salient since this is an important dimension of discrimination that is politically useful to emphasize, to wit, these two communities occupy similar social positions regarding many factors such as cultural representations, access to marriage benefits, housing, healthcare, and so on. However, the new taxonomy suggested by Dembroff cannot easily capture these common patterns of discrimination. And those who are either male/men and are (only) attracted to female/women, or female/women who are (only) attracted to males/men have some similar privileges that this new taxonomy cannot capture either. For all these reasons, I conclude that it would be useful to have a concept of sexual orientation according to which these are determined by the sex(es) and/or gender(s) of people one is attracted to, and also by one's own sex and/or gender. Therefore, I want to suggest that the following dispositional concept of sexual orientation is more useful politically than the one defended by Dembroff:

> *Dispositionalism***: A person S's sexual orientation is determined by the sex(es) and/or the gender(s) of persons for whom S is disposed to have sexual desires under the relevant manifesting conditions, plus S's own sex and/or gender.

In addition, this new characterization seems closer to the ordinary concept of sexual orientation, given that the distinction between "same-sex" and "opposite-sex" attraction seems to be part of the folk taxonomy of sexual orientation (although Dembroff is right that these labels can help to promote a binary conception of sex and gender as discrete categories, which is problematic).

It could be argued that for the purpose of achieving social justice, a "structural" view of sexual orientations could be the most useful. By "structural," I mean a kind of view similar to the accounts of gender and race that social constructionists such as Haslanger and others have offered. Haslanger provides a characterization of gender and race in terms of occupying certain positions within certain social structures of privilege and subordination:

> A group G is a gender (in context C) iff$_{df}$ its members are similarly positioned as along some social dimension (economic, political, legal, social, etc.) (in C) and the members are "marked" as appropriately in this position by observed or imagined bodily features presumed to be evidence of reproductive capacities or function.
>
> A group G is racialized (in context C) iff$_{df}$ its members are similarly positioned as along some social dimension (economic, political, legal, social, etc.) (in C), and the members are "marked" as appropriately in this position by observed or imagined bodily features presumed to be evidence of ancestral links to a certain geographical region. (Haslanger 2003, 252–53)

Likewise, we could offer a characterization of sexual orientations in terms of social hierarchies, as follows:

> A group is a *sexual orientation* (in context C) iff$_{df}$ its members are similarly positioned as along some social dimension (economic, political, legal, social, etc.) (in C) and the members are "marked" as appropriately in this position by observed or imagined features presumed to be evidence of a disposition to be sexually attracted to (or engage in sexual behavior with) people with the same or different sex assigned at birth.

A difficulty immediately arises: this structural view doesn't seem to capture the self-identification of some trans men and trans women, and therefore it is problematic. For instance, a trans woman who doesn't pass as a ciswoman and who is attracted to ciswomen would not count as having the same sexual orientation as a ciswoman who is attracted to other ciswomen.[5] This account does not seem to capture the relevant patterns of discrimination in this realm. For example, I believe that trans women who identify as lesbians and ciswomen who identify as lesbians are discriminated against in ways that are similar and should be recognized as being relevantly similar.[6] Therefore, I believe that the structural account of sexual orientations characterized above could satisfy some important political desiderata but would also fail to satisfy some central ones, such as doing justice to the self-identification of trans women.[7]

Dembroff has argued that a concept of sexual orientations based on someone's dispositions to instantiate certain sexual desires (as opposed to dispositions to engage in certain kinds of sexual behavior) is politically problematic. They write, "For these purposes, someone with the psychological features of a 'heterosexual' but queer behavioral dispositions can and should be protected from anti-queer prejudice" (Dembroff 2016, 21). That is to say, Dembroff suggests that what is politically relevant is someone's behavior, rather than her sexual desires and fantasies. I agree that someone's manifest behavior can be a focus of discrimination and stigma, so it is important to capture this. But at the same time, I also believe that someone with queer desires and fantasies who doesn't act on them (for instance, because she is repressed, or coerced into "heterosexual" behavior, or is not disposed to engage in "same-sex" behavior because of religious or health reasons) should also be protected from antiqueer prejudice. These people could also suffer discrimination, for example if they do not see their desires and experiences represented in society, or if they feel that, were they to express their desires, they would be stigmatized. So just having certain desires is enough to suffer discrimination and prejudice in the form of invisibility and isolation, in a way that is similar enough to those who are discriminated because of their sexual behavior. In my view, this pattern of similarity seems politically relevant and worth emphasizing. This is why I believe that a concept of sexual orientation based on someone's sexual preferences is more politically useful than a concept based on someone's dispositions to engage in sexual activities given certain inputs, independently of her other mental states.

In this chapter, I have compared several characterizations of sexual orientation, and I have argued that the following characterization best captures the ordinary concept:

Dispositionalism**: A person S's sexual orientation is determined by the sex(es) and/or the gender(s) of persons for whom S is disposed to have sexual desires under the relevant manifesting conditions, plus S's own sex and/or gender.

Relatedly, I have characterized sexual desire (for people with a certain sex and/or gender) as follows:

Hybrid View: A sexual desire (for men and/or women) involves the combination of a propositional attitude (of the form "S bears the relation of desiring toward proposition p") plus a disposition to be sexually aroused by, or sexually attracted to, men and/or women.

We have also discussed some possible benefits and harms of different concepts of sexual orientation, including several versions of dispositionalism and the structural account. In my view, all these different concepts do some important explanatory work and capture important political desiderata. More work is needed in order to investigate the ordinary concept of sexual orientation in different communities, and which concept of sexual orientation is the most politically useful, a consideration that could vary from context to context, depending on the relevant moral and political aims at issue.

Notes

1. This work has been funded by grants RYC-2012-10900 and FFI2015-66372-P. I have presented ancestors of this chapter at the Universities of Barcelona, Colorado Boulder, Michigan, Rutgers (via Skype), San Francisco State, and Stockholm, and at the Central APA in Chicago. I am very grateful to the audiences in all those occasions, especially Saray Ayala, Carolina Flores, Dan López de Sa, Meena Krishnamurthy, Rebecca Mason, and Cat Saint-Croix, for their useful feedback. Extra thanks to Robin Dembroff and Erin Mercurio for being my commentators at Stockholm and Chicago respectively, and for very helpful discussions.
2. See also Choi (2008).
3. See Heil (2012) for a summary of this line of argument, and Ashwell (2014) for an application of the argument to the case of desires in particular.
4. Here I focus on sexual desires that involve the sex and/or gender of the person(s) one is attracted to, given that our purpose is to capture the ordinary concept of sexual orientation. I do not intend to suggest that this is a central feature of our sexual desires in general, or that we cannot have sexual desires that are centered around other features.
5. A trans person is someone who does not identify with the sex that was assigned at birth. A cis person is someone who does identify with the sex that was assigned at birth.
6. See Jenkins (2016) for a similar objection to Haslanger's account of gender.
7. See Saul (2012), Bettcher (2013), and Díaz-León (2016) for similar arguments regarding accounts of gender. Perhaps we could modify the structural account as follows: A group is a *sexual orientation* (in context C) iff$_{df}$ its members are similarly positioned as along some social dimension (economic, political, legal, social, etc.) (in C) and the members are "marked" as appropriately in this position by observed or imagined features presumed to be evidence of a disposition to be sexually attracted to (or engage in sexual behavior with) people with the same or different *self-identification* in terms of sex-gender.

References

Ashwell, Lauren. 2014. "The Metaphysics of Desire and Dispositions." *Philosophy Compass* 9 (7): 469–77.
Bettcher, Talia M. 2013. "Trans Women and the Meaning of 'Woman.'" In *The Philosophy of Sex*, edited by Nicholas Powell, Raja Halwani, and Alan Soble, 233–49. 6th ed. Lanham, MD: Rowman & Littlefield.

Calhoun, Cheshire. 2002. *Feminism, the Family, and the Politics of the Closet: Lesbian and Gay Displacement*. Oxford: Oxford University Press.

Choi, Sungho. 2008. "Dispositional Properties and Counterfactual Conditionals." *Mind* 117 (468): 795–841.

Dembroff, Robin. 2016. "What Is Sexual Orientation?" *Philosophers' Imprint* 16 (3): 1–27.

Díaz-Léon, E. 2016. "*Woman* as a Politically Significant Term: A Solution to the Puzzle." *Hypatia* 31 (2): 245–58.

Haslanger, Sally. 2003. "Future Genders? Future Races?" *Philosophic Exchange* 34: 4–27.

Haslanger, Sally. 2006. "What Good Are Our Intuitions? Philosophical Analysis and Social Kinds." *Aristotelian Society Supplementary Volume* 80 (1): 89–118.

Heil, John. 2012. *Philosophy of Mind: A Contemporary Introduction*. 3rd ed. New York: Routledge.

Jenkins, Katharine. 2016. "Amelioration and Inclusion: Gender Identity and the Concept of *Woman.*" *Ethics* 126 (2): 394–421.

Ryle, Gilbert. 1949. *The Concept of Mind*. New York: Hutchinson's University Library.

Saul, Jennifer. 2012. "Politically Significant Terms and Philosophy of Language: Methodological Issues." In *Out from the Shadows: Analytical Feminist Contributions to Traditional Philosophy*, edited by Sharon Crasnow and Anita Superson, 195–216. New York: Oxford University Press.

Stein, Edward. 1999. *The Mismeasure of Desire: The Science, Theory and Ethics of Sexual Orientations*. New York: Oxford University Press.

Wilkerson, William. 2013. "What Is 'Sexual Orientation'?" In *The Philosophy of Sex*, edited by Nicholas Powell, Raja Halwani, and Alan Soble, 195–213. 6th ed. Lanham, MD: Rowman & Littlefield.

PART V
MEMORY AND EMOTION

17

Outliving Oneself

Trauma, Memory, and Personal Identity

Susan J. Brison

I died in Auschwitz, but no one knows it.

—Charlotte Delbo[1]

Survivors of trauma frequently remark that they are not the same people they were before they were traumatized.[2] As a survivor of the Nazi death camps observes, "One can be alive after Sobibor without having survived Sobibor" (Langer 1995, 14). Jonathan Shay, a therapist who works with Vietnam veterans, has often heard his patients say, "I died in Vietnam" (Shay 1994, 180). Migael Scherer expresses a loss commonly experienced by rape survivors when she writes, "I will miss myself as I was" (Scherer 1992, 179). What are we to make of these cryptic comments? How can one miss oneself? How can one die in Vietnam or fail to survive a death camp and still live to tell one's story? How does a life-threatening event come to be experienced as self-annihilating? And what self is it who remembers having had this experience?

How one answers these questions depends on, among other things, how one defines "trauma" and "the self." In this chapter, I discuss the nature of trauma, show how it affects the self, construed in several ultimately interconnected ways, and then use this analysis to elaborate and support a feminist account of the relational self.[3] On this view the self is both autonomous and socially dependent, vulnerable enough to be undone by violence and yet resilient enough to be reconstructed with the help of empathic others.

Trauma and the Undoing of the Self

There is a much clearer professional consensus among psychologists about what counts as a traumatic event than there is among philosophers concerning the nature of the self. A traumatic event is one in which a person feels utterly helpless in the face of a force that is perceived to be life-threatening.[4] The immediate

Susan J. Brison, *Outliving Oneself* In: *Feminist Philosophy of Mind*. Edited by: Keya Maitra and Jennifer McWeeny, Oxford University Press. © Oxford University Press 2022. DOI: 10.1093/oso/9780190867614.003.0018 psychological responses to such trauma include terror, loss of control, and intense fear of annihilation. Long-term effects include the physiological responses of hypervigilance, heightened startle response, sleep disorders, and the more psychological, yet still involuntary, responses of depression, inability to concentrate, lack of interest in activities that used to give life meaning, and a sense of a foreshortened future. A commonly accepted explanation of these symptoms of post-traumatic stress disorder (PTSD) is that, in trauma, the ordinarily adaptive human responses to danger that prepare the body to fight or flee are of no avail. "When neither resistance nor escape is possible," Judith Herman explains, "the human system of self-defense becomes overwhelmed and disorganized. Each component of the ordinary response to danger, having lost its utility, tends to persist in an altered and exaggerated state long after the actual danger is over" (Herman 1992, 34). When the trauma is of human origin and is intentionally inflicted, it not only shatters one's fundamental assumptions about the world and one's safety in it, but it also severs the sustaining connection between the self and the rest of humanity. Victims of human-inflicted trauma are reduced to mere objects by their tormenters: their subjectivity is rendered useless and viewed as worthless. As Herman observes, "The traumatic event thus destroys the belief that one can *be oneself* in relation to others" (Herman 1992, 53). Without this belief, I argue, one can no longer *be oneself* even to oneself, since the self exists fundamentally in relation to others.

How one defines "self" depends in part on what explanatory work one wants the concept of a self to do. Philosophers have invoked this concept in various areas of the discipline in order to account for a wide range of phenomena. The self is, in metaphysics, whatever it is whose persistence accounts for personal identity over time. One metaphysical view of the self holds that it is bodily continuity that accounts for personal identity and the other, that it is continuity of memory, character traits, or other psychological characteristics that makes someone the same person over time. There is also the view, held by poststructuralists, among others, that the self is a narrative, which, properly construed, is a version of the view that psychological continuity constitutes personal identity.[5] In ethics the self is viewed as the locus of autonomous agency and responsibility and, hence, is the subject of praise or blame. Most traditional accounts of the self, from Descartes's to contemporary theorists', have been individualistic, based on the assumption that one can individuate selves and determine the criteria for their identity over time independent of the social context in which they are situated. In contrast, feminist accounts of the self have focused on the ways in which the self is formed in relation to others and sustained in a social context. On these accounts, persons are, in Annette Baier's words, "second persons," that is, "essentially successors, heirs to other persons who formed and cared for them" (Baier 1985, 84).[6] In addition, the self is viewed as related to and constructed by others in an ongoing way, not only because others continue to shape and define us throughout our lifetimes, but also because our own sense of self is couched in descriptions whose meanings are social phenomena (Scheman 1983).

The Embodied Self

Although we recognize other persons most readily by their perceptible, that is, bodily, attributes, philosophers have been loath to identify the self with a body for a host of reasons.[7] A dead body cannot be said to be anyone's self, nor can a living, but permanently comatose, one. We do not typically use a bodily criterion of identity to determine who we ourselves are, and most of us, when imagining Locke's prince, whose soul "enters and informs" the body of a cobbler, would suppose the resulting person to be the prince (Locke 1974, 216). Some philosophers have been concerned to show that the self can survive the death of the body, but perhaps the primary reason philosophers have not identified the self with the body is an ancient bias against our physical nature. Plato praised philosophers for "despising the body and avoiding it," and urged that "if we are ever to have pure knowledge of anything, we must get rid of the body and contemplate things by themselves with the soul by itself" (Phaedo II.65c–67d). This rejection of the body has been most apparent in the disparaging of the female body, which has been presented as the antithesis to reason. Although, as Sara Ruddick notes, "there is nothing intrinsically masculine about mind and objectivity or anything feminine about passion and physicality, . . . philosophers have tended to associate, explicitly or metaphorically, passion, affection, and the body with femininity and the mind with masculinity" (Ruddick 1989, 194). How some bodies came to be viewed as "more bodily" than others is a puzzle that Ruddick answers by arguing that the lack of intellectual control over menstruation, pregnancy, labor, and nursing set such female bodily functions against reason, which was viewed as detached, controlled, and impersonal—that is, masculine.

Even Simone de Beauvoir, while arguing that "one is not born, but rather becomes, a woman," views childbirth and nursing as completely passive, and thus dehumanizing, processes, which keep women mired in immanence (Beauvoir 1953, 301). She suggests that "it is not in giving life but in risking life that man is raised above the animal; that is why superiority has been accorded in humanity not to the sex that brings forth but to that which kills" (Beauvoir 1953, 72). Although Beauvoir rejects the conclusion that this sex difference justifies male dominance, she nonetheless accepts the premise reducing childbirth to a purely "animal" function.[8]

Beauvoir was the first female philosopher I read and, as a teenager, I shared her disdain for (socially) compulsory marriage and maternity for women in this society. I still share her concerns about constraints on women's reproductive freedom, but I reject her view of pregnancy and motherhood as necessarily passive and tedious processes, even when voluntary. The work of Ruddick and other feminists who have been redefining motherhood has led me to see the liberatory potential in *chosen* maternity, childbirth, and childrearing. Reading Ruddick's *Maternal Thinking* in 1989, I recognized the ways in which my philosophical training had exacerbated my preexisting tendency to value the cerebral over the corporeal. In pursuing the life of the mind, I had accepted unthinkingly (because unconsciously) its incompatibility with the life of the (gestating and birthing) female body. My reading of Ruddick happened to coincide with a visit to a gynecologist who told me that I might have difficulty conceiving and that if I even suspected I would want to have a child someday I should start trying now. My philosophical bias against maternity, combined with a personal (and political) reaction against what I perceived as pressure to have a baby (as in the words of one academic woman's mother who said, "I'd rather be a grandmother than the mother of a Ph.D.") suddenly gave way to the startling realization that I might *want* to experience the particular kind of embodiment and connection pregnancy and motherhood provide, and that these things were not incompatible with being a philosopher. After years of considering my body little more than an unruly nuisance, I found myself wanting to yield up control over it, to learn what it had to teach me, to experience the abandon of labor and childbirth, what Margaret Walker has called "the willing or grateful surrender of 'I' to flesh" (Ruddick 1989, 212).[9]

Plato praised those "who long to beget spiritually, not physically, the progeny which it is the nature of the soul to create and bring to birth. If you ask what that progeny is, it is wisdom and virtue in general. . . . Everyone would prefer children such as these to children after the flesh" (*Symposium* 208e–209a, 209c–d). It occurred to me that this preference was not, after all, universal, and that, in any case, one did not have to choose between pursuing wisdom and virtue, on the one hand, and having children, on the other. My husband (who never felt as compelled to make such a choice) and I started trying to conceive, or, rather, as a friend put it more aptly, stopped trying not to. It was just six months later, however, that I was jumped from behind, beaten, raped, strangled, and left for dead in a ravine. The pleasures of embodiment were suddenly replaced by the pain and terror to which being embodied makes one prey.

I was no longer the same person I had been before the assault, and one of the ways in which I seemed changed was that I had a different relationship with my body. My body was now perceived as an enemy, having betrayed my newfound trust and interest in it, and as a site of increased vulnerability. But rejecting the body and returning to the life of the mind was not an option, since body and mind had become nearly indistinguishable. My mental state (typically, depression) felt

physiological, like lead in my veins, while my physical state (frequently, inca-
pacitation by fear and anxiety) was the incarnation of a cognitive and emotional
paralysis resulting from shattered assumptions about my safety in the world. The
symptoms of PTSD gave the lie to a latent dualism that still informs society's
most prevalent attitude to trauma, namely, that victims should buck up, put the
past behind them, and get on with their lives. My hypervigilance, heightened
startle response, insomnia, and other PTSD symptoms were no more psychological, if that is taken to mean under my conscious control, than were my heart rate
and blood pressure.

The intermingling of mind and body is also apparent in traumatic memories that remain in the body, in each of the senses, in the heart that races and
skin that crawls whenever something resurrects the only slightly buried terror.
As Jonathan Shay writes in his study of combat trauma, "Traumatic memory
is not narrative. Rather, it is experience that reoccurs, either as full sensory re-
play of traumatic events in dreams or flashbacks, with all things seen, heard,
smelled, and felt intact, or as disconnected fragments. These fragments may be
inexplicable rage, terror, uncontrollable crying, or disconnected body states and
sensations" (Shay 1994, 172). The main change in the modality as well as in the
content of the most salient traumatic memories is that they are more tied to the
body than memories are typically considered to be.

Sensory flashbacks are not, of course, merely a clinical phenomenon, nor are
they peculiar to trauma. Proust describes the pleasantly vivid flashbacks brought
on by the leisurely savoring of a tea-soaked madeleine (Proust 1981, 1:48–49).[10]
Trauma, however, changes the nature and frequency of sensory, emotional, and
physiological flashbacks. They are reminiscent of the traumatic event itself, as
Shay writes, in that "once experiencing is under way, the survivor lacks authority
to stop it or put it away. The helplessness associated with the original experience
is replayed in the apparent helplessness to end or modify the reexperience once
it has begun" (Shay 1994, 174). Traumatic flashbacks immobilize the body by
rendering the will as useless as it is in a nightmare in which one desperately tries
to flee, but remains frozen.

The bodily nature of traumatic memory complicates a standard philosophical quandary concerning which of two criteria of identity—continuous body
or continuous memories—should be used to determine personal identity over
time. Locke's bodily transfer puzzle in which we are asked to decide who survives
"should the soul of a prince . . . enter and inform the body of a cobbler" no longer
presents us with an either/or choice, depending on which criterion we invoke
(Locke 1974, 116). If memories are lodged in the body, the Lockean distinction
between the memory criterion and that of bodily identity no longer holds.[11]

The study of trauma replaces the traditional philosophical puzzle about
whether the soul can survive the death of the body with the question of whether

the self shattered by trauma can reconstitute itself and carry on in the world. It also reveals the ways in which one's ability to feel at home in the world is as much a physical as an epistemological accomplishment. Jean Améry writes, of the person who is tortured, that from the moment of the first blow he loses "trust in the world," which includes "the irrational and logically unjustifiable belief in absolute causality perhaps, or the likewise blind belief in the validity of the inductive inference" (Améry 1995, 126). More important, according to Améry, is the loss of the certainty that other persons "will respect my physical, and with it also my metaphysical, being. The boundaries of my body are also the boundaries of myself. My skin surface shields me against the external world. If I am to have trust, I must feel on it only what I *want* to feel. At the first blow, however, this trust in the world breaks down" (Améry 1995, 126). Améry goes on to compare torture to rape, an apt comparison, not only because both objectify and traumatize the victim, but also because the pain they inflict reduces the victim to flesh, to the purely physical. This reduction has a particularly anguished quality for female victims of sexual violence who are already viewed as more tied to nature than men and are sometimes treated as mere flesh. It is as if the tormenter says with his blows, "You are nothing but a body, a mere object for my will—here, I'll prove it!"

. Those who endure long periods of repeated torture often find ways of dissociating themselves from their bodies, that part of themselves which undergoes the torture. As the research of Herman (1992) and Terr (1994) has shown, child victims of sexual and other physical abuse often utilize this defense against annihilation of the self, and, in extreme cases, even develop multiple personalities that enable one or more "selves" to emerge unscathed from the abuse. Some adult victims of rape report a kind of splitting from their bodies during the assault, as well as a separation from their former selves in the aftermath of the rape.

Charlotte Delbo writes of her return from Auschwitz:

life was returned to me
and I am here in front of life
as though facing a dress
I cannot wear. (Delbo 1995, 240)

A number of Holocaust survivors, whose former selves were virtually annihilated in the death camps, gave themselves new names after the war, Jean Améry (formerly Hans Maier) and Paul Celan (formerly Paul Antschel) being among the most well-known. In a startling reappropriation of the name (literally) imposed on him during his incarceration at Auschwitz, one survivor retained and published under the name "Ka-Tzetnik 135633," meaning "concentration camp inmate number 135633" (Ka-Tzetnik 135633, 1989).[12] Others were forced to assume new names and national and religious identities (or, rather, the appearance of them) in order to avoid capture, and probable death, during the war. The dislocations suffered by what Rosi Braidotti (1994) has called "nomadic subjects" can be agonizing even when the migrations are voluntary or, as in the case of Eva Hoffman (1989), whose family moved from Poland to Canada when she was thirteen, involuntary, but unmarked by violence. Given how traumatic such relocations can be, it is almost unimaginable how people can survive self-disintegrating torture and then manage to rebuild themselves in a new country, a new culture, and a new language.

What can we conclude from these clinical studies and personal narratives of trauma concerning the relationship of one's self to one's body? Does trauma make one feel more or less tied to one's body? That may depend on one's ability to dissociate. Since I, like most victims of one-time traumatic events, did not dissociate during the assault, I felt (and continue to feel) more tied to my body than before, or, at any rate, more vulnerable to self-annihilation because of it.[13] Those who survived ongoing trauma by dissociating from their bodies may feel that an essential part of themselves was untouched by the trauma, but even they experience, in the aftermath, the physical intrusions of visceral traumatic memories.

These various responses to trauma—dissociation from one's body, separation from the self one was either before or during the trauma—have in common the attempt to distance one's (real) self from the bodily self that is being degraded, and whose survival demands that one do, or at any rate be subjected to, degrading things. But such an attempt is never wholly successful and the survivor's bodily sense of self is permanently altered by an encounter with death that leaves one feeling "marked" for life. The intense awareness of embodiment experienced by trauma survivors is not "the willing or grateful surrender of an 'I' to flesh" described by Walker, but more akin to the pain of Kafka's harrow, cutting the condemned man's sentence deeper and deeper into his body until it destroys him (Kafka 2009, 77–79, 96–98).

The Self as Narrative

Locke famously identified the self with a set of continuous memories, a kind of ongoing narrative of one's past that is extended with each new experience (Locke 1974). The study of trauma presents a fatal challenge to this view, since memory is drastically disrupted by traumatic events—unless one is prepared to accept the conclusion that survivors of such events are distinct from their former selves. The literature on trauma does, however, seem to support the view, advocated by Derek Parfit, that the unitary self is an illusion and that we are all composed of a series of successive selves (Parfit 1986).[14] But how does one remake a self from the scattered shards of disrupted memory? Delbo writes of memories being stripped away from the inmates of the death camps, and of the incomprehensibly difficult task of getting them back after the war: "The survivor must undertake to regain his memory, regain what he possessed before: his knowledge, his experience, his childhood memories, his manual dexterity and his intellectual faculties, sensitivity, the capacity to dream, imagine, laugh" (Delbo 1995, 255).

This passage illustrates a major obstacle to the trauma survivor's reconstruction of a self in the sense of a remembered and ongoing narrative about oneself. Not only are one's memories of an earlier self lost, along with the ability to envision a future, but one's basic cognitive and emotional capacities are gone, or radically altered, as well. This epistemological crisis leaves the survivor with virtually no bearings by which to navigate. As Améry writes, "Whoever has succumbed to torture can no longer feel at home in this world" (Améry 1995, 136). Shattered assumptions about the world and one's safety in it can, to some extent, eventually be pieced back together, but this is a slow and painful process. Although the survivor recognizes, at some level, that these regained assumptions are illusory, she learns that they are necessary illusions—as unshakable, ultimately, as cognitively impenetrable perceptual illusions.

In addition, though, trauma can obliterate one's former emotional repertoire, leaving one with only a kind of counterfactual, propositional knowledge of emotions. When alerted to the rumors that the camp in which he was incarcerated would be evacuated the next day, Primo Levi felt no emotion, just as for many months he had "no longer felt any pain, joy or fear" except in a conditional manner: "If I still had my former sensitivity, I thought, this would be an extremely moving moment" (Levi 1993, 152–153). Indeed, the inability to feel one's former emotions, even in the aftermath of trauma, leaves the survivor not only numbed but also without the motivation to carry out the task of constructing an ongoing narrative.

However, by constructing and telling a narrative of the trauma endured, and with the help of understanding listeners, the survivor begins not only to integrate the traumatic episode into a life with a before and after but also to gain some degree of mastery over the trauma. When I was hospitalized after my assault I experienced moments of reprieve from vivid and terrifying flashbacks when giving my account of what had happened—to the police, doctors, a psychiatrist, a lawyer, and a prosecutor. Although others apologized for putting me through what seemed to them a retraumatizing ordeal, I responded that it was therapeutic, even at that early stage, to bear witness in the presence of others who heard and believed what I told them. Two and a half years later, when my assailant was brought to trial, I also found it healing to give my testimony in public and to have it confirmed by the police, prosecutor, my lawyer, and, ultimately, the jury, who found my assailant guilty of rape and attempted murder.[15]

How might we account for this practice of mastering the trauma through repeated telling of one's story? The residue of trauma is a kind of body memory, as Roberta Culbertson notes, "full of fleeting images, the percussion of blows, sounds, and movements of the body—disconnected, cacophonous, the cells suffused with the active power of adrenalin, or coated with the anesthetizing numbness of noradrenalin" (Culbertson 1995, 174). Whereas traumatic memories (especially perceptual and emotional flashbacks) feel as though they are passively endured, narratives are the result of certain obvious choices (how much to tell to whom, in what order, and so on). This is not to say that the narrator is not subject to the constraints of memory or that the story will ring true however it is told. And the telling itself may be out of control, compulsively repeated. But one *can* control certain aspects of the narrative and that control, repeatedly exercised, leads to greater control over the memories themselves, making them less intrusive and giving them the kind of meaning that permits them to be integrated into the rest of life.

Not only present listeners but also one's cultural heritage can determine to a large extent the way in which an event is remembered and retold, and may even lead one to respond as though one remembered what one did not in fact experience. Yael Tamir, an Israeli philosopher, told me a story illustrating cultural memory, in which she and her husband, neither of whom had been victims or had family members who had been victims of the Holocaust, literally jumped at the sound of a German voice shouting instructions at a train station in Switzerland. The experience triggered such vivid "memories" of the deportation that they grabbed their suitcases and fled the station. Marianne Hirsch (1992–93) discusses the phenomenon of "postmemory" in children of Holocaust survivors and Tom Segev writes of the ways in which the Holocaust continues to shape Israeli identity: "Just as the Holocaust imposed a posthumous collective identity on its six million victims, so too it formed the collective identity of this new country—not just for the survivors who came after the war but for all Israelis, then and now" (Segev 1993, 11). The influence of cultural memory on all of us is additional evidence of the deeply relational nature of the narrative self.

The relational nature of the self is also revealed by a further obstacle confronting trauma survivors attempting to reconstruct coherent narratives: the difficulty of regaining one's voice, one's subjectivity, after one has been reduced to silence, to the status of an object, or, worse, made into someone else's speech, an instrument of another's agency. Those entering Nazi concentration camps had the speech of their captors literally inscribed on their bodies. As Levi describes it, the message conveyed by the prisoners' tattoos was "You no longer have a name; this is your new name." It was "a non-verbal message, so that the innocent would feel his sentence written on his flesh" (Levi 1989, 119).

Piecing together a dismembered self seems to require a process of remembering in which speech and affect converge. This working through, or remastering of, the traumatic memory involves going from being the medium of someone else's (the torturer's) speech to being the subject of one's own. The results of the process of working through reveal the performative role of speech acts in recovering from trauma: *saying* something about a traumatic memory *does* something to it. As Shay notes in the case of Vietnam veterans, "Severe trauma explodes the cohesion of consciousness. When a survivor creates a fully realized narrative that brings together the shattered knowledge of what happened, the emotions that were aroused by the meanings of the events, and the bodily sensations that the physical events created, the survivor pieces back together the fragmentation of consciousness that trauma has caused" (Shay 1994, 188). But one cannot recover in isolation, since "narrative heals personality changes only if the survivor finds or creates a trustworthy community of listeners for it" (Shay 1994, 188). Fortunately, just as one can be reduced to an object through torture, one can become a human subject again through telling one's narrative to caring others who are able to listen.

Intense psychological pressures make it difficult, however, for others to listen to trauma narratives. Cultural repression of traumatic memories (in the United States about slavery, in Germany and Poland and elsewhere about the Holocaust) comes not only from an absence of empathy with victims, but also out of an active fear of empathizing with those whose terrifying fate forces us to acknowledge that we are not in control of our own.

As a society, we live with the unbearable by pressuring those who have been traumatized to forget and by rejecting the testimonies of those who are forced by fate to remember. As individuals and as cultures, we impose arbitrary term limits on memory and on recovery from trauma: a century, say, for slavery, fifty years, perhaps, for the Holocaust, a decade or two for Vietnam, several months for mass rape or serial murder. Even a public memorialization can be a forgetting, a way of saying to survivors what someone said after I published my first article on sexual violence: "Now you can put this behind you." But attempting to limit traumatic memories does not make them go away; the signs and symptoms of trauma remain, caused by a source more virulent for being driven underground.

And so we repeat our stories, and we listen to others.' What Hoffman writes of her conversations with Miriam, her closest North American friend, could also describe the remaking of a survivor's self in relation to empathic others: "To a large extent, we're the keepers of each other's stories, and the shape of these stories has unfolded in part from our interwoven accounts. Human beings don't only search for meanings, they are themselves units of meanings; but we can mean something only within the fabric of larger significations" (Hoffman 1989, 279). Trauma, however, unravels whatever meaning we've found and woven ourselves into, and so listening to survivors' stories is, as Lawrence Langer describes reading and writing about the Holocaust, "an experience in *un*learning; both parties are forced into the Dantean gesture of abandoning all safe props as they enter and, without benefit of Virgil, make their uneasy way through its vague domain" (Langer 1995b, 6–7). It is easy to understand why one would not willingly enter such a realm, but survivors' testimonies must be heard, if individual and cultural recovery is to be possible.

To recover from trauma, according to psychoanalyst Dori Laub, a survivor needs to construct a narrative and tell it to an empathic listener, in order to reexternalize the event. "Bearing witness to a trauma is, in fact, a process that includes the listener" (Laub 1992, 70). And to the extent that bearing witness reestablishes the survivor's identity, the empathic other is essential to the continuation of a self. Laub writes of Chaim Guri's film *The Eighty-First Blow*, which "portrays the image of a man who narrates the story of his sufferings in the camps only to hear his audience say: 'All this cannot be true, it could not have happened. You must have made it up.' This denial by the listener inflicts, according to the film, the ultimately fateful blow, beyond the eighty blows that man, in Jewish tradition, can sustain and survive" (Laub 1992, 68).

Remaking Oneself

> A child gave me a flower
> one morning
> a flower picked
> for me
> he kissed the flower
> before giving it to me . . .
> There is no wound that will not heal
> I told myself that day
> and still repeat it from time to time
> but not enough to believe it.
>
> —Charlotte Delbo [16]

In the traditional philosophical literature on personal identity, one is considered to be the same person over time if one can (now) identify with that person in the past or future. One typically identifies with a person in the past if one can remember having that person's experiences and one identifies with a person in the future if one cares in a unique way about that person's future experiences. An interesting result of group therapy with trauma survivors is that they come to have greater compassion for their earlier selves by empathizing with others who experienced similar traumas. This, in turn, enables them to care for their future selves. They stop blaming themselves by realizing that others who acted or reacted similarly are not blameworthy. Rape survivors, who typically have difficulty getting angry with their assailants, find that in group therapy they are able to get angry on their own behalf by first getting angry on behalf of others (Koss and Harvey 1991).

That survivors gain the ability to reconnect with their former selves by empathizing with others who have experienced similar traumas reveals the extent to which we exist only in connection with others. It also suggests that healing from trauma takes place by a kind of splitting off of the traumatized self which one then is able to empathize with, just as one empathizes with others.[17] The loss of a trauma survivor's former self is typically described by analogy to the loss of a beloved other. And yet, in grieving for another, one often says, "It's as though a part of myself has died." It is not clear whether this circular comparison is a case of language failing us or, on the contrary, its revealing a deep truth about selfhood and connectedness. By finding (some aspects of) one's lost self in another person, one can manage (to a greater or lesser degree) to reconnect with it and to reintegrate one's various selves into a coherent personality.

The fundamentally relational character of the self is also highlighted by the dependence of survivors on others' attitudes toward them in the aftermath of trauma. Victims of rape and other forms of torture often report drastically altered senses of self-worth, resulting from their degrading treatment. That even one person—one's assailant—treated one as worthless can, at least temporarily, undo an entire lifetime of self-esteem (Roberts 1989, 91). This effect is magnified by prolonged exposure to degradation, in a social and historical context in which the group to which one belongs is despised. Survivors of trauma recover to a greater or lesser extent depending on others' responses to them after the trauma. These aspects of trauma and recovery reveal the deeply social nature of one's sense of self and underscore the limits of the individual's capacity to control her own self-definition.

What is the goal of the survivor? Ultimately, it is not to transcend the trauma, not to solve the dilemmas of survival, but simply to endure. This can be hard enough, when the only way to regain control over one's life seems to be to end it. A few months after my assault, I drove by myself for several hours to visit a friend. Though driving felt like a much safer mode of transportation than walking, I worried throughout the journey, not only about the trajectory of every oncoming vehicle but also about my car breaking down, leaving me at the mercy of potentially murderous passers-by. I wished I'd had a gun so that I could shoot myself rather than be forced to live through another assault.[18] Later in my recovery, as depression gave way to rage, such suicidal thoughts were quickly quelled by a stubborn refusal to finish my assailant's job for him. I also learned, after martial arts training, that I was capable, morally as well as physically, of killing in self-defense—an option that made the possibility of another life-threatening attack one I could live with. Some rape survivors have remarked on the sense of moral loss they experienced when they realized that they could kill their assailants (and even wanted to!), but I think that this thought can be seen as a salutary character change in those whom society does not encourage to value their own lives enough.[19] And far from jeopardizing their connections with a community, this newfound ability to defend themselves, and to consider themselves worth fighting for, enables rape survivors to move among others, free of debilitating fears. It was this ability that gave me the courage to bring a child into the world, in spite of the realization that doing so would, far from making me immortal, make me twice as mortal, as Barbara Kingsolver put it, by doubling my chances of having my life destroyed by a speeding truck (Kingsolver 1989, 59).

But many trauma survivors who endured much worse than I did, and for much longer, found, often years later, that it was impossible to go on. It is not a moral failing to leave a world that has become morally unacceptable. I wonder how some can ask, of battered women, "Why didn't they leave?" while saying, of those driven to suicide by the brutal and inescapable aftermath of trauma, "Why didn't they stay?" Améry wrote, "Whoever was tortured, stays tortured" and this may explain why he, Levi, Celan, and other Holocaust survivors took their own lives decades after their (physical) torture ended, as if such an explanation were needed (Améry 1995, 131).

Those who have survived trauma understand well the pull of that solution to their daily Beckettian dilemma, "I can't go on, I must go on."[20] For on some days the conclusion "I'll go on" cannot be reached by faith or reason. How does one go on with a shattered self, with no guarantee of recovery, believing that one will always stay tortured and never feel at home in the world? One hopes for a bearable future, in spite of all the inductive evidence to the contrary. After all, the loss of faith in induction following an unpredictable trauma also has a reassuring side: since inferences from the past can no longer be relied upon to predict the future, there's no more reason to think that tomorrow will bring agony than to think that it won't. So one makes a wager, in which nothing is certain and the odds change daily, and sets about "willing to believe" that life, for all its unfathomable horror, still holds some undiscovered pleasures.[21] And one remakes oneself by finding meaning in a life of caring and being sustained by others. While I used to have to will myself out of bed each day, I now wake gladly to feed my infant son whose birth gives me reason not to have died. He is the embodiment of my life's new narrative, and I am more autonomous by virtue of being so intermingled with him. Having him has also enabled me to rebuild my trust in the world around us. He is so trusting that he stands with outstretched arms, wobbling, until he falls, stiff-limbed, forward, backward, certain the universe will catch him. So far, it has, and when I tell myself it always will, the part of me that he's become believes it.

Notes

1. Delbo attributes this statement to one of her fellow deportees (Delbo 1995, 267).
2. This chapter was first published in 1997 and reprinted in *Aftermath: Violence and the Remaking of a Self*, 37–66 (Princeton: Princeton University Press, 2002). It is reprinted here with abridgements and slight modifications with the permission of the author and press.
3. In defending a feminist account of the relational self, I do not mean to imply that all relational accounts of the self are feminist. Some that are not (necessarily) feminist are those advocated by G. W. F. Hegel, Karl Marx, and contemporary communitarians.
4. This paraphrases Judith Herman's description of traumatic events (Herman 1992, 33). This description and the following discussion of trauma are distilled from Herman's book as well as from Janoff-Bulman (1992) and Shay (1994).
5. While some poststructuralists hold that the self is a fiction, not all do, and this is not, in any case, implied by the view that it is a narrative. I think the clinical studies and narrative accounts of trauma discussed below show that the self is not a fiction, if that is taken to mean that it is freely constructed by some narrator. No one, not even Stephen King, would voluntarily construct a self so tormented by trauma and its aftermath.
6. For other discussions of the relational self, see Jaggar (1983) and Meyers (1987, 1989, 1992, 1994). Virginia Held gives an excellent survey of feminist views of the relational self in so far as they bear on moral theory (Held 1993, 57–64).
7. An exception is Bernard Williams (1970), who presents a thought experiment that prompts the intuition that in at least some cases of so-called body transfer, we would identify with the surviving individual who has our body, and not the one who has our memory and other psychological characteristics.
8. Two critiques of Beauvoir's position on maternity and childbirth are presented in Ruddick (1989, 192–193, 275 n. 11) and Mackenzie (1996).
9. This quote is from an unpublished manuscript of Margaret Walker's titled "The Concept of the Erotic."
10. See also the discussion of charged memory in Proust in Glover (1988, 142–145).
11. If memories do not reside solely in the mind or in the body, but rather are a function of the way in which consciousness "inhabits" a body, then not only Locke's thought experiment, but also Sydney Shoemaker's (1975) and Bernard Williams's (1970) appear to be incoherent as described.
12. I thank Alexis Jetter for showing me the work of this author.
13. See Terr (1994) for an account of different responses to one-time and ongoing traumas.
14. Parfit, would not, however, agree with the relational account of the self I am defending here.

15. Of course, not many rape survivors are fortunate enough to have such an experience with the criminal justice system, given the low rates of reporting, prosecuting, and conviction of rapists. I also had the advantage of having my assailant tried in a French court, in which the adversarial system is not practiced, so I was not cross-examined by the defense lawyer. In addition, since the facts of the case were not in dispute and my assailant's only defense was an (ultimately unsuccessful) insanity plea, no one in the courtroom questioned my narrative of what had happened.

16. Delbo (1995, 241).

17. This is one of the positive aspects of a kind of multiple consciousness. Cf. Scheman (1993), Lugones (this volume), Matsuda (1989), and King (1988).

18. When I later mentioned this to my therapist, she replied, reasonably enough, "Why not shoot the assailant instead?" But for me that thought was not yet thinkable.

19. I should make a distinction here between the ability to kill in self-defense and the desire to kill as a form of revenge. Although I think it is morally permissible to possess and to employ the former, acting on the latter is to be morally condemned.

20. See Beckett (1965, 414). What Beckett actually writes is "you must go on, I can't go on, I'll go on," translating his original ending to *L'Innommable*: "*il faut continuer, je ne peux pas continuer, je vais continuer.*" I am grateful to Thomas Trezise for pointing out this passage.

21. For a discussion of Pascal's wager, see Pascal (1958); and for a discussion of "the will to believe," see James (1896).

References

Améry, Jean. 1995. "Torture." In *Art from Ashes: A Holocaust Anthology*, edited by Lawrence Langer, 121–136. New York: Oxford University Press.

Baier, Annette. 1985. "Cartesian Persons." In *Postures of the Mind: Essays on Mind and Morals* by Annette Baier. Minneapolis: University of Minnesota Press.

Beauvoir, Simone de. 1953. *The Second Sex.* Translated by H. M. Parshley. New York: Vintage Books.

Beckett, Samuel. 1965. *Three Novels.* New York: Grove Press.

Braidotti, Rosi. 1994. *Nomadic Subjects: Embodiment and Sexual Different in Contemporary Feminist Theory.* New York: Columbia University Press.

Culbertson, Roberta. 1995. "Embodied Memory, Transcendence, and Telling: Recounting Trauma, Re-establishing the Self." *New Literary History* 26: 169–195.

Delbo, Charlotte. 1995. *Auschwitz and After.* Translated by Rosette C. Lamont. New Haven: Yale University Press.

Glover, Jonathan. 1988. *I: The Philosophy and Psychology of Personal Identity.* London: Allen Lane, Penguin.

Held, Virginia. 1993. *Feminist Morality: Transforming Culture, Society, and Politics.* Chicago: University of Chicago Press.

Herman, Judith Lewis. 1992. *Trauma and Recovery.* New York: Basic.

Hirsch, Marianne. 1992–93. "Family Pictures: *Maus*, Mourning, and Post-memory." *Discourse* 15 (2): 3–29.

Hoffman, Eva. 1989. *Lost in Translation.* New York: Dutton.

Jaggar, Alison M. 1983. *Feminist Politics and Human Nature*. Totowa, NJ: Rowman & Allanheld.

James, William. 1896. *The Will to Believe and Other Essays in Popular Philosophy*. New York: Longmans, Green.

Janoff-Bulman, Ronnie. 1992. *Shattered Assumptions: Towards a New Psychology of Trauma*. New York: Free Press.

Kafka, Franz. 2009. *Franz Kafka: The Metamorphosis and Other Stories*. Translated by Joyce Crick. Oxford: Oxford University Press.

Ka-Tzetnik 135633. 1989. *Shivitti: A Vision*. Translated by Eliyah Nike De-Nur and Lisa Herman. New York: Harper & Row.

King, Deborah K. 1988. "Multiple Jeopardy, Multiple Consciousness: The Context of a Black Feminist Ideology." *Signs* 14 (1): 42–72.

Kingsolver, Barbara. 1989. *Homeland and Other Stories*. New York: Harper & Row.

Koss, Mary P., and Mary R. Harvey. 1991. *The Rape Victim: Clinical and Community Interventions*. 2nd ed. London: Sage Publications.

Langer, Lawrence. 1995. *Art from the Ashes*. New York: Oxford University Press.

Laub, Dori. 1992. "Bearing Witness, or the Vicissitudes of Listening." In *Testimony: Crises of Witnessing in Literature, Psychoanalysis, and History* by Shoshana Felman and Dori Laub, 57–74. New York: Routledge.

Levi, Primo. 1989. *The Drowned and the Saved*. Translated by Raymond Rosenthal. New York: Random House.

Levi, Primo. 1993. *Survival in Auschwitz*. Translated by Stuart Woolf. New York: Macmillan.

Locke, John. 1974. *An Essay Concerning Human Understanding*. Edited by A. D. Woozley. New York: New American Library.

Mackenzie, Catriona. 1996. "A Certain Lack of Symmetry: De Beauvoir on Autonomous Agency and Women's Embodiment." In *Texts in Culture: Simone de Beauvoir, "The Second Sex,"* edited by Ruth Evans, 122–158. Manchester: Manchester University Press.

Matsuda, Mari. 1989. "When the First Quail Calls: Multiple Consciousness as Jurisprudential Method." *Women's Rights Law Reporter* 11 (1): 7–10.

Meyers, Diana Tietjens. 1987. "The Socialized Individual and Individual Autonomy: An Intersection between Philosophy and Psychology." In *Women and Moral Theory*, edited by Eva Feder Kittay and Diana Tietjens Meyers, 139–153. Savage, MD: Rowman & Littlefield.

Meyers, Diana Tietjens. 1989. *Self, Society, and Personal Choice*. New York: Columbia University Press.

Meyers, Diana Tietjens. 1992. "Personal Autonomy or the Deconstructed Subject? A Reply to Hekman." *Hypatia* 7 (1): 124–132.

Meyers, Diana Tietjens. 1994. *Subjection and Subjectivity: Psychoanalytic Feminism and Moral Philosophy*. New York: Routledge.

Parfit, Derek. 1986. *Reasons and Persons*. Oxford: Oxford University Press.

Pascal, Blaise. 1958. *Pensées*. Translated by W. F. Trotter. New York: Dutton.

Plato. 2002. *Phaedo*. In *Five Dialogues: Euthyphro, Apology, Crito, Meno, Phaedo*, translated by G. M. A. Grube, revised by John M. Cooper, 93–154. 2nd ed. New York: Hackett.

Plato. 2008. *Symposium*. Translated by Robin Waterfield. Oxford: Oxford University Press.

Proust, Marcel. 1981. *Remembrance of Things Past*. Translated by C. K. Scott Moncrieff and Terence Kilmartin. New York: Vintage.

Roberts, Cathy. 1989. *Women and Rape*. New York: New York University Press.

Ruddick, Sara. 1989. *Maternal Thinking: Toward a Politics of Peace*. Boston: Beacon.

Scheman, Naomi. 1983. "Individualism and the Objects of Psychology." In *Discovering Reality: Feminist Perspectives on Epistemology, Metaphysics, Methodology, and Philosophy of Science*, edited by Sandra Harding and Merrill B. Hintikka, 225–244. Boston: D. Reidel.

Scheman, Naomi. 1993. "Though This Be Method, Yet There Is Madness in It." In *A Mind of One's Own: Feminist Essays on Reason and Objectivity*, edited by Louise Antony and Charlotte Witt, 145–170. Boulder, CO: Westview.

Scherer, Migael. 1992. *Still Loved by the Sun: A Rape Survivor's Journal*. New York: Simon & Schuster.

Segev, Tom. 1993. *The Seventh Million*. Translated by Haim Watzman. New York: Hill and Wang.

Shay, Jonathan. 1994. *Achilles in Vietnam: Combat Trauma and the Undoing of Character*. New York: Atheneum.

Shoemaker, Sydney. 1975. "Personal Identity and Memory." In *Personal Identity*, edited by John Perry, 119–134. Berkeley: University of California Press.

Terr, Lenore. 1994. *Unchained Memories*. New York: HarperCollins.

Williams, Bernard. 1970. "The Self and the Future." *Philosophical Review* 79 (2): 161–180.

18

Does Neutral Monism Provide the Best Framework for Relational Memory?

Iva Apostolova

My main goal is to identify the best metaphysical and epistemological framework to accommodate the relational model of memory to which I am sympathetic. The relational account of memory, preferred by many feminists, offers a way of looking at memory that decisively undermines the traditional archival model where the rememberer is a disembodied rational agent in a social vacuum who remembers episodes from her past life with various degrees of accuracy and where accuracy is the exclusive guarantor of the continuity of her own self. The relational account, in contrast, offers a paradigm of interpreting autobiographical memory that situates the rememberer within complex social networks, where individual memories are not only interpreted by others but also altered by the environment and the emotional states of all the rememberers involved. On the relational account, the rememberer is not only an autonomous agent, but also embodied, emotional, rational, and social all at the same time.

The relational account of memory is best equipped to deal with traumatic memory, which continues to be of significant interest to feminist philosophy. Traumatic memory, broadly understood, is the memory of an event (or events) that has a significant negative psychological or social impact on the individual or the group. Recent literature on trauma has described such negative impacts ranging from partial loss of short-term, long-term, or even operational memory, to recurring spatiotemporal confusion ("patchy memory"), to dramatic individual or social behavioral changes. Traumatic memory is little more than ignored by traditional accounts of memory, which operate almost exclusively from a viewpoint of one's past experiences where accuracy of the memory representation is measured against an alleged original experience. This rather simplified and overly abstract model of cognition cannot provide us with a nuanced and well-thought-out account of something as complex as trauma, whether individual or collective. In cases of trauma, the reliability of the rememberer's cognitive capacities is only one piece of the puzzle. The relational account of memory seems better suited to account for trauma because it incorporates factors beyond these capacities. What is more, by undermining the traditional model of memory, the

Iva Apostolova, *Does Neutral Monism Provide the Best Framework for Relational Memory?* In: *Feminist Philosophy of Mind*. Edited by: Keya Maitra and Jennifer McWeeny, Oxford University Press. © Oxford University Press 2022.
DOI: 10.1093/oso/9780190867614.003.0019

relational view offers not only a re-evaluation of our knowledge (of the past) but also a much-needed overhaul of traditional conceptions of the self.

The relational account of memory, however, is not without problems. One seriously stubborn problem is the threat of false memories known as the "semantic contagion" problem, which is the problem of interpreting one's past based on a current shift in one's circumstances or in the social context. In other words, the concern is that the reconstructive model of memory threatens to displace the notion of truth/veridicality and cause a loss of psychological and cultural control over one's past (Sutton 1998, 13). I propose Bertrand Russell's neutral monism as the most deserving framework to accommodate the relational view of memory while successfully addressing concerns of semantic contagion by reframing how we, as cognitive agents, relate to reality, including to other agents. The neutral monist account of memory is not incompatible with panpsychism, much preferred by some feminists for its capacity to avoid dualism in general and mind-body dualism in particular, among other benefits. I also argue that working from a genuine neutral monist vantage point spares us the need to adopt an either-or stance in regard to narrativism and episodism. In the current debate, narrativism gives preference to psychological over bodily continuity of the self, thus implying an undesirable cognitive dichotomy and hierarchy when viewed with a feminist lens.[1] Episodism, on the other hand, has been associated, in part, with the view that puts the very existence of a continuous self into question. A continuous, that is, synchronic and diachronic, self is not a required category as long as there are individual atomic memories present that measure up to a pre-established standard of accuracy. It is this standard of accuracy that guarantees that the subjective experience becomes an objective piece of knowledge.

The revised relational account of memory, which is within the metaphysical and epistemological framework of neutral monism, then, decisively rejects the idea of "places" where memories originate or are stored but, in contrast, operates with networks of relations between "events," the basic units of reality for the neutral monist. This adjustment, in turn, eliminates the dichotomy between experience and knowledge and dispenses with pre-established standards of accuracy; for the neutral monist, experience and knowledge are one and the same. For example, Sue Campbell draws our attention to the intersection of knowledge and experience illustrated by the human rights movement HIJOS (Hijos por la identidad y la Justicia contra el Olvido y el Silencio [Sons and Daughters for Identity and Justice against Forgetfulness and Silence]), started in the 1990s in Argentina and Guatemala (Campbell 2003, 373). HIJOS is known for organizing public demonstrations called "*escraches*" during which the demonstrators use different means, such as graffiti spray-painting, displaying photographs of the victims, and dancing to remind the public of their "disappeared" relatives. The government's ultimate goal is to obliterate from the collective consciousness anything that has to do with forced disappearances by either denying the facts of disappearance or, in some cases, denying the very existence of the people captured in the photographs carried around by the demonstrators. The goal of the protesters is twofold. On the one hand, they take the decisive and, in many cases, life-threatening, stance of rememberers. They remember and when they remember the disappearances *are* real. On the other hand, they, as rememberers, aim at changing the reality for all of us, even the ones who are unaware or simply born after the fact of the disappearance. My own autobiographical memory is *necessarily* modified and forever changed by my knowledge of the *escraches* precisely because my reality is forever changed. I no longer can ignore the fact that someone has chosen to remember, even at her/his/their own peril. I no longer can ignore someone else's trauma. This trauma has become a part of the collective consciousness, and, upon becoming aware of it, I have an obligation to change how I view the past.

The Relational Account of Memory

The relational account provides a viable alternative to the various models of memory and personal identity inspired by John Locke's insight that the self is continuous only if it accurately remembers and stores an original past experience. The "psychological continuity" model of memory, as well as the archival model, are based on this insight. As mentioned earlier, the relational account of memory has, however, been subject to the semantic contagion objection first raised by Ian Hacking. Hacking suggests that if we remove accuracy from the account of episodic memory, we are exposing the rememberer to "chronic suggestibility" where she is constantly reinterpreting her memories, thus leaving her in a state of confusion about her past. I believe that providing the appropriate metaphysical and epistemological framework will allow the relational model to successfully dispel this criticism in a general and categorical way. Linda Martín Alcoff, for example, proposes a way of dealing with the threat of semantic contagion in the case of sexual abuse memories by emphasizing the epistemological concept of truth, which she believes Hacking to have sidestepped (Alcoff 2011). While I agree with Alcoff's proposed critique, it is my conviction that Russell's neutral monism provides not only an epistemological framework, but also a metaphysical one that can successfully respond to the threat of semantic contagion and ground broader forms of relational memory.

To better understand the inspiration behind a relational account of memory, Campbell reminds us that the Anglo-European philosophical tradition has historically viewed memory, self, and personhood as intimately and inextricably interwoven (Campbell 1997, 52). Insofar as this is the case, undermining someone's remembering capabilities is also undermining their sense of self-respect and their social and moral status as persons. As a basis for her own view, Campbell takes the folklorist Kathrine Borland's interpretation of self as a "sense of self." The sense of self depends on a "reflective awareness of the self that is both partially achieved and made evident in the doubled presence of the self in expressions of memory, intention, and self-regard" (Campbell 1997, 55). In other words, my sense of self inevitably depends on, among other things, the fact that some of my experiences are past experiences or experiences of my past. It needs to be noted right away, however, that my sense of self is not built independently of what other people think of me. My personal story is always interwoven with other personal stories. What is more, as Susan James contends, my experience of the world is not initially integrated; it requires relations with others to become integrated and perceived as continuous (James, this volume). Taken from another angle, my person is determined by factors such as where I live; what culture(s) or subculture(s) I associate myself with or are dominant where I spend most of my time; what historical evidence I, personally, or the culture I associate myself with, accepts as valid and valuable; and so on.

If we interpret "person" as a socially constructed and socially constituted category, as I do, a relational notion of personhood seems fitting. Under this interpretation, a person possesses key cognitive abilities such as the ability to act, make decisions, and form intentions, which, in turn, lead to her/his/their ability to take moral responsibility for actions, a central component of personhood. All of these abilities are formed in relation to others, and so the other is partially constitutive of the self. The other, through her actions, helps me evaluate, re-evaluate, train, and retrain myself to gain the necessary self-respect and, through this, respect for others. The formation of intentions depends to a large extent on the ability to remember past actions and intentions. Many feminists, Campbell among them, share Daniel Dennett's interpretation of a responsible act as dependent upon the cognitive faculty of memory. Dennett's interpretation of the role of memory in constructing personal identity is an emendation of the overly rigid Lockean identity theory. For Dennett, being responsible for an action requires that I have been aware of this action in the past. Only then can I say that I intended to act the way I did, and give a reason for my action (Dennett 1978, 190–191). Remembering (understood broadly as recollecting an episode or even remembering that I have forgotten something), then, is a cognitive ability which, like all other cognitive abilities, is ongoing and depends upon others to function properly.

Remembering a past experience is not simply about repeating the order of events to myself; on the contrary, when I recollect something, I am integrating it into my current experiences. This integration almost always requires the presence of general knowledge, such as the knowledge that all of us experience the world from a gendered point of view. Remembering a particularly unpleasant bus ride, I remember that the bus was crowded, which made it uncomfortable. A part of the discomfort had to do with the mere fact that there were too many people gathered in a small space, and a moving one at that. But another part of it had to do with the fact that there were more male, college-aged passengers displaying behavioral patterns that I, as a woman, associate with rowdiness and aggression. Hence, my memory of the event is not classified in my mind as a "crowded bus ride" but rather as an "unpleasant bus ride due to predominantly male crowd." In this sense, as Campbell notes, upholding a sharp division between autobiographical memory and general knowledge can only obscure the complexity of autobiographical memory. At the same time, drawing a clean line between individual and collective memory prevents us from taking into account oppressive harms such as sexual abuse of women or other marginalized groups.

Understanding the nature of collective memory requires understanding that it is not simply the sum of memories of all individual members of the group. Collective memory, as Campbell notes, is above all a shared memory (Campbell 2003, 180). The shared/social nature of memory is well illustrated in the literature on testimony, for example. As any epistemologist would agree, an account of knowledge without an established sense of testimonial authority amounts to very little (it would include, perhaps, only a handful of a priori categories). As Lorraine Code points out, "Testimony . . . stands as a constant reminder of how little of anyone's knowledge . . . *could* be acquired independently" (Code 2000, 186). Thus, unique recollections of autobiographical events may have a symbolic or metaphorical value only, or they may acquire the function of reasons for future actions by the rememberer herself or any other member of the group (Campbell 2003, 49). A HIJOS member's personal and traumatic memory may become for others a symbol of government oppression, or it may motivate someone to become a human rights activist herself. Given all of this, denying me the status of a rememberer is denying me a key cognitive ability of integrating and interpreting my own biography, and from here, it is preventing me from forming and acting from a sense of self-respect. My sense of self-respect is not an abstract term or something that my legal rights will guarantee; it is an ability to move my body in space, to form views about the world, and to have a sense of past, present, and future. Furthermore, when confronted with something as complex as the experience of trauma, losing the status of a rememberer can take a more sinister turn toward gaining the status of a confabulator.[2]

The relational account of memory accepts the "reconstructive turn" in memory championed by Marya Schetchman (Schetchman 1994).[3] Schetchman argues against the psychological continuity theories of Sydney Shoemaker, Derek Parfit, and John Perry (1994, 3–7). All psychological continuity theories, she claims, oversimplify memory by representing it solely as a capacity to retrieve past events, thus making it into a purely psychological capacity and ignoring the element of embodiment, among others, present in memory. Schetchman's take on memory is echoed in Catriona Mortimer-Sandilands's examination of memory from the point of view of a patient with Alzheimer's. She writes, "The experience of memory is thus always already social, technological, and physical in that the conditions of the relationship between brain and object cannot help but be located in a complex range of conditions that offer the subject to the experience, and the experience to the subject" (Mortimer-Sandilands 2008, 274). It is not that a patient with Alzheimer's, she continues, does not have a functioning memory and thus, a self. Rather, it is that the memories that are valued under the current social conditions, namely, the coherent memories that provide us with a narrative self, are undermined in the patient, while at the same time, "the memories that are very much present to the person—the familiarity of what it feels like to walk, to touch, even to dance—are read as irrelevant, primitive, part of a diminished self" (Mortimer-Sandilands 2008, 275).

Schetchman's and Mortimer-Sandilands's criticisms aim to show the immense complexity of the seemingly simple relation of a "memory of" something. The constant influx of information that comes through our senses (body) at any given moment, needs to be processed and organized in order to be useful to its receiver *at all* (Schetchman 1994, 11). In this sense, accurate representation of discretely stored past episodes is hardly a priority.[4] Moreover, in looking into the nature of traumatic memory, we are faced with such phenomena as the loss of whole patterns of memory as a result of trauma where not only are discrete episodes altered, but so are one's future desires and expectations (Brison, this volume; James, this volume). On the contrary, in rewriting and reconstructing our pasts, we rearrange the different events and blur the boundaries between individual experiences to weave a tapestry of personal history. For this reason, the memories that contribute the most to our self-conception and help us form self-regarding attitudes are the ones that "stick" and not simply the ones that are stored. The existence of sticky memories also means that our current understanding of ourselves influences the way we remember events.

We need not forget, Schetchman urges, that a "memory of" is also emotionally charged. The emotional content of a given memory is a part of the significance memory plays in our personal history. We cannot expect that this significance could be captured by the close resemblance a given individual memory has to its originary source as the identity/archival model of memory proposes. This view would be too simplistic, not only leaving out such important issues as the role of detail recollection, emotional charge, and context reconstruction, but also overlooking aspects of the concepts of accuracy and truth/veridicality themselves. Building on Adam Morton's work on emotional accuracy and "repisodic" memory, Campbell warns us that there is more to accuracy than meets the eye. If we are bound to the idea of accuracy in memory, we need to pay attention not only to the veridical *representation* of a given past event but also to all the *possibilities* for representation that every event carries with it (Campbell 2003, 368).[5] Thus, we could, and sometimes even should, choose to re-remember and rewitness the past.[6]

Semantic Contagion

In his 1995 book, Ian Hacking, while claiming to adopt a reconstructionist account of memory himself, seems intensely concerned with recent narrative accounts of memory. Hacking labels the main problem "semantic contagion" and defines this as instances where the rememberer is exposed to "chronic suggestibility" and therefore reinterprets her past in light of new (social) interpretative categories (Hacking 1995, 249, 256). To put the problem of semantic contagion into the light of recent events, one could argue that the chain of public accusations of sexual misconduct of several high-profile Hollywood male celebrities, coupled with an increasingly pervasive climate of political correctness and heightened awareness of what constitutes appropriate and inappropriate sexual behavior, may "encourage" participants in sexual encounters, once thought of as consensual and appropriate, to "re-remember" these encounters as nonconsensual or inappropriate. For Hacking, such phenomena put the relational approach to memory in jeopardy. Campbell responds to Hacking by offering different reasons for why an important event could be falsely re-remembered: (1) either the event is not as important to one's life story as it might seem at first glance, or (2) the event is as important as is claimed, but it is not falsely re-remembered; it is simply re-remembered. An event that is important for one's biography cannot be isolated from other important events, including other people's memories of the same event (either as witnesses or listeners), and hence, false re-remembering would require altering a complicated network of past events that will ultimately lead to altering one's sense of reality and identity. Campbell concludes that Hacking's theory and the case studies on which it relies are, at the end of the day, informed by a revised version of the archival theory of memory, which holds that memory *should* resemble perception in that it *should* provide a mirror image of an isolated past episode; anything else is viewed as conceptually "contaminated." As Campbell suggests, framing the memory debates in terms of this revised version of archival memory prevents us from exploring newly emerging oppressive harms (Campbell 2003, 197–198).

Alcoff, on the other hand, points to "the communal nature of concept formation" to conclude that outside influence on my memories, such as a changed social perception of a phenomenon, will not create a significant distortion, that is, a contagion construed as a ground for confabulation within our personal memories (Alcoff 2011, 222). In support of her claim, Alcoff analyzes the case of Sigmund Freud's patient Dora and the incident where Dora was accused by Herr K. and Freud himself of projection and, essentially, confabulation.[7] Alcoff explains that if we are to follow the narrative of the accounts of the incident by all the parties involved, we notice that veridicality is really more a question of "negotiation" of one's "position within various social relations," among other things, as opposed to a correspondence to an isolated past event (Alcoff 2011, 216).

While Alcoff is very convincing in her analysis, and Campbell certainly may have a point that Hacking, despite his claim to the contrary, had tacitly adopted the good old archival model of memory, it seems to me that both responses are only partially capable of addressing the criticism that autobiographical memories are vulnerable to (drastic) changes in the political and social terrain, which may "taint," as it were, the veridicality of the memories themselves. If we want a more radical solution that does not commit us to either the hegemony of psychological continuity, or the nonexistence of subjectivity/selfhood, we need to show decisively that the epistemic value of accuracy of autobiographical memory does not consist in a simplified relation of correspondence between a recollection and an originary source. Russell's neutral monism points us in the right direction.

Russell's Neutral Monism

Russell claims that memory images, which are the truth-bearers and the meaning-carriers, need to be accompanied by certain types of cognitive feelings such as the feeling of pastness and the feeling of familiarity to be considered genuine memories. Russell never went as far as claiming that reality is panphenomenal, that is, that all of reality is grounded in perceptions and experiences (which, in my view, he should have), a thesis embraced by most panpsychists. But he did concede that "something can be done in the way of constructing possible physical worlds which fulfil the equations of physics and yet resemble rather more closely the world of perception than does the world ordinarily presented in physics" (Russell 1927a, 271). In support of this intuition, contemporary discussions of panpsychism have made use of Russell's neutral monism by pointing to how it manages (in virtue of claiming that the building blocks of reality are neutral) to avoid many of the snags panpsychism continues to face.[8]

Russell's neutral monist theory is a radical theory that does away with the dualisms between mind and body, knower and known, experience and reality, the phenomenal and the physical, memory and imagination, and, finally, memory and sensation. Although Russell himself never used the labels, it is my view that neutral monism draws a picture of a panpsychist, panexperiential, panphenomenal, and finally, panrelational reality that not only asserts the dynamic, reconstructive model of memory and does away with the classical model of personal identity by eliminating the subject of cognition, but also dethrones the hegemony of archival and scientific discourse in the memory debates. As such, I am convinced that neutral monism contributes to the "embodied cognition" thesis, broadly construed.[9]

Although Russell was familiar with the theory of Ernst Mach and Ralph Perry, he felt it was William James's ideas that were closest to his own view of neutral monism.[10] Neutral monism is at the same time a metaphysical and an epistemological theory aiming at explaining the relation, or, more accurately, bridging the gap between the physical and the psychological. It holds that mind and matter are made of the same "neutral stuff," which is more primitive than either mind or matter taken separately. In Russell's words, "the ultimate constituents of the world do not have the characteristics of either mind or matter as ordinarily understood: they are not solid persistent objects moving through space, nor are they fragments of 'consciousness'" (Russell 1921, 124). This primitive neutral stuff, however, should not be conceived as a third entity that has special properties to differentiate it from mind and matter alike. Neutral monism is instead like organizing entities in columns and rows. The same thing can appear in two different ways (for example, horizontally and vertically). Being a part of a column or row requires that the entity enters into at least two different relations (while, at the same time, there is no external limit to the number of relations an entity can enter into). Thus, under neutral monism, the object and the subject of cognition are different only depending on how the given theoretical framework (say, psychology or physics) incorporates them within its own goals and conceptual apparatus. As William James argues, experience/reality for consciousness has no "inner duplicity"; there is only "pure experience" within which things and thoughts are only points of reference for us (James 1904, 480).

Neutral monism promotes structuralism about physics (the idea that physics explains the world only in abstract, structural terms without engaging with the intrinsic nature of the basic entities of reality) and it champions monism about perception, which establishes that all we have access to is perception and everything else is inferred. It also accounts for all elements of reality such as events, particulars, and so on, in multiple ways depending on what our interest in them is, and how they are grouped. Thus, Russell's neutral monism seems to be inspired not by positing a new building block of reality, an inscrutable of sorts, but by the desire to explore the *relationship* and, eventually, blur the boundaries between knower and known, psychology and physics. Put otherwise, Russell's neutral monist theory has managed to flip the question of the relationship between reality and perception. Instead of asking how the physical entities (atoms, electrons, quarks, and other such particles) give rise to perceived color patches, it focuses on how the color patches we perceive make up the physical particles that we infer.[11]

In virtue of his conception of neutral monism, Russell's main claim could be labeled panpsychist (or panexperientialist) since he understands the difference between humans and inanimate objects as one of degree, not of kind. In *Religion and Science*, Russell writes, "Now we can only say that we react to stimuli, and so do stones, though the stimuli to which they react are fewer. So far, as external 'perception' is concerned, the difference between us and a stone is only one of degree" (Russell 1935, 130–132). Such panexperientialism suggests that the only reality to which I have direct access is phenomenal reality. In other words, physics or any other scientific discourse, for that matter, cannot give me anything other than an indirect account of reality. And so, when analyzing the veridicality of autobiographical memory, psychology alone, or any other science, for that matter, cannot get it right, as it were, and give us the complete picture. The so-called scientific picture of memory does little more than compartmentalize the individual's cognitive experiences, thus keeping the rememberer stuck in a loop of looking for a perfect match between a representation and its alleged originary source.

To go back to Alcoff's example with Freud's patient Dora and her encounter with Herr K., it is not that, as Alcoff herself remarks, the psychological terms of projection, repression, avoidance, and transference cannot add anything to the analysis of Dora's case. It is rather that the veridicality of her memory, and the reliability of Dora's own account of her social behavior, cannot be left to psychology to analyze and resolve. This qualification, however, does not and should not be read as suggesting that veridicality of memory is to be endorsed by the privileged first-person position of the experiencing individual self alone. To the contrary, neutral monism consistently undermines the privileged first-person, subject-driven vantage point of knowledge in favor of an integral experience where knowledge is a result of multiple crossing experience points. In other words, a relationalist with neutral monist underpinnings would not suggest that Dora is the sole authority on the veridicality of her recollection. If it were the case, epistemic solipsism would become an imminent threat. Dora's own recollection of the event in question is actually a *reconstruction* where factors like the behavioral and verbal reaction of the other participating parties during and after the event, the testimony of any witnesses, and so on, are an integral part of the fabric of her memory, and, in fact, inform the veridicality of her own reconstruction. Eliminating epistemic solipsism, however, should not come at the price of losing the uniqueness of individual memories. Thus, the neutral monistic account of memory will have to reconcile the uniqueness of autobiographical memories with the antirepresentational, antidualistic, and panphenomenal take on reality.

Neutral Monism and Memory

It is a fact that in the earlier part of his philosophical career, Russell held a traditional, dualistic view of knowledge where knowledge is a dual relation between
a subject and object of cognition (Russell 1912, 1992). However, it is also a fact
that, even then, Russell was very uncomfortable with the representational view
of memory where memories are the subject's representations of past sensory
stimuli caused by the object. This rejection of representationalism, however,
came at the expense of introducing a rather counterintuitive view of direct acquaintance with the past that was not a viable solution. Russell's attempt to account for all types of memory, including remote memory, implied that in such
cases direct acquaintance with the past can be taken seriously only if interpreted
metaphorically.

In light of this tension, as well as his growing dissatisfaction with the dualistic model of cognition, which he deemed metaphysically cumbersome and epistemically inefficient in 1918 in *Manuscript Notes*, Russell writes: "Imperative
to get rid of 'Subject.' / Involves abandonment of distinction between sense-data
and sensation. / Involves different theory of imagination and memory. / Tends to
make the actual object of memory (e.g.) more remote from the present mental
occurrence than on the old theory" (Russell 1986, 261–263). Russell follows
through with the "imperative" and pronounces the subject of cognition (the "I")
a "logical fiction," an unobservable, purely grammatical category that exists only
for ease of conversation (Russell 1986, 274). Since the subject is a "perfectly gra-
tuitous assumption" and therefore, we must "dispense with the subject as one of
the actual ingredients of the world," the functions of the subject end up being
assumed by memory, which puts it in the center of philosophical inquiry (Russell
1921, 142).

Dispensing with the cognitive subject, as radical a move as it may be, is one
thing, but actually navigating successfully through a subject-less terrain is another. On the one hand, the textual evidence shows that Russell was aware that
the subject (the "I") is not the same as the self and that the self has an important
function, but he failed to articulate this function as social and instead settled on
its being simply a "linguistically convenient" category (Russell 1921, 141). This
evidence, however, does not shed much light on the important distinction that,
for all intents and purposes, could be a part of the solution. On the other hand,
preserving the uniqueness of autobiographical memories appears to be challenged by the blurred lines between perception and memory, subject and object.
And so, with what was available to him, Russell introduced new terms that he
hoped would help him rebuild the picture of cognition.

Memory, Russell pronounced, is populated by a series of images. But since
these images alone cannot guarantee the veridicality of memory (and its

distinction from pure imagination), Russell adds two other elements that accompany images of past events, namely, "the feeling of familiarity" and "the feeling of pastness," which are referred to as "belief-feelings."[12] Although this term is not defined precisely, Russell makes clear that belief-feeling is not just another propositional attitude. There has to be something, Russell recognized, that guarantees that what I remember is *genuine*. "The image is not distinguished from the object existed in the past: the word 'this' covers both, and enables us to have a memory-belief which does not involve the complicated notion 'something like this,'" Russell writes in *The Analysis of Mind* (Russell 1921, 179). In other words, the belief-feeling is to replace any formal (rigid) form of (propositional) justification while, at the same time, avoiding the slippery slope of matching up representations with alleged objects.[13] To illustrate even more precisely how the new mechanism of memory operates, Russell introduces "akoluthic sensation," a term he borrows from Richard Semon (Russell 1921, 175). Akoluthic sensation is the in-between sensory stimulus and image; it is the not-any-more sensation and the not-yet-image. Akoluthic sensations point in the direction of "mnemic causation," which is a unique type of causation that guarantees the causal self-evidence, for the lack of a better phrase, of memories (Russell 1921, 157).

Despite my agreement, along with Sven Bernecker, that the label "mnemic" harms rather than helps Russell's task in that it appears to posit something mysterious and unexplainable in familiar terms, I see the introduction of the new type of causation based on akoluthic sensation as Russell's (one might even say "desperate") attempt to solve the problem of false memories without appealing to the notion of correspondence between something physical and something mental (Bernecker 2008, 41–46). Thus, if there is a mechanism that guarantees my unique access to my past, there should be, *ceteris paribus* and *rebus communibus*, no reason not to believe that what I remember is trustworthy. Pointing to the mnemic effects of a given behavior shows me that I have done two things: first, I have already identified the trustworthy/veridical memory as the end result of the causal chain of events, and second, I have, undoubtedly, formed expectations with regard to future behaviors. The formation of expectations is something that Russell considered an integral part of the mechanism of memory, although he never really explored its potential in depth (Russell 1921, 165, 185–186).[14]

Hence, my experience of the past and my knowledge of the past are one and the same, and, as such, there is no need to worry about the precarious transition from experience to knowledge, something that preoccupied classical epistemologists and philosophers of mind. This conclusion points in the direction of reconstruction and away from storage: in memory we *reconstruct* and *restructure* the past event and do not just store it. Although Russell did not have the relational model of memory available to him, no doubt missing out on considering the social dimensions of knowledge and the self, I believe he anticipated, especially toward the end of his career, some of the tenets of the relational account, which, as noted earlier, is compatible with the "embodied cognition" thesis, broadly construed.

Neutral Monism and the Relational Model

Although the notions of "embodied cognition" and the "extended mind hypothesis" are relatively recent theses in the philosophy of mind, I believe that Russell's neutral monism anticipated them in many ways. If I am right, this solidifies my claim that neutral monism proposes a more radical way than what is available to deal with the problem of semantic contagion, or more generally, the problem of false memories. Technicalities and historical subtleties aside, Russell's neutral monist epistemic framework looks at the world as sets of systems/structures that are accounted for by means of interconnectedness as opposed to rigid vantage points: "When we wish to describe a structure, we have to do so by means of terms and relations" (Russell 1927a, 276). This commitment necessitates the centrality of memory, which replaces, as it were, the subject of cognition. In order for this substitution to happen, however, memory must be reinterpreted and the memory-based model of personal identity must be reframed. The following passage from *The Analysis of Mind* demonstrates Russell's commitment to changing the way we think of the first-person vantage point once and for all: "It is supposed that thoughts cannot just come and go, but need a person to think them. . . . But I think the person is not an ingredient in the single thought: he is rather constituted by relations of the thoughts to each other and to the body" (Russell 1921, 18).

Each piece of knowledge is to be treated as a system/structure that depends on other structures right down to the elemental level of the classical "subject-object" relation. In other words, there is no (subjective) "place" that offers special, privileged access to knowledge by positing special mental relations. Thus, my autobiographical memories cannot be accounted for by the representational model where my current representations correspond to given past original events. I do not think that Russell would have had any heartache accepting that memory images are "incomplete contributors in a context-sensitive system rather than fixed determinants of output" (Sutton 2006, 282). In *The Analysis of Mind*, Russell often speaks of the role of philosophy in helping us account for the "integral experience" of reality, a continuous cognitive process as opposed to something given.[15] This prompted Russell's bold, although often ignored, proposition that a new, all-encompassing, branch of knowledge, which he called "chronogeography," should be in charge of the integral experience of reality (Russell 1927b, 228). The implications of this claim are twofold. On the one hand, psychology alone cannot answer questions concerning the mind, including those concerning memory. On the other hand, both psychology and physics are branches of chrono-geography, and not the other way around. There is therefore nothing to be lost and everything to be gained from adopting a philosophical attitude where the single privileged vantage point of knowledge of the world is once and for all eliminated.

Notes

1. For more on the narrativity of the self, see Brison (this volume).
2. For more details on the effects of denying women the status of rememberers, see Campbell (2003).
3. Schetchman writes, "A central function of our memory is turning the countless experiences with which we are bombarded into a manageable and comprehensible life history . . . . This will involve summarizing, condensing, and rewriting the facts remembered, and . . . such work is therefore pervasive in our autobiographical memories" (Schetchman 1994, 13).
4. Campbell reminds us that the content or accuracy of individual memories or historical facts may not add anything to the significance of a given memory. For example, a given memory may be significant through its place in a given cultural narrative or the themes and characters that populate that story (Campbell 2003, 51).
5. "Repisodic" as opposed to episodic memory is memory that has been reconstructed as a faithful memory by taking into account the context of, as well as emotional responses to, the remembered episode (Campbell 2003, 368).
6. The reconstructive turn in memory facilitates the "extended mind hypothesis" championed by Clark (1997), Clark and Chalmers (1998), and Sutton (2006), among others.
7. Alcoff (2011, 214–216).
8. Issues concerning Russell's neutral monism and some of the traditional problems that panpsychism faces, such as the grounding problem, physicalism, and mental monism, are among the ones discussed in Torin Alter and Yujin Nagasawa's collection (2015). See especially Stubenberg (2015).
9. For a discussion of the embodied cognition thesis, see Shapiro (2010, 2011). The embodied cognition thesis, in broad strokes, accepts that human cognition (understood as the product of the neurocognitive system) is determined by the boundaries and evolutionary development of the human body. In this sense, the human body is perceived as a constraint on and distributor and regulator of cognition.
10. For a detailed discussion of the origin of neutral monism and its three main versions, see Banks (2014).
11. See Stubenberg (2015, 86).
12. For the "feeling of pastness," see Russell (1921, 266). For the "feeling of familiarity," see Russell (1921, 161–162). Russell defines "feeling" as follows: "I use the word 'feeling' in a popular sense, to cover a sensation or an image or a complex of sensations or images or both" (Russell 1921, 187).

13. As Paulo Faria aptly points out, Russell was clear that the belief associated with the memory-image is to remain ambiguous in order to allow us to successfully distinguish between a genuine past and an imagined one (Faria 2017, 515).

14. Russell writes, "We might provisionally, though perhaps not quite correctly, define "memory" as that way of knowing about the past which has no analogue in our knowledge of the future; such a definition would at least serve to mark the problem with which we are concerned, though some expectations may deserve to rank with memory as regards immediacy" (Russell 1921, 165). Later he expands on this sense of expectation: "We do not, unless we are unusually reflective, think about the presence or absence of correlations: we merely have different feelings which, intellectualized, may be represented as expectations of the presence or absence of correlations. A thing which 'feels real' inspires us with hopes or fears, expectations or curiosities, which are wholly absent when a thing 'feels imaginary'" (Russell 1921, 185–186).

15. Compare with the embodied cognition thesis that integration of experience is a "synchronic and diachronic achievement, the hard-won and fragile product of ongoing cognitive work" (Sutton 2006, 285).

References

Alcoff, Linda Martín. 2011. "Experience and Knowledge: The Case of Sexual Abuse Memories." In *Feminist Metaphysics: Explorations in the Ontology of Sex, Gender, and the Self*, edited by Charlotte Witt, 209–223. Dordrecht: Springer.

Alter, Torin, and Yujin Nagasawa. 2015. "What Is Russellian Monism?" In *Perspectives on Russellian Monism*, edited by Torin Alter and Yujin Nagasawa, 422–451. New York: Oxford University Press.

Banks, Erik C. 2014. *The Realistic Empiricism of Mach, James, and Russell: Neutral Monism Reconceived*. New York: Cambridge University Press.

Bernecker, Sven. 2008. *The Metaphysics of Memory*. Dordrecht: Springer.

Campbell, Sue. 1997. "Women's 'False' Memory and Personal Identity." *Hypatia* 12 (2): 51–82.

Campbell, Sue. 2003. *Relational Remembering: Rethinking the Memory Wars*. Lanham, MD: Rowman & Littlefield.

Clark, Andy. 1997. *Being There: Putting Brain, Body, and World Together Again*. Cambridge, MA: MIT Press.

Clark, Andy, and David Chalmers. 1998. "The Extended Mind." *Analysis* 58: 10–23.

Code, Lorraine. 2000. "The Perversion of Autonomy and the Subjection of Women: Discourses of Social Advocacy at Century's End." In *Relational Autonomy: Feminist Perspectives on Autonomy, Agency, and the Social Self*, edited by Catriona Mackenzie and Natalie Stoljar, 181–212. New York: Oxford University Press.

Dennett, Daniel. 1978. "The Conditions of Personhood." In *The Identity of Persons*, edited by Amélie Oksenberg Rorty, 197–196. Berkeley: University of California Press.

Faria, Paulo. 2017. "Russell's Theories of Memory." In *The Routledge Handbook of Philosophy of Memory*, edited by Sven Bernecker and Kourken Michaelian, 519–527. London: Routledge.

Hacking, Ian. 1995. *Rewriting the Soul: Multiple Personality and the Sciences of Memory*. Princeton, NJ: Princeton University Press.

James, William. 1904. "Does 'Consciousness' Exist?" *Journal of Philosophy, Psychology, and Scientific Methods* 1: 477–491.

Mortimer-Sandilands, Catriona. 2008. "Landscape, Memory, and Forgetting: Thinking through (My Mother's) Body and Place." In *Material Feminisms*, edited by Stacy Alaimo and Susan Hekman, 265–287. Bloomington: Indiana University Press.

Parfit, Derek. 1984. *Reasons and Persons*. New York: Oxford University Press.

Perry, John. 1975. "Personal Identity, Memory, and the Problem of Circularity." In *Personal Identity*, edited by John Perry, 135–158. Berkeley: University of California Press.

Russell, Bertrand. 1912. *The Problems of Philosophy*. London: Hackett.

Russell, Bertrand. 1921. *The Analysis of Mind*. London: George Allen & Unwin.

Russell, Bertrand. 1927a. *The Analysis of Matter*. London: George Allen & Unwin.

Russell, Bertrand. 1927b. *An Outline of Philosophy*. London: George Allen & Unwin.

Russell, Bertrand. 1935. *Religion and Science*. London: Thornton Butterworth.

Russell, Bertrand. 1986. "Manuscript Notes." In *The Collected Papers of Bertrand Russell, Volume 8*, edited by John G. Slater, 247–271. London: George Allen & Unwin.

Russell, Bertrand. 1992. *Theory of Knowledge: The 1913 Manuscript*. London: Routledge.

Schetchman, Marya. 1994. "The Truth about Memory." *Philosophical Psychology* 7 (1): 3–18.

Shapiro, Lawrence A. 2010. "Embodied Cognition." In *Oxford Handbook of Philosophy and Cognitive Science*, edited by Eric Margolis, Richard Samuels, and Stephen Stich, 118–146. New York: Oxford University Press.

Shapiro, Lawrence A. 2011. *Embodied Cognition*. New York: Routledge.

Shoemaker, Sydney. 1984. "Personal Identity: A Materialist's Account." In *Personal Identity* by Sydney Shoemaker and Richard Swinburne, 67–132. Oxford: Basil Blackwell.

Stubenberg, Leopold. 2015. "Russell, Russellian Monism, and Panpsychism." In *Perspectives on Russellian Monism*, edited by Torin Alter and Yujin Nagasawa, 58–90. New York: Oxford University Press.

Sutton, John. 1998. *Philosophy and Memory Traces: Descartes to Connectionism*. Cambridge: Cambridge University Press.

Sutton, John. 2006. "Introduction: Memory, Embodied Cognition, and the Extended Mind." *Philosophical Psychology* 19 (3): 281–289.

19

The Odd Case of a Bird-Mother

Relational Selfhood and a "Method of Grief"

Vrinda Dalmiya

Old Stories, New Contexts: Grief and Selfhood

I begin with an ancient tale of death and a broken friendship, a tale involving emotions of grief, revenge, attempted reconciliation, and ultimately, the rejection of forgiveness.[1] This story is embedded as a minuscule part of the longer Sanskrit epic the *Mahābhārata*, which is about a destructive fratricidal war between the Pāṇḍava and the Kaurava clans. After a problematic victory in a bloody battle, Yudhiṣṭhira—the eldest Pāṇḍava—is groomed to ascend to the throne. But he is reluctant and has many questions about the possibility and strategies of ruling well under the circumstances. Our story is one of several narrated to him as part of his "education" to become a good king. Let me summarize the episode as follows:

> Pūjanī, a mysterious bird-mother lived in the palace as a friend of King Brahmadatta. She and the Queen gave birth to sons on the same day and the two infants resided together in the palace. Every day, Pūjanī flew across the seas and brought back two special fruit—one for her baby bird and the other for the human prince. With this unique nourishment, the prince gradually grew strong and healthy. One day tragedy struck the royal household: in play, the prince threw his bird companion to the ground and killed it. Flying home from her foraging mission, Pūjanī spotted her son lying dead on the ground. Crazed with grief and rage, Pūjanī gouged out the prince's eyes with her claws, blinding him for life.
>
> The episode continues as a long and complex dialogue between Brahmadatta and Pūjanī. Reassuring her of forgiveness, Brahmadatta asks Pūjanī to continue living in the palace as before. Pūjanī argues that given what had transpired, it was in her best interests to leave since neither of them could ever move beyond the memories of violence and injury that they had caused in each other's lives. The narrative concludes with Pūjanī ending her friendship with the king, flying away from the palace, and, as the text says, "disappearing into the beyond."[2]

Vrinda Dalmiya, *The Odd Case of a Bird-Mother* In: *Feminist Philosophy of Mind*. Edited by: Keya Maitra and Jennifer McWeeny, Oxford University Press. © Oxford University Press 2022. DOI: 10.1093/oso/9780190867614.003.0020

The heart of this tale is in the nuances of the dialogue between Brahmadatta, the father of a blinded prince, and Pūjanī, the mother of the baby bird killed in play. But the setting of the exchange is interesting also. Intriguingly, this conversation between parents overtly negotiating their personal tragedies is deemed significant for the would-be king Yudhiṣṭhira's concerns about governance. The precise political message Yudhiṣṭhira learned (or was expected to learn) in the epic is not something we are concerned with. But since the *Mahābhārata* was intended to be retold, reinterpreted, and made relevant for different times, my project explores other possibilities in its contemporary telling/hearing. Note that the very name *Pūjanī* in Sanskrit means "worthy of being worshiped." Can the bird-mother be exemplary for feminists? Does her grief and its complex entanglement with various other psychological states bring out the political dimensions of maternal mourning in the aftermath of violence? And more specifically, what is the nature of selfhood and subjectivity that follows from Pūjanī's foregrounding her grief in the way she does in the episode?

Judith Butler's essay "Violence, Mourning, Politics" shows how grieving is permission to construct ourselves as related to those we grieve for, and hence, is a way of including them in our ethico-political world (J. Butler 2004). For instance, the Women in Black movement—a small group of Israeli Jewish women marching silently with Palestinian women (in black clothing) to protest Israeli occupation of Palestinian lands—delinks grief from narrow nationalist agendas and signals a broader global responsiveness by "performing" a politics of mourning for those designated as Other.[3] In the *Mahābhārata* too, we find an entire chapter at the end of the battle (the *Strī Parva*) devoted to the wailing of women from both sides of the warring factions. This public display of grief amid dismembered corpses of fallen heroes could well be a narrative attempt to break down the politically constructed binaries of us/them, friends/foes. But Pūjanī's grief is different. It is not publicly staged in the above sense and is not even caused by a willfully motivated injury like an act of war. In fact, Pūjanī positions herself as a bereaved *mother* but one who became violent *herself* and who, as we shall see in her laments, appears to entrench rather than dissolve the categories of "human" as against "bird" or "us" against "them." We explore how her maternal positioning can illustrate a new ethical order "from within the scene of intimacy" and gesture toward a self-construction that is open to men as well as women, while also supporting the agency of women to be nonmothers if they so desire (Das 2010, 4).

The fact that maternal selfhood need not necessarily entrench regressive views of femininity is clear in recent feminist work. For instance, Cynthia Franklin and Laura Lyons analyze the legal and social responses to the murder of Gwen Araujo initiated by her mother's grief and go on to investigate resources in a *mother's* loss that subverts even the heteronormativity associated with motherhood (Franklin and Lyons 2008, 2016).[4] More recently, the Mothers of the Movement in the United States show how Black motherhood can be mobilized against racism and structural police brutality. The Pūjanī story becomes interesting when framed by such attempts to depersonalize and politicize maternal response to loss. The episode situates maternal grief thickly in a complex affective cartography that includes deeply self-reflexive ruminations about sources of violence in the mother's own self. Mourning, tinged as it is here, by rage, revenge, and rejection of forgiveness, becomes an opportunity to explore the relational complexity in maternal subjectivity, the functioning of grief in such self-constructions, and the ways in which a grief-fueled selfhood can relate ethically to others.

My hypothesis is that Pūjanī becomes "worship-worthy" for feminists by establishing the self as a "feeling thing" through what can loosely be called (with a Cartesian nod) a "method of grief"—a self that is constituted by volatile emotions because it is embodied and dependent on others. Some commentators read the episode we are concerned with here as the classical debate between free will and determinism, with Pūjanī owning her responsibility in the unfolding of the tragedy and Brahmadatta pushing for a more fatalistic determinism (Woods 2001). But our questions are: Does Pūjanī's "going away" from the palace (after rejecting the king's forgiveness) exemplify an empowering agency significant for relational selves? And why is her departure, which after all is rejection of a relationship, such a natural consequence of her grief?

Two Alternative Accounts of Grief and Selfhood

In the tangle of multiple relations in our story, grief both pulls apart as well as reinstates the bonds of (different) relational selves. Let us look more closely at this dialectic of binding and rupturing of relationships initiated by the emotion.

Grief, Harm, and Retreat from a Relational Nexus

The Pūjanī-Brahmadatta dialogue is overtly about demarcating "appropriate" trust from its misplaced, irrational forms. Pūjanī's refusal of Brahmadatta's overtures alerts us to the dangers of hasty trust. According to Annette Baier, trust is "accepted vulnerability to another's possible but not expected ill will . . . towards one" (Baier 1994a, 99). What makes trust risky is not knowing what to expect from others or "the *opaqueness* to us of the reasoning and motivation of those we trust and with whom we cooperate" (Baier 1994b, 15; emphasis added). Thus to the extent that we cannot know or rely on a person's "good motivations," we ought not to trust her and craft ourselves "in relation" to them. Pūjanī seems to build on this insight when rejecting Brahmadatta's pleas for continued friendship.

Being knowingly injured by someone is a clear indication of their ill will toward us and is enough reason to distance ourselves from them (*Mahābhārata* 12.139.42). Expecting "goodwill" from such persons is, in Pūjanī's evocative words, like "continuing to walk with sores on the soles of our feet" (*Mahābhārata* 12.139.76). But the step from being harmed to absence of trust is hardly unproblematic not only because sores on the soles of our feet sometimes can and do heal, but because the king in the story had not harmed Pūjanī at all. In fact, *he* had been wronged by *her*! So Pūjanī's wariness of Brahmadatta must lie elsewhere. The text suggests that *victims* of wrongdoing (like Brahmadatta) are like simmering embers ready to burst into flame at any time or like a fire under the sea that periodically spouts out in volcanic eruptions (*Mahābhārata* 12.139.44/ 45). Such imagery highlights the emotional instability of those who have been harmed, which in turn generates opacity about their motives. It is no longer safe for Pūjanī to associate with Brahmadatta, who is now unpredictable *as the father of a boy vengefully blinded by her*.

Interestingly, this argument against trusting people *we* have harmed is powerfully self-reflexive: it construes not only the king as untrustworthy, but also Pūjanī herself. Pūjanī in the text explicitly traces her violent action to the love of her son. Her first reaction to seeing her dead child is extreme grief—she "burns with sorrow" and admits that everything else—her being buffeted by vengeful emotions—follows as a consequence (*Mahābhārata* 12.139.59). The sense of unbearable risk here comes not only from the opacity of a grieving Other but from the opacity of her own motives *to herself.* Pūjanī is unable to trust herself. Her heinous act of blinding the prince reveals her *own* undependability. Since sustainable trust relationships are grounded not only in our expecting that the trusted will not harm us, but also in the confidence that we will not harm them, the argument now is that victimhood destroys the *self-trust* necessary for maintaining relationality. The volatility of grief thus undermines relational selfhood from points of view of both the aggressor and the aggrieved. As the former, Pūjanī retreats from the king. But its logic places her in the unenviable position of retreating from herself with self-doubts about her competence to maintain a relational subjectivity with him.

Grief, Love, and Affirmation of the Relational Nexus

An alternative narrative about grief is also possible. Martha Nussbaum has written evocatively about her grief at her mother's death. It, she says, "felt like a nail suddenly driven into my stomach" which was accompanied by a "vague and powerful anger—at the doctors, for allowing this crisis to occur . . . above all at myself, for not having been able to stop this event from happening" (Nussbaum 1997, 232–233). For Nussbaum too, this viscerally experienced anguish slides into other emotions, which together become the grasp of a value-laden absence in her life. Apprehending the fact that someone important to us is no more cannot take the form of a cool and detached judgment. She rhetorically asks: "Can I assent to the idea that someone tremendously beloved is forever lost to me, and yet preserve emotional equanimity?" (Nussbaum 1997, 243). Emotional upheaval *is* the recognition of loss, reinforcing that a person who is lost *matters* to one. Grief in its various manifestations therefore becomes a means of acknowledging the *importance* of things for us and consequently, our neediness and our dependence on those whom we "do not fully control" (Nussbaum 1997, 232). In this way, it is a cognitive route to our relational selfhood rather than an impetus for its dismantling.

The grieving Pūjanī comes face to face with how much her (now dead) son mattered. A cross-temporal coherence of discrete mental events marks the *value* of the baby bird in her life: the bird-mother had previously felt joy when the little chick was born, was happy when it flourished, sad when it was frustrated, and her actions were routinely organized around its interests. Grief presupposes this affective history. It signals for Pūjanī the singularity of her life *in terms of someone valuable to her*, and thus in grieving its loss, she comes to accept the relationality of "being a mother of that baby bird" as self-defining.

The irony here is that grief (caused by death) brings home the relational identity of the griever only when one of the relata in the relationship is destroyed by the loss of the loved one. So it could be objected that grief at best is access to a past (relational) selfhood in the moment of its unraveling. Butler puts this poignantly: "I not only mourn the loss, but I become inscrutable to myself. Who 'am' I without you? . . . [W]hat I have lost 'in' you, that for which I have no ready vocabulary, is a relationality that is composed neither exclusively of myself nor you" (J. Butler 2004, 22). And this could be why, according to Butler, grief fails to *give* or present us a "relational identity." Rather, as she argues, we *lose* our relationality and hence, our very self, when we grieve.

However, I wonder if "what I have lost *in* you" needs to be parsed as "in losing you, I have lost my relationship" or even "in losing you, I have come to realize that I could have had a relationship in you." It could well mean "in losing you, I have come to realize the importance (for me) of the relationship with you." In other words, I wonder whether deaths always entail termination of a relation rather than a *change* in them. As diachronic processes, relationships may continue in new forms and can even survive the destruction of a relata. "Being the daughter of Betty Craven" presumably remains a central plank of Nussbaum's life even after her mother, Betty Craven, died. Martha *continued* as the "daughter of," but of the (now) deceased, Betty. At the end of a marriage, for example, we may (or may not) choose to define ourselves as "ex-wives." If we do, we continue to be constituted by the marriage, but now by a marriage-*as-past* and, hence, a changed relationship. This is an open-endedness where our narratives determine whether the relationship to a lost one *ends* or is merely *transformed* by their passing. In the latter case, mourning for those we have lost is consistent with continuation of a self-consciously embraced relational self with the dead.

Accordingly, death of a child need not imply termination of the relationship of motherhood. The 1949 journal of a Soto Zen Buddhist practitioner, Nakayama Momoya, whose son was killed in World War II, brings this out vividly. Momoya charts her descent into a Pūjanī-like near-madness due to sorrow, which is gradually replaced by peacefulness on meeting her Buddhist teacher. But significantly, her descriptions of enlightenment and calm differ from traditional Buddhist doctrines of giving up "clinging." Recall Buddha's handling of a mother's loss of a child in the story of Kisa Gotami. When the bereaved Kisa Gotami begged the Buddha to bring her son back to life, he sent her in search of a handful of mustard seeds from a household that had not been visited by death. Of course, going door to door, Kisa Gotami found no such place. But she did confront the universality of loss in the process, and this enabled her to reconfigure her personal pain. Understanding that attachment to impermanent things (like her son) inevitably led to sorrow, Kisa Gotami overcame attachment itself. However, there is no such transcendence in Moyoma's account of attaining peace. She specifically mentions her efforts of working *with* her (dead) son and speaks "not of transcending or universalizing her love for her son, *but as remaining in his presence forever*" (Ohnumo 2012, 203). Here, it is the relational stance to a particular individual (her son) that transformed into Buddha Mind. We see this possibility also in non-Buddhist contexts when ordinary locutions reference grief as a "commemoration" or "a way of keeping the love alive," thereby attesting to a continuation of a relationship with the deceased (Solomon 2007, 74). Thus, Pūjanī need not, and does not, "go missing" in her relational identity as a mother when her son dies. Her grief signifies recreation of a (maternal) relational identity, but with the new role of ensuring that her son does not disappear from the social world in the way that he did from the physical one.

Selfhood through a "Method of Grief"

The duality in the metaphysical functioning of grief accounts for the oddness of Pūjanī advocating both an acceptance and rejection of relational identity. Note that her grief signaled and reinforced her love/bond with her child, yet it led her to seriously disassociate from the king, thus making the two relations hitherto central in her life incompatible. Note also that this reiterates the worry that intimacy and a caring identity are parochial and unable to generate a politics or augment relations to distant or nonfamilial others. However, further complexities in the story help us move beyond such objections. Remember that *both* Brahmadatta and Pūjanī are grieving parents (of course for different reasons), yet it is Pūjanī alone who finds trusting the king "as impossible as fixing a shattered clay pot" (*Mahābhārata* 12.139.69). Brahmadatta, on the other hand, wants to retain his friendship and connection to her even after the tragic incidents. Thus it seems that our protagonists experience the personal tragedies involving their children differently, thereby constructing very different *kinds* of grief-fueled identities. I attempt to explain this difference through what could be called a "methodic" function of grief. The suggestion is that Pūjanī's attitude to her anguish, unlike Brahmadatta's stance to his sorrow, displays a mixture of metaphysical and epistemic elements reminiscent of Descartes's method of answering the question "What am I?"

The Cartesian cogito emerged as the indubitable Archimedean anchor in a sea of universal doubt: the manner of its exposure also established its nature. Since the very attempt to doubt everything led to the cogito, its certainty lay in its being a substance with the essential property of doubting/thinking. The universality of doubt established the self as a "thinking/doubting thing"—with doubting encompassing the entire range of "thought." In a parallel fashion, grief is simultaneously the epistemic means of registering a selfhood *and* defines the specific nature of the self that is so established. Pūjanī encountered herself through a brush with maddening pain and rage-induced violence—an encounter that decimated her self-trust. Though her emotional volatility made her distrust her competence in maintaining ethical relations, it simultaneously brought home the certitude of her maternal identity—an identity constituted by the relation with her child. Because of this she was prone to upsurges of emotion that tracked events in *its* (the child's) life. Thus, unruly and unpredictable passions that generated her self-mistrust also enabled her to recognize herself *as a mother*. This amounted to the certitude of her being a thing hurtable by what happened to her child. Like the Cartesian doubter, Pūjanī, in confronting her volatility, came to know herself as a relational subject and, therefore, as inherently emotional and reactive. Consequently, the literally *self*-presenting state of grief made perspicuous a relational subject that is a "feeling thing"—of course, with felt grief standing in for a range of emotions, including joy and rage.

The consequences of this are interesting. First, a feeling thing is not determined through a single emotion in "referential isolation." In a different context, Agnieszka Jaworska argues for the connection of emotions with selfhood and shows how it is implausible to grieve for someone without also experiencing "the joys, fears, hopes, regrets etc. characteristic of caring about the same object"

(Jaworska 2007, 562). Grief references the continuity and coherence of an agent's life by tracking the intentional object of different emotions felt across times. The connection of various emotions to a common intentional object/person establishes a pattern that highlights what is of importance to a subject (which incidentally, Jaworska calls "caring"). Because of this, grief ends up "speaking for the agent" and there is no need to move to self-reflexive second-order (rational) *endorsements* of first-order desires in order to determine identity.

Second, such a feeling thing is bound to another in a way such that misfortunes in the *other's* life (the limiting case of which is its death) make her susceptible to emotional upheavals. Pūjanī's self embraces *dispositional* grief—a self with a constitutional openness to sorrow— even in its violent forms caused by misfortunes of an Other. This openness to being affected also introduces opacity in self-consciousness. Note that some philosophers of mind have long noted the co-existence of a fundamental anonymity with self-awareness. Dan Zahavi, for instance, mentions at least five different ways in which ignorance can be reconciled with self-givenness (Zahavi 2002). When Pūjanī speaks of past experiences of harm affecting our current motivations long past our ability to retrieve them consciously, she references one of the ways Zahavi has in mind. However, the self-opacity in question here also has a temporal dimension. Our identities spill into the future. Given our constitutive tendency to be emotionally affected by uncertain futures, we become unpredictable, unreliable, and opaque even to ourselves. Everything that goes into the making of who I am is not known to me now.

Finally, because of the centrality of emotions, maternal bonds (even when nonbiologically conceived) emerge as essentially embodied connections. Pūjanī, in knowing herself as a feeling thing, knows herself as a parent-*with-a-body*. It is significant that after the death of her child, she who had lived in the palace quite happily before begins to think of Brahmadatta and his son in terms of their species-specific bodied configurations and social locations *that are different* from hers. The particular, individualized friendship between Pūjanī and Brahmadatta now gets embedded in power-infused hierarchies emanating from the social categorizations of their respective bodies. The king and the prince are perceived as members of the Kshatriya group—a warrior caste known for aggression (*Mahābhārata* 12.139.16–19). They are also "human," while Pūjanī is a "bird," the natural hunting target for "humans" (*Mahābhārata* 12.139.60). Tensions in their relational nexus are now naturalized in terms of the prevalent social constructs and norms associated with these bodily differences. Pūjanī thus becomes very much a *bird*-mother living and interacting dangerously with *human* actors who conceive members of her kind as prey or food.

But herein is a problem. Emphasizing the corporeal interrelationality of maternal identity, once again, questions the plausibility of a continued relationship with a dead child. In what sense can Moyoma or Pūjanī survive the deaths of their respective children as relational beings when the relationality is corporeal and the *body* of one of the relata is made absent by death? In response, I refer to a fascinating paper by Jane Ribbens McCarthy and Raia Prokhovnik that distinguishes between the "enfleshed" Other and embodiment to argue for a material relationship even with the dead:

> With the death of a loved one, the biological body of "you" is buried or cremated, while material presence of "you" is not wholly erased but remains in significant ways. But also, and crucially, the "us" remains as an embodied relationality, held with "me" in many embodied forms; the "us" is *written into* "*my*" *body*, and continues to have material presence after death. (McCarthy and Prokhovnik 2013, 11; emphasis added)

This hints at how a truly relational perspective leads us to relax the boundedness of material bodies themselves. Construed relationally, the *materiality* of a body is not simply that of a biological entity but can survive as corporeal traces—including those of grief and emotionality—left in another body. If bodies also are "relational" and "open" to other *bodies*, then death is the cessation of an "enfleshed" person, but it allows for a continued material connection in and through these other bodies. I preserve, for example, the purse my mother was using when she died because it carries *her touch*. Though deceased, the child has left its material presence that can be felt through its "traces" in (say) her mother's bodily being. Such bodily traces of the deceased are like genetic imprints working through other bodies across times and sometimes can be stronger than conscious memory.[5] Thus in embracing the dispositions to feel a whole range of emotions, Pūjanī can, without paradox, endorse an embodied relationality with her now dead child.

Such self-construction of a "feeling thing" through what I have been calling the method of grief stands in stark contrast to Brahmadatta's perception of himself. Brahmadatta keeps his emotions (and hence his embodied entanglement with his son) at arm's length. When he confronts himself as bound-with-his-child through his own grief, his response is to retreat to intellectual self-reflectiveness and philosophical analysis. He rationalizes away the emotions produced by the bond to his son and quickly shifts to the position of a cool-headed "friend," benefactor, or moral judge, thus vacating the location of a "parent." Grief for him is *episodic*. He retreats from acquiescing to the ongoing affective vulnerabilities that come along with accepting oneself as a thing that must feel in response to what happens to another. He therefore, need not mistrust himself as participating in relations of trust because he does not give up on rational self-control. Unlike the Cartesian, he never succumbs to the universality of doubt or self-mistrust.

However, Brahmadatta, in shifting focus away from the tragedy of his son and its emotional effects on him, also rationally explains away *Pūjanī's* vengeance. In this he tries to tame Pūjanī. She becomes someone he has cognitively grasped and, therefore, someone who can no longer surprise with hurtful behavior. These moves enable Brahmadatta to shore up his defenses against the perils of dependency that come with friendship and love. Maybe as the ruling power, the myth of control and invincibility is habitual for him, and he is expected to forge relations of pragmatic and reason-based solidarity. The king's political sovereignty and moral high ground come to mark a *disembodied* (though relational) selfhood.

But now we face another quandary. Pūjanī, in recognizing herself through the "method" of grief, seems to undermine her agentive significance. A self, configured in terms of maternal grief, is inherently untrustworthy (because of being inherently volatile) and thus is unreliable as an ethico-political agent. How then can Pūjanī's acceptance of her opacity to herself be empowering? Continuing with the Cartesian parallel is helpful here. After emerging from universal doubt, Descartes's "thinking thing" went on to *bring back belief in an external world.* This, of course, was done with the help of a God. But note that Cartesian proofs of God relied on innate ideas within the cogito/thinking thing. Could Pūjanī's acceptance of herself as a feeling thing through her self-mistrust bring back her agentive confidence? And could the seeds of such confidence and moral agency lie within *her* starting point—the world of a caring, (dispositionally) grieving mother open to emotional upheavals?

To answer this, we take a closer look at the vulnerabilities of the corporeal relational self. On the ontological or *metaphysical* plane, an embodied relational self is exposed to physical death and violence and routine discursive erasures by being socially constructed in unpalatable ways (J. Butler 2016). Such selves live with unpredictable violence inflicted on them and, as we have seen, with unpredictable violences that they themselves initiate on others in response. But note that physical violence here is coupled with uncertainty and not-knowing. This introduces an *epistemic vulnerability* in the lives of corporeal relational selves. So now our question is whether such metaphysical and epistemic vulnerabilities could be a resource for unique modes of ethico-political functioning. Could Pūjanī's "disappearing into the beyond" be both an exemplification of and search for a form of agency that is oddly consistent with being "out of control" and the "unknowing" inherent in being a feeling thing?

Uncertain Agency

According to our reading the narrative does not end with a bird-mother's paralysis because of self-doubt. She acts in leaving the king, and her exit from the palace is a resistance to the reason-based and emotion-denying identity being foisted on her. This is a constructive agential move consistent with her vulnerability and unknown-ness to herself. The story's abrupt end and *silence* about where Pūjanī went and whether she lived happily ever after, only deepens the unknowing surrounding her exit.[6]

Butler has shown how metaphysical vulnerability or openness to physical harm lies at the heart of some political actions (J. Butler 2016). Nonviolent passive resistance, for example, presupposes *exposing our bodies to injury*, and thereby vulnerability to police brutality or imprisonment constitutes the distinct political agency of a peace march or protest. Though Butler also notes that "by virtue of the subject's *opacity to itself* it sustains some of its most important ethical bonds," the connection between epistemic vulnerability or the opacity of the self and action is less clear (J. Butler 2001, 22). The attempt to build uncertainty into the heart of political action reworks doubt as a motivator. Vacillating between options can be experienced as creative and can enable an imaginative experimentation with oneself. This allows for a receptivity to possibilities that are usually closed off by certainty. But for such openness to facilitate rather than stymie action (as in the case of Buridan's ass), we need to resort to psychological resources other than certain belief. Being reasonably sure or believing that a particular option leads to the desired goal can no longer explain action. In fact, the analysis of action now moves beyond its usual belief-desire formulations.

In the absence of belief, it is the normative importance of our projects that compel action.[7] The agent is impelled by value (rather than calculations of success), and she experiments with imagined scenarios whose implications may well be still hazy. What if poor women from the South get to set global economic agendas? What if supporting caring labor is the primary objective of a democracy? Such *imaginings* of a different world entertain what is not the case and what might never come to be the case, and yet motivate action. This is the stuff of *hope*. Moving toward unknown, not fully known, and maybe even unlikely yet important futures with hope, lies at the heart of political activity in societies that are trying to rectify unprecedented forms of oppression and attempting to transcend collective prejudice. When political progress is geared toward producing the radically "new" and the new is by definition what is yet to be known, it must involve uncertainty-fueled action.

In the context of our story, Pūjanī's acceptance of the epistemically vulnerable self opens up the possibilities of repositioning herself in truly creative and new ways. She can leave the palace for an *imagined* and *hoped*-for future—where corporeal relational selves will be nurtured and accommodated rather than violently foreclosed by pregiven scripts, where though she cannot "be" without the possibility of being volatile, there can be social arrangements to contain the harm caused by such unreliability. This experimental search takes Pūjanī away not only from the palace, but from the narrative world of the epic itself, making it a deeply self-reflexive moment where the *Mahābhārata* self-critically apprehends its own limits and gestures (imaginatively and hopefully?) toward a "beyond." Note that Brahmadatta's world, which Pūjanī leaves behind, is also the *Mahābhārata*'s general virtue-theoretic framework of aiming at *individual* self-cultivation through control of desires and emotion. Surrendering to one's relationality in a method of grief signals the limits of such self-transformation: violence-proneness caused by being relationally constituted cannot be "cultivated away." Rather the search shifts to newer democratic and institutional structures that allow for anger, rage, and helplessness while also mitigating the harm they can cause. Pūjanī's odd stand on forgiveness begins to make sense in this context.

Selves and the Limits of Forgiveness

The method of grief as discussed so far is an ontological and epistemic move in the philosophy of mind that enables us to both make and know ourselves as relational. However, it has consequences for moral psychology—including the virtue of forgiveness. Analyzing forgiveness in this *Mahābhārata* story is complicated because Pūjanī is both the aggressor (who needs to be forgiven) and a victim (who needs to forgive). The oddness of Pūjanī is that she champions moral responsibility and unabashedly owns her act of vengeance but rejects forgiveness, which is a very acceptable "reactive attitude" toward a wrongdoer. Sidestepping the vast literature on the phenomenology and political ramifications of forgiveness, our brief comments focus on the intertwining of social power with forgiveness. This once again reinforces that a corporeal feeling thing does not feel in a vacuum but that its emotions are calibrated with meanings attached to its body. Situating forgiveness within a world of uneven privilege complicates the virtue in surprising ways. Forgiveness implies that we "forswear the resentment" of having been harmed and opt not to retaliate even though we could have (Strawson 1974, 6). Further, we forgive in spite of the possibility of the forgiven act reoccurring. This is either because we have confidence in being able to protect ourselves if it does happen again, or because we trust that the act will not be repeated. On the first option, forgiveness indexes a fearlessness born of power. This is a power that Brahmadatta as a king has. But then paradoxically, the king's forgiving Pūjanī only reinforces why she is (and needs to be) afraid of him in the first place and resists a continued cohabitation. On the second option—a trust that Pūjanī's vengeful act (born out of love and anger) will not recur—Brahmadatta adopts a stance *not* shared by Pūjanī about herself. After all, the loss of her son made the relationally constituted bird-mother dispositionally prone to explosive emotions. The king's forgiveness is now unacceptable because it is based on rejecting who Pūjanī is—a "feeling thing" and all that this entails.

Note that the discussion has moved from the person who is forgiving to what it is like for a person to be forgiven—more specifically to what it is like for a *corporeal relational self* to be forgiven by someone who believes himself to be a self-contained and rationally self-regulating unity. Peter Strawson's analysis of reactive attitudes generates a destructive dilemma for our protagonists. Brahmadatta could adopt the "objective attitude" of thinking Pūjanī to be psychologically deranged or "abnormal" and thereby take her action off the moral hook. Alternatively, he could treat her as responsible for her actions but retain the "participant attitude" of choosing to truly forgive her vengeance. Both stances turn out to be unviable for Pūjanī. The rejection of the first is straightforward enough. It is an objectification that denies Pūjanī's status as a moral agent and does nothing to acknowledge or affirm the ethico-political subjecthood of a grieving mother. On the second option, Pūjanī's *action* is a misstep of an otherwise legitimate moral actor. Brahmadatta could endorse the conclusion that the motivation displayed in her vengeance "might properly be resented," yet go on to "repudiate that attitude for the future (or at least for the immediate future)" (Strawson 1974, 6). But herein lies the problem: this stance toward the bird-mother drives a wedge between the act being forgiven and the actor— Pūjanī's action is treated as a lapse not truly reflective of herself. But as we have tried to establish, the dispositional roots of grief and violence (and hence, the possibility of the reoccurrence of the latter) lie in *who Pūjanī relationally is*. In this way, accepting the king's forgiveness amounts to delinking Pūjanī's moral selfhood from her identity *as* a mother. In reading through the dialogue, it has always struck me as odd that Pūjanī does not overtly express guilt at what she has done even though she accepts "responsibility" for it. Lament as a trope is central in the epic but is strangely absent in this episode. Is forgiveness meaningless because Pūjanī does not experience its correlative emotion of guilt? Of course, insisting on forgiveness could well be a means of inducing guilt in the person being forgiven—an attempt to make her come to realize that what she has done makes her blameworthy. But Pūjanī from the very beginning fully accepts herself as responsible for the violence. Could the oddness of her response be an attempt to contain the harm of violence without necessarily giving up on a self constituted by this potentiality for violence? Could she be gesturing to a way in which forgiveness sometimes undermines the agentive selfhood of the person being forgiven? Could the issue for Pūjanī be not so much about forgiving or being forgiven, as about (not) forgetting? Pain suffered because of the loss of (or on behalf of) some others stays with us when these others constitute who *we* are—when they leave traces in our very bodies. Forgiveness, at best, negotiates past and present violence but is too thin a mechanism for forward-looking harm or open-ended futures infused with possibilities of harming. Corporeal relational selves need to contend with such futures. Pūjanī can be seen as leaving the palace—and the space of forgiveness—to "fly into the beyond" in search for alternatives. She could be staging the delicate balancing act of trying to build community by holding together both the violence-proneness and the more positive relational possibilities of materially and relationally constructed selfhoods.

The Relationality of Care

In conclusion, we draw together these reflections on the bird-mother of the *Mahābhārata* to consolidate the subject position of a *mother* as a site for normative transformation. The ethics of care begins from "within the scene of intimacy" in the mother-child relational nexus. But of course, motherhood can be forced, oppressive, romantic, essentialistic, apolitical, or prepolitical. Shifting to the *grief* of a mother as a starting point is more robust. It establishes the relational identity central in care ethics as an intuitively "owned" Archimedean point, rather than being biologically or sociologically imposed, and then deromanticizes it by recognizing its inherent tendencies toward violence.[8] The relational identity of a bereaved mother as a "feeling thing" has three important consequences. First, emotions are indexed to particular contexts and are inflected by crisscrossing vectors of power that make "being a mother" a nonessentialized intersectional location. *How* a mother feels the grief (or joy) arising from a primal dependency, *whether or not* she can forgive, *what form* her rage, violence, and disappointments take, all depend on her social location. Second, emotions are motivational forces. Thus, identities supervenient on patterns of emotional resonance devolve into plans and policies of *acting* in accordance with what and who are important to them. Because of this a caring maternal identity thus positions itself as a "care claimant" involved in the political activity of demanding from, and seeking changes in, the normative and social infrastructural order within which she is a relational self (S. Butler 2012). Finally, volatile emotions make such selfhood epistemically vulnerable or opaque even to itself. Accordingly, actions stemming from a maternal subjectivity highlight uncertainty and agentive forms that are not only consistent with but are made possible by the not-knowing associated with it. Being/acting as a mother involves collective sensibilities, and democratic institutions to accommodate them involve structural interventions based on imagination and hope. Changing norms of grievability is, of course, a way of including the socially excluded and stemming violence against them. But this strategy is effective because grief stakes out a particular kind of relational identity with those we grieve for. However, as we see in the case of Pūjanī, this identity is unstable and uncertain of itself. It therefore expresses itself not in certain doxastic states but through political interventions relying on imagination and hope that can dare to be transformative of the all too familiar neoliberal order.

Notes

1. I am grateful to Elyse Byrnes, Arindam Chakrabarti, Keya Maitra, and Jen McWeeny for helpful comments.
2. This is an abridged version of the story as it occurs in the *Āpaddharmaparva* of the *Mahābhārata* (Kinjawadekar 1979, 12.139). Subsequent references to the epic will give the section (*parva*), followed by the chapter and then the verse. For a more detailed textual analysis of the dialogue see Dalmiya (2018).
3. See also Athanasiou (2005).
4. Gwen Araujo, a teenage transgender woman, was murdered on October 4, 2002, in Newark, California.
5. The editors have pointed me to an interesting paper by Catriona Mortimer-Sandilands (2008) that explores how selfhood is maintained through embodied connections with the environment in spite of memory loss in the early stages of Alzheimer's disease.
6. I have been influenced by Emily Hudson's (2013) interpretation of the significance of silences in the text.
7. See Mollendorf (2006).
8. For a discussion of violence in care, see Simplican (2015).

References

Athanasiou, Athena. 2005. "Reflections on the Politics of Mourning: Feminist Ethics and Politics in the Age of Empire." *Historein* 5: 39–57.

Baier, Annette. 1994a. "Trust and Antitrust." In *Moral Prejudices: Essays on Ethics* by Annette Baier, 95–129. Cambridge, MA: Harvard University Press.

Baier, Annette. 1994b. "What Do Women Want in Moral Theory." In *Moral Prejudices: Essays on Ethics* by Annette Baier, 1–17. Cambridge, MA: Harvard University Press.

Butler, Judith. 2001. "Giving an Account of Oneself." *Diacritics* 31 (4): 22–40.

Butler, Judith. 2004. "Violence, Mourning, Politics." In *Precarious Life: The Powers of Mourning and Violence* by Judith Butler, 19–49. London: Verso.

Butler, Judith. 2016. "Rethinking Vulnerability and Resistance." In *Vulnerability in Resistance*, edited by Judith Butler, Zeynep Gambetti, and Liticia Sabsay, 12–27. Durham, NC: Duke University Press.

Butler, Samuel A. 2012. "A Fourth Position of Care." *Hypatia* 27 (2): 390–406.

Dalmiya, Vrinda. 2019. "A Case of Relational Autonomy in the *Mahābhārata*: The Story of Pūjanī." *Sophia* 58 (2): 239–254.

Das, Veena. 2010. "Sexuality, Vulnerability and the Oddness of the Human: Lessons from the Mahabharata." *borderlands e-journal* 9 (3): 1–17.

Franklin, Cynthia, and Laura Lyons. 2008. "From Grief to Grievance: Ethics and Politics in the Testimony of Anti-war Mothers." *Life Writing* 5 (2): 237–250.

Franklin, Cynthia, and Laura Lyons. 2016. " 'I Have a Family': Relational Witnessing and the Evidentiary Power of Grief in the Gwen Araujo Case." *GLQ: A Journal of Gay and Lesbian Studies* 22 (3): 437–466.

Hudson, Emily. 2013. *Disorienting Dharma: Ethics and the Aesthetics of Suffering in the Mahābhārata.* Oxford: Oxford University Press.

Jaworska, Agnieszka. 2007. "Caring and Internality." *Philosophy and Phenomenological Research* 74 (3): 529–568.

Kinjawadekar, Pandit Ramchandrashastri Sastri, ed. 1979. *The Mahābhārata* with *Bharata Bhawadeepa Commentary by Nilkantha.* New Delhi: Oriental Books Reprint Corporation.

McCarthy, Jane Ribbens, and Raia Prokhovnik. 2013. "Embodied Relationality and Caring after Death." *Body and Society* 20 (2): 18–43.

Moellendorf, Darrel. 2006. "Hope as a Political Virtue." *Philosophical Papers* 35 (3): 413–433.

Mortimer-Sandilands, Catriona. 2008. "Landscape, Memory and Forgetting: Thinking through (My Mother's) Body and Place." In *Material Feminisms*, edited by Stacy Alaimo and Susan Hekman, 265–287. Bloomington: Indiana University Press.

Nussbaum, Martha. 1997. "Emotions as Judgments of Value and Importance." In *Relativism, Suffering and Beyond: Essays in Memory of Bimal K. Matilal*, edited by P. Billimoria and J. N. Mohanty, 231–251. Delhi: Oxford University Press.

Ohnuma, Reiko. 2012. *Ties That Bind: Maternal Imagery and Discourses in Indian Buddhism.* Oxford: Oxford University Press.

Simplican, Stacy Clifford. 2015. "Care, Disability, and Violence: Theorizing Complex Dependency in Eva Kittay and Judith Butler." *Hypatia* 30 (1): 217–233.

Solomon, Robert. 2007. *True to Our Feelings.* Oxford: Oxford University Press.

Strawson, P. F. 1974. "Freedom and Resentment." In *Freedom and Resentment and Other Essays* by P. F. Strawson, 1–25. New York: Methuen Publishing.

Woods, Julian. 2001. *Destiny and Human Initiative in the Mahābhārata.* Albany: State University of New York Press.

Zahavi, Dan. 2002. "Anonymity and First-Personal Givenness: An Attempt at Reconciliation." In *Subjektivität—Verantwortung—Wahrheit*, edited by David Carr and Christian Lotz, 75–89. Frankfurt am Main: Peter Lang.

20

Equanimity and the Loving Eye

A Buddhist-Feminist Account of Loving Attention

Emily McRae

The subject of this chapter is loving attention, a way of paying attention to others that is motivated by care, respect, and kindness. This way of attending, integral to Mahayana Buddhist philosophy of mind and ethics, is also central to many influential feminist conceptions of moral perception. By focusing specifically on loving attention, I hope to show that attention is rarely neutral, that our ways of attending have affective and normative valences. We do not simply attend; we can attend approvingly or disapprovingly, compassionately or cruelly, lovingly or arrogantly. This implies that failures of attention are not always explained by the absence of attention, but that we can also fail by attending in the wrong kind of way.

Drawing on both feminist and Buddhist philosophical traditions, I offer an account of loving attention that highlights the ways in which these traditions of theorizing attention can complement and improve each other. By putting these Buddhist and feminist theories of attention in dialogue, my aim is to expose blind spots in both theories and possible ways of addressing them. In particular, I will argue that Buddhist accounts can benefit from feminist insights into the effects of systems of oppression on the ways we attend or fail to attend to each other. The interplay between social, political, and economic power and attention is not adequately addressed in Buddhist accounts of attention. On the other hand, the Buddhist focus on the cultivation of attention, including loving attention, help address important questions that often remain unanswered in feminist literature: How can I transform my attention in a liberatory way? What specific practices and skills are necessary for such a transformation? I argue that Buddhist moral psychological and epistemological skills of equanimity and mindfulness help construct a more compelling account of the cultivation of loving attention. These skills, especially equanimity, are necessary components for understanding how one could change from an unloving, arrogant perceiver to someone who can lovingly attend to others.

Emily McRae, *Equanimity and the Loving Eye* In: *Feminist Philosophy of Mind*. Edited by: Keya Maitra and Jennifer McWeeny, Oxford University Press. © Oxford University Press 2022. DOI: 10.1093/oso/9780190867614.003.0021

Attention and Loving Attention

In Buddhist philosophy of mind, attention (Sanskrit: *manasikāra*, Tibetan: *yid la byed pa*) and the related phenomena of concentration (Sanskrit: *samādhi*, Tibetan: *ting nge 'dzin*) and mindfulness (Sanskrit: *smṛti*, Tibetan: *dran pa*) are defined in terms of the ability of the mind to take an object and the resulting qualities of that mind so directed. Attention, or what I will refer to here as "bare attention," is simply the mind's ability to be directed to an object. According to Abhidharma Buddhist accounts of mind, bare attention is one of five "omnipresent" mental factors since every mental state is directed to an object (Dreyfus and Thompson 2007; Bodhi 1993, 81). Such bare attention can be fleeting or even momentary, too quick and trivial for us to notice or appreciate. Of course, the mind also has the ability to attend to an object over time, the skill of concentration. Another related skill is the mind's ability to "pay attention" (as opposed to simply "attend"): the capacity to remember that we are attending to something and to not become distracted. This is the skill of mindfulness. Neither concentration nor mindfulness is present in every moment of mental cognition, but is instead a skill that is cultivated, especially in the context of meditation (Dreyfus and Thompson 2007).

Western approaches to attention, at least folk psychological ones, tend to emphasize its function of bringing into focus one object out of many possible objects of awareness, to foreground an object and thereby relegate other possible objects to the background or periphery of one's awareness. William James famously claimed that attention is "the taking possession by the mind, in clear and vivid form, of one out of what seem several simultaneously possible objects or trains of thought. Focalization, concentration, of consciousness are of its essence" (James 1981, 403–404). Sebastian Watzl summarizes this "intuitive" (which he contrasts with "scientific") view of attention: "attention is the selective or contrastive aspect of the mind: when you are attending to something you are contrasting what you pick out with what remains in the background" (Watzl 2011, 843).

The kind of attention I will be concerned with here—loving attention—assumes both the "bare attention" (Tibetan: *yid la byed pa*) of the Buddhist tradition and focalization of consciousness that we see in James's and other Western accounts. At the very least, it is the mind's ability to direct to an object, which structures one's consciousness by highlighting the object in some sense while pushing other objects of awareness into the background. Our mind can be directed to an object, or foreground an object, in a variety of ways and for a variety of reasons, some moral and some not. I do not share Iris Murdoch's sense that attention itself is just or moral: we can attend cruelly or uncharitably by seeing only mistakes or faults, and we can attend for cruel purposes, such as to more effectively manipulate someone.

Loving attention structures our consciousness by bringing positive, compassionate, and sympathetic views of others to the foreground and allowing uncharitable, unsympathetic, or self-centered habits of perception to recede to the background. It includes both the selection of an object and the sympathetic or loving interpretation of that object. This is because failing to attend lovingly not only is due to focusing solely on negative objects but also can be due to attending negatively to an otherwise positive object. It is possible (and not uncommon!) to maintain uncharitable interpretations even of another's good qualities: using a resentful interpretative framework, for example, generosity becomes showing off, honesty is heard as rudeness, helpfulness comes off as obsequiousness, and so on.

Loving attention is related but not equivalent to the more widely discussed concept of "loving perception" or "moral perception," more generally. Margaret Holland distinguishes moral perception—the construal of a situation as moral and the recognition of morally salient features of that situation—from moral attention (Holland 1998, 301). Following Murdoch and Simone Weil, Holland defines moral attention as a normative concept, an "inner moral activity" that includes both "an effort to set aside dispositions that tend to distort perception and an effort to see what is independent from oneself" (Holland 1998, 306, 309). Moral attention, she argues, is the ability to change our moral perception for the better. This is true, I think, of loving attention. It not only is perceiving someone lovingly, but also implies some degree of inner work: one must *select* objects of attention, *construe* or *interpret* those objects in a loving way, and, Buddhist ethicists would argue, *habituate* oneself to these activities through cultivation practices. Because I focus on cultivation and transformation, "loving attention" suits my philosophical purposes better than "loving perception." Nevertheless, since the concepts overlap and often used interchangeably, I will draw on feminist and Buddhist discussions of loving perception to develop my account.

Loving Gazes, Arrogant Gazes

That the basic ways we attend to others—the ways we perceive and interpret other people, what we notice and what we don't (or refuse to) notice—is not morally neutral is one of the simplest but profound insights from feminist and critical race theory.[1] In these literatures, modes of attention are often discussed in terms of visual metaphors (the "gaze" or the "eye") that are used to explain broad patterns of interpretation (often immediate and reactive) in the context of systems of oppression. For many feminist theorists as well as antiracist theorists, the fact that the gaze is morally loaded demands that we develop a broader understanding of perception and attention in ethics; we need to understand the moral contours of how we see each other (perception) and the inner activity of changing how we see each other (attention).

Marilyn Frye distinguishes what she calls the arrogant eye—the paradigmatic perception of women by men in a phallocentric patriarchal society—from a more transformative and affirming way of seeing others, which she calls the loving eye. Men with arrogant eyes "organize everything seen with reference to themselves and their own interests" (Frye 1983, 67). For such a person, everything, including other people, is "either 'for me' or 'against me'" (Frye 1983, 67). This reduces others either to tools for meeting one's desires or obstacles to the satisfaction of one's desires. This reduction is accomplished *in the act of perception*, through the "gaze" itself (Mulvaney 1975; Yancy 2008; Fourlas 2015).

The problems with the arrogant eye are both epistemic and ethical: such a self-centered mode of perception not only falsifies the object of perception (the epistemic problem), but also "coerces the objects of his [the perceiver's] perception into satisfying the conditions his perception imposes" (the ethical problem) (Frye 1983, 67). When we are gazed at arrogantly, this creates significant pressure to conform to the (inaccurate) assumptions that are motivating and conveyed through the gaze. Consider, for example, George Yancy's example of the hostile, racist gaze of a white woman toward him, an African American man, in an elevator. Although her gaze, through which Yancy was perceived as a threat, a hypersexual predator and criminal, did not upend his sense of self, it did impose restrictions on his behavior: "It is through her gaze that I become hypervigilant of my own embodied spatiality. . . . My movements become and remain stilted. I dare not move suddenly. . . . I feel trapped" (Yancy 2008, 14–15). Even when we do not accept the narrative that the gaze implies, we are not free of its coercive effects.

According to Frye, arrogant perception refuses to see the other as a distinct individual, existing in her own right, with her own desires, needs, and goals. The loving gaze requires us to recognize the distinctness of the other without grafting her identity onto ours (Frye 1983, 75). María Lugones argues that, while Frye's account captures some kinds of arrogant perception, it cannot easily explain the arrogance of white women's gaze toward women of color: "[White women] ignore us, ostracize us, render us invisible, stereotype us, leave us completely alone, interpret us as crazy. All of this while we are in their midst. . . . Many times white women want us out of their field of vision" (Lugones, this volume, 109). This failure of love is not well described by the failure of seeing the other as independent; rather, it is a failure that comes from an overemphasizing difference and distinctness, which results in a profound failure of empathy and identification. Love, according to Lugones, requires a desire for mutual understanding, an empathic learning from others that is based on a deep recognition of our interdependence (Lugones, this volume, 109–110). The loving gaze, then, must recognize the *independence* of the other, the fact that she is not reducible to our projections onto her that are based on our own desires and needs. It must also recognize the *interdependence* of the other, that fact that she is not different in kind, that there are realities that we share or could come to share with each other.

Buddhist Accounts of Loving Gazes

The idea that there is, as Yancy has put it, an "ethics of perception," would not be controversial for many Indo-Tibetan Buddhist philosophers, who tend to place importance on the moral and epistemic qualities of the gaze (Yancy 2014). The eighth-century Indian master Śāntideva's advice —"Whenever catching sight of others, look on them with an open, loving heart"—is not just a practical tip for the aspiring bodhisattva, but exposes something deeper about the moral and epistemic significance of the loving gaze. The nineteenth-century Tibetan master Patrul Rinpoche comments on this verse:

> Even when you simply look at someone else, let that look be smiling and pleasant rather than an aggressive glare or some expression of anger. There are stories about this, like the one about the powerful ruler who glared at everyone with a very wrathful look. It is said that he was reborn as a *preta* living on left-overs under the stove of a house, and after that, because he had also looked at a holy being in that way, he was reborn in hell. (Patrul Rinpoche 1994, 199)

I interpret these stories of the *preta* and the hell-being not only as cautionary tales; they are also expressions of the ethical and epistemic importance of the loving and compassionate gaze and the dangers of arrogant and resentful ones.

In general, love is defined in Buddhist contexts as the earnest desire for the happiness and causes of happiness of another being (*Path of Purification* IX.91, 93, 98; Patrul Rinpoche 1994, 198–201; McRae 2017b). The relevant sense of happiness here is a robust one, including not only another's feeling happy, but also their overall well-being, and presence of the conditions and causes for their happiness and well-being in the future. Although this definition captures the intuitive heart of love in Buddhist traditions, it is important to remember that love in this context is not a mere desire. It is a committed orientation toward the well-being and happiness of another that includes cognitive, affective, and conative aspects. In Patrul Rinpoche's account of love, he argues that love requires activities of the mind (thinking about others in the right kinds of ways), speech (talking about and to others in the right kinds of ways), and body (seeing others and behaving toward them in the right kinds of ways).[2]

I have argued elsewhere for the primacy of moral perception and attention in Buddhist moral psychology, and so will not rehearse those arguments here (McRae 2017b). I will only emphasize that, in the context of Indo-Tibetan Buddhism, love is transformative: changing the way we see others is a central component of learning to love them. Love requires seeing positive qualities of others, or at least not refusing to see them, and the committed attention to their well-being (Heim 2014). The fifth-century Buddhist scholar Buddhaghosa focuses specifically on how love changes the way we see others; one of love's main functions is to "see virtues" in others (*Path of Purification* IX.98). We do not make up virtues to project into them, but rather remain open to seeing the ones that are there. Buddhaghosa notes that if we fail to find a single positive quality of another, we can cultivate compassion for them by attending to the ways they must suffer from their complete lack of good qualities (*Path of Purification* IX.20)! Many Tibetan Buddhist contemplative practices that are designed to cultivate love focus on changing the way we habitually perceive others, training us, for example, to imagine others as our children or parents.[3] The function of these contemplative practices, as I see it, is to change our deeper habits of attention by introducing new frames, such as "child" or "parent," to apply to others and, in so doing, intervene in habits of apathy and arrogance that usually characterize the ways we attend to others.

Drawing on both Buddhist view of loving attention and feminist ones, I offer, and aim to defend in the remainder of the chapter, the following as an account of loving attention: loving attention is the direction of awareness toward another person (or sentient being) that structures one's consciousness in a way that recognizes the positive qualities of others and makes possible sympathetic interpretations of the other. It allows one to appreciate the interdependence of self and other without reducing the other to the self (or vice versa). Loving attention ultimately clarifies an otherwise warped and damaging view of the other (as instrument to my happiness, as irrelevant to me, and so on). It is transformative, both epistemically and ethically: we become better knowers and better moral agents by attending lovingly. As such, it is an epistemic and moral skill that we can and should cultivate.

The Accuracy of Loving Attention in the Context of Oppression: Feminist Contributions to Buddhist Theory

There is, among some proponents of loving attention, such as Murdoch, a sense that loving attention is more accurate and just than modes of attention that are arrogant or self-centered (Murdoch 1970, 33).[4] In her analysis of Murdoch, Holland distinguishes the qualification of "accurate" from "just": the accuracy of attention is seeing "something as it actually is," whereas the justice of attention is "seeing fairly" by considering "the relevant background and other factors which contribute to developing an overall understanding" (Holland 1998, 309). In my own account, I credit loving attention with clarifying (rather than distorting) perception, which includes both accuracy and justice, in Murdoch's sense.

But the clarifying potential of loving attention is far from obvious. In Murdoch's famous example of a mother-in-law who actively changes her perception of her (lower class) daughter-in-law from "sometimes positively rude, always tiresomely juvenile" to "refreshingly gay," "spontaneous," and "delightfully youthful," she claims that this new, loving way to attend is ultimately more just (Murdoch 1970, 16–18). But why? Maybe the daughter-in-law really is a tiresome person and this redescription of her as refreshing and gay is not only less accurate, but a self-deceptive, delusional coping mechanism that allows the mother-in-law to construct a (false) narrative about her family life that she can live with.[5] Because of its inaccuracy, such a redescription could be dangerous if, for example, it blinds the mother-in-law to the real ethical misconduct of the daughter-in-law.

Of course, the mother-in-law in this example recognizes her own tendencies toward snobbery and her jealous desire for her son's attention, and, in changing her perception of her daughter-in-law, she is attempting to correct those biases (Murdoch 1970, 17). So, we could argue that accuracy is explained less by the narrative it projects onto others ("refreshingly gay"), than by the biases it corrects in the self (snobbery and jealousy). As Murdoch puts it, loving attention is "the effort to counteract such states of illusion" (Murdoch 1970, 36).[6] This is also what many Buddhist moral psychologists and ethicists would say. According to the *Ornament of the Mahāyāna Scriptures*, love dissolves the "mind-made knot" of dysfunctional mental states (17.19). It is because it can reduce biases caused by dysfunctional mental states such as hatred, anger, envy, and arrogance, that loving attention clarifies, rather than obscures or distorts, our perception of others.

This response makes sense of many cases of loving attention, including Murdoch's mother-in-law case, since built into that case was the assumption of real anti-daughter-in-law bias in the mother-in-law's habits of thinking and feeling (Murdoch 1970, 18). But the bias in this case is based on the overvaluing of the self and the tendency to find only fault with the other. If this is our tendency, then loving attention would help clarify our perception of the other, since it would, as Buddhist ethicists say, provide an antidote to that particular kind of misperception. But what if our problem is not overvaluing the self and finding fault with others but, rather, undervaluing the self and excusing others' bad behavior? As Sandra Bartky has argued, when we are accustomed to identifying with the beloved's narratives and providing him with the emotional support that maintain them, we make ourselves vulnerable to epistemic and moral bias (Bartky 1990). We can learn to accept "the world according to him" (what Bartky calls an "epistemic lean"). If the "world according to him" contains significant immorality, then over time one may be unable to determine when the beloved's actions are more seriously immoral (what Bartky calls an "ethical lean") (Bartky 1990, 111–113). Could loving attention dissolve the mind-made knot of *these* afflictions? This is complicated by the fact that undervaluing the self and pre-emptively forgiving others' bad behavior can sound virtuous (especially in the context of Buddhist ethics), which obscures their epistemic and ethical dangers.

We could say that the "undervaluing the self" cases are not different in kind from the "overvaluing the self" cases, since the obsession with the self is at the root of both. As Maria Heim has argued, self-loathing, on at least some Buddhist views, is understood as a problem of self-centeredness (Heim 2009). Whether one is self-aggrandizing or self-loathing, there is still an inflated concern with the self, a way of understanding others that is refracted through the lens of one's own, self-absorbed narrative. The content of self-absorbed narratives may vary—from arrogant narratives of being better than others to self-deprecating or despondent narratives of being worse than others—but they are all, in the end, narratives centered on the self.

But there is another resource in Buddhist and feminist, especially Womanist, philosophy to respond to the danger that loving attention may further distort perception and judgment in the context of oppression: self-directed loving attention. Alice Walker famously claimed that a Womanist "Loves herself. Regardless" (Walker 1983, xi).[7] Self-directed loving attention is about seeing ourselves chari-tably and fairly, being committed to our own lasting happiness and the causes of that happiness, and seeing how we are dependent on others—and them on us—but not reducible to others. This imperative—to love oneself, regardless—is not as antithetical to the Buddhist ideal of universal care as it may seem. Buddhaghosa argues that, in order to effectively love others, we must direct loving attention to oneself: "May I keep myself free from enmity, affliction and anxiety and live happily" (*Path of Purification* IX.8). He considers the objection that this self-love might "conflict what is said in the texts" insofar as self-directed love may seem selfish, but ultimately rejects the objection. This initial, self-directed love functions as an example, he argues, that makes the other-directed loving atten-tion possible. By making oneself an example, we become more sensitive to others' similar desires for happiness (*Path of Purification* IX.10).[8] In Mahayana Buddhist ethics, self-directed love can be more directly justified as it is part of one's larger moral commitment to care, since the call to attend lovingly to all sentient beings who suffer also applies to oneself.

Although self-directed loving attention is not incompatible with the broader Buddhist ethical projects, Buddhist ethical prescriptions about loving attention need more nuance if we want to apply them to the context of oppression. A practice of self-directed loving attention may be fruitful (and life-saving) for a member of an oppressed group who is at risk of undervaluing herself and excusing the bad behavior of others. A practice of other-directed loving attention may be central for a member of an oppressor group who is a risk of arrogant perception. Of course, many of us belong to both oppressed and oppressor groups, as in the case of white women who are often both the victims and perpetrators of arrogant perception. This suggests a need for even more sophistication in how we think about and practice loving attention, since in such cases one may need to alternate between a focus on self-directed loving in some situations and a focus on other-directed loving attention in others. This is one area in which feminist and critical race moral psychology can supplement Buddhist conceptions of loving attention by exposing the ways they fail to fully account of the role of power and domination in understanding loving attention.

The Cultivation of Loving Attention: Buddhist Contributions to Feminist Theory

Loving attention, on this Buddhist-feminist account, is transformative: it changes how we see, how we understand others and ourselves, how we interpret events, and how we respond to those events. But how do we effect that transformation? What mechanisms, skills, or practices make the transition from arrogant perception to loving attention possible? There is not, in Western philosophical (including feminist) literature, much emphasis on the cultivation of loving attention. Murdoch, in her mother-in-law example, drops some clues about how such a change may occur —for example, by locating one's own biases and intentionally creating new narratives that counteract these biases—but the mother-in-law seems to be able to change her perception of her daughter-in-law by a simple act of the will, upending her habitual modes of perception in one decisive mental act.[9] Although this could happen, it seems unrealistic to expect that all arrogant perception, especially perception that is based in and reinforced by systems of oppression, could be so easily transformed.

Lugones offers one possible practice of loving attention: world-traveling, immersing oneself into another's "world" in order to better understand the other and oneself. Traveling to another's world, and (re)understanding both the other and the self through that travel, requires playfulness and an openness to discovery (Lugones, this volume). It is unclear whether world-traveling is a practice that cultivates loving attention or a practice that is made possible by loving attention (or both). Either way, the question of cultivation is relocated rather than resolved, since we still ask, how do we learn to world-travel? How do we become motivated to world-travel?

The basic issue here extends beyond Lugones's account of world-traveling. It is about the skills that are required to make us receptive to others in a non-self-centered way. To advise an arrogant perceiver that she must learn from others is not likely to be effective since part of what it means to arrogantly perceive others just is to assume that we know all there is to know about them, that our projection onto them fully captures who they are. It is necessary to think, then, about *how* it is we are able to learn from others and how the assumptions of arrogant perception are undermined.

Cultivating loving attention requires a shift in one or more of the following: (1) what we pay attention to; (2) how we pay attention; (3) the purpose of our attention; and (4) the fact of attention, that is, that we are paying attention at all. Loving attention requires us to pay attention to admirable qualities of others and sympathetic interpretations of their situation with an eye toward their continued happiness, or as Buddhist ethicists would say, we need to attend to the happiness of others and the causes of that happiness. But it is not only the content of the attention that matters for loving attention, the quality of the attention matters, too. Two qualities in particular stand out: that the attention is reasonably sustained (not fleeting) so that it can inform our related habits of thinking, feeling, and action, and that the attention has an affective component as *loving* attention. Third, the purpose of and motivation for loving attention is not self-centered. This is the quality of loving attention that both Frye and Lugones focus on: loving attention does not reduce others to the self, nor does it construct others as fundamentally different in kind from the self. Finally, loving attention demands that we pay attention in the first place, that is, it counteracts indifference, apathy, and problematic habits of ignoring.

Equanimity, Mindfulness, and the Cultivation of Loving Attention

Buddhist ethics tend to prioritize the cultivation problem and develop sophisticated theories of moral psychology to address it. Changing one's mode of attending in the four ways outlined above requires the development and practice of certain supplementary skills. Each of these skills militates against particular obstacles to cultivating loving attention. The main obstacle to the first of the four ways of shifting our habits of attention—changing what we pay attention to—is negative emotionality, such as jealousy, envy, hatred, or resentment, that habituates us to focus on negative qualities in others. Obstacles to the other three aspects of changing our attention are apathy or indifference (obstacles to 2 and 4), distraction or not paying attention (obstacle to 2), and self-centeredness (obstacles to all, but especially 3). In Buddhist ethical traditions, these obstacles to the development of loving attention have clear antidotes, the most relevant of which, for our purposes, are equanimity and mindfulness. Both are themselves cultivatable, and Buddhist ethicists generally offer many techniques to develop these skills.[10]

In Indo-Tibetan Buddhist ethics, equanimity (Pāli: *upekka*, Tibetan: *btang snyoms*) is defined as freedom from craving and aversion, particularly about others.[11] Equanimity is potent since it can effectively respond to negative emotionality, self-centeredness, and indifference, that is, it can be understood as an antidote to most of the obstacles to loving attention. Mindfulness is the skill of the intentional placement of attention and the vigilance required to maintain that attention (Garfield 2012, 1–2). The moral and epistemic power of equanimity and mindfulness to respond to the obstacles to loving attention is not immediately obvious, so I will discuss each obstacle in turn.

In Indo-Tibetan Buddhist moral psychology, craving (the affective attitude of wanting) and aversion (the affective attitude of not wanting and not tolerating) form the basis of what we would call negative affective states (what Buddhists call "affliction"), such as hatred, resentment, pride, envy, and jealousy. For example, envy is characterized by aversion to another's success and craving that success for oneself; jealousy by craving the ownership of another person and the aversion to being "denied" that ownership; and resentment by aversion to another on the basis of a real or imagined wrongdoing or fault and the craving for their unhappiness. Since habits of craving and aversion are foundational to the development of negative emotionality, as freedom from craving and aversion, equanimity functions as an antidote to various kinds of negative emotionality that could preclude or inhibit more virtuous emotionality. When we have some mental space from our craving and aversion reactions, then, even when negative affective states arise, we are less likely to act on them or have them color our interpretation of others.

By undermining the power of negative affective states, equanimity creates cracks in the armor of arrogant perception. Arrogant perception—the sense that the other is not worth knowing (if only because we assume we already know everything about her)—is itself expressive of an afflictive affective state, arrogance. It is also conditioned and maintained by other negative affective states, such as (possibly unconscious) fear of the other, deep insecurity about oneself, and anger toward and resentment of the other when she acts in unexpected or "unacceptable" ways, as determined by the arrogant perceiver. Arrogant perception, then, includes various kinds of negative emotionality. Equanimity practices are designed to undermine the power of these states by creating a nonreactive mental space where we develop the freedom to refrain from identifying with the craving and aversion associated with such states. By not identifying with feelings of superiority or fear of others, for example, we are able to pursue other methods for relating to others, including loving attention.[12]

Equanimity is also an antidote to self-centered modes of attention, particularly self-centered projections of others, because it is freedom from craving and aversion, which are expressions of, and mechanisms for the maintenance of, self-clinging. Craving, on the Buddhist view, is fundamentally about the self (what I want, what I think I need or deserve), as is aversion (what I do not like, cannot stand, or cannot tolerate) (McRae 2013). The self-centeredness of craving and aversion explains why craving and the related quality of attachment are not considered to be love, or partially constitutive of love, on the Buddhist view: craving and attachment are fundamentally self-centered because they understand the other person (the object of craving and attachment) in terms of the self (that is, in terms of what I need or want, how I see myself, and so on.). Love is different because it attempts to understand another person in a way that is not filtered through one's own desires (McRae 2017a, 507).[13] This insight is shared by Frye and Lugones, who insist, in different ways, that the loving gaze is one that transcends self-centered projections or imaginings of the other. Equanimity helps explain how that transcendence of the self-centered perspective could happen: by developing some freedom from our most basic narratives of self-centeredness ("I want!" "I don't want!") we become more receptive to others' needs and aims simply because we are not always chasing after our own.

Even if we accept the liberatory potential of equanimity for overcoming negative emotionality and self-centered distortions of others, it may not be clear how equanimity could help overcome the obstacle of indifference. Insofar as equanimity decreases or eliminates craving and aversion, it would seem to make us less invested in others and therefore more likely to ignore them (McRae 2017a, 495–497). This is a particular problem for the cultivation of loving attention, since one of the obstacles to such attention—and one of the characteristics of arrogant perception—is ignoring the other, the complete failure to notice her. Even if equanimity could help with the previous two obstacles to the cultivation of loving attention, if it has the side effect of increasing our indifference to others, then it may undermine the development of loving attention.

That equanimity could undermine or inhibit love is a danger that Buddhist ethicists anticipated. For Buddhaghosa, indifference and apathy ("ignoring faults and virtues") is the near enemy of equanimity (Path of Purification IX.101). Patrul Rinpoche warns of mistaking what he calls "mindless impartiality" ("just think[ing] of everyone . . . as the same") for real equanimity (Patrul Rinpoche 1994, 198). Indifference and mindless impartiality can be avoided if we remember that equanimity is not about others; it is about freedom from our own feelings about and reactions to other, understood through the moral psychological concepts of craving and aversion. Suppose that, when having a conversation with someone, I think to myself, "Wow. This guy is really annoying." I may even start to feel some associated physical sensations, such as antsy-ness, fidgeting, or feelings of heat. Applying equanimity to this situation would be to dissociate from the judgment that this guy is an annoying person, that annoyingness is some essential quality of him or this conversation. It would also be to not take so seriously my own cravings ("I got to get out of this conversation!") and aversions ("I can't stand this person!"). This mental freedom does not make me indifferent to him; on the contrary, it makes me more likely to be able to engage with him in a genuine and caring way. As I see it, one of the subtler (and superficially paradoxical) insights of Buddhist accounts of equanimity as a moral skill is that sometimes we have to care less in order to care more.

The final obstacle to loving attention is the fact that sometimes we simply are not paying attention at all. It is not that we are attending to wrong things about the other, or in the wrong ways, but that we are simply failing to attend to another. This is a form of arrogance, as Lugones argues, but is not obviously helped by equanimity practices that uproot craving and aversion: if I barely notice that you are in the room, I'm unlikely to form cravings or aversions toward you. When we are simply not paying attention, or barely paying attention, to others, another skill is needed: mindfulness, the ability to place one's attention and the careful maintenance of that attention. Garfield calls mindfulness "the necessary mechanism for focusing the mind on the morally relevant dimensions of moral situations and on one's own moral responsibility" (Garfield 2012, 4). It is what combats "the natural tendency to mindless action" (Garfield 2012, 6). This is because immoral actions—including actions that maintain systems of oppression—are not always caused by hostile or even fearful motivations. Sometimes they are "mindless," caused by negligence, distraction, or forgetting. Without mindfulness "it is possible to remain utterly inattentive to one's own moral life, failing to notice situations that call for moral response, failing even to recognize one's own moral attitudes, dispositions and motivations" (Garfield 2012, 6). Mindfulness, then, is a corrective to failing to pay attention at all, or paying insufficient attention.

Buddhist philosophers and feminist philosophers have, in different ways, argued for the epistemic and moral significance of loving attention and dangers of arrogant, self-centered habits of attention. Drawing on both traditions, I have attempted to give an account of loving attention that can respond to some of the worries that are articulated in feminist literature (the dangers of loving attention in the context of oppression) and those that are articulated in Buddhist traditions (the ways in which we can cultivate or fail to cultivate loving attention). With regard to the latter, I have argued that mindfulness and equanimity together allow us to cultivate loving attention by responding to particular obstacles to such cultivation. These skills are conceptually well-suited to respond to the obstacles to loving attention: equanimity, as freedom from craving and aversion, is the right kind of concept to address the obstacles of negative emotionality, self-centeredness, and indifference; mindfulness, as the placement and careful maintenance of attention, is well-suited to respond to the obstacle of not paying attention and not holding attention.

Notes

1. See Fourlas (2015), Frye (1983), Lugones (this volume), Murdoch (1970), Mulvey (1975), Snow (2005), and Yancy (2008).
2. See Patrul Rinpoche's story of the sage Asanga for an illustration of the importance of the loving gaze (1994, 211–212).
3. See, for example, Khenpo Ngawang Pelzang (2004, 140–143).
4. I use "loving attention" where Murdoch would simply use "attention." On Murdoch's view attention is by definition loving: "I use the word 'attention,' which I borrow from Weil, to express the idea of a just and loving gaze directed upon an individual reality" (Murdoch 1970, 33).
5. See Snow (2005).
6. Murdoch equates "attention" and, what I would call, "loving attention" (1970, 33). For problems with defining attention as loving and just, see Bommarito (2018).
7. See also Edwards (2016) and Harris (2012).
8. See also Harris (2012) on the intersections of Womanist and Buddhist conceptions of and practices of self-love.
9. In fact, the fact that this moral change is entirely internal, an act of the individual agent's will, is central to her overall argument in *The Sovereignty of Good* (Murdcoch 1970).
10. For two excellent examples, see *Path of Purification* and Patrul Rinpoche (1994), which each discuss methods of cultivating equanimity.
11. See McRae (2017a).
12. That equanimity enables love (and other positive mental states, such as compassion and joy) is a core feature of the Buddhist moral psychological concept of the four boundless qualities (*brahmavihāras, tshad med gzhi*): equanimity, love, compassion, and sympathetic joy. See *Path of Purification* (part IX), Patrul Rinpoche (1994, ch. 2, part 1), and McRae (2017a, 2017b).
13. This gets tricky in cases when the desire seems altruistic, such as wanting another's suffering to end. But it is important to distinguish between wanting another's suffering to stop for her own sake and wanting it to stop because you experience it as burdensome. Consider, for example, wanting a child to stop crying because you want her to be happy and wanting her to stop crying because her crying is inconvenient or unpleasant for you. The first, but not the second, is conducive to loving attention. I thank Nic Bommarito for pressing me on this point.

References

Bartky, Sandra. 1990. "Feeding Egos and Tending Wounds: Deference and Disaffection in Women's Emotional Labor." In *Femininity and Domination: Studies in the Phenomenology of Oppression* by Sandra Bartky, 99–119. New York: Routledge.

Bodhi, Bhikku, ed. 1993. *A Comprehensive Manual of Abhidharma.* Seattle, WA: Buddhist Publication Society.

Bommarito, Nicolas. 2018. "Attention." In *Inner Virtue* by Nicolas Bommarito, 127–170. New York: Oxford University Press.

Buddhaghosa. 1991. *The Path of Purification.* Onalaska, WA: Buddhist Publication Society.

Dreyfus, George, and Evan Thompson. 2007. "Asian Perspectives: Indian Theories of Mind." In *The Cambridge Handbook of Consciousness*, edited by Philip Zalazo, Morris Moscovitch, and Evan Thompson, 89–114. Cambridge: Cambridge University Press.

Edwards, Kirsten. 2016. "Learning to (Re)member as Womanish Curricular Transcendence." In *Race, Gender and Curriculum Theorizing: Working in Womanish Ways*, edited by Denise Taliaferro Baszile, Kirsten T. Edwards, and Nichole A. Guillory, 53–70. New York: Lexington Books.

Fourlas, George. 2015. "Being a Target: On the Racialization of Middle Eastern Americans." *Critical Philosophy of Race* 3 (1): 101–123.

Frye, Marilyn. 1983. "In and Out of Harm's Way: Arrogance and Love." In *The Politics of Reality: Essays in Feminist Theory* by Marilyn Frye, 52–83. Freedom, CA: Crossing Press.

Garfield, Jay. 2012. "Mindfulness and Ethics: Attention, Virtue, and Perfection." *Thai International Journal of Buddhist Studies* 3: 1–24.

Harris, Melanie L. 2012. "Buddhist Meditation for the Recovery of the Womanist Self, or Sitting on the Mat Self-Love Realized." *Buddhist-Christian Studies* 32: 67–72.

Heim, Maria. 2009. "The Conceit of Self-Loathing." *Journal of Indian Philosophy* 37 (1): 61–74.

Heim, Maria. 2014. "Buddhaghosa on the Phenomenology of Love and Compassion." In *The Oxford Handbook of Indian Philosophy*, edited by Jonardon Ganeri, 171–189. New York: Oxford University Press.

Holland, Margaret. 1998. "Toughing the Weights: Moral Perception and Attention." *International Philosophical Quarterly* 38 (3): 299–312.

James, William. 1981. *The Principles of Psychology, Volumes I and II.* Cambridge, MA: Harvard University Press.

McRae, Emily. 2013. "Equanimity and Intimacy: A Buddhist-Feminist Approach to the Elimination of Bias." *Sophia* 52 (3): 447–462.

McRae, Emily. 2017a. "Equanimity in Relationship: Responding to Moral Ugliness." In *A Mirror is for Reflection*, edited by Jake Davis, 336–351. New York: Oxford University Press.

McRae, Emily. 2017b. "The Psychology of Moral Judgment and Perception in Indo-Tibetan Ethics." In *Oxford Handbook of Buddhist Ethics*, edited by Daniel Cozort and Mark Shields, 335–358. New York: Oxford University Press.

Mulvey, Lisa. 1975. "Visual Pleasure and Narrative Cinema." *Screen* 16 (3): 6–18.

Murdoch, Iris. 1970. "The Idea of Perfection." In *The Sovereignty of Good* by Iris Murdoch, 1–45. New York: Routledge & Kegan Paul.

Patrul Rinpoche. 1994. *Words of My Perfect Teacher.* Translated by Padmakara Translation Group. Lanham, MD: Altamira Press.

Pelzang, Ngawang Khenpo. 2004. *A Guide to the Words of My Perfect Teacher*. Translated by Padmakara Translation Group. Boston: Shambala.

Śāntideva. 1995. *Bodhicaryāvatāra*. Translated by Kate Crosby and Andrew Skilton. New York: Oxford University Press.

Snow, Nancy. 2005. "Iris Murdoch's Notion of a Loving Gaze." *Journal of Value Inquiry* 39 (3/4): 487–498.

Walker, Alice. 1983. *In Search of Our Mother's Gardens*. Orlando: Harcourt Books.

Watzl, Sebastian. 2011. "The Nature of Attention." *Philosophy Compass* 6 (11): 842–853.

Yancy, George. 2008. *Black Bodies, White Gazes: The Continuing Significance of Race*. Lanham, MD: Rowman & Littlefield.

Yancy, George. 2014. "Interpretive Profiles on Charles Johnson's Reflections on Trayvon Martin: A Dialogue between George Yancy, E. Ethelbert Miller and Charles Johnson." *Western Journal of Black Studies* 38 (1): 1–12.

Contributors

Iva Apostolova is an associate professor of philosophy at the Dominican University College in Ottawa, Canada. She is a contributor to and coeditor of *Ageing in an Ageing Society: Critical Reflections* (Equinox, 2019) and an author of articles published in *Feminist Philosophy Quarterly, Russell: The Journal of Bertrand Russell Studies*, and *Bioethics*.

Lynne Rudder Baker was Emerita Professor of philosophy, formerly Distinguished Professor, at the University of Massachusetts Amherst. In addition to her five books, published by Cambridge University Press, Oxford University Press, and Princeton University Press, she published numerous articles and book chapters and lectured all over the world. Lists of her publications and presentations may be found at www.people.umass.edu/lrb.

Susan J. Brison is professor of philosophy and Eunice and Julian Cohen Professor for the Study of Ethics and Human Values at Dartmouth College. She has held visiting positions at Tufts, NYU, and Princeton and fellowships from the National Endowment for the Humanities and the Mellon Foundation. The author of *Aftermath: Violence and the Remaking of a Self* (Princeton University Press, 2002), she has published numerous articles on gender-based violence and on freedom of expression in scholarly journals and in the popular press.

Judith Butler is Maxine Elliot Professor in the Department of Comparative Literature and the Program of Critical Theory at the University of California, Berkeley. She is the author of seventeen books, including *Gender Trouble: Feminism and the Subversion of Identity* (Routledge, 1990) and *The Force of Nonviolence* (Verso, 2020). Butler is also active in several human rights organizations, currently serving on the board of the Center for Constitutional Rights in New York and the advisory board of Jewish Voice for Peace.

Ashby Butnor is an assistant professor of philosophy at Colorado State University. She is the coeditor, with Jennifer McWeeny, of *Asian and Feminist Philosophies in Dialogue: Liberating Traditions* (Columbia University Press, 2014). Her teaching and research interests include East Asian philosophies, phenomenology, care ethics, feminist epistemology, and the ethics of global poverty.

Vrinda Dalmiya is professor of philosophy at the University of Hawai'i, Mānoa. She is the author of *Caring to Know: Comparative Care Ethics, Feminist Epistemology, and the Mahābhārata* (Oxford University Press, 2016) and coeditor of *Exploring Agency in the Mahābhārata: Ethical and Political Dimensions of Dharma* (Routledge, 2018). Her articles have appeared in journals like *Hypatia, Sophia, Journal of the Indian Council of Philosophical Research*, and *Journal of Social Philosophy*.

E. Díaz-León is an associate professor of philosophy at the University of Barcelona. Before this, she taught at the University of Manitoba. She received her PhD from the University of Sheffield. She specializes in philosophy of mind and language and philosophy of gender, race, and sexuality. Her articles have appeared in the *Australasian Journal of Philosophy, Ergo, European Journal of Philosophy, Hypatia, Mind, Philosophical Studies, Proceedings of the Aristotelian Society*, and *Ratio*, among others.

Paula Droege is a teaching professor in the Philosophy Department at Pennsylvania State University. Her research on philosophical theories of consciousness proposes an essential role for temporal representation in conscious states. She is the author of *Caging the Beast: A Theory of Sensory Consciousness* (John Benjamins, 2003), *The Evolution of Consciousness: Representing the Present Moment* (Bloomsbury, 2022), and articles on the role of consciousness in memory, free will, and delusion. Her work in feminism focuses on the relation between epistemic and structural constraints on autonomy.

Gabrielle Benette Jackson is a lecturer in philosophy at Stanford University. She is a specialist in philosophy of mind, phenomenology, and feminist philosophy, with an interest in recent cognitive science. Jackson's work has appeared in *Phenomenology and the Cognitive Sciences* and *European Journal of Philosophy*, among other publications.

Anne J. Jacobson's interdisciplinary research draws on philosophy of mind/cognitive neuroscience, feminist philosophy, and the history of philosophy. Recent philosophical work includes *Keeping the World in Mind: Mental Representations and the Sciences of the Mind* (Palgrave MacMillan, 2013) and the coedited *Neurofeminism: Issues at the Intersection of Feminist Theory and Cognitive Science* (Palgrave Macmillan, 2012). She has been the director of the University of Houston's Center for Neuro-Engineering and Cognitive Science from 2005.

Susan James is professor of philosophy at Birkbeck College, London. Among her publications are *Passion and Action: The Emotions in Early-Modern Philosophy* (Oxford University Press, 1997), *The Political Writings of Margaret Cavendish* (Cambridge University Press, 2003), *Spinoza on Philosophy, Religion and Politics: The*

Theologico-Political Treatise (Oxford University Press, 2012), and some papers on the history of feminist philosophy.

Janine Jones is an associate professor of philosophy at University of North Carolina Greensboro. She is author of the articles "Caster Semenya: Reasoning Up Front with Race" (2014) and "When Black Female Presence Is (Seemingly) Not Invited to *The Second Sex*" (2019), among others, and coeditor of *Pursuing Trayvon Martin: Historical Contexts and Contemporary Manifestations of Racial Dynamics* (Lexington Books, 2014). She is on the editorial board of *Simone de Beauvoir Studies* and is a member of the Black Internationalist Unions, a unit of the Abolition Collective.

Amy Kind is the Russell K. Pitzer Professor of Philosophy at Claremont McKenna College. She has authored two introductory textbooks: *Philosophy of Mind: The Basics* (Routledge, 2020) and *Persons and Personal Identity* (Polity, 2015). She has also edited two volumes, *The Routledge Handbook of Philosophy of Imagination* (Routledge, 2016) and *Philosophy of Mind in the 20th and 21st Centuries* (Routledge, 2018), and has coedited two collections, *Knowledge through Imagination* (Oxford University Press, 2016) and *Epistemic Uses of Imagination* (Routledge, 2021).

María Lugones was professor of Latin American and Caribbean area studies and comparative literature at Binghamton University, where she also directed the Center for Philosophy, Interpretation, and Culture. She was the author of *Pilgrimages/ Peregrinajes: Theorizing Coalition against Multiple Oppressions* (Rowman & Littlefield, 2003) as well as a number of foundational articles in feminist philosophy, queer theory, and decolonial studies. She was the recipient of the Society for Women in Philosophy Distinguished Woman Philosopher Award in 2015.

Matthew MacKenzie is professor of philosophy and department chair at Colorado State University. He specializes in Buddhist philosophy, classical Indian philosophy, and the philosophy of mind, with a special focus on consciousness and self-consciousness. His articles have appeared in *Philosophy East and West*, *Phenomenology and the Cognitive Sciences*, *Asian Philosophy*, and *Journal of Consciousness Studies*, among other journals. He is the author of *Buddhist Philosophy and the Embodied Mind* (Rowman & Littlefield International, 2022).

Keya Maitra is the Thomas Howerton Distinguished Professor of Humanities and professor of philosophy at University of North Carolina Asheville. Her articles have been published in *Hypatia*, *Asian Philosophy*, *Philosophy in the Contemporary World*, *Southwest Philosophy Review*, *International Journal of Philosophical Studies*, and many anthologies. She is the author of two books, *Philosophy of the Bhagavad*

Gita: A Contemporary Introduction (Bloomsbury Academic, 2018) and *On Putnam* (Cengage Learning, 2003), and a coauthor of *Ethics of Governance: Moral Limits of Policy Decisions* (Springer, 2021).

Emily McRae is an associate professor of philosophy at the University of New Mexico. She specializes in Tibetan Buddhist philosophy, ethics, moral psychology, and feminism. She has published articles in both Western and Asian philosophical journals, including *American Philosophical Quarterly*, *History of Philosophy Quarterly*, *Journal of Religious Ethics*, and *Philosophy East and West*. Together with Jay Garfield, McRae published a translation of the nineteenth-century Tibetan master Patrul Rinpoche's *Essential Jewel of Holy Practice* (Wisdom Books, 2017).

Jennifer McWeeny is an associate professor of philosophy at Worcester Polytechnic Institute. She specializes in phenomenology, philosophy of mind, philosophy of gender, feminist philosophy, and decolonial studies. McWeeny is coeditor of two books: *Speaking Face to Face: The Visionary Philosophy of María Lugones* (State University of New York Press, 2019) and *Asian and Feminist Philosophies in Dialogue: Liberating Traditions* (Columbia University Press, 2014). She is a recipient of the Fulbright US Scholar National Research Award (France, 2019–20) and Editor in Chief of *Simone de Beauvoir Studies*.

Diana Tietjens Meyers is Professor Emerita of Philosophy at the University of Connecticut Storrs. She has held the Laurie Chair at Rutgers University and the Ellacuría Chair of Social Ethics at Loyola University Chicago. She currently works in four main areas of philosophy: philosophy of action, feminist ethics and aesthetics, and human rights. She has published five monographs. The most recent of those is *Victims' Stories and the Advancement of Human Rights* (Oxford University Press, 2016).

Jennifer Radden is Emerita Professor of philosophy at the University of Massachusetts Boston. She has published extensively on mental health concepts, the history of medicine, and ethical and policy aspects of psychiatric theory and practice. Her books include *On Delusion* (Routledge, 2010) and *Melancholic Habits: Burton's Anatomy & the Mind Sciences* (Oxford University Press, 2017).

Naomi Scheman is Professor Emerita of Philosophy and of Gender, Women, and Sexuality Studies at the University of Minnesota. Her account of the social construction of psychological phenomena, begun in her doctoral dissertation in 1978, informs her subsequent work in feminist epistemology and metaphysics, much of which has been collected in two volumes: *Engenderings: Constructions of Knowledge, Authority, and Privilege* (Routledge, 1993) and *Shifting Ground: Knowledge and Reality, Transgression and Trustworthiness* (Oxford University Press, 2011).

Index